William S. Burroughs, the world-renowned author of *Naked Lunch, Junky, Queer, Cities of the Red Night, The Place of Dead Roads, The Western Lands, Interzone, The Cat Inside* and *The Letters of William S. Burroughs 1945–1959,* is a member of the American Academy and Institute for Arts and Letters, and a *Commandeur de l'Ordre des Arts et des Lettres* of France. He lives in Lawrence, Kansas.

Oliver Harris gained a Double First in English at Christ Church, Oxford, and wrote his doctoral dissertation on William S. Burroughs. His articles have appeared in *New Statesman, Harpers & Queen,* and the anthology *William S. Burroughs: At the Front.* Currently a lecturer in American Literature at the University of Keele, he lives in Oxfordshire with his wife and two daughters.

THE LETTERS OF

WILLIAM S. BURROUGHS

1945 TO 1959

EDITED AND
WITH AN INTRODUCTION

OLIVER HARRIS

PICADOR

First published 1993 by Viking Penguin, a division of Penguin Books USA, Inc.

First published in Great Britain 1993 by Picador
This edition published 1994 by Picador
an imprint of Macmillan General Books
25 Eccleston Place London SW1W 9NF
and Basingstoke

Associated companies throughout the world

ISBN 0 330 33075 6

Grateful acknowledgement is made for permission to reprint the following
copyrighted works:
Letters to Allen Ginsberg: 1953–1957 by William S. Burroughs.
Originally published by Full Court Press, New York. © 1982
by William S. Burroughs.
By permission of Wylie, Aitken & Stone.
Selections from *Naked Lunch* by William S. Burroughs. Used by permission of
Grove Press, Inc.
The Yage Letters by William S. Burroughs. Copyright © 1963, 1975 by
William S. Burroughs.
Reprinted by permission of City Lights Books.

3 5 7 9 8 6 4 2

A CIP catalogue record for this book is available from
the British Library.

Printed and bound in Great Britain by
Mackays of Chatham PLC, Chatham, Kent

Acknowledgments

I would like to thank:

James Grauerholz for his wide-ranging editorial assistance and whole-hearted support; William Burroughs and Allen Ginsberg for their cooperation in providing invaluable information; the estate of Jack Kerouac; Gregory Corso; David Stanford at Viking Penguin; and my agent, Deborah Rogers.

Robert H. Jackson, James P. Musser, and Gary Nargi, for providing copies of letter manuscripts from their private collections.

The staff of the following university libraries, for their assistance and for providing copies of letter manuscripts from their collec-tions: Marilyn Wurzburger, Head of Special Collections at Arizona State University, Tempe; Bernard Crystal, Assistant Librarian for Manuscripts at the Butler Library, Columbia University, New York; and Cynthia Farar, Assistant to the Research Librarian at the Harry Ransom Humanities Research Center, University of Texas, Austin.

Ron Padgett and Anne Waldman, editors of *Letters to Allen Ginsberg, 1953–1957*.

Grove Press, for permission to quote from *Naked Lunch*; City Lights Books, for permission to quote from *The Yage Letters*; and Viking Penguin, for permission to quote from *Junky, Queer*, and *Interzone*.

In addition, thanks to Alan Ansen, and to Lucien Carr, Peter Elvins, Terence Mckenna, Barry Miles, Rogers Scudder, and Tao

Elvins Wolfe, for their kind correspondence and helpful information.

And finally, special thanks to Ian MacFadyen for his knowledge, enthusiasm, and support, and most of all to Jenny, Ella, and Mia, for making all the hard work and sleepless nights worthwhile.

—Oliver Harris

Contents

1 9 5 4

Introduction

What is it that makes these letters of William Burroughs so extraordinary? A writer's early correspondence ordinarily promises two things. First, a kind of draft literary autobiography. The reader hopes for a running record of the genesis of the writing, and a bank of raw material from which the features of the author's experience can be drawn. A writer's early letters also promise the emergence of a certain quality of prose, the development of a distinctive voice. In the years covered by this volume, William Burroughs disappoints on neither count. His letters model that instantly recognizable, unmistakably Burroughsian voice, the unique drawl that mixes mandarin intellect and hipster humor. And if they are often damned funny, it is because they must outlaugh despair, outbid damnation, and find delight in a life that was often deluged by disaster. For these are exorbitantly vocal, prodigious letters, voluminous not so much in length or number as in drama. Typically written in a state of emergency, they evoke an exotic zone where every external event, every new encounter and environment, no matter how colorful or calamitous, is matched by Burroughs' own capacity for the extreme. Reporting back from that physical and emotional front line with self-dramatizing relish, his letters reveal clues to illuminate the life, and keys to open up the texts. But their content does more than chronicle, their style more than impress, and the whole is greater than the sum of their always original and often remarkable parts. What makes these letters of William Burroughs extraordinary, as extraordinary as either the facts of his life or the qualities of his fiction, is the central role that they played in both.

In the decade and a half they cover, more often than not, in one way or another, the action turns on the letters themselves. Incriminating letters, intercepted by the police in New Orleans, April 1949, and again a decade later in Tangier, April 1959. Letters through which Burroughs evolved as a writer during the mid-1950s, rehearsing his routines and expropriating them to form fiction. Letters that were lifelines, cast across continents and oceans, converting the isolation of addiction and exile into the workshop of creativity. And dead letters returned unanswered, provoking crisis. At times William Burroughs was, quite literally, a man who lived by writing; *un homme de lettres*.

The letters not only provide a context but form a text in their own right, because the years from 1945 to 1959 frame the rise and fall of letter writing as integral to Burroughs' fiction making. The epistolary novel he wrote close to this volume's chronological center, in 1953, was the embodiment of a progressive merger of life, letters, and literature. When editing his own correspondence again two years later, he found that it already possessed a continuity to fit the aesthetic framework of his work-in-progress: "Funny though how the letters hang together. I figure to use one sentence and it pulls a whole page along with it."

The result here is a curious paradox. A book of correspondence, even that of the most conventional novelist, does not invite sequential reading, because the reader looks for fragments, not coherence. And yet this volume, which concludes with both the publication of Burroughs' fragmentary antinovel, *Naked Lunch,* and the discovery of the technique that made a methodology of its madness, the cut-ups, does require chronological reading. It does so precisely because these letters *do* tell a story, and because they themselves show, rather than tell, how Burroughs started from narrative and arrived at antinarrative. To travel that route as it was taken is to experience the extraordinary course of Burroughs' investment of creativity in his correspondence. When, at the heart of this volume, he writes, "Maybe the real novel is letters to you," Burroughs was thinking of one particular reader, but now speaks to all. The letters gradually generate their own narrative, finally shape their own significant form. The one, inescapable editorial intervention in the present volume has been the decision where to end it, the choice of the last letter. For the rest, no criteria but the broadest—quality and the intention to be representative—have been used, with very few editorial deletions.* The first letter was the earliest available for selection.

On July 24, 1945, William Seward Burroughs wrote from St. Louis to Irwin Allen Ginsberg in New York, enclosing a nearly identical letter to Jean Louis Kerouac. An American triumvirate of diverse backgrounds and ages—a middle western WASP aged thirty-one, an East Coast Jew aged nineteen, and a French Canadian Catholic, twenty-three—Burroughs, Ginsberg, and Kerouac had by then known one another some eighteen months. During that time, the three men had shared the same New York apartment, Burroughs had conducted lay analytical sessions with his junior partners, and had introduced them to the esoteric in literature and the exotic in street life. Although after the following year the trio would never again spend more than a few months together in the same country, let alone at the same address, already they had embarked on lifelong friendships. And although it would be another five years before any of them had anything published, before Kerouac succeeded in inspiring Burroughs to write a book of his own, or before Ginsberg would serve first as his agent and then as a substitute Muse, already they had laid the literary foundations for what became known as the Beat Generation. Their alliance was Burroughs' starting point as a writer. And because his movements were about to open up a gulf that only letters could bridge, the end of their season together is also this volume's starting point. That July, the world was also less than two weeks away from Hiroshima.

Written on the brink of turning points both personal and global, literary and historical, the 1945 letter to Ginsberg that opens this volume appears strangely tight-lipped. Like the one enclosed with it to Kerouac, its language is stilted, its tone almost formal, the impression left by its French valediction one of affectation rather than affection. It is the only letter to Ginsberg (or Kerouac) where Burroughs does not sign off "Love," "As ever," or without some personalized version of his name—until, that is, the final letter in

---

* All editorial insertions in the dates and addresses of letters are indicated in brackets.

the volume, over fourteen years later. There, writing from Paris on October 29, 1959, Burroughs signs off not with a customary expression of intimacy but with his full name, in lower case, impersonally: william seward burroughs. These first and last letters to Ginsberg are like bookends. Distant as strangers, yet companions in that very impersonality, as if their symmetry sought to bracket all that passed between them.

Given the period covered by this volume, it is natural that letters to Allen Ginsberg should predominate. Until the new decade of 1960, by which time Burroughs was engaged in cutting himself off from his past, Ginsberg was not only by far the most consistent recipient but also the most dedicated custodian of his correspondence. Indeed, had Ginsberg not been such an assiduous archivist, with both eyes set firmly on the future, little of Burroughs' material would have survived the often careless, chaotic circumstances of its production. For Burroughs, writing to Ginsberg was one of only two constant habits throughout a decade and a half of constant, turbulent change. The other habitual companion, whose shadow remained with him until the end, was the old Chinaman, junk.

When William Burroughs recounted the history of his pre-1945 years in the preface to *Junkie* (1953),[1] the self-characterization is marked by a lack of, and quest for, motive, direction, need. In his teens, he had "drifted into solo adventures" of juvenile risk-taking before going to Harvard, where he "majored in English literature for lack of interest in any other subject." Afterwards, he "drifted around Europe for a year or so," then "fooled around taking graduate courses in psychology and Jiu-Jitsu," and "played around the edges of crime." When his autobiographical sketch reaches the mid-1940s, there is no mention of writing or writers, no place for his new relationships with Ginsberg and Kerouac, or with his common-law wife, Joan Vollmer. The focus is strictly on the immediate subject and the fact of his possession by it: "You become a narcotics addict because you do not have strong motivations in any other direction [. . .] I drifted along taking shots when I could score. I ended up hooked [. . .] You don't decide to be an addict." The

---

1. Note that *Junkie* was re-edited and republished in 1977 as *Junky*. For ease of reference, all textual citations in footnotes are of this version.

years of indulgent drifting were over, a decision had been made, a "special need" acquired, a direction—downward—found, and its dictates followed.

The letters in this volume start, then, shortly after Burroughs had begun his indenture to narcotics. As early as the second letter, September 1, 1946, we hear what will become a familiar refrain: the announcement that he has given up his addiction, entirely. With each year that follows, with each relocation, first from one state to another and then from continent to continent, the refrain persists, punctuated with increasing frequency by both renewed determination to kick and mounting despair at ever doing so. Two years later, he was planning a novel tactic to break the habit: "My latest idea is to go to some other city and have dwindling quantities mailed to me." The prospect of cure by correspondence, like his hope to afford a sanitarium from the profits of his carrot crop, has its amusing side. But the comedy was cruelly pathetic, as when, in 1954, he resorted to hiring friends who confiscated his clothes and prevented access to pharmacies, a method borrowed from Coleridge via De Quincey. All told, more than a decade passes before a breakthrough is achieved. Addiction is not merely a recurrent subject of Burroughs' letters, it is their matrix.

The last five years of the 1940s chart Burroughs' legally enforced movements down through America, from New York to New Orleans, from New Orleans to East Texas, and from East Texas finally over the border into Mexico. Shortly after arriving in Mexico City, Joan would write to Ginsberg, quoting a friend's remark: "I'd rather be on the outside looking in, than on the inside looking out."[2] Burroughs' letters up to this point are those of an outsider still stuck on the inside; a professional farmer and family man, landowner and landlord, but one fundamentally isolated from his neighbors: "There seems to be no one of any interest around," he writes in 1948, "or if such people exist, I can not find them." Uncannily predicting his itinerary for the next ten years, he considers removing to "Central America, S. America, or possibly to Africa." In the meantime, Burroughs' dissatisfaction with America inspired a pro-

2. Joan Vollmer Burroughs to Allen Ginsberg, October 31, 1949, Mexico City (Ginsberg Collection, Columbia University, New York).

ductive confrontation with bureaucracy, and a hostile conflict with legal and cultural norms. His distinctive philosophy and politics are already deeply felt and lucidly articulated, and always working against the grain of his environment.

Addiction provided a crude yet effective yardstick with which to measure social interference, but Burroughs recruited oppositional or marginalized figures to delineate his position. In particular, he identified with and borrowed from Wilhelm Reich and Alfred Korzybski, whose radical psychosexual and semantic practices challenged mainstream thinking. Because they challenged the mainstream, Reich and Korzybski were also sticks with which to beat and berate Ginsberg in the course of Burroughs' lectures on language, socialism, ethics, medicine, and mysticism. "Allen, please do me one favor. Get Korzybski's *Science and Sanity* and read it. Every young man should get the principles of Semantics clear in his mind *before* he goes to college (or anywhere else for that matter)." And again, debating Ginsberg's visionary experiences, Burroughs insists on semantic clarity, concrete examples, empirical knowledge, reflecting his own commitment to experimental verification: "Mysticism is just a word. I am concerned with *facts* on all levels of experience." If the tone is often that of an impatient teacher correcting a lazy student, what is also striking is the rapier accuracy, the precision at once chilling and comic: "Human, Allen, is an adjective, and its use as a noun is in itself regrettable." Burroughs was not a man to compromise friendship—even with one so junior to him in years and experience, and one balanced at the time on a tightrope of psychiatric treatment—by pulling his verbal punches.

But there are early gaps in the carapace of Burroughs' famously iconoclastic cynicism, moments when the sharpness of his pen is matched by a softness of the heart. He attacks Neal Cassady's behavior as an "absolute nadir in human relations," in order to stand up for "a decent, honest, well-meaning, well-mannered Jewish girl like Helen [Hinckle]": "I would be much more inclined to throw Neal out than her if it came to a choice." As such letters reveal, while Burroughs was an early misanthrope, his notorious misogyny, and anti-Semitism, were later acquisitions.

The new decade of the fifties dawned for Burroughs in Mexico.

There, conditions were "about where the US was in 1880," as if, anticipating the expeditions into Central and South America, his geographic movements south were regressions in time, quests in older cultures, hotter climes, for mythical America's "glorious Frontier heritage." In fact, it was the heat of the law that drove Burroughs across the border, and it was a final, calamitous transgression that would force him out again.

At first, Mexico was "a fine, free country," where a man like Burroughs could relax, as in his native land he could not. The untenable social position of the addict and homosexual was reversed, and Burroughs' lost haute-bourgeois status ironically reinstated, in a nation where "the cops recognize you as their superior and would never venture to stop or question a well dressed upper class character like myself." The state of anxiety-free exile, which would not endure long, was also the condition of Burroughs' first serious engagement with writing, which would.

On arrival in Mexico his letters speak of opening a bar, or buying a farm. It is not until March 1950, on receipt of a copy of Kerouac's first novel, that Burroughs even notes, almost en passant, that he has begun his own. He doubts the salability of his book (then called *Junk*), "owing to the criticism of the Narcotic dept. it contains," but there is a teasing blank space in his letters where the writer's first anxieties and ambitions might be expected to appear. His hopes, when expressed, are modest, his creative rationale likewise. After working on the manuscript for a year, Burroughs' most significant remark was to ally its writing to his environment: "I don't mean it as justification or deterrent or anything but an accurate account of what I experienced during the time I was on junk [. . .] For one thing the book was written in Mexico. It is difficult for anyone living in the States to realize how meaningless such a concept as 'justification' is down here." Unconcerned with either defensive or aggressive impulses, Burroughs intended neither to justify nor to deter but, disinterestedly, to document. In revision, he would cut out all theory and domestic relations in order to "confine [himself] to straight narrative," like a soldier to the boredom of the barracks. A year later, he was "only glad" the publishers "don't want to hash up the story itself," a relief seven years and a world away from the compulsively interrupted course of *Naked Lunch*, and Burroughs' frenetic relish as "captain of this lushed up hashhead subway."

Looking back in 1965, Burroughs recalled that when he had started to write *Junkie*, "there didn't seem to be any strong motivation [. . .] I didn't feel compelled. I had nothing else to do." His writing debut came about with an initial absence of will that —ominously, prophetically—parallels his first use of narcotics. The situation appears to repeat two years later, when Burroughs started writing *Queer* to take his mind off the absence of his then boyfriend: "I have been working on a new novel (with Marker away and no one around I can talk to I have need of distraction)." When he echoed these lines in a following letter, the meaning exceeded his intention: "With Marker away I got another habit." Another habit, but of a different kind. "I ended up hooked . . . You don't decide to be"—a writer.

"While it was I who wrote *Junky*," Burroughs later commented, "I feel that I was being written in *Queer*." The shift from active to passive mood coincides with a marked change in the nature of his letters. Although that change is only inferential at first—not seen directly but alluded to, because it takes place outside his correspondence with Ginsberg, which is all that survives from this period—the letters change with his fiction: from the dry, measured, impersonal tone of *Junkie* toward the vulnerable, personal self-exposure of *Queer*. That shift also mirrors Burroughs' state of narcotic possession, while translating it not, as the books' titles superficially suggest, into sexual need but into a creative dependency. In May 1952, he observes of a particular routine: "It was the turning point where my partial success was assured. If I had not achieved the reckless gaiety that charges this fantasy, Marker would have refused to go with me to S.A." What he also notes is that the routine came to him "like dictated," a fact confirmed but complicated by a glance at *Queer*, where Burroughs appears under his *nom de plume*, Lee, and Marker as Allerton: "Lee paused. The routine was coming to him like dictation [. . .] Mary and Allerton left. Lee was alone in the bar. The monologue continued." The published text prefers failure over success, absence over presence. The routine turns autonomous, becomes as independent of author or audience as any text. Allerton is an alibi. The real need was elsewhere.

What divides *Junkie* from *Queer*, what makes the novel documenting Burroughs' addiction lead to a novel whose writing begins to resemble an addiction, was the killing of his wife. Joan's only contribution in these letters comes in one of the last before her death, and takes the form of postscript comments on Burroughs' sexual life, written in pencil "so the old boy can erase it if he sees fit." It is hard to imagine any gesture so self-effacing yet so indelible, or to conceive a more grimly pathetic entrance that is also an exit. As for Burroughs' first surviving comments on the event's meaning to him, rather than on its legal effects, three and a half years and as many thousand miles of water separate them from the tragedy itself. In his introduction to *Queer* on its publication in 1985, he confirmed that "the book is motivated and formed by an event which is never mentioned, in fact is carefully avoided: the accidental shooting death of my wife, Joan, in September 1951."

The shooting was a turning point. Before it, Burroughs' biography reads like a balance sheet with every new entry in the debit column. After it, his life reads like a novel, albeit a novel such as few would wish to write, and none perhaps but Burroughs could live, and survive. It is from this point on that he begins to see in his letters, as in his writing, new significances, to see their interdependence. On the simplest level, he could now anticipate a future. "Better save my letters," he writes in April 1952, "maybe we can get out a book of them later on when I have a rep." Two months later, his despair at Marker's failure to reply implies the deep-seated, personal needs that his writing sought to satisfy: "Of course I am attempting black magic [. . .] I have written five or six letters to him with fantasies and routines in my best vein but he doesn't answer [. . .] I just wrote because it was as near as I could come to contact with him like I was talking to him." The routines evolved in his letters, and they were an act of threatening courtship, love-letters, black-mail. When Marker's rejection seemed final, Burroughs contemplated never writing again. Yet Allerton, as the anonymous listener inside the narrative of *Queer*, is wooed precisely because rejection is inevitable. When Allerton walks out of the book,

William Lee becomes Coleridge's Ancient Mariner in search of a Wedding Guest, finding one whose absence is taken for granted. The routines continue as soliloquies, as written performances for the reader. Looking ahead to *Naked Lunch,* the comedy turns coercive, becomes both compulsive and repulsive: "Gentle reader, I fain would spare you this, but my pen hath its will like the Ancient Mariner."

Two years later, at the virtual dead center of this volume, Burroughs again writes in a state of crisis brought on by a failure of his correspondent to reply, and by the return to sender of his own letters. In April 1954, he pleads with Kerouac: "The withdrawal symptoms are worse than the Marker habit. One letter would fix me. So make it your business, if you are a real friend, to see that he writes me a fix. I am incapacitated. Can't write. Can't take interest in anything." "He" was by then Allen Ginsberg, and the routines Burroughs was writing to him were early episodes of *Naked Lunch.* Burroughs' letters gradually constitute a unique epistolary erotic, an economy in which love serves as a literal pre-text: "Whenever I encounter the impasse of unrequited affection," he wrote in the same letter to Kerouac, "my only recourse is in routines." As dependent on Ginsberg, an ocean away, as he was on junk, Burroughs let his routines become the harvest of a grim reaping of his own erotic and emotional failure. His letters begin like emissaries in the hope of recognition from Whitman's "great Camerado, the lover true," but they end up like the dead letters of Melville's *Bartleby:* "On errands of\life, these letters speed to death." For by the time *Naked Lunch* was published in 1959, Burroughs had begun to sever the human relation of writer to reader through the mechanical texts produced by his cut-up methods. His habit of writing to Ginsberg would end, though the need to write would not.

An essential determinant of the role played by Burroughs' letters was simply the physical distances that divided him from Ginsberg, or from anyone else with whom he could meaningfully communicate. Although his letters never doubt the value of leaving America, they often admit the price paid, while hinting at the necessary isolation of the traveler. Burroughs' expatriation, which coincides with his writing, was only partly enforced by his legal and social violations, by his heroin addiction and homosexuality. Also, there were exceptions, as in Kerouac's visit to Mexico in the summer of 1952. But Burroughs' portrait of Kerouac as a paranoid houseguest who stole his host's share of the bread rolls hardly suggests a welcome meeting of minds, or a respite from his status as a "pernicious foreigner." Then again, when he finally escaped his legal limbo in Mexico at the end of 1952, Burroughs returned to America not to visit New York but to set off from Florida for the jungles of Central America, quoting Shakespeare: "Let determined things to destiny hold unbewailed their way." He chose not to visit Ginsberg but to travel still further away from him and write back. What resulted from the next six months was "In Search of Yage," part one of the epistolary novella *The Yage Letters* (1963).

Comparing the two texts, the reader will recognize that much of the material published as "fiction" under that title is reproduced as correspondence here. Comparison confirms the limited extent of Burroughs' reworking, the selective cannibalization of his letters and notes to fabricate a narrative out of his itinerary. The cumulative, cutting comedy of these anthropological, political, and erotic anecdotes, was, largely, original to the actual letters. Like most of those that follow, these are more than a writer's letters; they are a major part of the writing itself. Their quality as fiction derives from Burroughs' growing investment in the letter form, and signals the strange but steady merger of his letters with his life.

The quest for the reputedly telepathic drug had been prepared for in the closing lines of *Junkie*, where yagé is hesitatingly promised as the "final fix." In the course of revision, significant omissions were made, the most dramatic effect of which was to defer the quest beyond the drug's acquisition. "Yes," Burroughs wrote, "Yage is the final kick and you are not the same after you have taken it. I mean literally." But this dramatic discovery was retrospectively deleted, in recognition that the botanical Grail could not satisfactorily conclude his picaresque search for transforming knowledge. Significantly, as Burroughs notes, the yagé vine itself did not travel well: "Yage is not a transportable kick." The chemical enlightenment promised as an end in itself in 1953 would, by the time *The Yage Letters* appeared a decade later, be displaced by a process of writing—through additional texts that once again, though now far more radically, reedited the old ones, and so exemplified Burroughs' cut-up methodology.

Also blue-penciled from the original "Yage" letters were all references to Burroughs' parallel but unsuccessful attempts to write a narrative account of his misadventures. The significance of maintaining an epistolary form lies in its contrast to his previous writing. As published, *Junkie*, *Queer*, and *Yage* retain a chronological continuity with overlapping material that only serves to heighten their formal distinctiveness. The first was written in the first person, the second in the third person, and the third in the form of letters. Having failed twice to find what he called "a suitable medium," Burroughs was led to try the one form he always used and had already mastered: the epistolary form itself.

When he started to write *Queer*, Burroughs had intended it to use the "same straight narrative method" of *Junkie*, only to find that by shifting person, and by writing after withdrawal from narcotics, the muted, flat register of the self-contained addict exploded into the manic garrulity and emotional excess of his routines. The resulting fragmentation of narrative, allied to the sudden appearance of Burroughs' personal voice, brings the book closer to the inherently episodic, conversational form of his letters. The introduction and redundancy of *Queer*'s internal audience in turn led to a structure for "In Search of Yage" that reproduced the conditions of its composition: an isolation from the absent reader bridged by letter writing. The result, the fictional letters of William Lee, generates a fictional Allen Ginsberg to receive and read them. As Voltaire said of God, if Ginsberg did not exist, it would be necessary to invent him. Burroughs unconsciously suggests as much a year later, in the striking phrase that unexpectedly reverses roles: "Maybe the real novel is letters to you."

Reading through Burroughs' letters to Ginsberg up to August 1953, it comes as a shock to be reminded that, for over six years, their relationship had been conducted entirely by correspondence. When they did finally meet in New York that September and, fittingly, began editing the "Yage" letters together, Ginsberg described the result as "a great psychic marriage": "His new loquaciousness is something I never had the advantage of," he told Neal

Cassady, "he is very personal now, and gives the impression of suffering terribly and continuously."[3] It is tempting to think that their passionate embrace came about not despite but because of the fact that for so long the relationship had existed purely on paper. There is a hint of this in the signatures of Burroughs' letters. In April 1952, he had, after much deliberation, settled on the pseudonym William Lee. (In itself this was a curiously ambivalent choice, given his stated desire to disguise his identity from his mother, whose maiden name was Lee. Conversely, Burroughs liked the Oriental overtones, but could not discard his Anglo-Saxon forename.) For the next year, the letters are signed simply Bill: Bill Burroughs, or Bill Lee, it is not clear. But from May 1953 every other letter is signed Willy Lee. This might, innocently, be explained as befitting letters half intended for fictional use. Yet that of August 17, the last before Burroughs reached New York, and clearly personal in content, also concludes with the signature of his fictive persona. Whether the question of identity did or did not confuse Ginsberg, it certainly appears to have confused Burroughs. It would be almost another four years before Kerouac could write "he, Burroughs (not "Lee" any more)."[4] In any case, the end of the six-year geographical gap between Burroughs and Ginsberg produces, in this volume, a lacuna that lasts from August to December 1953, by which time Burroughs was halfway to Europe, and their marriage of minds had terminated in abrupt physical divorce.

The letters resume in Rome, where, cursing the cold, Burroughs finds himself huddled in his room preparing for the journey to Tangier by reading H. G. Wells's *The Invisible Man*. After references to Wells's "Country of the Blind" as an index of his alienation in Peru, and to *The Time Machine* in the context of *yagé* as "space-time travel," what could be more appropriate, more prescient, more sinister? It is as though the next chapter of his life were already written, and Burroughs had seen the script. In *Naked Lunch:* "The Spanish boys call me *El Hombre Invisible*—the Invisible Man . . ."

---

3. Allen Ginsberg to Neal Cassady, September 4, 1953, in *As Ever: The Collected Correspondence of Allen Ginsberg and Neal Cassady*, edited by Barry Gifford (Berkeley: Creative Arts Books, 1977).
4. Jack Kerouac to Lucien and Cessa Carr, February 28, 1957, Tangier (Carr Collection, Columbia University).

First Rome, and then Tangier, provoke the seasoned traveler into outbursts of contempt for the local culture, prompted in each case by the previous reports of American writers: by "that lying bastard" Gore Vidal, whom Burroughs had recently, if briefly, met in New York; and by Paul Bowles "(that shameless faker)," whose Tangerine novel *Let It Come Down* he certainly knew. Nine months later, Burroughs was still complaining that he had "generally received a cool reception in Europe and Tangier," as if he had been led to expect the red carpet and a ticker tape parade. His judgment of foreign parts, as of people, could be called capricious, were it not so integral to his personality. His verdicts, sometimes based on first impressions, sometimes not even on that, are ever extreme but often reversible. Bowles in particular would dramatically improve on actual acquaintance. Some would be condemned by, but others survive, the special and recurrent sin of failure to return a letter. And so on arrival in Rome, finding "neither [Alan] Ansen nor any word from him," Burroughs planned to proceed to Africa, railing: "As for Ansen, I hope I don't see him there or anywhere else [. . .] Whose idea was it Ansen should go with me? Jack's I believe. He always was an expert in unconscious sabotage." Three days later, he and Ansen were "reconciled."

The severity of Burroughs' spontaneous opinions led to numerous editorial cuts in the now out-of-print volume of correspondence that overlaps much of these following years. The reader already familiar with *Letters to Allen Ginsberg 1953–1957* (where the letter quoted above appears, in expurgated form) will also discover other substantial and frequently highly significant omissions rectified here. In addition, previous mistakes—such as the misdating of several letters, and occasional errors of transcription or printing—have been made good, without, hopefully, the introduction of new ones. More than the earlier letters, those from the Tangier period present a considerable challenge to any editor, given the circumstances of their writing. When Burroughs' typewriters were not pounded to the brink of breakdown, his pen was regularly misguided by one or another drug. Many letters also underwent copious annotation or deletion, while the status of certain ones was problematized by Burroughs' practice of appropriating them to form sections of his work-in-progress. He used his intimate letters also as an author's notebook, as a diary of his desperate addiction and equally desperate writing cure, as a personal, twentieth-century Journal of the Plague Year.

When Burroughs arrived in Tangier the New Year of 1954, it was an international zone and free port, technically not a part of Morocco at all. Whereas the rest of the country was divided between France and Spain, Tangier was uniquely colonized by eight jealous yet indifferent foreign powers. The result was a hybrid neither African nor Western, a "city with many identities and therefore none."[5] It was both a collage where anything went, and a place that was a kind of no-man's-land and that attracted a similarly displaced personnel. "Junkies, queers, drunks. About like Mexico," Burroughs notes of his fellow expatriates. "Most of them came from some place else for obvious reasons." To the south of the zone stretched the deserts of the Dark Continent, but with its easy proximity to Gibraltar and mainland Europe, Tangier was not quite the land of the Foreign Legion. Nevertheless, by seeking to regain in Morocco the legal and cultural license he had enjoyed and lost in Mexico, Burroughs had put the Atlantic between himself and Ginsberg.

After only four months in Tangier, he was heavily addicted again, and was spurred into sending his few close friends a stream of letters because of the silence of the one who mattered most. Neal Cassady wrote to Ginsberg, begging "for godsake allen, write him, I get practically daily letters from him wailing your desertion of him, he's desperate, believe me."[6] The previous day, April 22, Burroughs was consumed by the tragic, raging tantrums of King Lear, striking through—but not out—the lines: "Allen's neglect will drive me to some extravagance of behavior. I don't know what I will do but it will be the terror of the earth." In Shakespeare's play, what follows is "Storm and tempest." Three hundred and fifty years later, Burroughs' storm was safely disposed of in a tea-cup. "Bill is all taken care of," Ginsberg wrote back to Cassady. "He just never got my letters & began imagining all sorts of things.

---

5. Richard F. Patteson, *A World Outside: The Fiction of Paul Bowles* (Austin: University of Texas Press, 1987), p. 47.
6. Cassady to Ginsberg, April 23, 1954, in *As Ever*.

He sure is lonely or imagines himself such and I guess it drives him off the road at times."[7] It was, in Ginsberg's words, "a gratuitous crisis," a simple mix-up of lost letters and broken communication. However genuine Burroughs' expressions of fear for his safety, what they also, inescapably, suggest is that the fear was for the loss of his only audience, the only receiver out there for his nightly transmissions. Two years later, little had changed: "This letter is the only writing I have done in a week now. In the grey Limbo of junk I seem to depend on you as my only point of reference, in fact the only strong emotional contact I have left." When Burroughs quoted Kerouac's reply to his April 22 letter, and admitted that there were "only a few people in the world I want to see," the question was to the point: "If I love Allen why don't I return and live with him?"

Burroughs stayed on in Tangier until September 1954, his addiction eating up his parents' $200 monthly check, and leaving him on the edge of poverty and illness. The extremity of his living conditions was exaggerated in his letters through his routines, as if by outbidding reality he could find remedial distraction in comedy and fiction. So the disease that grips him in July leads Burroughs into a virtuoso digression, starting from his own suffering and desertion by his old friend Kells Elvins: "Pain worse by the minute. And Kells would have to leave *exactly* when I need him. Eric has a hard luck story worth three of that . . ." The three stories that duly follow, a series of mounting medical atrocities, were included near verbatim in *Naked Lunch,* but divorced from the personal anxieties out of which they grew and transplanted from their original epistolary context. The parodic excesses of his material may have been pitched at Ginsberg, but letters such as this confirm what the reader who instinctively shares the cruel comedy of Burroughs' writing also knows: that it is a necessary therapy, self-administered. "I am just writing along to put off the misery I will feel when I stop writing," he comments the following month, "I know it's there waiting for me . . ."

A novelist invents a world and peoples it with his own creations. In Tangier, Burroughs found his characters and locale ready-made,

---

7. Ginsberg to Cassady, May 12, 1954, in *As Ever.*

but the contrary quality of the city, its artificially dense cultural juxtapositions, its fragmented expatriate society, did not add up to a novel. A city so cosmopolitan yet so small could almost shut out the individual past, but not quite sustain the present or build a future, and the result for Burroughs was exactly as Paul Bowles had described it: "The place was a counterfeit, a waiting room between connections, a transition from one way of being to another, which for the moment was neither way, no way."[8] In the interim, spurned even by Bowles, and despite the visits of friends, Burroughs pictures a daily life reduced to various basic routines involving letters themselves. In the morning, mounting the twisting medina paths up to the American legation to collect his mail, on the days when there was any mail to collect. Then crossing the Socco Chico, with its teeming café life, to post his letter to Ginsberg at the Spanish post office. Or maybe taking the longer walk across the Socco Grande markets to the British post office, from which transatlantic mail deliveries were more efficient. Finally, back to his room at one end of a crooked alleyway, in a building where his neighbors read from right to left if they could read at all. And sitting there over his typewriter, writing and rewriting another letter to Ginsberg, a muezzin from the nearby mosque wailing the prayer call through the open shutters of a window whose only view was of a cul-de-sac.

Burroughs looked to his letters for distraction: "It is really a deprivation to be without intelligent conversation. I evolve concepts, but no one to communicate with. Well enough, I am getting garrulous." The routines that came to him lacked any immediate human outlet, and he needed an audience to satisfy his material, like a stage performer turned inside out, because, as he told Kerouac that September, he was "not self-sufficient." And so Burroughs made his abortive return to the States in the fall of 1954, when Ginsberg again rejected him—by letter. Burroughs' reply that October describes the bizarre, circular intensity of his correspondence: in it he tells how rereading Ginsberg's letter inspired a "tremendous dream"—the first part of which is specifically about letters—which

---

8. Paul Bowles, *Let It Come Down* (London: John Lehmann, 1952; London: Peter Owen, 1984), p. 151.

he then recounts. Almost demanding interpretation, the dream juxtaposes homosexual self-contempt with a realization of the recurrent
fear of intercepted mail, while the typed pages are so mixed up that
the dreamer is left vainly "looking for *the end of the letter* and a
signature." The dream depicts a nightmare of confused identity and
broken communication that ironically anticipates Burroughs' cut-
up texts.

On his return to Tangier, Burroughs wrote back: "I need you
so much your absence causes me, at times, acute pain. I don't mean
sexually. I mean in connection with my writing." The displacement
of erotic need onto paper makes the agony of Ginsberg's absence
all the greater for being essential to it. Coming to think of his writing
as both the means to a cure and its reward, Burroughs would find
that salvation from addiction was to require another year of solitary
suffering. It was hardly surprising that he should build his fiction
around his letters, material that already had a reader.

In October 1955, his letters record a temporary, but dramatic
and creative, recovery. Regrettably, the precise nature of the letter
sequence coded A, B, and C, has been obscured—partly because
these long letters were extensively reworked at the time but have
survived incomplete, and partly because the first, recently published
as selections, has not been included here. What is clear, however,
is the extent to which Burroughs' transcription and editing of his
own letters not only provided content for his work-in-progress but
also organized its structure and developed his creative strategy.
Describing the simple "gimmick" that allowed him to "use all
letters, including love letters, fragmentary material, anything," he
recognizes the resulting mosaic form. This then posed inevitable
aesthetic questions about his medium, because "the mosaic method
is more suitable to painting than writing."[9] On thinking next about
the pictures of Paul Klee, his comment that one is an "exact copy
of what I saw high on Yage in Pucallpa when I closed my eyes,"
recalls his letter from Pucallpa of June 18, 1953: "The effect can not
be put into words [. . .] I could *paint* it if I could paint." The
drug-induced visions thereby relate to the "cryptic significance of

---

9. *Interzone* (New York: Viking Penguin, 1989), p. 126. The line derives from a
letter, dated October 20, 1955, not printed here.

juxtaposition" attributed to his chapter of letter selections, a phrase that reappears in *Naked Lunch* after his admission: "So I got an exclusive why don't I make with the live word? The word cannot be expressed direct." In other words, Burroughs was working toward transcending his own verbal medium via references to another, visual medium. Editing his correspondence produced an approximation of collage that looked forward to the specifically *collagiste* method of the cut-ups. But in 1955, this line of development was checked by the lack of any artistic input or context, and by the resumption of his habit.

When he reached England and began the apomorphine treatment in 1956, Burroughs knew that the death-in-life of addiction had to end: "This time I'll make it if it kills me." Cure, when it came, meant rebirth. Back in Tangier that October: "I don't see our roles reversed exactly but expanded and altered on both sides. I have entered a period of change more drastic than adolescence or early childhood." Suddenly, a breakthrough takes place on all fronts. Like a dam bursting, his writing pours forth: "Interzone is coming like dictation. I can't keep up with it." And no longer regarding himself as an ill-omened pariah in Tangier, Burroughs announces it as his "dream town" and himself possessed by a Revelation. In the routine that follows, he breaks into the dynamic hip style of Lord Buckley to demolish religious leaders, clearing the path for "Pop Lee Your Friendly Prophet." At a time when Tangier itself was poised to lose its license—the abolition of the international zone was only days away—Burroughs found his own in "the most beautiful city in the world, or at least it's always young and fair to me." The only thing missing now was the presence of his old comrades Ginsberg and Kerouac, and they would be there in four months, together with Peter Orlovsky and Alan Ansen.

Their visit that spring of 1957 causes another lull in Burroughs' letters, as they set to work with him on his manuscripts, and his own energies turned away from new correspondence. The first to arrive, Kerouac took a room above Burroughs' in the Villa Muniria and put his speed-typing skills to good use, only to find that the material began giving him nightmares. Since Burroughs' behavior had become as outlandishly self-parodic as his writing, and proved equally alienating, it was no surprise that Kerouac soon fell homesick, and he left shortly after the arrival of Ginsberg and Orlovsky, who moved into his old room. Six hours a day Ginsberg worked on the still-chaotic texts, using his unique familiarity with the material to select additions from three years of Burroughs' letters to him. Ansen aided the collective effort with his scholarly expertise, and after two months, they had organized the mess into a 200-page manuscript.

Burroughs' short-lived reunion with Kerouac and Ginsberg brought out the emotional tensions in their relationships: he admitted to Kerouac that contact with him had sometimes been a proxy for direct communication with Ginsberg; while Burroughs' obsession with Ginsberg naturally created strains due to the presence of his lover, Orlovsky. But the reunion is also a reminder of what Burroughs had missed during the 1950s and would continue to miss out on—the growing momentum of publicity and publication that raised the flag of the Beat Generation in the United States. Burroughs was not there in San Francisco when Ginsberg first read "Howl," nor would he be there in New York when Kerouac's *On the Road* grabbed the headlines. When Ginsberg and Kerouac left Tangier that spring and summer, they made trips through Europe but returned home. When Burroughs also left for Europe, he would return to Tangier.

At first, his trips to London and Copenhagen appeared mistakes, but then the pieces began to fall into place. Reviewing his work, he saw no place in it now for letters, or for forms of structuring that resembled an epistolary novel. So, in September 1957, he reacts strongly to Ginsberg's suggestion for linear continuity, considering "any attempt at chronological arrangement extremely ill-advised." Burroughs rejected precisely the narrative unity of an autobiographical novel, because he wasn't interested in the false continuities of traditional fictional time, story, or identity. He was interested in a form that reproduced his experiences both of Tangier and of his work's composition: his drug-induced sensitivity to the place's strange collage of histories and cultures resulted in sudden, heightened intersections of dream and reality; and this corresponded to the fusions and reversals of past and future, fact and fantasy, that came about from transcribing, cutting, and selecting from a mass of fragmentary material drawn from his letters. Two years earlier, Burroughs had noted that "*Junk, Queer,* and *Yage,* reconstructed my past." *Naked Lunch*'s abrupt transitions and contradictions intended the opposite; vaulting time and identity through schizophrenic deconstruction. Hence the significance of his development, that October 1957, of a theory "that contains the key to addiction, cancer and schizophrenia," to account for, if not to organize, his new material. Many of Burroughs' speculative ventures into medical science were actually highly prescient, if pointless. In *Naked Lunch:* " 'I thought of that three hundred years ago.' 'Your plan was unworkable then and useless now . . . Like Da Vinci's flying machine plans . . .' " At a creative level, his readiness to consider scientific theory as integral to his writing, though fruitless in terms of a practice at the time, would, however, prophesy a later shift: the breakthrough from content to technique.

After three months of frantic writing and self-analysis that winter in Tangier, Burroughs had shed another skin: "I feel myself not the same person. I am about ready to leave Tangier." The promise of a new identity demanded a new locale, a break with the past. And as his biographer notes, it was "the first time in many years that he was leaving a place voluntarily, without the threat of police or legal action to spur him to flight."[10]

It was unfinished business that took Burroughs to Paris in January 1958. He was now ready to resolve his relationship with Ginsberg, who had been living there since the previous September, and to resume psychoanalysis. When he arrived, Ginsberg was stunned by the transformation. The "Satanic Bill" of old, he wrote, "in front of my eyes turned into an Angel!"[11] It was a greeting as friends they had waited years to achieve. Now Burroughs could lay his emotional burdens and traumas on the analyst's couch. When Gregory Corso heard of this, he wrote warning: "They'll kill you, and perhaps that's what you wish, perhaps you don't want to write

10. Ted Morgan, *Literary Outlaw: The Life and Times of William S. Burroughs* (New York: Henry Holt, 1988), p. 271.

11. Ginsberg to Peter Orlovsky, January 20, 1958, in *Straight Hearts' Delight: Love Poems and Selected Letters 1947–1980,* edited by Winston Leyland (San Francisco: Gay Sunshine, 1980).

anymore."[12] Whatever Burroughs wanted, the normalization of his former relationship with Ginsberg—so crucial to his past creativity—combined with the apparent success of psychoanalysis, certainly did shift his attention away from letter and fiction writing. In October 1958, he juxtaposes further radical analytical progress with his equal need for a corresponding aesthetic breakthrough: "Analysis is coming to spectacular climaxes. I am completely dissatisfied with all the work I have done in writing and with the whole medium." Only the month before, Burroughs and Corso had joined forces on a magazine project, but it failed to materialize—failed for, among other reasons, one that is instructive.

It was bound to fail because, as Corso informed Ginsberg, "our content will be of the most sordid, vile, vulgar, oozing, seeping slime imaginable." This was, for Burroughs, already superannuated. Over a year before, in Tangier, Ginsberg and Kerouac had suffered nightmares retyping his material, so that when Kerouac came to fictionalize the scene in *Desolation Angels,* the speech of Bull Hubbard rings true: "It's a matter of catharsis where I say the most horrible thing I can think of—Realize that, the most *horrible* dirty slimy awful niggardliest posture possible—By the time I finish this book I'll be as pure as an angel . . ." In terms of content, Burroughs had well and truly reached the final frontier of depravity. Next month, despite dramatic advances on other fronts, he admitted: "But I still can't get a line on writing . . ." In the same letter, Burroughs described the work of his Parisian hotel neighbor, not primarily a writer but a painter: "I see in his painting the psychic landscape of my own work. He is doing in painting what I try to do in writing." The neighbor was Brion Gysin.

After Ginsberg's departure from Paris that summer, Burroughs started to become friendly with the man who had cold-shouldered him in Tangier, and whom he once dubbed a "paranoid bitch on wheels." Before they achieved what Gysin later termed "psychic symbiosis,"[13] Burroughs found another extraordinary character in

12. Gregory Corso to Burroughs and Ginsberg, February 1958, Venice (Ginsberg Collection, Columbia University).

13. Brion Gysin in Gysin and Terry Wilson's *Here to Go: Planet R-101* (San Francisco: Re/Search Publications, 1982), p. 166.

Jacques Stern. The passionate praise for Stern during this period seems almost a dry run for Gysin. Stern was classed as a great writer and a mystic master of therapeutic techniques, and Burroughs urgently needed to evolve the psychology and literary method of *Naked Lunch* beyond their grounding in addiction and withdrawal. Burroughs was, quite simply, ready and waiting for a new focal point, a new source of ideas. Stern himself would fade away, and Gysin fulfill his promise. Significantly, Burroughs set his own desire for writing that had the "urgency of bullfighting" next to his report that Gysin's "life and sanity" were at stake when he painted. It recalls his earlier identification with the goals of another painter: "I am trying, like Klee, *to create something that will have a life of its own, that can put me in real danger, a danger which I willingly take on myself.*"[14] Exactly three years later, the excitement of Burroughs' direct and intuitive identification with Gysin's work was double-edged: the painter's apparent success only highlighted his own continuing artistic limbo, as suggested by the distinction between what Gysin "is doing" and what Burroughs was trying to do. Meanwhile, there was the piecemeal publication of *Naked Lunch*.

There is a curious irony to the events leading up to the appearance of Burroughs' most famous work. Paris was the only place where the book could then have been published, and Maurice Girodias of Olympia Press perhaps the only one to consider doing it. Yet Girodias had already rejected the manuscript before Burroughs arrived, so that, in April 1958, it was to San Francisco and City Lights that he turned. Despite Burroughs' suggestions for a selection that "avoided the more obscene sections which would involve difficulties of a legal nature," Lawrence Ferlinghetti also rejected it. It was only the appearance of excerpts in American magazines, with the media attention they attracted, that convinced Girodias to change his mind and Olympia Press to publish. In keeping with the material's disorderly composition, the book's final form was influenced by the order in which it was sent to the printers, one last act that Burroughs later called an "accidental juxtaposition."[15]

14. In *Interzone*, p. 128. See note 7, page xxxix.
15. From "An Interview with William S. Burroughs" (March 1974), by John Tytell, in *The Beat Diary*, edited by Arthur and Kit Knight (California, Pa., 1977), p. 42.

By the time of its publication, Burroughs was already moving ahead and, with newfound "power and confidence," about to enter yet another period of drastic change. From late 1958, letter by letter, a momentum had been building up, an energy of metamorphosis escalating, a psychic thunderstorm brewing. When fed into his subsequent writing, it could only seem fantasy, but Burroughs' letters insist otherwise. In the week of *Naked Lunch*'s launch, he wrote: "What I am putting down on paper is *literally* what is happening to me as I move forward. This is no land of the imagination [. . .] And dangerous in a most literal sense."

The publication of *Naked Lunch* was a watershed for Burroughs. It was the culmination of years spent in "total humiliation and failure" and their conversion into success: "I have been on the outside," in July 1959, he told Ginsberg, who needed no reminding, "I don't figure to go back." But this volume does not end there, because within three months, Burroughs traded the two old relations that had brought him to Paris in 1958 for two new ones that would keep him there after 1959. He had entered into a new dominant friendship to match that of the last decade, and a new form of therapy to mirror his long-running engagement with professional analysts, and both coincided with a creative turning point. It was a point where Burroughs turned the page on his past and started a new book all in one swift motion.

The "new method of writing" that Burroughs announces in the final letter to Ginsberg was the prototype for a range of methods he would spend the next decade intensively exploring: cut-ups. Though their practical operation lies beyond this volume's horizon, an essential, neglected element of their genesis is disclosed here. When Brion Gysin handed him the first, accidental cut-up products, Burroughs had two reasons for acting the way he did: "I showed the first texts to Burroughs hoping to hear him laugh out loud as I had. He took off his glasses to reread them even more intently, saying: 'You've got something big here, Brion' [. . .] He recognized immediately that this was a tool of enormous importance to him."[16]

To begin with, Burroughs had been excited by Gysin's artistic knowledge and experience. Gysin had studied Japanese and Arabic

---

16. Brion Gysin, in *Here to Go*, p. 186.

calligraphy, seen Max Ernst at work on his frottages during the war, and been expelled from the Surrealists by André Breton in 1935. He was already well versed in the history of multimedia art movements and in the techniques of such Paris-based luminaries as Marcel Duchamp, Man Ray, Henri Michaux, Benjamin Péret, and Tristan Tzara, all of whom Burroughs had met socially with Ginsberg and Corso in June 1958. In Tangier, Burroughs and Gysin had had little in common. In Paris, Gysin opened up an entire artistic context that Burroughs knew and sought only superficially. Although this background—and any discussion of Dada or Surrealist methods—is absent from Burroughs' correspondence at the time, his letters do confirm the direct impact of Gysin's current pictorial practice, to the extent that he tried his own hand at drawing. Almost thirty years before going public as a painter, Burroughs produced the calligraphic cover for the first edition of *Naked Lunch*. Claiming in April 1959 that some of his drawings were "positively alive," and in May that to "really dig" them "you must be tea high," again recalls his earlier sense of kinship with Klee's visionary pictures and its implied relation to the mosaic form of letter selections. Still, as a writer, Burroughs could not simply pick up Gysin's brush and run with it, however urgent his desire for a new medium. But with a pair of scissors he could, and did, directly apply visual, material methods to his texts.

Secondly, Burroughs' letters show that Gysin was responsible not only for the aesthetic means of his new method but also for its therapeutic ends. At its inception, the cut-up principle was directly related to L. Ron Hubbard's "science of mental health" known as Scientology. Radically simple, if not simplistic, Scientology slammed the door on Burroughs' years of psychoanalytical treatment, despite its apparent success at the time. And because the psychology of Hubbard's *Dianetics* was mechanistic, it allowed Burroughs to develop and, crucially, *combine* in one practical method the artistic, therapeutic, and scientific levels of his previous writing. Above all, Scientology promised self-sufficiency. Burroughs' next book, the collaborative pamphlet *Minutes to Go,* advertised the cut-up method as a creative and therapeutic manual, offering a simple way to convert patients into physicians and readers into writers: "do it yourself."

The sudden news of this convergence of artistic and remedial methods deriving from Gysin would, in itself, have been enough to open up a distance between Burroughs and Ginsberg. "I can not explain this method to you," Burroughs writes, "until you have necessary training." But as the two final letters make explicit, the new developments were accompanied by a more personal estrangement. The "biographical" note in his penultimate letter, introduced with the warning that Ginsberg had mixed him up "with someone else doesn't live here any more," begins with a renunciation of his former identity: "I have no past life at all [. . .] Remember?" he asks, before answering his own question with an echo of Bartleby's menacing refrain, "I prefer not to." Mirroring the biographical note "by 'myself,' " his last letter "isn't written for 'you' exactly": "Pay no attention to above." After years spent less desiring than needing exactly that—attention, an audience—Burroughs reversed the entire dynamic of his past letters and previous fiction. Coinciding with his physical assault on the very medium of written communication, and with the dismissal of his most intimate reader, the so-called death of the author has never been enacted so literally.

The last time Burroughs had had to write a "biographical sketch," seven years earlier in April 1952, he had signed off combining his lately coined *nom de plume* with the most personal affection for Ginsberg: "Magnums of Love, Willy Lee—That Junky writin' boy, Bill." In the seven years they had been corresponding since 1945, they had moved a lot closer together, and were about to move, through letters, much closer still. Another seven years on, Burroughs uses only the same, absolutely impersonal signature that concludes his third-person, cut-up "biographical exegesis" to also terminate his next, and this volume's last, letter to Ginsberg. The autobiographical, the epistolary, and the creative lines run and join together. The letter cycle comes full circle.

Oliver Harris
August 1991
Oxfordshire, England

1945

July 24, 1945
[700 South Price Rd.
Clayton, Mo.][1]

Dear Allen,

I thank you for your card which I was happy to receive on returning from a business trip to Chicago.

Apparently the authorities decided to be charitable in your case or perhaps they considered your inversion so deeply ingrained that it could only be described as physical.[2]

Where did you secure the C?[3] My own supply is utterly depleted.

More delays in regard to the Merchant Marine. They demand a new document: my Army Medical Record which can only be secured by filing a petition with the Department of Demobilized Personnel Records in North Carolina. *Quelle Blague alors!* I am sending a letter to Jack [Kerouac] via you. He did not think to put an address on his letter.[4]

Veuillez acceptez mes sentiments de plus cordiales. Je vive à te revoir,

William Burroughs

---

1. The address was that of Burroughs' parents since 1926.
2. The authorities: Columbia University. Having written obscene graffiti on the windows of his room in Livingston Hall, Ginsberg, on the morning of March 17, 1945, was visited by Dean Fermin, who found Kerouac (then banned from the campus) in his room. Ginsberg was suspended subject to a psychiatric report.
3. C: cocaine.
4. Burroughs wrote to Kerouac welcoming his plan to get a job as a merchant seaman. In fact, Kerouac's plan, the result of parental pressure, came to nothing, and he ended up working as a soda jerk in the drugstore under his parents' Ozone Park apartment. Burroughs and Kerouac met up in New York that August for V-J Day.

1946

Sept. 1, 1946
10036 Conway Road
St. Louis 5, Mo.[1]

Dear Allen,

Thanks for your letters. I was glad to hear from you.

The Goldstein menage[2] sounds typically depressing. No doubt you will be admitted to Columbia. McKnight is just playing hard to get.[3]

I have given up junk entirely and don't miss it at all. Giving my attention to money making enterprises variously engaged in patent medicines and household appliances. This patent medicine deal is one long beef with the Pure Food and Drug Dept. They are trying to impede the sale of my fluoride tablets for tooth decay. "Death County Bill's Tooth and Bone Tablets from The County Without a Toothache."[4] I am concocting an aphrodisiac which the Dept. will probably regard with even less enthusiasm. Please let me hear from you soon again.

As Ever,
Bill

What's the latest scope on Lucien?[5]

---

1. The address is that of Burroughs' parents' gift shop, close to their home on South Price Road. In June, as punishment for a narcotics misdemeanor, Burroughs had been "sentenced" by a judge to spend the summer with his parents. His arrest is described in *Junky*, pp. 26–27.

2. Goldstein ménage: on the top floor of the Ninety-second Street apartment house where Ginsberg lived were the ex-wife of popular author Harry Golden, and her son; the writer Charles Peters also rented a room in the house.

3. Nicholas McKnight, dean of Columbia University, who had suspended Ginsberg from Columbia. Ginsberg had just applied for readmission. Following a psychiatric report, McKnight accepted his enrollment in the September term.

4. In Deaf Smith County, around Amarillo, the water, loaded with lime and phosphate, is supposed to cure bad teeth. They say, "If you drink a little, the lime will first build up under your fillings, then pinch them out."

5. Lucien Carr: he had lately been released from Elmira State Reformatory, having served two years for the manslaughter of David Kammerer in August 1944. Burroughs and Kerouac had been indicted as material witnesses. Burroughs knew Carr, and Kammerer, from St. Louis.

Oct. 10, 1946
10036 Conway Road
St. Louis 5, Mo.[6]

Dear Allen,

Thanks for your information in regard to Joan.[7] I have sent her a money order c/o Garver.[8] If you see her tell her I will be in N.Y. towards the end of this month and may bring her back with me to Texas where I will likely spend the winter. Money to be made here like picking fruit off the trees. Grapefruit that is. I expect to clear about $10,000 this winter in the mail order citrus business. I am leaving here in a few days for St. Louis to divorce my wife[9] and extort some financial backing from the family. My best to Lucien. See you at the end of this month. *Pin Joan down on her address.*

As Ever,
Bill

---

6. Contrary to the letter heading, Burroughs was writing from Pharr, Texas.

7. Joan Vollmer-Adams: Burroughs had been living with her since early 1946, and by November she was titling herself Mrs. W. S. Burroughs. In October, Joan had been admitted to Bellevue Hospital, and Burroughs had become concerned when a letter to her was returned. He did collect Joan, on the thirty-first, and brought her back to Texas. They stayed first with Kells Elvins, Burroughs' boyhood friend from St. Louis, with whom he had rented a house in Pharr, Texas. Elvins owned farmland in the Rio Grande Valley, and Burroughs succeeded in promoting money from his parents to buy fifty acres nearby. He and Joan found their own ninety-nine-acre farm near New Waverly, East Texas, forty miles north of Houston.

8. William Maynard Garver, introduced to Burroughs by Herbert Huncke, who had met Garver in Riker's Island. To finance his heroin habit, Garver stole and then pawned overcoats. In *Junky*, Garver appears as Bill Gains, p. 41, etc.

9. By wife Burroughs meant Ilse Herzfeld Klapper. Burroughs' marriage had been one of convenience, made in July 1937 in Athens, in order to allow Ilse, a German Jewess, to flee the Nazis. (They had met in Dubrovnik, on a trip Burroughs made to Europe in 1936.)

1947

Feb. 19, 1947
[New Waverly, Texas]

Dear Allen,

Received your letter. Gratified to learn of your liaison with Cassady.[1]

As regards your psychiatric difficulties, I am not at all surprised. These jerks feel that anyone who is with it at all belongs in a nut house. What they want is some beat clerk who feels with some reason that other people don't like him. In short, someone so scared and whipped down he would never venture to do anything that might disturb the analyst. I think you would do better with the Reichians who sound a good deal more hip.[2]

I would like some of that hay. Enclose $20. Allen, this is very important. *Please save any seed that comes with the stuff. When you buy it in bulk, ask your friends to do the same, and sound down the connection about the price of some seed.* I am afraid this seed I have has been sterilized by the government. What a dirty, underhanded, bureaucratic trick. And send along all the seed you can get your hands on. I think Vickie saves them.[3]

Be careful how you send the hay. Put a phoney name and return address on the package.

---

1. Ginsberg had met and fallen for Neal Cassady the previous month.
2. On March 11, Ginsberg wrote to Wilhelm Reich, describing his "psychic difficulty" as a homosexual and asking him to recommend an analyst. Ginsberg also recounted his lay analysis at the hands of Burroughs, a year earlier, as having left him "with a number of my defenses broken, but, centrally unchanged, with nothing to replace the lost armor." (Quoted in Barry Miles's *Ginsberg* [New York: Simon & Schuster, 1989], p. 96.)
3. Vickie Russell: a/k/a Priscilla Arminger, the daughter of a Detroit judge, and an underworld friend of Herbert Huncke. She appears as Mary in *Junky*, p. 12, *et ff.*

Garver has redeemed himself, and came up with a fairly believable story and the stuff, so Huncke and I are briefly with it.[4]

As Ever,
Bill

---

4. Herbert Huncke: born 1916, Greenfield, Massachusetts, a prominent Times Square junky hipster. He had been staying with the Burroughses since the previous month, and stayed on until that September. Huncke appears as Herman in *Junky*, p. 5, *et ff*.

[*March 11, 1947*
New Waverly, Texas]

Dear Allen,

Thanks for your letter.

As regards Garver, I cannot regard his behavior in a charitable light. He actually had the gall to come on hurt because I doubted his "integrity," and refused to send more money until I saw some stuff from the last $10. When for the pay off he writes me he is sending that tincture and never did send it.[5] To my way of thinking he really came up crummy.

I am not sick and I do not want you to even try and connect. Thanks for your offer, but I don't want you taking any chances when I don't really need it.

I doubt if the poppy seed is sterilized since they sell the right kind of poppy seed in seed stores. Only you can't get it by the pound. For some idiotic reason the bureaucrats are more opposed to tea than to stuff. Here in Texas *possession* of tea is a felony calling for 2 years. Texas has a number of such special felonies.

Sorry you can not get any tea seed. Like I say, I fear this seed I have is no good at all, any of it. The poppies are growing but the weed hasn't shown, and I am fairly sure won't show. I may have to run a still here to make expenses. So send along the poppy seed please.

Let me hear from you again soon. It is practically Summer down here, and king size scorpions, Tarantulas, Ticks, chiggers and mosquitos are emerging in droves. I killed 10 scorpions yesterday. The house is overrun with huge rats as big as possums. I shot one who was too fat and got wedged in his hole, but the survivors are legion and gun shy. I am contemplating the purchase of a ferret.

As Ever,
Bill

---

5. Tincture: probably paregoric, a weak, camphorated tincture of opium.

[*August 8, 1947*
New Waverly, Texas][6]

Dear Allen,

Was glad to hear from you, grieved but not surprised to learn of your difficulties. Enclose $10 to relieve immediate necessities.[7]

2 unimportant-looking letters arrived and were forwarded to Denver. 1 more today. I opened one thinking it might be Norman.[8] Someone named Charlie, and his message nothing to my purpose. I guess Norman is not going to answer. Gives him too much anxiety no doubt. Anyway the crop is ripening and the samples I have taken most encouraging, so I will scrape by without Norman's hard-to-get advice.[9]

No complications arose from the parental visitation, on the contrary a shower of benefits.

I enjoyed your poem.[10]

---

6. This letter was dated July 10 by Burroughs, but the postmark on the envelope is Aug. 8, 1947, and the later-mentioned "parental visitation" by Burroughs' parents, Mort and Laura, to the farm in Texas occurred after the birth of William Burroughs III, Burroughs and Vollmer's son, on July 21, 1947, in Conroe, Texas.
7. At the end of his Columbia term, Ginsberg had gone by bus to Denver to spend the summer with Neal Cassady, who had just started living with Carolyn Robinson (later Cassady), and was still married to, and sleeping with, Luanne Sanderson. Despite initial financial difficulties, Ginsberg soon found a job and an apartment.
8. Norman: known by Burroughs through another friend, Jack Anderson, who like Norman worked on the docks in New York City. It was from Norman that Burroughs had acquired a quantity of morphine syrettes in January 1945. He appears as Norton in *Junky*, pp. 1–2.
9. Advice: i.e., on how to dry and "cure" marijuana.
10. Ginsberg had written an ode for the birth of Burroughs' son, a rhymed verse epic that took him six days to complete, which he did in late July and sent to Burroughs.

Keep me informed of developments. I fear your position in Denver is somewhat precarious.

As Ever,
Bill

P.S. I bought my own scale. Lost the envelope with new address so using old until I hear from you.

1948

Feb. 20, 1948
Privy Moving Day
Weed Co. Texas[1]

Dear Al,

Back here for several weeks and feeling O.K. at last. I had to go to Lexington for the cure. Stayed 2 weeks and was sick 3 weeks more after I got out. Put it down, kid, put it down.[2]

Please find out how much $ you need to have that stuff packed and sent down here. You can reverse the express charges, or maybe packing charges too. Let me know and I will send $ to extent necessary.

I have conducted some successful experiments with weed concentrates. By the way could use some more seed if you run across some with a good pedigree. Will take up to a quart at $25 per pint. Let me know what the score is and be careful.

Frankly I don't trust that kind of straight genital Reichians from here to Benny Graff. Feller say when a man gets too straight he's just a god damned prick.[3]

Did you deliver my Xmas present to Huncke and Phil?[4] Wish I had it back now.

Well since I have to live in this hole I figure to live cheap. Bought two hogs to fatten on slops. Getting in some chickens right soon.

---

1. Weed Co.: actually New Waverly.
2. Burroughs entered the Federal Narcotic Farm in Kentucky after spending the winter in New York picking up a habit from Bill Garver. His experiences in Lexington feature in *Junky*, pp. 60–68.
3. That winter, Ginsberg had begun twice-weekly sessions with one of the analysts recommended by Reich, Dr. Allan Cott in Newark. Ginsberg lasted three months. Benny Graff was a Reichian patient who later became a junky and an informer.
4. Phil White: a thief and junky from Tennessee. Appears as Roy in *Junky*, p. 5, etc. Burroughs met both Huncke and White during his first involvement with narcotics in 1945. He "worked the hole"—pickpocketed on the subway—with White, whose moniker "the Sailor" derived from his having recently returned from sea. The present was probably a small ball of homemade opium from Burroughs' poppies, collected by Ginsberg during a visit to New Waverly in August 1947.

We got wolves here now. Moved down from the big wood north of Pine Valley.

I received a present from Garver. Give him my best regards if you see him. Give 'em to anybody else too. They don't cost nothing, feller say.

The Honest Hog Caller
Will Burroughs

P.S. Send your address. Lost it.[5]

---

5. At the time, Ginsberg was living in a room at 536 West 114th Street, opposite Columbia.

June 5, 1948
[New Orleans]

Dear Jack and Allen,

Glad to hear from you all and to learn of successful completion of the novel.[6] I wrote a letter to old 27th St. address which, no doubt, will be returned here.[7]

Your letter left something to be desired from the standpoint of information. I would appreciate news of: Garver, Carlos, Hunky, Phil, Hal, Lucien and, of course, yourselves.[8]

I'm selling out in New Waverly and moving to New Orleans. Have bought some farm land in Rio Grande Valley which should bring in a sizeable bundle of gelts come cotton picking time. Someone else is doing the work on a share basis.

I lost my Texas driving license for driving while drunk and public indecency.[9] Find things very uncool in Texas. So will take out Louisiana citizenship, and return only to look over my holdings. Since I won't be in Waverly will not be able to receive visitors there. May buy a house here. In fact negotiating in that direction now, since I must have some place to stash these brats.[10] If I get a house here, will be ready to receive visits.

I still have a crop left at the farm. Will go back there to get it in a week or so, but may find the harvest unadvisable for reasons of security. Please let me hear from you *soon*. Present address is: *111 Transcontinental Drive, New Orleans 20, La.*

Will be here a few more weeks, I guess.

As Ever,
Bill

---

6. *The Town and the City*, a draft of which Kerouac had finished in May.

7. In the fall of 1947, Ginsberg had rented a room on West 27th Street, though he was now living at West 114th Street.

8. Hal Chase: from Denver. Burroughs had met him through Joan in 1944, when Chase was an anthropology student at Columbia. Carlos was one of Burroughs' former junk customers.

9. Caught *in flagrante* with Joan in their parked car outside Beeville, Texas, Burroughs was arrested, fined $173, and bailed out by his parents after a night in jail.

10. Brats: Julie Adams, Joan's three-year-old daughter from her first marriage, and Billy, her son by Burroughs.

Oct. 14, 1948
[509 Wagner St.
Algiers, La.]

Dear Allen,

I sent a letter to your brother in regard to the shipping charges.
Have not heard from him.[11]

My farming enterprise looks very good. I believe I told you that
Kells [Elvins] and I have incorporated our holdings, bought equipment, and hired a manager. The first crop comes off in a month.
If commodity prices hold up for 6 months we will clean up. Should
realize about $15,000 clear for each of us in the next 6 months.

Let me know where and I will send you some tea. I still have
a habit, but plan to go somewhere for a cure when I get some $
from the first crop. Joan sends her best.

As Ever,
Bill

It seems very doubtful to me that Huncke will ever make any
attempt to repay Durgin.[12] I think any policy of appeasement in
that direction will be disastrous, and can only lead to fresh impu-
dence and impositions.

---

11. Ginsberg's elder brother, Eugene Brooks.
12. In May, Ginsberg had sublet an apartment at 321 East 121st Street, Harlem,
from Russell Durgin, a Columbia University theology student. Ginsberg had
allowed Huncke to move in, and he promptly ransacked Durgin's valuable book
collection. The incident was used in John Clellon Holmes's 1952 novel, Go, where
Durgin appears as Verger, Huncke as Ancke, and Ginsberg as Stofsky.

Nov. 9, 1948
[509 Wagner St.
Algiers, La.]

Dear Allen,

I was glad to hear from you.

Financially things look very good. In these inflation times I couldn't be in a better spot. Our first crop will come off in about a week. Peas. We should gross about $5000 on this deal. Lettuce and carrots are coming along. I should be in the $ by Xmas. Our real cash crops (cotton and tomatoes) will come in next Spring and Summer. Also have an oil deal on, which may mean quick $.

I am very dissatisfied with living conditions here. There seems to be no one of any interest around, or if such people exist, I can not find them. I am still trying to devise some method to break the habit. My latest idea is to go to some other city and have dwindling quantities mailed to me. Stuff is too easy to buy in N.O.

I have been considering the possibility of moving out of the U.S.A. to Central America, S. America, or possibly to Africa. May also move back to N.Y. or its environs.

Looking for a job that pays any money is going to prove discouraging.[13] The only type wanted now is technicians. General intelligence is regarded as a highly undesirable characteristic. (I am referring to you, of course. I am not looking for a job.)

I will send along some weed. Please give some (about 10 sticks) to Brandenburg.[14] I am going to raise some more this Spring for my own use, so I will attempt to raise enough for commercial purposes. Make everything pay is my motto. To this end, I am looking around now for some cheap land in this vicinity.

I think Gilmore's indignation a bit thick in view of his own check dodging proclivities. Does he now consider himself com-

---

13. Ginsberg, after graduating from Columbia, was unable to find a job except as copyboy or dishwasher.
14. Bob Brandenburg: a small-time hoodlum, who in 1945 had introduced Burroughs to his roommates Huncke and Phil White. He appears in *Junky* as Jack, p. 3, etc.

pletely cured?[15] I can not share his enthusiasm for Sullivan who, it seems to me, has distinguished himself chiefly by introducing a somewhat more confusing terminology.[16] I think, also, that he partakes of the naïve conviction that anyone who is "fully analyzed" will turn out to be a nice liberal. Have you resumed analysis? You might have a go at the Washington School. Myself I am about to annunciate a philosophy called "factualism." All arguments, all nonsensical considerations as to what people "should do," are irrelevant. Ultimately there is only fact on all levels, and the more one argues, verbalizes, moralizes the less he will see and feel of fact. Needless to say, I will not write any formal statement on the subject. Talk is incompatible with factualism.

Jack might do well to collaborate with some professional writer who has facility and knows how to edit. Some one who could reduce Jack's writing to marketable proportions.

Glad to hear of your success with Lucien. My regards to all.

As Ever,
Bill

---

15. William Scott Gilmore, born 1911, a friend of Burroughs' from Harvard during the 1930s. Cured: of either neurosis or homosexuality.
16. The neo-Freudian, Harry Stack Sullivan, who died the following January.

Nov. 30, 1948
[509 Wagner St.
Algiers, La.]

Dear Allen,

Glad to hear from you. I will be leaving in a few days for the Valley to look after my interests there, and may extend my trip into Mexico. I hope to rid myself of the habit in the course of this trip. Taking along a pint of P.G. and a large supply of goof balls to taper off.[17] Also 20 caps and plenty of weed. Speaking of which I will be sure to send yours along before leaving.

It seems to me that you harbor some semantic confusions on the subject of crime. "Crime" is simply behavior outlawed by a given culture. There is no connection between "crime" and ethics: the sadistic atrocities of the Nazi S.S. were not "criminal." I do not see a connection between lying and violation of the law. In fact there is more lying in the course of a "regular job" most of which require a constant state of pretense and dissimulation. The necessity of a continual misrepresentation of one's personality is most urgent in such lines as radio, advertising, publicity, and, of course, television. Personally I find pushing junk a great deal more restful and less compromising from an ethical standpoint. (As you know I have been a "journalist" and an advertising man.) The line between legitimate and criminal activity has broken down since the war. Most everyone in business violates the law every day. For example, we farmers in the Rio Grande Valley depend entirely on Mexican laborers who enter the Country illegally with our aid and connivance. The "civil liberties" of these workers are violated repeatedly. They are often kept on the job at the point of gun (at cotton picking time when delay may mean loss of the entire crop). Workers who try to leave the field are shot. (I know of several instances.) In short my ethical position, now that I am a respectable farmer, is probably shakier than when I was pushing junk. Now, as then, I violate the law, but my present violations are condoned by a corrupt government.

---

17. P.G.: paregoric. Goof balls: Nembutal capsules, a barbiturate.

I have been thinking seriously of leaving the U.S.A. for South America, or perhaps Africa. I intend to look around a bit, and if I find some place to my liking, transfer the family there. I am buying a small tract of land in a swamp near N.O., where I will build a house.

Joan is fine and sends her best regards. Willie is talking now.[18]

It seems that Vickie is really on the skids.[19] I find her acts of violence especially distasteful in that they are obviously performed from a desire to harm others rather than from practical considerations of monetary gain. I abhor unnecessary violence. It is the mark of a small and undisciplined nature. Give my regards to Lucien, Brandenburg and all. I am writing Jack.

As Ever,
Bill

P.S. Please give Brandenburg some of the weed.

---

18. William Burroughs III was then aged sixteen months.
19. Burroughs had heard reports that Vickie Russell had lately turned to mugging.

Nov. 30, 1948
[509 Wagner St.
Algiers, La.]

Dear Jack,

Sorry to be slow in answering your letter.

Allen tells me you are making progress in the sale of your novel.[20] If you succeed in publishing one book, and get a name, you will have easy going from there on. So stick with it and use every contact you have. Sooner or later you will find a publisher.

I'm just setten around waiting for things to grow. I've got peas coming off any day (100 acres). Lettuce and carrots on the way. Taking a trip down to the Valley in a few days, and may go on into Mexico. I want to stay out of N.O. long enough to get this Chinaman off my back. (Kick my habit.)

I have a feud on with the nabors, a termite nest of Dagos, which may develop into a shootin' war. I'm ready. I've got enough guns here to stand off a siege. Shooting is my principal pastime.

Come on down any time. There's plenty room in this house, and I am building another out in a piece of swamp I bought. A sort of hunting lodge.

If all my crops come in on schedule, I will be rolling in $ by cotton picking time. The only thing worries me is the ———— government will put the snatch on such a big hunk of what we sons of the soil wring out of the earth. I am so disgusted with conditions I may leave the U.S.A. altogether, and remove myself and family to S. America or Africa. Some place where a man can get something for his money, and live in proper style. Here you have to scrimp no matter how much you make, and can't even get decent service. It's almost impossible to get anyone to do anything. Unions! That's the trouble, Unions!

[*Letter unsigned; possibly incomplete.*]

---

20. Kerouac's novel: *The Town and the City*.

Dec. 2, 1948
[509 Wagner St.
Algiers, La.]

Dear Allen,

Your letter does not make it quite clear where I should address mail. The only address on the letter is the York Ave. address.[21]

What about the tea? I just packed it, and now realize that I do not know where to send it. Let me know and I will mail it along.

I was afraid you would encounter difficulties getting a job. All they want now is technicians. The only way out is to work for yourself. I may be able to give you a job in a year or so if all goes on schedule. I plan to put $ back into real estate. For years I have wanted to buy a rooming house in N.Y.C. Perhaps I will be able to realize that wish. You could manage some property for me.

Enclose article about the Texas labor situation. The Rio Grande Valley is one of the few remaining areas of cheap labor in the U.S.A. The only alternative to cheap labor ($2.00 per 12 hour day) is mechanization, requiring a large initial outlay for expensive equipment and processing plants. Machine-picked cotton requires special processing: a plant costing circa $300,000. If Valley farmers had to pay a living wage for farm labor they would be ruined. A farm worker's Union is the farmer's nightmare. If anyone wants to live dangerously in a noble cause, let him organize farm labor in Texas. Maybe Jerry Rauch would like to take on the job.[22]

As Ever,
Bill

I do not mean to convey the impression that Kells and I sit under a palm leaf sun shelter, rifle in hand "suppressing" the workers. The whole deal is handled by labor and vegetable brokers. For example, I will make a deal with a labor broker, paying him so much per lb. to get my tomatoes picked and delivered to the veg-

21. From October, Ginsberg had been living in a three-room cold-water flat, belonging to Walter Adams, at 1401 York Avenue.
22. Jerry Rauch had been Ginsberg's roommate at Columbia in the winter of 1943.

etable broker who buys them. (Often the vegetable broker has his own pickers and handles the entire operation.) The broker backs a truck up to the Rio Grande and loads it with Mexican "Wetbacks" as they swim or wade across the border. He drives them to the field and gets the job done. Some brokers go in for rough stuff, some don't. I recall one broker mentioning casually that "his foreman had to shoot 2 wetbacks last night." But like I say, I don't have anything to do with it personally.

1949

Jan. 10, 1949
[509 Wagner St.
Algiers, La.]

Dear Allen,

Mrs. Hinckle is here for the past week:[1]
"Gathering her brows like the gathering Storm,
Nursing her wrath to keep it warm."
Tam O'Shanter—R. Burns.

Can't say as I blame her much. What kind of a character is this Hinckle to leave his wife here without funds, then not even bother to let her know what his intentions are? If I had not been here to help out she would have been forced to return to San Francisco. I seriously consider this kind of irresponsible behavior intolerable. Such people assume that someone else will do what they should be doing. After all Mrs. Hinckle is not my responsibility. I don't object to her staying here, and she has been very conscientious about paying her way as far as she is able. But it is certainly up to Hinckle to *get down here right now*. I don't see any excuse for the delay. He must have known Neal and Jack had no intention of leaving immediately.

My first crop of peas froze 5 days before harvest time. $5000 lost. (Actually only $300 lost—the cost of seed and labor.) I mean the crop would have brought $5000 if it had not been destroyed by frost.

. Better luck with the lettuce. We sold 8 acres in the field at $250 per acre = $2000 = $1000 for me. That helps. We are gambling with 4 acres of lettuce which may bring $1500 per acre if it comes in. Carrots will come off next—30 acres. Then our real cash crops which are cotton and tomatoes.

I am dead sick of sitting around. May open a bar if I get the $. Putting out feelers in the local junk market. You can't beat junk

---

1. Helen Hinckle, on her honeymoon, had been waiting in New Orleans for her husband and Neal Cassady to return from their coast-to-coast trip. Burroughs rescued her from a brothel in which, almost penniless, she had been left. In *On the Road*, where Kerouac recounts the trip, she appears as Galatea Dunkel.

for quick $. I've never seen such a swarm of junkies as exists in N.O. They underbid each other for your business. That is why it is hard to kick here. You don't have to look for it. It comes looking for you. Every time a pusher is knocked over (which happens daily. N.O. is famous for its stool pigeons), 2 jump into his place. A veritable hydra.

Please let me hear from you. *Did you receive the tea I sent?* If so or not *let me know*. It was sent to 114th St.[2]

As Ever,
Bill

---

2. Ginsberg's old room at 536 West 114th Street.

Jan. 16, 1949
[509 Wagner St.
Algiers, La.]

Dear Allen,

I sent a telegram and a letter to the York Ave address. Receiving no reply to either (both communications being of an urgent nature), I assumed you were not staying at this address. So I am writing c/o your brother.

I would like to know what gives with the Hinckle-Kerouac-Cassady expedition. Does this Hinckle character expect to billet his wife on me indefinitely? His performance is an all time record for sheer gall and irresponsibility. I have never so much as laid eyes on Hinckle. Behavior like his would stretch a close friendship. And all this without one word of apology or explanation.

She has been here about 2 weeks. During this time he has never communicated with her on his own initiative. All contact has been the result of her prolonged and expensive endeavors via long distance. *Has he left N.Y. yet* ?? He promised to leave over a week ago, and she sent him $10 (about her last, I think), to help him get here. Since then no Hinckle, no word.

How Hinckle treats his wife is none of my concern. When his neglect takes the form of deserting her without funds (what money she has did not come from him), and expecting me to take over until such time as he gets tired of fiddle fucking around N.Y. and decides to come down here, it ceases to be a personal matter between him and his wife. She has been a perfect guest, and very conscientious about helping out and paying as far as she was able. This in no way excuses his unpardonably irresponsible and ill-mannered behavior.

If you see him please tell him how I feel about this matter, and don't mince words either. Helen is his wife. I expect him to come down here *right now* and look after her.

It has occurred to me that they may be in trouble. The combination of Neal and a new car is highly suggestive.[3] Please let me hear from you *right away*.

As Ever,
Bill

P.S. *Did you get the tea?*[4]

---

3. Cassady had used Carolyn's savings to purchase a brand-new maroon Hudson.
4. Ginsberg wrote back denying responsibility for Mrs. Hinckle, and asking Burroughs for another package of marijuana, having already smoked his way through the first one with Jack and Neal.

Jan. 30, 1949
[509 Wagner St.
Algiers, La.]

Dear Allen,

Thanks for your letter.

Neal, Luanne and Jack left here 2 days ago headed for Frisco, routed through Tucson where they hope to put the bite on a party name of Harrington for a sawbuck.[5] Al and his wife Helen are staying on in N.O. perhaps for several months. Al has a job beginning tomorrow.

I can not forego a few comments on the respective and comparative behavior of the several individuals composing this tour, a voyage which for sheer compulsive pointlessness compares favorably with the mass migrations of the Mayans. To cross the continent for the purpose of transporting Jack to Frisco where he intends to remain 3 days before starting back to N.Y. . . . Obviously the "purpose" of the trip is carefully selected to symbolize the basic fact of purposelessness.

Neal is, of course, the very soul of this voyage into pure, abstract, meaningless motion. He is The Mover, compulsive, dedicated, ready to sacrifice family, friends, even his very car itself to the necessity of moving from one place to another. Wife and child may starve, friends exist only to exploit for gas money . . . Neal must move. To shift into less figurative gear: He takes $1000 (which could have been a down payment on a house to take care of his family), makes a down payment on a car, leaves his wife and child without $ one, cons other people (Luanne, Kerouac) into sending a few $ for their support while he refuses to do a lick of work, or even send his wife a single letter. Then he arrives here and has the unmitigated gall to expect me to advance $ for the continuation of this wretched trip. It so happened I was broke and not in condition to advance anything even had I been so inclined. As a matter of

---

5. Alan Harrington: a friend of Kerouac's and a fellow young writer, through whom he had met John Clellon Holmes in New York the previous summer.

principle I would not have contribúted one cent, if I were wallowing in $.

When he saw it was no go, he cooled off in his relations with me. Clearly I was of no use in the Great Move. Al also failed him, holding out $30 wired him by his family. But Jack sent home for $25 (which he should have kept for himself and remained in N.O.) and the car had gas and oil to move again. How far I don't know. It has been driven too far too fast. The rods are loose. It is in urgent need of about $100 in repairs. The wind up is he will probably lose the car, when he fails (as he inevitably will) to keep up the payments. He owes $2000 on the car. I doubt if anyone would give more than $2000 for it now. So it looks like he will end up minus the car minus $1000.

As I understand it Al (at Neal's instigation) married Helen to get money for The Voyage: money which was not forthcoming or at least not in the expected quantities. Having outlived her usefulness, she was to be abandoned in Tucson. His performance strikes me as an absolute nadir in human relations. No one deserves to be treated in this way—certainly not a decent, honest, well-meaning, well-mannered Jewish girl like Helen. I would be much more inclined to throw Neal out than her if it came to a choice. During the time she has spent here, she has made every effort to pay her way in money when she had it, also by helping with the housework, baby sitting and general errands. Now it seems that Al (who is not a bad sort) will undertake her support. He acts like he is quite fond of her, which is an agreeable surprise to me.

Incidentally I was very favorably impressed with Jack Kerouac. He seems much more sensible, more sure of himself than I ever remember him as being. Certainly he has changed in the past 6 months and the change is good.

Thank you for the offer to stay with you in N.Y. Riker's Island maintains (or did) an arrangement whereby addicts commit themselves to the Hospital for 30 days. They get no cure, just confinement. Once in there is no getting out before the 30 days are up. I thought you were familiár with this arrangement, of which Bart and Phil White (to name a few) availed themselves.[6] I was consid-

---

6. Bart: a junky friend of Bill Garver's and former customer of Burroughs' in New York. As Old Bart, he appears in *Junky*, p. 46.

ering this rather drastic step, but will try once more (starting to-morrow) here. I do not at present have money for any cure via trips to foreign climes. 6 months at Lexington is out of the question, private joints are prohibitive—$100 per week up—way up.

An outrage that such disorderly rabble roam the streets to pounce on unoffending strangers (I refer to the 6th Ave incident). It is to deal with such contingencies that I always carry a gun. I don't figure to take any shit off anybody . . . Let alone some snot-nosed punk. Joan sends her best regards.

As Ever,
Bill

P.S. Just received your letter with enclosures for various members of the expedition. Like I say they are gone. Appalling weakness on the part of Kerouac and Luanne to drive all the way to Frisco, arrive there without a cent, to face the problem of raising money for immediate return. Unless they show more firmness than they have in the past, Neal will con them out of the money as quick as they make it. Payments are due on the car, you know. If you will send me the Frisco address I will forward the material intended for Neal, Jack and Luanne. But probably it would be simpler for you to write yourself direct. As for the Huncke plan, I consider it, to say the least, unlikely of success.[7] If you prevail on him to get a job at all it will be a latter-day miracle. The more obligation Huncke is under to anyone, the more anyone has done to help him, the more certain he is to steal from or otherwise take advantage of his benefactor. It works out like an algebraic equation. Raise (X) (benefits), you raise (Y) (resentment) = Everything of value seized and disposed of. Well it's your decision.

---

7. Ginsberg was planning to take in the homeless Huncke upon his impending release from Riker's Island, and give him an ultimatum to find a job.

Feb. 7, 1949
[509 Wagner St.
Algiers, La.]

Dear Allen,

Thanks for your letter.

You evidently have a deep block on the subject of farming. Mere lack of knowledge could not account for your staggering ignorance of agricultural operations. Ruined by *one freeze* in *January* in an area that makes two complete crops a year, three if need be? Ruined when our main cash crop—cotton—will not go in the ground for another month? Ruined when I own 50 acres of the finest land in the Valley—worth $400 per acre now and land prices going up? No, we are not ruined. As it happened, the freeze worked out to our advantage, owing to the alertness of my partner, Kells. At the first sharp drop in temperature, without waiting for the Weather Bureau Warning which was *12 hours late,* he rounded up a batch of Wetbacks, got right out to the field and covered (plowed under) 25 acres of tomato plants (we had 50 acres in tomatoes). Thus he saved 25 acres from the freeze which will be worth as much or more than the whole 50 acres, because he was one of the few farmers to act promptly and save his tomato crop. The 25 acres that he could not save we will place in cotton—one of the surest cash crops. $200–400 per acre. Our 30 acres of carrots were not damaged. It looks like we are the Lord's Anointed, so far. We will have about 150 acres to put in cotton.

My opinion of Neal is about identical with Lucien's, though, in deference to your sensibilities, I never put the matter quite so bluntly. They were not here very long, and did not have time to do much of anything. Like I say, Neal had planned to replenish the exchequer here. When he saw no $ were forthcoming, he couldn't leave quick enough, and acted as though I had lured him here on false pretenses. He didn't unlock any "charm" or "graceful human nature" around here.

Al and Helen [Hinckle] have moved into an apt. on Esplanade Ave. They both have jobs and seem to be doing fine. As you suggest, they may well become permanent party here.

As to Luanne's intentions, I know almost nothing. She did speak of planning to come back to N.Y. with Jack. But someone said she will never tear herself away from Neal and Frisco. So that's all I know.

I had a card from Jack & Neal today. The address is *109 Liberty Street*, Frisco.

Glad to hear Lucien is getting along well. Give him my best regards. It looks like Huncke has taken umbrage at your offer. That will not likely prevent him from attempting further impositions when he is released.

I am involved in 2 lawsuits.[8] But they won't get anything out of me. If need be I will duck out of the State.

As Ever,
Bill

P.S. You may console yourself that Neal does not confine his impositions to "frustrated fruits" or enamoured females. Apparently anyone will do. I think he has deteriorated since I last saw him in N.Y. He does not even bother any longer to hide his machinations. I have the impression he lacks any clear notion of how he appears to others. Can he really think people are *that* dumb? I guess he can.

---

8. One or both of these lawsuits probably had to do with the "tenant trouble" mentioned in the following letter of March 15, 1949.

March 15, 1949
[509 Wagner St.
Algiers, La.]

Dear Jack,

Thanks for your letter. I have been slow answering because I am very busy right now. The fact is I am in process of moving, having bought a place in the French Quarter consisting of 2 houses and a patio. We will live in one and rent out the other. I have been occupied with painting and repairing this place so as to get a good price for it. Expect to sell this house and move into the other within the next month.

I was interested in your information about Neal. I do not see anything out of the way in his view-point if he follows through consistently. If he does not *feel* "responsibility" towards others he does not have any. Of course he can not *claim* anything from others under the conditions he has himself created. I do not believe he understands this. I suspect he feels that others are under some mysterious *obligation* to support him. Most inveterate moochers are convinced that while they have no obligations towards anyone else ("owe nothing to anybody"—Huncke) that others have a moral obligation to supply their needs. But to return to the concept of "obligation," the word only has meaning in terms of a specific relationship; it must be an expression of voluntary, spontaneous feeling. A conflict between "obligation" and feeling is impossible. Which is another statement of the fact that the only *possible* ethic is to do what one *wants* to do. This is the conclusion to which psychoanalysis leads, though many practitioners of analysis shrink back from this final but inescapable step. Because in the end people will do what they want to do, or the species will become extinct. That is what I believe.

How is Huncke? Give him my regards. Allen's message in your letter was rather strange. Seriously, I doubt his sanity. Any word from Neal?[9] Hinckle and his wife finally left for Frisco.

---

9. Kerouac had been back in New York for a month, having returned from seeing Cassady in Denver.

I am having tenant trouble already. Two insufferable fruits live in the back house on my new property, and I find to my surprise and indignation that I can not evict them without removing the premises from the rental market. I tell you we are bogged down in the octopus of bureaucratic socialism. Please let me hear from you soon.

As Ever,
Bill

March 18, 1949
[509 Wagner St.
Algiers, La.]

Dear Allen,

I am in process of moving, having acquired a property in the French Quarter consisting of 2 houses and a patio. We will live in the front house, the back house is occupied by 2 loathsome tenants. So I am now a landlord body and soul. Scrap rent controls, I say. . . . To dictate to a man what he can and can't do with his own property is *Un-American Socialism*. Such insidious measures leave the back door of the Ship of State ajar so that the cur of Communism can slink in and plunder the American ice-box. My tenants are fat and sassy now, but come March 31 at midnight *RCED Day* (Rent Control End Day)—and I'll be waiting up with a stop watch to raise the rent or out they go.

Putting this house up for sale, and have been busy painting the old whore up to look young and alluring. I expect to get $9000.

Meanwhile the farm is producing that old green stuff. I expect at least $2000 for my cut of 30 acres of carrots which are about ready to come off. Then I will settle back to wait for the real pay-off from tomatoes and cotton. (*Just received call from McAllen.[10] $500 for my share, and lucky to get that. Bottom fell out of carrots. Most farmers had to plow them under.)

Allen, please do me one favor. Get Korzybski's *Science and Sanity* and read it.[11] Every young man should get the principles of Semantics clear in his mind *before* he goes to college (or anywhere else for that matter). The doctor says "your mystical experiences are just hallucinations," and you think he has said something.[12] Did he

10. McAllen, Texas, near Pharr, where Kells Elvins was based.
11. Count Alfred Habdank Skarbek Korzybski, *Science and Sanity: An Introduction to Non-Aristotelian Systems and General Semantics* (Lancaster, Pa.: International Non-Aristotelian Publishing Co., 1933). In 1939, Burroughs attended a series of lectures at the recently opened Institute of General Semantics in Chicago given by Korzybski, who died in 1950.
12. In the summer of 1948, Ginsberg experienced visions in which he heard a God-like voice reading William Blake's poetry aloud to him.

say in *terms of fact* what an hallucination is? No—because *he does not know*. No one knows. He is just throwing around verbiage. Frankly I was (and am) dubious of your mystical experiences because of their *vague character*. I am suspicious of "universal forces" etc. Naturally they exist, but we can only attain knowledge of such matters by concrete examples and operations. Take the question of time. Did you know that telepathy is independent of time as it is of space? (Space and time are, of course, inseparable.) Therefore everything that has ever or ever will be thought is *now* available to *all* minds . . . Past and Future are purely arbitrary concepts.

Well what is Herbert [Huncke] doing besides living on you? If he does get any $ you will likely be the last to see any. Is this Little Jack referred to Little Jack Melody?[13] I remember him. A pretty solid character. How is Vickie [Russell], by the way? Still on stuff? I am. I had hoped to go to a sanatorium for a 10 day cure on my carrot money. Now that hope is blasted. Guess I will just take a train for some strange city with a pint of P.G., plenty of goof balls and stay until kicked. The pushers have been giving out a reduction cure here lately. I don't have much of a habit, unless milk sugar is habit-forming. I may go in the Business again as a silent backer.[14] God knows I need the money. Apart from stuff I am on a pistol buying kick.

I will send some weed tomorrow.

Now this business about Joan and myself is downright insane. I never made any pretensions of permanent heterosexual orientation. What lie are you talking about?[15] Like I say I never promised or even *implied* anything. How could I promise something that it is not in my power to give? I am *not* responsible for Joan's sexual life, never was, never pretended to be. Nor are we in any particular mess. There is, of course, as there was from the beginning, an impasse and cross purposes that are, in all likelihood, not amenable to any solution.

---

13. Little Jack Melody: Vickie Russell's gangster boyfriend. Burroughs knew him from his Henry Street days in New York, 1945.
14. Burroughs soon joined with an acquaintance in New Orleans to deal heroin.
15. Ginsberg had accused Burroughs of "living a lie" with Joan, because of their incompatible sexual orientations.

Glad to hear of Jack's possible success.[16] Herbert's picture of the Universe, by the way, is an excellent representation of his own position—a particle moving about hitting other particles. Lucien's talents might be of use to put on an animal act. Where did he come by this ability? Can he talk to *horses?*

As Ever,
Bill

P.S. What is the tea situation in N.Y.? Good tea is to be had here for around $30 per lb. Any possibility of quick profitable turn over? Please look into this. We could both make a few $.

---

16. On March 29, Kerouac's *The Town and the City* was accepted by editor Robert Giroux at Harcourt Brace, with a $1,000 advance.

April 16, 1949
[509 Wagner St.
Algiers, La.]

Dear Allen,

Just took a fall. Possession. The bastards are trying to send me to the State joint at Angola which is one of the worst in the South.

They shook down the house and found some of our correspondence on the subject of tea. This info was made available to the Feds, who questioned me at tedious length, and were, I think, finally convinced that no large scale operations were involved. However, they may have called the N.Y. office and mentioned your name and address which they have from the letters. (Incidentally they did *not* find your next to last letter, and do not suspect any pushing.) I doubt if you will ever be bothered, but best keep clean, and remember Graff *might* drop around some time when he has nothing else to do. Little Jack [Melody] should know the score too, if he plans to stay there. I don't wish to be responsible for anyone's misfortune.

My own case does not look too good, but we are trying for a *nolle prosse*. The stupid cops went out to my house without a search warrant, which is the reason the Feds refused to accept the case. I don't want to take it to a jury if any other course is open. If convicted I am subject to 2–5 years in Angola, which is definitely not a Country Club.

While the case is pending, of course, I have to avoid any contact. One stick, one cap now could send me away for 7 years as a second offender. (Junk felonies add up in this State.) So I am back on lush. I kicked a good part of my habit in a Precinct Cell. (It shouldn't happen to anyone but a Narcotic agent.) Then went to a Sanatorium for a week. Good as new now.[17]

My immediate plans are uncertain, but I doubt if I will remain

---

17. Link, Burroughs' lawyer (who appears as Tige in *Junky,* pp. 94–104), had arranged the sanatorium cure immediately after his arrest. According to Joan, Burroughs' father was "about to swoop down upon [us] from St. Louis with the intention of hospitalizing Bill elsewhere for at least six months." (To Allen Ginsberg, April 13, 1949, Ginsberg Collection, Columbia University.)

here, because they won't let me alone. They have orders to question "known addicts" when and wherever encountered. One of the guys that was in with me is now back with more charges against him. I am subject to a shake anytime and 72 hours in a Precinct, me and anybody with me for the offence of standing on a street corner.

All these misfortunes descended on me because a fucking uniform cop in a radio car recognized someone in the car with me. And *he* is out on the street with no charges against him.[18]

Convey my congratulations to Jack. I would have written him except I haven't been able.

Let me hear from you soon. Regards to all and sundry, and keep clean.

As Ever,
Bill

---

18. On April 6, Burroughs was stopped by police in a stolen car near Lee Circle, New Orleans. The incident is described in *Junky*, where the friend recognized by the police appears as Pat, and the other friend as Cole, pp. 80–104.

May 27, 1949
[Pharr, Texas][19]

Dear Jack,

Very glad to hear from you.

As a professional farmer, I will say a few words on the subject of buying a farm.[20] Settle this question clearly. Are you looking for (1) a place to live? or (2) a money-making deal? If No. 1, don't pay for good farm land. If No. 2, keep in mind that labor, machinery and operating costs, are still going up, while commodity prices are in general going down, and subject to inexplicable and unforeseeable fluctuations and collapse. The law of supply and demand no longer holds. Scarcity of a commodity does *not* insure a high price. In the future I will not plant anything without a government support price on it. We can only make money here by paying 15¢ per hour for our labor on some of the best irrigated farm land in the world. Even so this Valley is full of bankrupt farmers, who have been wiped out in the last 2 years. So proceed with caution. If land is good it is high. Livestock is something I can't talk about, except to say this: cattle is strictly a rich man's deal. Anyone who plans to start with a few and build up a herd is in a category with characters who plan to beat the races.

I would appreciate all details of "*L'affaire Ginsberg*," and news of all and sundry in N.Y. or wherever.[21]

My own plans are in a state of flux. Will most likely be here (we have rented a house) 'till cotton-picking (circa Sept. 1, before we get all our $). Then, *quien sabe?* I may take a trip through Mexico and Central America to view the Mayan antiquities. May stay down there and live cheap for a spell. May return to N.Y. May go to Angola. (The Courts resume business in Sept.)

Please let me hear from you very soon. Things are real dull here.

---

19. In early May, Burroughs had moved his family to a rented house in Pharr.
20. Kerouac and Cassady were toying with the idea of buying a ranch together.
21. Ginsberg was arrested on April 21 after an incident involving another stolen car. This one, with Ginsberg and Vickie Russell as passengers, was full of stolen clothes, and driven by Little Jack Melody, who was on parole at the time and without a driver's license.

I don't even have a car. The Revenooers put the snatch on it in N.O. They are making efforts to condemn it, but I expect eventually my lawyer will wrest it from their sticky clutches. Meanwhile I am immobilized in this Valley of heat and boredom.

As Ever,
Bill

June 24, 1949
Route 1
Pharr, Texas

Dear Jack,

Thanks for your letter. What's with Al talking about the Wrath of God?[22] Has he flipped his lid? We got the W. of G. down here in the shape of Border Patrol Agents deporting our Field Hands, and D of A Bureaucrats telling us what, where and when to plant.[23] Only us farmers have other names for it. And if any obscenity bunch of bureaucrats think we're going sit on our ass and let the W. of G. take over, they will learn that we are not Liberals.

If I was in Al's place I would say "Go ahead and place your charges, if any." His present position is insufferable. Imagine being herded around by a lot of old women like Louis Ginsberg and Van Doren.[24] Besides I don't see why Van Doren puts in his 2 cents' worth. Snivelling old Liberal Fruit. (Have you noticed all these fuckin' Liberals will show their old yellow fangs when they think they can get by with it. All Liberals are weaklings, and all weaklings are vindictive, mean and petty.) I don't see anything to gain from this Medical Center deal, a lot of New Deal Freudians.[25] I wouldn't let them croakers up there treat my corn let alone my psyche.

I have just done reading Wilhelm Reich's latest book *The Cancer Biopathy*. I tell you Jack, he is the only man in the analysis line who is *on that beam*. After reading the book I built an orgone accumulator, and the gimmick really works. The man is not crazy, he's a fucking genius.[26]

---

22. Ginsberg told Kerouac the Wrath of God had descended upon him, after his arrest and consequent trouble with the Columbia authorities.
23. D of A: Department of Agriculture.
24. Louis: Allen's father. Mark Van Doren: one of his professors, who had spelled out the choice facing Ginsberg as: live inside society or join the criminal subculture.
25. Ginsberg took the advice of his university professors and pleaded insanity, ending up in the Columbia Presbyterian Psychiatric Institute, on West 168th Street, which he did not finally leave until February 1950.
26. *The Cancer Biopathy*, translated by Theodore P. Wolfe (New York: Orgone Institute Press, 1948). Reich first built an orgone energy accumulator in 1940, as

Our cotton looks good. Start picking July 1. I ought to realize about $15,000 on the deal, but the obscenity government will put the snatch on about $6,000 of that, to pay their obscenity bureaucrats to mind other people's business.

Still no car. They filed a claim, my man filed an exception, a date was set for a preliminary hearing etc. etc. Bathtard thonsa bithes.[27] This seizure of property is a violation of the Constitution. If I had the money I'd take it to the Supreme Court. The bastards might as well tear up the Constitution. They've taken it all back in Bureau Decisions. They may be the W. of G. to Al, but they're just a lot of overpaid (at any price) bureaucrats to me. A cancer on the political body of this country which no longer belongs to its citizens.

Well, I will see you either in N.Y. or here. Come down any time if you like. We have plenty of room. Please let me hear from you very soon. Anything new on your book?

As Ever,
Bill

---

a research tool to study orgones (a neologism conflating *orgasm* and *organism*), but later saw its potential to treat illness. The box, lined with metal on the inside and organic material on the outside, had been the subject of prolonged investigation by the FDA since the fall of 1947. Although they failed to find dissatisfied users and to prove fraud, they succeeded in discrediting Reich and banning his "gimmick."
27. The paretic phrasing of Politte Elvins, Kells's syphilitic father.

Sept. 26, 1949
Kells Elvins
Route One
Pharr, Texas

Dear Jack,

I was somewhat taken aback by your account of Neal's behavior. Evidently he is approaching the ideal state of absolute impulsiveness.[28]

I am just back from Mexico City where I have rented an apartment preparatory to moving down there with the family.[29] Mexico is very cheap. A single man could live good for $2 per day in Mexico City liquor included. $1 per day anywhere else in Mexico. Fabulous whore houses and restaurants. A large foreign colony. Cock fights, bull-fights, every conceivable diversion. I strongly urge you to visit. I have a large apt. could accommodate you. Tell Neal to come too if he is heeled. I have to watch the $. Despite the temptations of Mexico I am still on the lush wagon.

I don't see why Al is wasting time with those Liberal jerks. Is he rational? Any news of Huncke, Garver, etc? How is Lucien?

Jack, I wonder if you could do something for me? You know this gadget made by the Reichians called the accumulator? Could you find out from Al or somebody what it looks like. I want especially to know its shape, where and if there is a window, how one gets into it.

Please let me hear from you soon. If I am gone to Mexico, mail will be forwarded. Better be very careful what you say as it may be opened and read. No references to junk or weed.

As Ever,
Bill

P.S. What is the housing situation in N.Y. now?

---

28. Cassady had entered a so-called blank period of reckless behavior that summer and fall.
29. Refers (apparently) to the apartment Burroughs rented at 26 Río Lerma, Mexico City (see letter of March 10, 1950).

Oct. 13, 1949
[Mexico City]

Dear Allen,

I was glad to receive your letter, and to learn that you are rational.

I would like to visit N.Y. but it is out of the question at present. I don't know what gave Jack the idea my affair in N.O. was straightened out. The case comes up Oct. 27, with every indication of an unfavorable outcome.

We made out pretty well on the cotton, but operating and machinery costs are so high we did not end up with much. Fall vegetables will be coming off in 2 months or so.

Mexico City is a fine town. Prices here are about ⅓ what they are in the States. In fact I would like to live down here, and don't see how I can afford to live anywhere else. Will not be able to make any decision until after the 27th.

There is no doubt that the life of a writer is ideal, if you can manage it. I am very anxious to see Jack's novel. I don't imagine he could be persuaded to leave N.Y. and make a trip down here, later on if I do return. I am sure he will be very successful from all indications. Soon he will have to start worrying about income tax. (3% in Mexico.)

Joan took the loss of her medicine surprisingly well, and feels better than in years.[30] I myself have been strictly on a lush kick despite every opportunity to pick up on anything and everything. I just don't want any. Besides, I have not money to waste.

Gilmore is still in N.Y. Heard from him not long ago. Too bad about Huncke and Co.[31] By the way did you receive that letter of warning I sent you after my own fall? I too made the mistake of

---

30. Joan's "medicine" consisted of Smith Kline and French Benzedrine inhalers, two per day. She couldn't get them in Mexico, though she could get tequila at forty cents a quart. She wrote Ginsberg: "I'm personally fine also, although somewhat drunk from 8 am on . . . I shan't attempt to describe my sufferings for 3 weeks after the benzedrine gave out, but with thyroid tablets, Reich and faith, I made it." (October 31, 1949, Ginsberg Collection, Columbia University.)
31. Huncke—alone—drew a prison sentence: five years.

having correspondence in my quarters which fell into official hands. Well, I have learned more caution.

I am not giving an address here, because I will not be at it by the time you could write. You may not hear from me for some time. My best regards to all.

As Ever,
Bill

Nov. 2, 1949
[Mexico City]

Dear Jack,

Thanks for the letter. I also heard from Al, and was relieved to discover he is rational.

My case in New Orleans looked so unpromising that I decided not to show. So I figure to be in Mexico quite some while. I think it's 5 years before a case is cancelled out by the statute of limitations. I may go into farming down here. Also considering the project of opening an American Bar on the border. (Mexican side, of course. I *no sabe* U.S. side of The Border.)

I was certainly gratified to hear of your success as a novelist, and meeting all them celebrities. [. . .] What is this Vidal character like?

Be mighty glad to see you down here. You won't make a mistake visiting Mexico. A fine country with plenty of everything cheap. One of the few places left where a man can really live like a Prince.

I sure would appreciate it if you could find out where in Mexico City those accumulators are. I can not locate them. Regards to all. Keep me posted. Write: c/o Kells, Pharr, Texas.

As Ever,
Bill

March 20, 1952
Orizaba 210—apt 5
Mexico, D.F.

Dear Allen,

I have been working on a new novel (with Marker away and no one around I can talk to I have need of distraction). Novel could be part II of *Junk* (is, however, complete in itself). Dennison main character, but I have shifted to 3rd person narrative.[7] Relationship of Allerton and Dennison (Marker and myself though both Allerton and Dennison are to be regarded as derived from rather than copied from the originals) seems to be the central theme. Same straight-forward narrative method as I used in *Junk*. Might drop a few soundings to see if anyone who read *Junk* would be interested. (Needless to say, the publishers who objected to *Junk* on grounds of immorality are not to be regarded as hot prospects to buy my current work. Still and all it *is,* in a sense, a novel of reformation. Tells how Dennison got off the junk and why.) I hope you will accept an agent's fee if you score. I know this sort of thing is a lot of trouble and I appreciate your efforts. [. . .]

I have not found anyone who knew Hoffman. By the way, Peyote poisoning presents symptoms similar to polio.

Decided to dedicate *Junk* to Phil White (under his correct name) if it is ever published. Guess A.L.M. (Adelbert Lewis Marker) is slated for dedication in present work.[8] My best to Lu.

Garver never showed. If he is coming I wish he would do so instead of hovering over me like this. Please let me hear from you soon.

By the way I glanced through a book called *The Homosexual in America*.[9] Enough to turn a man's gut. This citizen says a queer

---

7. The novel was *Queer*. Kerouac had used the pseudonym Will Dennison for Burroughs in *The Town and the City*.
8. In fact, since *Queer* was to remain unpublished for more than three decades, Burroughs used the dedication "To A.L.M." in *Junkie* when it was published in 1953. The dedication was dropped for *Junky*.
9. Donald Webster Cory, *The Homosexual in America: A Subjective Approach* (New York: Greenberg, 1951).

learns humility, learns to turn the other cheek, and returns love for hate. Let him learn that sort of thing if he wants to. I never swallowed the other cheek routine, and I hate the stupid bastards who won't mind their own business. They can die in agony for all I care. I like very few people, as a matter of fact, and what happens to people I don't like, like the song say, "tis their misfortune and none of my own,"[10] which is why I never could be a liberal except in a situation where the majority was made up of people I liked, in which case there wouldn't be any political problems on account of problems arise because people is stupid and let themselves get pushed around. (There's a flaw in my argument if you can find it, young man.)

Love,
Bill

---

10. A reference to the traditional American cowboy song: "Get along, little dogies, get along./ You know Oklahoma will be your new home./ Get along, little dogies, get along./ 'Tis your misfortune, and none of my own."

March 26, 1952
ORIZABA, 210—apt 5
Mexico, D.F.

Dear Jack,

I do not know how much longer I will be here. I am classified as a "pernicious foreigner" and the Immigration dept. will request my departure as soon as the case is settled. Doubt, however, if I make it out of here [in] under 3 weeks. When I do leave will head South for Ecuador, unless Marker and I decide to sail his 23 ft slope (whatever the hell a slope is) down to Ecuador.[11] [. . .]

Glad to hear of advance on your novel. Allen is trying to sell mine as pocket book original.[12] Meanwhile I am writing on another novel, since I got nothing else to do. This is a queer novel using the same straight narrative method as I used in *Junk*; it is in fact a sequel or part II to *Junk*. Dennison is still main character, but I shift to 3rd person. I doubt if your publisher would be interested. I think, however, that this novel is more saleable than *Junk*, and has a wider appeal. It is, in fact, more sensational, but the two stories are really complementary and should go together. Part I is on the junk, Part II off.

And let me tell you, young man, that I *did not* "leave my sexuality back somewhere on the Opium road." That phrase has rankled with me all these years. I must ask of you, if I am to appear in your current opus, that I appear properly equipped. With male facilities.

Jesus, man, you sure can pick your women. You needn't have cautioned me not to reveal address to Kells' wife.[13] She and me

---

11. Slope: sloop.
12. Kerouac had just received a $250 advance for a paperback novel from Ace Books, owned by Carl Solomon's uncle, A. A. Wyn. Kerouac offered Solomon, who was acting as an editor, a 160-page extract of *On the Road*, as well as the novel on which he and Burroughs had collaborated in 1944, which was "entitled (I think), I WISH I WERE YOU, and is 'by Seward Lewis' (they being our respective middle names)." (Kerouac to Carl Solomon, April 7, 1952, Ginsberg Collection, Columbia University.) The contract was never taken up.
13. Elvins's wife: Marianne Woolfe. Kerouac's concern about his address being known followed the birth, in February, of his daughter, Janet, and the subsequent

don't hardly say hello. I gather she don't like me. Well wives generally don't. Well, I hope to see you soon. Please write to me what your plans are. My best to Neal.

As Ever,
Bill B

P.S. Another thing. I am not entirely happy about appearing under the name of Old Bull Balloon. I can not but feel that the epithet Bull contains an uncomplimentary reference, and I am by no means old. You'll be equipping me with white hair next book.

I guess i will have to change the name Dennison in my current book. You see my mother read your book, and, of course, spotted me. In short Dennison is become a little transparent. But it is hard to get away from your name entirely. I thought of Sebert Lee, but Sebert is like Seward and Lee is my mother's name. I guess it will do though.

---

breakup of his marriage to Joan Haverty. Kerouac was worried about being traced by the Brooklyn Uniform Support of Dependents and Abandonment Bureau, and sued for child maintenance.

April 3, 1952
Orizaba 210—apt 5
Mexico, D.F. `

Dear Jack,

I can't make any definite arrangement with you because I don't know when or how or by what route I will leave Mexico.[14] When I do know will inform you. Also it is not for me to decide how long I will remain in Mexico. Once the case is settled, the Immigration dept. allows me 5 days to pack up and get out of the country with the alternative of forcible deportation to the U.S. [. . .]

I am relieved to hear of the liquidation of Old Bull Balloon, and the advent of Bill Hubbard. My novel is coming along. Expect to finish it in 2 or 3 months more as I don't write from scratch in fact I can't. When I write it is simply a question of putting down in some sequence what is already there. The excerpts from your novel sound mighty fine.[15] Of course, the *Finnegans Wake* kind of thing can only be fully appreciated in context of the whole work, which in the case of this kind of writing more than any other, is an actual amoeboid-like organism.

With Marker away I got another habit. Start cutting down tomorrow. With plenty codeine there's nothing to kicking a habit. Done it 5 times in the past 2 years. This habit I got partly for my health. I was convalescent from jaundice and wanted to cut out drinking completely for a month or so.

Been seeing a lot of bull-fights. Good kicks. Going to a cock fight this evening. I like my spectacles brutal, bloody and degrading.

Why this arbitrary date the 18th for your arrival here? Why don't you come right on down here now? Right at the moment legal proceedings are immobilized by Holy Week. I asked the secretary how come no court this week and she say: "Because we are Christians" (unlike some other people who shall be nameless).

---

14. Kerouac had written back at the end of March asking Burroughs to take him to Ecuador with Marker.

15. Kerouac's novel, although then titled *On the Road*, would later be published as *Visions of Cody*.

I am due in court Monday, and if the ballistic experts are there, and the judge ain't in Acapulco, and Jurado shows, maybe I will be acquitted or convicted or something definite. No word from Allen. My best to Neal.

As Ever,
Bill

April 5, 1952
Orizaba 210—Apt 5
Mexico, D.F.

Dear Allen,

You really are a sweetheart. I could kiss you on both cheeks. We should get used to calling each other sweetheart. I understand it is the standard form of address between agent and author, but this time I mean it. Of course I *insist* you take 10% commission, and I leave the finances to you. I will send a note to Wyn[16] but exactly how shall I address it? Meanwhile I will send along a power of attorney just for luck if I can find out how to do it. The Embassy should know.

About the new novel. This is, in some ways, a more difficult job than *Junk* and a great deal harder for me to evaluate. I would like your opinion before the publisher sees it. The 3rd person is really 1st person. That is the story is told from viewpoint of Lee. (I have decided to drop Dennison because Ma read Kerouac's book. Lee is the name. I guess 1st name will be William though that is getting close again.) When someone walks out of the room where Lee is, he is gone until Lee sees him again. There is nothing in the story Lee isn't there to see, you understand, exactly as in 1st person. The subject matter makes 3rd person convenient and at times mandatory. Take this passage for example. Lee has undressed preparatory to laying an Indian: "Though he was near 40 he had the thin delicate body of an adolescent."

O.K., I do have the same physique I had at 18, which is uncommon and significant in delineating the character. But wouldn't I feel silly putting the above passage in the 1st person? I will however experiment with 1st person as I write.

Now *Junk* is, of course, complete without this part I am writing, but the two sections do complement each other. I have some misgivings about the present work. Sex and love are difficult subjects.

---

16. After several rejections, Ginsberg had persuaded Carl Solomon and his uncle to accept the manuscript of *Junkie*, obtaining an $800 advance from Ace Books.

There is always impairment of the critical faculty, and what is interesting to me may not be of interest to others.

I really prefer the final version I sent you to the original. I do not feel that the part about Reich and the philosophical sections belong there cluttering up the narrative. They should be relegated to an introduction or a post script of miscellaneous observations. What I will do is this. I will go over that material I cut out and prepare from it a post script, adding to it some observations I have made subsequently. I will also look over *Junk* to see if any changes or additions are indicated. I certainly hope you do get sent down here as a consultant as I could really use your help and criticism on what I am writing now.

I was delighted to hear of your good fortune with your poems. The excerpts sound fine, send me more in next letter.[17] [. . .]

I figure to go to Panama when I leave here and maybe raise hogs with Marker. Food prices are high as U.S., but the land is fertile, cheap, and plentiful. They can't keep 'em on the farm in Panama. They all want to come in the city and be pimps. It's a perfect set-up. I may buy a place down there and I hope you will be able to visit me. Panama is only $50 by boat from New Orleans—Ecuadorian line—or $50 by air from Miami. I will enclose some kind of a note to Wyn pending more formal authorization. Thanks again Allen. I was really getting desperate as I want to take care of Willy and have him with me and also Marker, of course.

Love,
Bill

[. . .]

---

17. In January, Ginsberg had sent several poems derived from his notebooks to William Carlos Williams. Williams's enthusiastic reply inspired Ginsberg to discover more poetry in his journals, and initiated a lasting relationship with the elderly poet. On April 4, Ginsberg took a selection of poems to Williams, who wrote an introduction to what was the manuscript of *Empty Mirror*. It took almost ten years for the collection to be published.

[*April 1952*
210 Orizaba, Apt. 5
Mexico City]

Dear Jack,

In all likelihood I will be here still the 22 of this month and am looking forward to your visit. If I have to leave before then I will leave directions with Kells Elvins at the Turf Club. Due in court tomorrow. Like the Immortal Bard say, "Tomorrow and tomorrow and tomorrow."

I think the title *Queer* for second section is only terrific. The title had me baffled. I want to get *Junk* out as soon as possible because of current interest in the subject. Consequently, I will do whatever they prefer as regards second section. You say don't let them hurry you, but my bargaining position will not be better with the passing of time. They know I can't find another publisher. I am completely unknown. So I will accept their conditions on this deal. After all, the advance money is not the kind of money I am looking for. So why squabble about a few hundred dollars? Anyway it is up to Al to make those decisions. I trust his judgment and acumen to get the best deal possible for me. He certainly is a good friend. You know he was willing to continue as my agent without commission? I of course insisted he accept the commission, and I am going to lay a bonus on him.

I have been living very quiet lately. A bad liver and the limitations imposed by my legal situation. (Bail here amounts to probation. Nobody checks on you, parole officers are unknown in Mexico, but if you get in any additional trouble your bail can be revoked and your person reincarcerated). I even go out without my piece now like a *petit bourgeois*.[18] I detest limitations of any kind, and intend to establish my ass some place where I am virgin on the police blotter. I hope you will come along with me. We will get rich and live like sultans—like the song say (Tea for Two), "A girl for you and a boy for me." What I want to do is buy a house— probably in or near Panama City—which will serve as my head-

18. Piece: i.e., pistol.

quarters. From there I have transportation to all S. and Central America and West Indies. If I later find someplace I like better I can always move. In any case I do not want to go back to the States. I will settle some place down here. You know I have been happier down here than I ever was before in my life. I feel like I took off a strait jacket. You don't realize how much the U.S. is dragging you until you are out of it and feel the difference.

Been working intensive on new novel. Just applying last touches to sketch of my dear friend Hal: "His face showed the ravages of the death process, the inroads of decay in flesh cut off from the living charge of contact. He had aged without experiencing life like a piece of meat rotting on a pantry shelf. Moor (Hal's *nom de my plume*) was literally kept alive and moving by hate, but there was no passion no violence in Moor's hate. His hate was a slow steady push, weak but infinitely persistent, waiting to take advantage of weakness in another."[19] Later, speaking of Hal's hypochondria: "But he was sick, and his sickness was death . . . A faint greenish steam of spiritual rot surrounded his body. Lee (that's my handle) thought he would glow in the dark."

Frank has gone back to the States. I think he plans to work in Alaska. About 15 citizens of the Mexico City College crowd have gone up there. Thank God I am a man of letters and don't have to expose myself to the inclemencies of near Arctic conditions. I am looking forward to see you so make it as pronto as you possibly can. By the way I just thought did you ever meet Frank's wife? My God she is an American bitch that won't quit. I never yet see

---

19. The lines appear almost verbatim in *Queer*, p. 6. Compare the description of Joe Varland's eyes in F. Scott Fitzgerald's 1927 short story "A Short Trip Home": "They were helpless yet brutal, unhopeful yet confident. It was as if they felt themselves powerless to originate activity, but infinitely capable of profiting by a single gesture of weakness in another."

On the subject of plagiarism: "In a moment of hasty misjudgement a whole paragraph of description was lifted out of this tale where it originated, and properly belongs, and applied to quite a different character in a novel of mine. I have ventured none the less to leave it here, even at the risk of seeming to serve warmed-over fare.—F.S.F." In *Bernice Bobs Her Hair* (Harmondsworth: Penguin, 1968), pp. 109, 106.

her equal. Frank does not have one friend he can take to the house. She has forbidden him to eat out as she does not want he should take in any nourishment unless she is there to watch him eat it. Did you ever hear the like of that? Needless to say my place is strictly out of bounds to Frank and he always has that hunted look when he comes to see me. I don't know why American men put up with such shit from a woman. Course I am no expert judge of female flesh, but she has "Lousy Lay" writ all over her scrawny, unappetising person. Jesus, I am coming on like an old bitch.[20] Well I will be seeing you and I hope soon.

As Ever,
Love,
Bill

P.S. I am glad in a way that Laughlin did not take *Junk* as I will sure make more $ with a publisher who is strictly commercial. Did you ever meet Laughlin, by the way, and if so how do you dig him? He's a hard cat to dig. Have you read Gore Vidal's latest— *The Judgment of Paris*? Funny in places. The man is primarily a satirist and should avoid philosophising and tragedy. Why will people insist on attempting what they are not fitted to do? A man who writes beautiful prose will insist to produce excruciatingly bad poetry and so forth. Is Gore Vidal queer or not? Judging from the picture of him that adorns his latest opus I would be interested to make his acquaintance. Always glad to meet a literary gent in any case, and if the man of letters is young and pretty and possibly available my interest understandably increases. By the way what ever became of Al's normality program? I haven't heard anything about it lately. I certainly was glad to see him pull out of that let's-take-our-place-in-a-normal-society dive. I thought the nut croakers had fucked him up permanent and reconstructed him in their own dreary image. But he's the same old Al now. I imagine the doctors feel he has "relapsed." I got a lot out of analysis myself, but I got it largely in spite of the strenuous efforts of the therapists to prevent me from

---

20. This passage appears, nearly verbatim, in *Queer*, pp. 54–55—but the addition was made during Burroughs' final manuscript revision in 1985.

realizing my, to them, reprehensible potentialities. Analysis is an instrument of tremendous possibilities, but, like most every thing else at the present time, it is in the hands of cowardly, weak, stupid and vicious men.

My best to Neal

April 14, 1952
Orizaba 210 apt. 5
Mexico, D.F.

Dear Allen,

I enclose the signed power of attorney.

As to finishing second novel in 2 months: I do not exactly know how far along I am. I have a lot of material in rough form and do not know exactly how long it will take me to get it in final form. I *could* promise it in two months, yes. I would prefer to have them go ahead and publish *Junk*. And take my time on the other novel, which, as planned, would include my trip to Ecuador with Marker. So tell them whatever you think is best. If you think it is best to give them *Queer* in two months I guarantee it will be ready in that time. Specifically, I have about 10 pages of the beginning ready to go, and about 60 pages of rough draft some of which can be used without any alterations, some of which requires a good deal of work. So whatever you decide is O.K. with me. I am pushing right along on the second novel anyway, as I have nothing else to do, and I prefer to work intensively. One thing, I have not decided on ending for second novel. Perhaps the ending just hasn't occurred yet.

I don't care what prefaces, apologies or explanations they paste on the deal, so don't worry about that. I am only glad they don't want to hash up the story itself. I will write to Wolberg and ask him if he wants the job, if not get someone else. Like I say, I don't care what they do along that line.

As for publisher's introduction, I would rather you wrote it as I want to give all my time to the second novel. I will send you a brief autobiographical sketch. Perhaps you can use some of it directly. I give you free hand there, as in making all arrangements. Incidentally I think *Queer* is excellent title. I personally think it would be a better idea to publish *Queer* as a sequel to *Junk* rather than together, but in this life we have to take things as we find them as the torso murderer said when he discovered his victim was a quadruple amputee. The financial arrangements are O.K., go ahead and sign the contract, and whatever you tell them I will deliver it on time.

Love,
Bill

P.S. About death of Joan. I do not see how that could be worked in. I wish you would talk them out of that idea. I will take care of her disappearance. I did not go into my domestic life in *Junk* because it was, in the words of Sam Johnson, "Nothing to the purpose."

I want to get this letter right off. You will have the autobiographical material in a few days. Also I want to read the poetry you sent me over at leisure, and will comment at that time. *Did you receive the two insertions I sent to go in Junk?* Please let me know as this material is important. Yes I have copy of *Junk*. [. . .] I will write again in few days. A friend here has written a technical book on painting. What agent handles that kind of deal? If you want the agenting on this deal, you can have it, of course, but does not look red hot to me.

[*April 22, 1952*
210 Orizaba, Apt. 5
Mexico City]

Dear Allen,

I begin to understand the rift between publisher and author. The publisher's demands are not only highly irritating but contradictory as well. For example, they don't want to publish books separate or together so far as I can make out, and the question of person is confusion's masterpiece. I quote: "Necessities preclude publishing book together one part in first person one in 3rd." I wonder precisely what person they expect *Queer* to be in—and exactly where (since it is neither joined nor separate to *Junk*) they mean to publish it? I feel as if I was being sawed in half by indecisive fiends who periodically attempted to shove me back together. I am going to continue *Queer* in 3rd person and send it along like that. If they want it switcheroo'd to 1st person, O.K. Can do. On one point I am in agreement: I do not favor any delay in the publishing date.

Now as to this biographical thing, I can't write it. It is too general and I have no idea what they want. Do they have in mind the—"I have worked (but not in the order named) as towel boy in a Kalamazoo whore house, lavatory attendant, male whore and part-time stool pigeon. Currently living in a remodelled pissoir with a hermaphrodite and a succession of cats. I would rather write than fuck (what a shameless lie). My principal hobby is torturing the cats—we have quite a turnover. Especially in Siameses. That long silky hair cries aloud for kerosene and a match. I favor kerosene over gasoline. It burns *slower*. You'd be surprised at the noises a cat can make when the chips are down"—routine, like you see on the back flap? Please, Sweetheart, write the fucking thing will you? PLUMMM. That's a great big sluppy kiss for my favorite agent. Now look, you tell [Carl] Solomon I don't mind being called queer. T. E. Lawrence and all manner of right Joes (boy can I turn a phrase) was queer. But I'll see him castrated before I'll be called a Fag. (HE WANTS TO CALL PART II *FAG*. IMAGINE!) That's just what I been trying to put down uh I mean *over*, is the distinction between us strong, manly, noble types and the leaping, jumping, window dressing cocksucker. Furthechrissakes a girl's gotta draw the line somewheres or publishers will swarm all over her sticking their nasty old biographical prefaces up her ass.

Seriously, Sweetheart, I do have to concentrate and I can't be distracted from *Queer* by vaguely menacing Kafkian demands for notes and insertions and biographical indications of unspecified length and subject matter. I am a writer not a prestidigitator. I do not manipulate a typewriter with my feet nor do I write on a blackboard with the pus drips outta my prick. I sit down—preferably—at a typewriter or pad and pencil (I favor number 2 pencils in a plain yellow Venus. Is that the kind of biographical data they want?) and write one thing at one time. So pick up on the action, Pops: I will send along some "material" see what I mean? It's too general. For example, I think of the Anderson period (How could I ever have been interested in that?),[21] well I take one incident as indicating set-up and wrote a short story (incomplete of course. What ya think I am, a hack?) I enclose story with some mighty sorry biographical material. I have to write specific, Al. They wanta hear about how I cut the end joint off my little finger? Wanta know how it feels and looks to cut off a finger joint? (You'd be surprised how much blood comes out.) O.K. I'll tell them. Say, maybe that's an angle. Just hit the highlights in this biographical monster. Talk that up to Sol. But when they ask me to write a "biographical sketch" I feel like a personnel manager just said, "Tell me about yourself." So please, Al, pin them down or see what you can do with the deal utilizing the material I have sent you. I am trying to get *Queer* in shape to show them. A lot of work and I been sick lately. No energy no appetite and nobody to bring me milk toast except Old Dave [Tercerero] looks in now and then and makes a run for me to the grocer. Marker wrote he isn't coming with me to S.A. He plans to take Army Exchange civilian job in China or Europe. I am deeply hurt and disappointed. I will try to change his mind but I don't know. Please send any money you wring out of those vampires going around sucking off the talents of we authors, to me in the form of a check payable to me.

---

21. Reference is to Jack Anderson, on whom Burroughs had a crush in the early 1940s, which led to his cutting off the last joint on his little finger. See story "The Finger" in *Interzone*.

I am hooked again. And all on account of the Pusher and my own stupidity. I don't see how a man who lives by battening on his fellow humans can look into a shaving mirror. He doesn't often by the looks of him. You see I got back on the junk wagon in order to pack in the sauce so my liver could rehabilitate itself like a convict, and now I find out junk is the worst thing there is for the liver.

I wrote to Wolberg already. No answer yet. He'll want to be paid I feel sure, and rightly too. Us writers got to stand together or we'll be had in all 72 (an arbitrary number I just hit on) positions for gratis.

Translate me into all languages if you can. It makes me feel so delightfully international.

Wherever Hal is and whatever sickness he claims to have, I hope he rots for being so bitchy when I tried—in a perfectly straight forward manly way—to get in his pants. He is a bitch that won't quit. I worked him into *Queer* under the name of Winston Moor. That was really a labor of love my dear.

Get with those technicolor peyote kicks Daddy O and shoot me that solid address.[22]

I am enjoying your poems, especially Night Apple. My dear I simply must read the short story about your affair with a Mongolian hair-lipped idiot in Dakar. It sounds too too Truman Capoty. A hunch back blowing you at the same time?

I simply must get to work. Just squandered three hours writing to you and Marker. Better save my letters, maybe we can get out a book of them later on when I have a rep. So good night for now, Sweetheart. I enclose a short story which is sort of sample of high-light technique in biography. After all it is the highlights that matter. Who cares what shade of yellow my piss is when I wake up in the morning? And some assorted material. Write me what they want *now*.

> Magnums of Love
> Willy Lee—That Junky writin' boy
> Bill

P.S. Story and "material" under separate cover.

---

22. Earlier that month, Ginsberg had taken peyote for the first time.

April 26 [*1952*]
Orizaba 210
apt. 5, MEX, D.F.

Dear Al,

Just heard from Wolberg. He declines assignment on grounds he knows nothing about drug addiction, he is busy writing a book himself, and he thinks it's a silly idea anyway. So tell them to look for someone else. It really is pretty raw to hold up the entire advance pending delivery of *Queer*. I suppose an author has to put up with that sort of thing until he gets a reputation. But they are definitely going back on what they said at first.

I have been working day and night on *Queer*. I have now 25 pages complete, and about 70 pages more in long hand notes. I figure the 70 will simmer down to about 40 to 50 pages more, making 75 in all. Look here, might as well just put these 75 pages on the end of *Junk* and publish as one novel. That is, if they approve the additional material. Personally I think the shift to third person is indicated and adds greatly to the interest. Look at it like this: On junk you are concerned primarily with self, so first person is best instrument; but off the junk you are concerned with relationships and 1st person is not adequate to say what I have to say. Why the Hell can't you shift persons in the middle of a book? So it hasn't been done, well let's do it. Anyway I am going to present it third person. If they want to change it, all right, but I think the change would entail considerable loss.

No sign of Jack. He is overdue here. I am very tired. Working 'till all hours. I will send *Queer* along in a few days. I will get as much as I can in finished form, and indicate the rest with notes and synopses.

Love,
Bill

P.S. I am sick lately, no energy and no appetite. (I do get hungry but can't bring myself to sit down alone in a restaurant and eat through a meal, so break two eggs in milk and that is dinner.) How I miss Joan! Also discouraged and hurt, because of Marker and I got no relaxation, nobody to talk to. I shouldn't be crowded like this. Elephants and authors have long, vicious memories.

May 15, 1952
Orizaba 210 apt 5
Mexico, D.F.

Dear Allen,

I sent off the 60 pages of *Queer* to you yesterday air mail registered. Please let me know as soon as you receive the MS. [. . .]

As you know Jack is here. I am very much impressed by ON THE ROAD. He has developed unbelievably. He really has a tremendous talent, no doubt about it.[23] My friend Kells was arrested for weed along with a segment of the hip set. The stuff was planted on Kells. Time to move on South. This is getting like the good old U.S.A. People sending in lists, arrest and search without warrant, planted evidence. A movement is underway, led by a frustrate queer teacher of psychology, to purge Mexico City College of queers and hipsters. One woman turned in her own husband for smoking tea. She made a mistake. Nobody else will lay the unappetising old beast. All very disquieting and Un-Mexican. Pressure from the States, the source of bum kicks, headwaters of Drag River. Why can't people mind their own fucking business?

Jack and I are going back into the mountains for a few days with old Dave and his woman.[24] Some kind of fiesta. I want to dig the mountains and do some shooting with my new .38 Colt revolver that I bought for the Ecuadorian jungles.

Would like to hear all details on Genet. I think we should organize an international rescue brigade to liberate his talented ass by force of arms. I haven't given up yet on Marker. He may change his mind and come with us to Ecuador or wherever we go.

---

23. Kerouac mailed 530 pages of *Visions of Cody* to Carl Solomon on May 17, and it was that manuscript which Burroughs must have seen and liked. Kerouac returned the judgment, writing to Ginsberg: "His 'Queer' is greater than 'Junk' . . . Bill is great. Greater than he ever was." (May 10, 1952, Ginsberg Collection, Columbia University.) In a following letter, Kerouac noted that he was just then starting to sketch "a book about Bill," and *Doctor Sax*.
24. Old Dave's (much younger) woman was a Catholic Indian, called Esperanza Villanueva.

Did I tell you I learn from Wolberg: "I can't find anything out about Yage. The U.S. Army is conducting secret experiments with this drug." Next thing will be armies of telepathy-controlled zombies marching around. No doubt about it. Yage is a deal of tremendous implications, and I'm the man who can dig it. So let us hear from you. Jack sends his love. What with all the codeine you want without RX in any *bodega*, it is a relatively simple matter to send the Chinaman on his way. I made it 3 or 4 times already the codeine route. Nothing to it. Those bastards Stateside don't want people to cure themselves. They aim to incarcerate all undesirables, that is anyone who does not function as an interchangeable part in their anti-human Social Economic set up. Repressive bureaucracy is a vast conspiracy against Life.

Love,
Bill

P.S. Can you think up a good first name for me? Lee is O.K. for last name but Bill Lee is a little too close. I am thinking of the Old Folks you understand.

[*May 23, 1952*
210 Orizaba, Apt. 5
Mexico City]

Dear Allen,

Thanks for your very encouraging letter. I see you really understand what I attempt to say. Writing must always remain an *attempt*. The Thing itself, the process on sub-verbal level always eludes the writer. A medium suitable for me does not yet exist, unless I invent it.

I have gone over *Queer*, adding, cutting out, altering. I am sending a retyped complete revision of the 60 pages, which supercedes the MS. you now have. I am sending also a page or so to be inserted in *Junk* and instructions for a few alterations in *Junk*. This material you will have in a week.

I am making arrangements to leave Mexico. I can not wait for process of law to take its interminable course. May lose my bond money (all that remains from sale of Texas land), but *I must go. I must find the Yage*. Plan expedition to Colombian jungles.

The Oil-Man and Slave Trader routines are not intended as inverted parody sketches à la Perelman,[25] but as a *means* to make contact with Allerton and to interest him. The Slave Trader routine came to me like dictated.[26] It was the turning point where my partial success was assured. If I had not achieved the reckless gaiety that charges this fantasy, Marker would have refused to go with me to S.A. The point is these fantasies are vital part of the whole set-up. You can point this out if Wyn thinks they are irrelevant.

Whatever arrangement is O.K. by me. If they want to put this 60 pages on end of *Junk* to make one novel, O.K. Or I will go on with *Queer*. Point out to Wyn how I produced those 60 pages *on schedule*, really writing from scratch. The point is I want contract before I can do any more. I do not pretend to write for myself.

How is your poetry deal progressing? I am going to go over

---

25. S. J. Perelman, the humorist and writer.
26. Both routines appear in *Queer*, pp. 29–33 and 66–70: "Lee paused. The routine was coming to him like dictation." (P. 66.)

what you sent me line by line, but do not have time now as I want to get this letter in the mail. Kells was released with apologies, the others are out too. A very minor fracas. Mexico is trying to make noise like anti-narcotic drive, but their heart isn't there. A good % of the NAR agents blast, and Mexicans naturally prefer to mind own business. The cops who arrested Kells waited *outside* while he dressed. (Contrast letter-reading U.S. Laws.) [. . .]

Incidentally you mention as best lines Page 52. I think so too. This states the theme of the book.

For some reason I have forebodings about this S.A. expedition. Don't know why except it seems a sort of final attempt to "change fact." Well, *a ver* (we shall see).

Love,
Bill

P.S. I think Richard Lee is best. The name Al somehow does not suit me. James not bad. Would like something with more of an old Anglo-Saxon ring like my real middle name, Seward. We will think further on it.

June 4, 1952
210 Orizaba apt 5
Mexico, D.F.

Dear Allen,

Thanks for your letter. I hope we get a prompt decision on the MS. I will send along the revised MS. of *Queer* and some insertions for *Junk* and some name changes.

Watch your semantics young man. How can you arrive at criteria of "actuality" in "experience of feeling"? Neither Melville nor his Ahab were concerned with validity of intensity. Intensity is by its very charge valid for he who experiences it. When I say "madness" I mean what I see in a nut house: beat, resigned, dim, diffuse, nowhere people. No fire no intensity no life. There is madness & madness if you want to stretch the word. *Madness is confusion of levels of fact.* A peyote hallucination is a *fact,* but it is not on the same fact-level as an external material object. Madness is not *seeing* visions but *confusing* levels.

Of course I am attempting black magic. Black magic is always an attempt to force human love, resorted to when there is no other way to score. (Even curse is last attempt at contact with loved one. I do not contemplate any curse, that is absolute end of wrong line. ~~The picture of him slipping further and further away from me, laughing talking thinking of me less and less is intolerable picture of indifference.~~ The curse is last attempt to regain attention.) I want his love, but even more I want he should recognize my love for him. By indifference he cuts me off from expressing life, from my way of expressing life, from life itself. In short I am aware of wanting human love. I am aware that the attempt to coerce love fails if it succeeds and fails if it does not succeed. But the chance is there to accomplish some work "not unbecoming men that strove with Gods"—"Ulysses," Tennyson. *Because the end is not known.* Possibility of human love *by accident by the way,* possibility of change of direction. But the result of sitting on your ass and saying: "I might as well accept the fact that I can't score for any. Love isn't for me. I will give up attempt or bring attempt in line with reality, and with a sigh of cow-like resignation, take the Mongolian idiot that pimp reality hands me, or take nothing, or take the woman with the official federal stamp of approval, clear and sharp and unforgeable and indelible, deep pressed into her unexciting haunch."—is *known* and nowhere.

I am not being hincty, Allen. I appreciate your letter and admit the sense of what you say and the above is in no sense any rebuttal of your statements, but a clarification of my own position. As you say "the importance is the trip through river of fact." Incidentally I was not thinking in terms of *transcendence* but in terms of actual *change*. Some new and *usable* techniques.

I have been looking over your poems. *River Street Blues* I like, especially the swimming hole by the river and the whole desolate scrap heap of dreary U.S. industrial set up is almost telepathically conveyed so you remember the picture but not the words. Only the stanza about Neal "You can have me if you like but don't expect too much" is verbal level and perfect dreary touch in context or stands alone. In "Raw Mouth" "Sadness of long highways" excellent line.

My plans for leaving Mexico would have no conceivable bearing on possible return to U.S. But I don't think I will ever want to go back there. I intend to settle somewhere in S.A. if it comes to realizing plans for the future. I want to own land and a house there and a boat and raise my own necessary herbs and medicines and hunt and fish and have Willy with me and maybe Marker will change his mind and come too and I will live the life of Riley. You know, the first time I wrote the above I wrote it straight. Reading it over I said: "That is Illusion." Marker isn't coming. That is clearer with every day that passes and no letter from him. I have written five or six letters to him with fantasies and routines in my best vein but he doesn't answer ~~and I feel like I am making a nuisance of myself.~~ I told him I didn't expect him to answer all my letters, I just wrote because it was as near as I could come to contact with him like I was talking to him and I hoped at least he would be amused by the letters because they were funny, but he didn't answer that letter. I also sent him a book for his birthday, and I sent him clippings from newspapers and magazines I think might interest him. No answer. I guess the relation is too much strain on him and he wants to drop it. Even though I promise him not to make any scenes. I guess he doesn't want love from me.

Must take out life insurance. Willy and Marker beneficiaries. Of course I may score for the Yage in a South American drug store without any danger or trouble at all. I don't know what will happen. By the way tried peyote. Interesting. Everything looks like a peyote when you are high on this God awful stuff. I have never been so painfully sick. That peyote came up solid out of my stomach like a ball of hair. I thought I would not get it out. I suffered excruciating spasms of the asposegus or whatever you call it, and it took me 10 minutes to get that peyote out of my stomach, and clogged my throat all the way up like I was a tube of tooth paste. I hope Yage doesn't turn out to be one of these nausea kicks.

We ran into a bunch of young U.S. hipsters down here. Most of them went back to the States yesterday. A nice bunch of kids except for the one who is still here. He is a junky named Wigg who is said to play a cool bass fiddle.[27] Hè is strictly on the chisel though he has gold and always mooching junk, saying: "No I don't want to *buy* any. I'm kicking. I just want half a fix." I have had all I can stand still for from this character. Driving around in a new $3000 Chrysler and too cheap to buy his own junk. What am I the *Junkie's Benevolent Society* for the Chrissakes? He is ugly as people get.

I may get all the bond money back at that. Things look good right now. But with the money or without the money I leave this month. Direct to Panama. Then, *Quien sabe?*

Love,
Bill

P.S. I have not done any more on *Queer*. Waiting to hear what Wyn wants. Besides don't feel much like writing now. I want to kick the habit, but not much drive to quit.

---

27. Kerouac to Burroughs, May 1955: "Guess who I saw in the Village, Wig Walters, Cash in yr novel, Wig was a little fatter, older, still trying to be mysterious but I can see through him now—he is however a serious jazz artist and was waitlin [*sic*] on bass with a gang of new musicians who are the wave of the future, in Café Bohemia." (Ginsberg Collection, Columbia University.)

"Cash" appears in *Junky*, pp. 143–45. "Wigg" appears in *Queer*, p. 55, but this addition was made in Burroughs' final manuscript revision in 1985, from this letter.

June 23, 1952
Orizaba 210—apt. 5
Mexico, D.F.

Dear Allen,

Please let me know what is going on up there. I would have left Mexico by now except the court secretary went on a 15 day vacation and took my file along. If Wyn intends to publish JUNK, if he expects me to write footnotes or make any alterations, he should let me know at once. When I reach S.A. I will be unavailable for long periods, as I intend to dig unexplored areas.

I can not understand this delay. The initial arrangement, as I understood it, was immediate advance and contract. Then they want to see what I have written on QUEER; when they receive that they will send along advance right away. With great effort I got 60 pages ready in a few weeks. That was over a month ago. I have heard nothing since. Needless to say I will not do anything more without advance and contract.

So please write me when you receive this letter. There is very little time left. I have not heard from Marker in two months. I don't know why he won't write to me. Enclose a poem I wrote to Marker.

I want to get out of Mexico. There is nothing more for me to do here. Jack returns to U.S. July 1st. I am going on to S.A. alone. I offered to pay Marker's expenses if he would come with me. No answer. I guess he means no. Still trying to kick habit. Not much incentive. Please write to me. I have not heard from you in weeks.

Love,
Bill

To M.
I gave you all I had.
I got no stash left.
Kick this one cold.
You can't turn me on.
You got a route different from mine.
You can't fix me if you want to.
I let it happen like I let the habit happen.
I knew it would hurt.
I didn't care.
O.K. So you won't.
So you can't.
Nothing to come down with.
Kick it cold.
I won't be sick forever.
Muscles twitch to rest.
The gut unknots and turns over.
"I'm hungry"
Some habits take your gut along on the way out
Like a mushroom bullet.
So I'm cured so I'm off.
Where can I go alone?
What I got left to take anywhere?
I gave it all to you.
You never wanted it.
You never asked me anything.
It was my idea.
You say I got no grounds to complain.
Maybe not. I don't know.
Brought it on myself.
I guess I did.
I'm no accidental citizen walking down Accident Street
And a brick falls on his sconce.
I'm no Innocent Bystander bystanding when the riot starts.
I acted the only way I could act.
I end up nowhere with nothing.
Please don't lecture me because you are lucky and I'm not.

Please don't hurt me so I can't help wanting to hurt you.
At least wish me luck.
And let me stay ready to help you any way I can.

P.S. It looks like he won't even wish me luck or say good-bye.

[*Early July 1952*
210 Orizaba, Apt. 5
Mexico City]

Dear Allen,

I received the $180 for which many thanks.[28] Without your able mid-wifing my brain-child would have been still-born.

Bill Garver arrived with blood all over his pants where he had been using a safety pin coming down on the plane. His first words were: "How do you say enema in Spanish?" Same old Bill. I also received an epistle from Bill's *ex*-pal Joe Lucas. It was a masterpiece, commencing: "This will enlighten you about Bill Garver and what a shit-heel he is . . . Sneaked out owing me $150 after I supported him for years." Ending: "Every word is *true*. He is a real no good prick."

I am taking a little vacation in the country. I will send along a version of the remaining work on *Junk* in a few days so Wyn can look it over and there will be time for corrections before the August 15 deadline. I am due in Court on August 5 for final Judgement.

Bill says it's Hell in U.S. 8 years for an eye-dropper in Washington. This Nar[cotics] is just a stalking horse like Anti-Semitism. The real significance of these scandalous laws is political.

Love,
Bill

P.S. It would be convenient for all concerned if I had more time to give to the additional material Wyn wants. This last minute scramble is not my fault. I only wish I had been told what I have just been told 2 months ago. I would have had it done and done right by now. As it is I am rushed, there is going to be some sloppy work—I am also kicking, really kicking now—and it can't be helped. I will do the best I can. No word from Jack. He owes me a bread, butter, bed, weed, liquor and loan letter. *Did you receive last 25 pages of S.A. section of Queer?* Please answer.

---

28. The money represented the first $200 installment of Burroughs' advance for *Junkie*, less Ginsberg's commission.

July 13, 1952
Orizaba 210 apt. 5
[Mexico City]

Dear Allen,

Sending along the MS. under separate cover. I hope they are satisfied. If they had told me what they wanted three months ago I would not have been rushed like this and there would have been ample time for alterations.

I think the material is all clear enough. I enclose a chapter on a Mexican queer bar which they can use or not as they see fit. It is to be inserted back in the original manuscript of JUNK at page 150 as indicated. If they are retaining the chapter on the queer bar in New Orleans, then this chapter should go in to complement. Of course I was rushed on the material herewith submitted. It is the best I could do on such short notice. I have inserted references to my wife here and there. She does not disappear. She has no bearing on the story and therefore she is only mentioned casually and occasionally. The last reference is: "My wife and I were separated at this time." Now if they insist, I can insert a drunken car accident and some jail scenes. I know that it would be an artistic error and that it does not belong in this book. If they want it I will write it. Alternatively they could simply cross out all references to her. Like I say she has no bearing on the story whatever. Please let me know right away when you receive the manuscript. I am sending it airmail registered.

I will definitely be out of here next month. According to Mexican law, all cases must be decided within one year and my year is up Sept. 8. So this is really the end.

I have heard nothing from Jack. He left here borrowing my last $20 which he promised to pay immediately he arrived in the U.S. That was almost 2 months ago.[29] To be blunt, I have never had a more inconsiderate and selfish guest under my roof. I certainly would not consider making any jungle expeditions with Jack. If I had not received the $180 I would have become a public charge.

---

29. Burroughs amended the original, which read: "That was over a month ago."

Thanks a million for the info on Yage. That was exactly what I wanted to know, and could not find out here.

Let me hear from you.

Bill Garver is here. I have him pretty well squared away. In *Junk*, the New Orleans Section, is a reference to Lindy the Pimp. Change this name to *Lonny* the Pimp. Lindy is a real name. We must watch these names. Change Johnny Irish to plain Irish or Jimmy Irish. He is dead but he may have heirs. Old Bart can stay Bart. He is dead—heart trouble—and he has no relatives.

I was really surprised and shocked by Jack's behavior. For example, I had asked him to keep the grass—I had bought it—out of the apartment in case of a shake, except what he was using. I didn't want a whole bag of it there. I pointed out to him that: (1) I was out on bail and in trouble already; (2) It was my apartment; (3) I had a habit. So what does he do? He wants Dave [Tercerero] to bring him the bag so he can hide it somewhere *without telling me*. Dave told me about this plan and I put a stop to it.

. That was only one of many such incidents showing a complete lack of any consideration. After staying in my place a month without putting out one cent, and borrowing my rent money to leave, he has not sent me so much as a post card.

I am not a difficult person to get along with, and I am willing to make every allowance for eccentricities, but I simply can not get along with Jack. Unless he undergoes some radical transformation, I do not want him to visit me again. I think someone should tell him. He needs analysis. He is so paranoid he thinks everyone else is plotting to take advantage of him so he has to act first in self-defense. For example, when we were out of money and food, I could always rely on him to eat all the food there was if he got the chance. If there were two rolls left, he would always eat both of them. Once he flew into a rage because I had eaten *my half* of the remaining butter. If anyone asks him to do his part or to share on an equal basis, he thinks they are taking advantage of him. This is insane. He simply does not see the facts correctly.

Love,
Bill

[*Sept. 18, 1952*]
210 Orizaba, apt. 5
Mexico, D.F.

Dear Al,

Just a note to ask what is score now. I heard from Jack. Says he saw Huncke and Brandenburg in N.Y. Is now in Calif. with Neal. He says we are good friends. I guess I have to forgive him everything. But his visit was a strain on my nerves. Marker is back. I don't know whether I am glad or not. I guess I am. He was here 5 days before he came to see me, and I was Hurt and couldn't help making somewhat of a scene. He said he values my friendship and I guess he does after his fashion. Then he says: "Why can't we just be friends without no sex?" I explained it was too much strain on me, I couldn't make it that way, but just once in a while like once or twice a month, so finally he comes around to agree to that. Needless to say, the strain is still considerable, but since he is here I can't help but see him even if it is ruining my digestion, sleep and nerves.

Bill Garver is here, and the same as ever. I am really on my way South real soon. Don't want to discuss the details of my case. It's too dull. Poor Bill G. got some poison H. and went completely off his nut for 2 days. I felt like a male nurse. It was awful. Can't write more now. Going to see Marker.

Love,
Bill

P.S. Please let me know what is score with Wyn. I am flat broke from wining and dining Marker. Living on Bill G. who wants his quart of whole blood every time he lends me 10 pesos. Jack's address in case you want to know is:

c/o Cassady
1047 E Santa Clara St.,
San Jose, Calif.

Oct. 6, 1952
210 Orizaba apt 5
[Mexico City]

Dear Allen,
    Thanks for the check. I did not think too much of the last section, but if they are satisfied that is the important thing. After all *Queer* was out of place according to any frequent viewpoint, and they want to sell the book. So be it.
    I don't see myself writing any sequel to *Queer* or writing anything more at all at this point. I wrote *Queer* for Marker. I guess he doesn't think much of it or of me. I only have a few days left here. The decision will be in this week. He just left town with one of the dullest characters around here (no queer relationship). I would be appalled at the prospect of having lunch with him. Well if he prefers the company of dull characters there is not much I can do. I expect I will be gone before he returns.
    Cannot say that I found your advice very helpful. Like telling someone with a habit not to take the withdrawal symptoms seriously, only with a habit you know it can only last so long. I do regard this deal as more or less final since I did everything I possibly could and failed completely. Always before there was reserve so that I could withdraw intact. This time I did not reserve anything or maintain any defences. I don't see myself going through this deal again, and of course the possibility of mutual attraction is remote. Commercial sex leaves me absolutely cold. It would not be question of accepting a second best, but of accepting something I simply don't want.
    I am off the junk except for a little codeine. Intend to cut that out too within the next week. Junk doesn't interest me any more. Also I am not drinking at all.
    I think all writers write for an audience. There is no such thing as writing for yourself. Only they never find out who the audience is. When you find out who you are writing for I think you stop writing. Like now I don't want to write a story I want to talk to Marker.
    No plans except to go on to Panama and make a lot of money.

Needless to say I am not at all choosy as to how I make it. Most people simply aren't human so far as I am concerned. I don't care what happens to them. I have not learned any lessons of charity.

As for Jack, I do not feel up to the role of mediator at this time. I do not feel kind towards him. Old Garver is here of course and he bores me to death, but he means well and he has a certain amount of money, so we plan to go in business together in Panama. He is on the nod a good part of the time, and I can pretend to listen and he is too far gone to know the difference. The man is a wreck. He will fumble five minutes for a word.

Sorry you are not having any luck with your book,

Love,
Bill

P.S. Oct. 14, 1952 (First wrote Oct. 14, 1914 which would be before I was born.)[30] Marker never wrote so much as a card. I am waiting to leave. Don't feel any better. What about French translation of *Junk*? See what you can do. No more word from Jack. I can't understand Wyn delaying publishing date on *Junk*. The sooner they publish the better the timing. Well it's their deal. [. . .]

Can't seem to eat anything solid. Only milk and have to force that down. Lost 10 pounds since he left. ~~Perhaps I should thank him for teaching me not to ever try that again.~~

I am not cut out to be a writer. I am essentially active, and will always seek solution in activity.

Love,
Bill

---

30. Another error, since Burroughs was born February 5, 1914.

Nov. 5, [1952]
Orizaba 210
apt. 5
[Mexico City]

Dear Allen,

I hope this is my last letter from Mexico. Expect final judgment between the 7–10 of current month.

Marker and I reconciled. I went up to see him and paid his way back to Mexico City for a few days.[31] He likes me well enough in his way. I know how far his way is from my way. [illegible] have sex even if he doesn't like it, and just does it to oblige once in a while. Do you know Kafka's Penal Colony? Where the officer says after six hours of the script writing in the flesh of the scriptee, we offer him a little rice pap: "And not one in my experience ever refused the rice pap."[32]

Any news on *Queer* or French translation of *Junk* or anything? What about your book? Run of bad luck lately. Pocket picked for $200 the other day. Chinaman half in and half out of the door. Codeine and goof balls, and complete discouragement. All I want is out of this miserable cold town. Oddly did have very satisfying sex experience last night with Mexican kid on straight physical level and no nonsense. Dave [Tercerero] is here now trying to get me back on.

Three years in this town and no one I want to say good-bye to when I leave, except Marker. It seems people get stupider and more worthless every day. I heard from Jack. Still in Calif. rolling up a stake.

---

31. "Up" being Jacksonville, Florida.
32. These lines were heavily crossed out, rendering a first sentence illegible. In the margin Burroughs wrote: "Changed my mind on this passage." The reference to "In the Penal Colony" alluded to his readiness to accept any relationship with Marker rather than none at all. See "In the Penal Colony," in *The Collected Short Stories of Franz Kafka*, edited by Nahum Glatzer (Harmondsworth: Penguin, 1988), p. 150.

When I leave here head straight for Panama. After that *quien sabe?* Maybe things will be better down there. Write soon.

Love,
Bill

Garver sends his dim goof-balled best.

[*Dec. 15, 1952*]
Cobble Stone Gardens
Laura Lee Burroughs
Mortimer Burroughs
233 Phipps Plaza
Palm Beach, Florida

Dear Allen,

Jurado killed someone and skipped the country. They tried to shake me down for more $ so I followed Jurado's example. Took off with an Ex Commy also wanted for paper hanging—bum checks in case you haven't heard the expression—in Mexico, Cuba and U.S.[33] We had a few close calls on the trip up, but made it O.K. I am visiting with family for Xmas. Above address will find me until the 1st more or less. Please write. Jack is in Mexico at 210 Orizaba.[34]

Love,
Bill

---

33. Tex "the Trotskyite" Riddle, who, according to Burroughs, suggested they might as well pull a bank robbery before leaving, and hide out in Bolivia.
34. Kerouac and Cassady had driven down from San Jose together. Cassady left before Burroughs' own departure, and Kerouac stayed on, but was gone before Christmas.

Dec. 23 [*1952*]
233 Phipps Plaza
Palm Beach

Dear Allen,

Thanks for the letter. There has been no change in my plans. I am leaving for Panama in a week or so, and thence will proceed to the Putumayo headwaters. In the words of the Immortal Bard: "Let determined things to destiny hold unbewailed their way."[35]

My income has survived the treachery and fall of Jurado. I lost only the bond money. I should never have expected to recover peso one of that money knowing the Mexicans as I do. Jurado fled to Brazil in shame and ignominy. He murdered a 17 year old youth who inadvertently damaged Jurado's fish-tailed Cadillac. I have a few bones to pick with that loud-mouthed bum if I ever see him again.

After three years' absence I had expected some *impact* on revisiting the U.S. But nothing happened. I don't like it here. I don't dislike it. I feel that my home is South of the Rio Grande. Mexico City is more home to me than any other place, but that is out for a year or so. They may have some kind of warrant out for me.

I am taking the cure. No nar[cotics]. Cortisone, which is the very latest thing and works like crazy. The croaker says my health is perfect.

What an appalling idea to sandwich my book in with the memoirs of a narcotic agent.[36] Oh well. Let them do what they like. But I can't see the point of further delays.

Garver is in Panama where they serve P.G. in dippers. He writes

---

35. *Antony and Cleopatra,* act 3, scene 6, 84–85.
36. Six months later, *Junkie* was published by Ace in their Double Book series together with a reprint of the 1941 nonfiction account *Narcotic Agent* by Maurice Helbrandt. These were the memoirs of a onetime agent for the Federal Bureau of Narcotics, U.S. Treasury Department, his book described on the front cover as: "Gripping True Adventures of a T-Man's War Against the Dope Menace." The binary contrast of the two back-to-back books was made all the clearer by *Junkie's* subtitle: *Confessions of an Unredeemed Drug Addict.* When re-published as *Junky,* the subtitle was dropped.

he is happy there and wants me to go in the pig raising business with him. After all a man has to settle down some place some time. So why not on a little pig farm in Panama with old Garver nodding over his P.G. on the veranda?

Marker is still in Mexico. I think he plans to join me in S.A. or Panama. Address in Panama will be c/o U.S. Embassy or my address here will always be forwarded. Merry Xmas,

Love,
Bill

[*Dec. 24, 1952*]
Cobble Stone Gardens
Laura Lee Burroughs
Mortimer Burroughs
233 Phipps Plaza
Palm Beach, Florida

Dear Allen,

This P.S. on letter I just mailed.

(1) No I will not linger in U.S. or visit N.Y., much as I would like to see you and Lucien.

(2) Mail to: c/o U.S. Embassy, Panama, R[epública] de P[anamá], or to Florida for forwarding. Please advise Jack I am not writing him direct as mail to him may be opened. An old Mex law trick. If you send him my address, please disguise my name so two do not appear in conjuncture in letter to Jack.

(3) Parents settled in Palm Beach. Doing well. Willy with them.[37]

(4) I saw Holmes' article.[38] O.K. in an obvious way.

(5) What *is* this disgraceful job of yours? Are you a towel boy in a whore house? Peddling unlicensed condoms on 42nd St? or what? Why all the blushes? You're old enough to be acquiring a brass plate.[39]

(6) The U.S. *politically?* Good Lord, I never thought about it. Sometimes I think the whole Communist Party & Russia was cooked up by the reactionaries to forever discredit the left. Oh well, I am not much interested in politics, though an old-fashioned, bomb-throwing terrorist movement might be amusing.

---

37. Willy: i.e., Burroughs' son.

38. John Clellon Holmes, whose "Beat" novel *Go* had been published with great success earlier in 1952, wrote an article entitled, "This Is the Beat Generation," which appeared in the *New York Times* on November 16.

39. Probably refers to the job Ginsberg started that October with George Fine Market Research. This *was* on Forty-second Street, and the commercial accounts on which Ginsberg worked as an analyst did include cosmetics and deodorants, though not condoms.

Little Surrealist sketch. A woman in white uniform with a chrome-plated machine appears in J. E. Hoover's office: "I have come to give Mr. Hoover a sample high colonic wash courtesy of the Fox Massage Studios Inc." She plants a time bomb up his ass. High up.

1953

Jan. 10, 1953
Panama

Dear Allen,

Just got my ass, or what's left of it, out of the hospital after an operation for piles. The Doc tells me I am pileless for life now, so I did the right thing to get operated, but it is a gruesome, painful deal, and I went in the hospital junk-sick. My skivvies disappeared in surgery, a sinister conjuncture of circumstance. I am off the junk now and convalescing. Still leave a little pool of blood when I sit down like I was menstruating. I had to buy maroon slacks to cope with the situation.

Enough of this foolery. I will leave here for Colombia when I am in condition to travel—10 days from now, more or less—and find the Yage. 1st to Bogotá for info. Then to the Putumayo. Meanwhile, staying at beach near here. For the next 10 days I can be reached c/o *U.S. Embassy, Panama, R de P*. After that, Florida address will always reach me in time.

Garver was here but he left for Mexico and I was glad to see the last of him. He really hates to see anyone quit the junk. At the last moment, after I had spent 2 hours in midday heat buying paregoric for him, when he knew he would likely not see me again and I was of no further use, he has the gall to talk against Joan, which he never did before in my hearing. Garver prides himself on "not being vicious." Check. He is no more vicious than he dares to be at any given moment:

> "Willing to wound yet afraid to strike,
> Just hint a fault and hesitate dislike,
> Reserved alike to blame or to commend,
> A timorous foe, and a suspicious friend."
>
> Pope.[1]

---

1. From Alexander Pope's "Epistle to Dr. Arbuthnot": "Willing to wound, and yet afraid to strike, / Just hint a fault, and hesitate dislike; / Alike reserved to blame, or to commend, / A tim'rous foe, and a suspicious friend."

Let me hear from you. I am alone out here. I feel 100% better without junk. It *is* horrible stuff and no mistake. My best regards to Lucien.

As Ever,
Bill

March 1, 1953
Hotel Niza
Pasto, Colombia

Pasto Leprosy Capital of Colombia. Leprosy is not of the coastal regions here but of the high mountains. A leprosy area is always a blighted area. You feel it on entering, "This is a terrible *place*."

Dear Allen,

I am en route back to ugh Bogotá—another leprosy place—having collected nothing but a malignant strain of malaria peculiar to the Putumayo. I have been surrounded by medicine men, (The most inveterate drunk and liar and loafer of the village is always the medicine man. A horrible crew.), jailed by the police, rolled by the local hustler (Imagine finding a genuine how-much-you-gonna-give-me-hustler in the Amazonian jungle. I did lay him at least but it cost me $20. $10 fee and $10 he rolled me for.), and finally prostrated by malaria.

The trip was star-crossed from the jump. When that idiot of a *Colombian* Consul misdated my tourist card Jan. 20, 1952 instead of Jan. 20, 1953. Clearly an error in view of dates on plane ticket etc, but try to explain that to a backwoods Colombian official. I did not discover this error until I reached Puerto Assis, 2 days from Mocoa the capital of Putumayo by bus and canoe. More accurately the police discovered the error and called it to my attention. I was detained 8 days in Puerto Assis, while sepulchral telegrams issued periodically from Mocoa: "The case of the foreigner from Florida will be resolved," and finally, when I had persuaded the locals to let me continue my journey, and had a good man lined up to take me to the Yage area, another telegram; "Let the foreigner from Florida be returned to Mocoa." In Mocoa they got like a jail and put me in it. But I explained the error to the Chief of Police, seemingly an intelligent man, and was released next day, only to be set upon by malarial parasites. Now I am about flat on my ass and must return to Bogotá where I hope there is some money waiting for me. If not I will become what is known in bureaucratic circles as a "public charge." I intend to have my tourist card reassembled and return. Travel in Colombia is difficult even with the soundest of credentials. I have never seen such ubiquitous police. Love to Jack and Lucien. I may run up to N.Y. when this trip is over. Is *Junk* on the stands yet?

As Ever,
Love,
Bill

March 3, 1953

P.S. Back in Bogotá where The Institute (in the person of Doc Schultes) and the U.S. Embassy rallied to my assistance.[2] The matter of my misdated tourist card is now settled, and I am armed with a paper signed and sealed by Ministers and Secretaries of the Colombian Foreign Office. So I will return like MacArthur and this time there will be no nonsense. Bogotá horrible as ever. I feel very much brought down for some reason that is hidden from me, and have a bad feeling about my impending return.

Thanks for your letter. They are up to their old tricks: 2 books, 1 advance. By all means tell them to *go ahead and publish Junk(ie) as is*. I have written nothing yet. I can't write out in the bush. God knows when I will be in condition to write up the trip or how much I will have to say. I think definitely separate book should receive separate advance. Why can't they go ahead and publish *Junkie* as is and later issue an edition with Yage part added? I don't know yet whether Yage will be book in itself. Oh well I am just confusing the issue further. Tell them to go ahead and publish *Junkie*. Right now I do not choose to write. When I return from

---

2. Dr. Richard Evans Schultes, a renowned psychobotanist. He gained his doctorate, researching into peyote, from Harvard in 1937, a year after Burroughs had graduated there.

this trip I can be more definite. [. . .] I received some $ from the Old Folks. My old Ace in Hole. Know the Song? "Some write home to the Old Folks for coin, And that's their Old Ace in the Hole."[3]

P.S. Dr. Schultes is going with me.

---

3. On the other hand: "My name'd be mud / Like a chump playing stud / If I lost that old Ace in the Hole."

March 5, 1953
Bogotá

Dear Allen,

Returning to the Putumayo today. I have attached myself to an expedition—in rather a vague capacity, to be sure—an expedition of varied purposes and personnel: Dr. Schultes; three Swedish photographers who intend to capture a live anaconda; two Englishmen from the Cocoa Commission (whatever that is), and 5 Colombian "assistants." A whole truck-load of gear is on the way down, boats and tents and movie cameras and guns and rations. Seems like a fairly decent crew of people, but strictly 4-ply. (The Swedes went on ahead and I haven't seen them yet. They are probably bounding about the Putumayo in shorts.) Schultes is the only one who comes on at all. He likes to chew coke with the Indians, and is not above amorous dalliance with indigenous females. But I have rarely met two more irretrievable squares than the Cocoa Commission. I expect to be down there a month. Write me c/o U.S. Consulate, Bogotá.

Like I say, tell them to *go ahead and publish Junkie*. Can always bring out later addition with Yage material.

This country has got like martial law. Cops frisk you getting on and off trains, busses, planes. They search your luggage anywhere anytime. I nearly got a nervous breakdown travelling with a piece in my suitcase. Twice they missed it by inches. Love to Jack and Lucien. I will write when I get out of the bush.

Love,
Bill

April 12, 1953
[Bogotá]

Dear Allen,

Back in Bogotá. Mission accomplished. I have a crate of Yage with me. I know how the witch doctors prepare it. I have taken it three times. (1st time came near dying.) I am not going to take any more until I extract the pure substance free of nauseating oils and resins. A large dose of Yage is sheer horror. I was completely delirious for four hours and vomiting at 10 minute intervals. As to telepathy, I don't know. All I received were waves of nausea. The old bastard who prepared this potion specializes in poisoning gringos who turn up and want Yage. "You've come to the right place," he says. "Just drink this straight down." But he won't resort to any such unethical practices as slipping datura or strychnine or rat poison in your drink. Just Yage and he drinks the same amount. (There is apparently considerable tolerance acquired.) He killed a citizen a month before I picked up with him. I later took smaller doses. Very similar to weed including aphrodisiac results. But any dose you can feel is nauseating, impairs coordination, and gives one a chill. The Institute is going to help me extract the alkaloids and I will conduct further experiments with the pure stuff.

We separated from the Swedes unfortunately. Our expedition boiled down to Dr. Schultes, the two Englishmen from the Cocoa Commission, and two Colombian botanists. The friction that develops in all expeditions was not long in manifesting itself, in the form of a progressive coolness between the Cocoa Commission and the Colombians. A clash of purposes and temperaments with myself sitting uneasily on the fence suspect by both parties of secretly adhering to the other. (Incidentally I was all wrong about the Cocoa Commission. They turned out to be charming and far from square.) Throughout the trip I was treated like a V.I.P. (Very Important Person), travelling free of charge in military planes, sleeping in the Governor's house, eating in the officers' mess. I think they were under the misapprehension I was attached to one of the Commissions or a representative of the Texas Oil Company travelling incognito. (The Texas Co. was there 2 years ago, found no oil and pulled out. But everyone in the area believes firmly the Texas Co. will return. Like the Second Coming of Christ and about as unlikely.)

Spent 5 days on a Colombian gun boat on the Putumayo River. To say the Colombians run a loose ship is an understatement. As Dr. Cope (Cocoa Com.) remarked: "Wouldn't surprise me to see someone shit on the deck and wipe his ass with the flag." Finally ended up in the hottest spot in all Colombia. Right on the edge of the war where they take your luggage apart and read your letters. And me with that piece in my suitcase. I thought, "Well I've had it this time." But just as they were closing in on my luggage, Schultes (I thought he was miles away in Bogotá) drove up in an Official Car and my luggage was loaded in it without a suitcase opened. (I tell you Schultes is specially assigned to my protection.)

You will see my picture in *Life* one of these days. A reporter from *Life* came down just as I was on the way out. He is doing a story on Yage. Looks like I am scooped. Queer to be sure, but about as appetizing as a hamper of dirty laundry. Incidentally I have been turned down—charmingly but firmly—all over the Amazon area. (Once by a soldier I was drinking with in the sentry box.) At present trying to make time with the Point IV chauffeur, who drove me up to Bogotá in the Official Car. (Point 4 is some kind of an agricultural Commission down here that Schultes works for.)[4] I will be leaving Bogotá in 10 days so send mail to my Florida address, *202 Sanford Ave, Palm Beach, Florida.*

I been trying to talk the *Life* reporter into doing an article on the Auca—hostile Indians of Ecuador. Never even photographed. Myself to go along as guide and interpreter. I told him I know the area like the palm of my hand, and speak the indigenous dialects fluently. (Fact is I have become a shameless impostor.) I can always rattle off some kind of gibberish and then say, "These are Chickua Indians from the North. They speak a different dialect." I really think I have him interested in the idea. He is going to write a story

---

4. Point Four was the last item announced by President Truman in his inaugural address of January 1949. A part of U.S. foreign policy for Communist containment, it offered technical and industrial aid to underdeveloped nations in Latin America, Asia, and Africa.

on Schultes, Yage and some kind of puberty rites connected with the use of Yage in the Vaupes area. This citizen has dyspepsia already, and I would like to be there when he takes Yage.

Another idea I suggested to him was to go in the area occupied by the Liberals, interview and photograph. (If the Liberals don't shoot you on the way in, the Conservatives will shoot you on the way out.) What gives with *Junkie*? Regards all around.

Love,
Bill

P.S. The remark attributed to Dr. Cope epitomizing the lax conditions obtaining in the Colombian Navy is really my own and derives from a dream that came to me in 17th Century English. "The English and French delegates did shit on the floor and tearing the Treaty of Seville into strips with much merriment did wipe their backsides with it, seeing which the Spanish delegate withdrew from the Conference."

This expedition is so far more picaresque and Abneresque than Ahabesque.[5] Imagine a reporter from *Life* taking pictures of Ahab from a helicopter or televising the pursuit of the White Whale. The reporter did arrive in a plane and my first knowledge of his presence was when I saw him taking my picture.

Stood up by the Point 4 chauffeur last night. I guess it's no go.

I don't know what I will do now. May go on to Ecuador and definitely want to see Lima, Peru. Plan to be back Stateside in 2 months and will try to have the Yage material in some sort of shape by then, but tell Solomon *to go ahead and publish Junkie now*. The search for Yage turned out to be a pushover. Everyone grows it in their back yard and you can buy all the Yage you want right in Mocoa which is accessible by bus. Another thing, the Amazon area is much more populated than is generally supposed. It is very easy to go down the Amazon to the Atlantic. You go by motor launch down to Brazil where you can take a steam boat on down. The only areas really untouched are those occupied by hostile Indians.

---

5. Abneresque: the comic strip character, as in *Naked Lunch* (p. 2): ". . . carrying *The News* as a prop. 'Only thing I read is Little Abner.' " (Note that all citations of *Naked Lunch* refer to the Grove Press edition, 1992.)

So I am looking for a live one to finance expedition into these areas. *"A ver."* We shall see.

This *Life* character is a bit of a shit by the way. "We got two kinds of publicity, fellow" he says. "Favorable and unfavorable. Which do you want?" With such shameless blackmail he mooches his way around demanding discounts, free transportation etc. But who am I to talk? Case of the pot and the kettle, what? My dear Allen, I never advocated fighting the Institute unless there was irreconcilable conflict of interests.

April 22, 1953
Quito

Dear Allen,

Had to leave Colombia since my visa expired. Plan to return there in 2 weeks. Met a pretty young Liberal—I gave him my piece as contribution to the Cause—and contracted to help him leave Colombia. (The Conservatives will not give him exit permit. They are waiting for a pretext to kill him and confiscate his coffee plantation.)

There simply is nothing to be said in favor of the Conservatives. Every intelligent, sympathetic person I met in Colombia was a Liberal. The doctor who treated my malaria, the people who interceded for me with the police, the German who helped me score for Yage, even the hustler who rolled me for $10, all the boys I took an interest in, Liberals every one. The Conservatives are not only a bunch of shits they are *all ugly*. I never saw anything like it. The Nacional Police, which is back-bone of Conservative Party, is the most unanimously hideous body of young men I ever laid eyes on. (Colombian boys are by and large very comely.) They—the police—are a special breed that looks like the end result of atomic radiation. There are thousands of these horrid knaves in Colombia, and I literally only saw *one* I would consider eligible—and he appeared ill at ease as if he knew not how to conduct himself in the midst of such a vile rout. The Conservatives have also armed a disgusting crew of civilian hoodlums. I saw them in action throwing glasses, grabbing the waitresses, yelling "*Viva los Conservadores!*" in a Liberal café, hoping to provoke someone so they could shoot him. Loud-mouthed drunken bums. Imagine the Times Square boys armed and turned loose on the public.

I have a premonition I may get myself in trouble when I return to Colombia. However it is *impossible* to remain neutral, and I will help this boy no matter what. Always was a pushover for a just cause and a pretty face. Wouldn't surprise me if I end up with the Liberal guerillas.

Even Doc Schultes, who is so rep Conservative in Boston he

thinks Sacco and Vanzetti were guilty, is a Liberal sympathizer in Colombia.[6]

No money has been forthcoming for expeditions to contact the hostile Indians. My last week in Bogotá was flat broke and reduced to the shoddy expedient of stealing my drinking alcohol from the University laboratory placed at disposal of the "visiting scientist." About the cheapest trick of the year I think. I extracted some pure Yage. Results uncertain so far. Send mail to Florida. I am very much in transit. I have $50 to live on 'til next month. Living in flop houses. I could have sold that piece for $150. Oh well. He needs a gun more than I need money. The present situation in Colombia is even worse than I thought. Many of them are former officers in Franco's army who took the cloth after a six week cramming course. (And do they lead the life of Riley.) The majority of Colombian priests have come over from Spain since Franco took over. I-always say no good ever comes out of Spain. The best people in S.A. are the Indians. Certainly the best-looking people. My boy is at least 70% Indian. The other 30% I can't pin down.

As Ever,
Bill

P.S. As you see my search for Yage has been complicated by other factors. I am trying to get something done. I think Yage is a telepathic drug, but I can't be sure. There are things of which I can not bring myself to speak. More later when experiments conclusive. Need someone to check results with me.

---

6. Nicola Sacco and Bartolomeo Vanzetti: Italian-American anarchists executed, amid great international protest, in Massachusetts, 1927.

May 5, 1953
[Lima]

Dear Allen,

This finds me in Lima which is enough like Mexico City to make me homesick. Funny thing all my nostalgia is for Mexico. That's home to me and I can't go there. Got a letter from Jurado. I am sentenced in absentia. I feel like Romans felt when they were exiled from Rome.

Situation is this: I will stay here about 2–3 weeks and write up what I have now and send it along to you. I need to return to jungle and spend at least a month living with Yage-taking Indians, which I have not been able to do so far because of delays and running out of money. It doesn't have to be the Auca (I just figured Auca would provide a combination of features). So see what you can do about $, and write me c/o U.S. Consulate, Lima, Peru.

You know this story on Yage in *Life* is a break for us. Free publicity. The U.S. will be Yage conscious for sure when that issue hits the stands. Let me hear from you right away.

As Ever,
Love,
Bill

May 12, 1953
Gran Hotel Bolívar
Lima, Peru

Dear Allen,

I spent one night in this hotel and laid in a stock of their stationery of which this is the last. So it goes to you, sweetheart,
my favorite agent. What is going on up there? Am I in the
stalls yet and if not why not? Write me what the score is. I
will be here a month or so. Have been working on the Yage
section. So far it isn't exactly inspired. But such as it is I will
be able to send it along in another two weeks more or less.
(Meanwhile I need money at least to buy a second-hand typewriter.)
I think the section will come to about 30–50 pages. Can't be
sure yet.

Lima is the promised land for boys. I never saw anything like
it since Vienna in '36. But you have to keep an eye on the little
bastards or they'll steal all your fucking valuables. (I lost my watch
and $15 in the service.) Oh well the watch didn't run anyway. I
never had one that did. I have not seen here any queer bars (hope
I don't see any), but in the bars around the Mercado Mayorista—
Main Market—any boy is wise and available to the Yankee dollar.
Last night I checked into a hotel with a beautiful Indian to the great
amusement of the hotel clerk and his friends. (I don't think the
average U.S. hotel clerk would be amused at such an occurrence.)
Yes, they have Yage here and a short trip from Lima. I plan to go
when I finish the Yage section.

Lima also has an extensive Chinatown, good restaurants, pleasant climate, the cheapest living I hit in S.A. In short I wouldn't
mind settling down here, but I still like Mexico better. Now please
write me exactly what is going on. Love to all.

Love,
Willy Lee

P.S. This town looks like you could score for junk. In Colombia
and Ecuador nobody ever heard of such a thing. A little weed among

the Coast-wise negroes, coca—but only in leaf form—among the Indians—but no junk at all.

Write c/o U.S. Consulate, Lima, Peru. Incidentally you most always see some blood in these louche Peruvian bistros. Ramming a broken bottle in your opponent's face is standard practice. Everyone does it here.

May 23, 1953
[Lima]

Dear Allen,

Enclose a skit I dreamed up.[7] (The idea did come to me in a dream from which I woke up laughing.) Family converted the $270 into traveller's checks and remitted it to me.[8] Rolled for the check that same night by a kid I picked up. Losing all my fucking valuables in the service. (The checks are, of course, no loss as American Express refunds the $, and the kid could not cash them anyway without a U.S. passport.)

Recovering from a bout of Pisco Neuritis. First Caqueta Malaria, then Esmeraldas Gripe, now Pisco Neuritis. (Pisco is local liquor. Seems to be poison.) Looking for a second-hand typewriter, and will send along what I have with prospectus. Can't leave here for another week or so until my neuritis clears up completely.

May 24

Ho hum dept: Rolled again. My glasses and a pocket knife. This is a nation of kleptomaniacs. In all my experience as homosexual I have never been the victim of such idiotic pilferings of articles no conceivable use to anyone else. Glasses and traveller's checks yet! I'm afraid I will never learn. Trouble is, I share with the late Father Flannagan—he of Boy's Town—the deep conviction that there is no such thing as a bad boy.[9]

---

7. Note that when edited and later published in *The Yage Letters* (p. 42), the word "skit" was replaced by the term "routine." At the time of its composition, Burroughs evidently had not fully conceptualized such texts as "Roosevelt After Inauguration" as a specific literary form. The five-page text of "Roosevelt" was enclosed with this letter.
8. The $270 represented the second part of the advance on *Junkie*, $300 less Ginsberg's commission.
9. Reference is to the highly successful, highly sentimental 1938 MGM film *Boys' Town* starring Spencer Tracy and Mickey Rooney.

I will send along what I have written when I get a typewriter —I should have it in N.Y. in 10 days or so.

Got to lay off the sauce. Hand shaking so I can hardly write, so must cut short.

Love,
Bill

Sunday May 30 [*1953*]
[Lima]

Dear Allen,

Woke up with an honest boy and my valuables—or what's left of them—intact. Found him without a lamp too. That was lost in the service a week ago.

I studied Zen Buddhism at one time. This "flashing" is what a writer tries to do. But seems like there is always something (words perhaps) between us and the fact. Humility is indeed beatness, a compulsory virtue that no one exhibits unless he has to. I like your poem.[10] Thought of writing a story about a sage who returns from the mountain a lecherous drunken old man chasing young boys. The story is flash-back from jail where sage is languishing for indecent exposure. Point is some old bum in jail for molesting a child may be "the Sage." *Quien sabe?* Not me. The older I get the less I *sabe*, the less wisdom, maturity and caution I have.

A few self flashes. Shadow boxing with a young kid in a louche Peruvian bistro (Haven't you any dignity at *all?* Obviously not), making a pass at 13 year old Indian boy right in front of his father, brothers and uncles, dragging home two ragged brats. All I remember is they were young. Woke up with the smell of youngness on my hands and body.

Now if I was wise and listened to a psychoanalyst, I would give up young boys and be an assistant professor somewhere sitting around hatching a cancer of the prostate (that fucking croaker in Panama bungled my ass—I'll sue him), and accepting reality.

Instead if I live to 80 will be demonstrating judo to some young boy in some louche bistro. Like the Poet say: "God keep me from ever being a wise old man praised of all." Yeats, "Poet's Prayer."[11]

---

10. At the end of April, Ginsberg had been inspired by Chinese paintings in the New York Public Library to start studying Zen Buddhism. The poem Burroughs refers to may have been the beginning of "The Green Automobile," a long-lined celebration of Ginsberg's love for Neal Cassady that eventually ran to thirty-four stanzas.

11. W. B. Yeats's "A Prayer for Old Age": "God guard me . . . From all that makes a wise old man / That can be praised of all."

I am working on Yage and will send along about 20 pages this week, leaving to your discretion how much if any to show the boys in the front office. Jack is crazy. Why should a publisher take all his books? If someone is willing to publish *On the Road,* he should jump at it like a hungry pike. [. . .] Congrats to Lu on forthcoming child. Must get to work on Yage.

As Ever,
Love
Bill

June 5, 1953
[Lima]

Dear Allen,

Sending along what I have done on Yage. This is still in rough form subject to corrections and additions. As to what else will be covered: Ecuador briefly, and Lima and Peru Jungle if I ever get there. I feel like a text book on tropical diseases. Will watch my hygiene in future. Now have some obscure brand of dysentery, and waiting results of lung x-ray. Doc says he don't like the sound of that left lung.

So use your judgment Sweetheart, as to what you show or tell them.

Been living quiet. What with all these diseases and my ass fucked up by that incompetent Spic croaker in Panama.

Well I'm not going to fool around here much longer. Today I ask the Doc; am I or am I not in jungle shape within next week? If he says no, I am cutting back via Panama—where I will stop off to have words with that croaker and sue the Avianca Company for that error in my tourist card. I should get at least $500. The incompetent spic bastards. Will also hit Mexico on way back. Yes, Jurado beat the rap again. He always lands on his big feet. Love to the boys.

Love,
Bill

June 6, 1953
[Lima]

Dear Allen,

Leave for jungle Tuesday for good or for bad in sickness or in health. Doc says no active T.B. Just old scars from childhood. Billy Bradshinkel's ghost still unlaid.[12] Feel nostalgia for U.S., a flood of memories: Like when I was the cheapest thief in New York and Phil [White] and I made a teenage sailor for his locker key and came home with a bag of dirty laundry, and I smelled the handkerchiefs to see if the kid had jacked off in them, lust flickering like heat lightning through junk haze. *Ah ma folle jeunesse!*

Ecuadorian miscellanea:

Esmeraldas: Hot and wet as a Turkish bath, and vultures eating a dead pig in the main drag and everywhere you look there is a nigger scratching his balls.

The Police in Las Playas: You will recall I was arrested there when I beached a balsa raft, suspect to have floated up from Peru with a young boy and a tooth brush. (I travel light. Only the essentials.) The withered face of cancerous control. Ecuador is really on the skids. "For this I will never follow thy fading fortunes more."[13] Let Peru take over and civilize the joint so a man can score for the amenities.

Guayaquil: Every morning a swelling cry goes up from the kids who sell cigarettes in the street. "*A ver Lookies!*"—"Look here Luckies!"—Nightmare fear of stasis. Will they still be saying "*A ver Lookies*" 100 years from now? Horror of being *stuck* in this place. This fear follows me like my ass. A horrible, sick feeling of final desolation.

Peru: Vultures circle over Lima and roost on the buildings. A peculiar violet evening sky. Here the evening lasts several hours. Everybody in Lima has active T.B. or old scars.

---

12. See *The Yage Letters*, pp. 9–11, for more of the Billy Bradshinkel routine.
13. *Antony and Cleopatra*, act 2, scene 7, 80–81: "For this, / I'll never follow thy pall'd fortunes more. / Who seeks and will not take, when once 'tis offer'd, / Shall never find it more."

I live in an empty shop on the outskirts of town, with a vast rubbly lot all around. At all hours people are lined up in the lot along adobe wall shitting. I gather sanitary facilities are inadequate in slum districts. You see this all over Lima, a city of open spaces, shit strewn lots and huge parks, vultures wheeling in a violet sky and young kids spitting blood in the street. Some innaresting monuments. One to Chavez—whoever he may be. Naked boys with wings twisting around a cone straining up as if trying to goose each other. Really Mr. Chavez! And all alone on a pedestal in the island separating two wide streets a life sized bronze 15 year old boy, completely naked playing marbles. Heats me pants every time I pass him on the bus.

Saw a Peruvian bull-fight. Dreary butchery. One bull he stuck the sword in 5 times before the poor beast succumbed to cachexia. Vultures over the ring flapping their wings irritably in frustration.

A cop walking along leading a young man by the *hand.* Is it a prisoner or just holding hands? Went to a Turkish bath. The sheer copper bronze beauty of the young Indian body leaves one breathless—if one shares my predilections.

They got codeine pills like Mexico in the drug store. Chinaman stay away from my door! Sent you Yage MS. Write me what you think.

Think I will skip Auca this trip. For one thing need an ass that works in case I have to sacrifice my virtue inna service. Just thought of punch line for Reggie in *Queer,* who lost his intestines in the service. "I regret I have but one ass to give for my country."[14]

Love,
Willy Lee

---

14. U.S. patriot Nathan Hale's last words: "I regret that I have but one life to give for my country."

Junio 18, 1953
Pucallpa

Dear Allen,

Hold the presses! Everything I wrote about Yage subject to revision in the light of subsequent experience. It is *not* like weed, nor anything else I have ever experienced. I am now prepared to believe the *Brujos* do have secrets, and that Yage alone is quite different from Yage prepared with the leaves and plants the *Brujos* add to it. I feel rather like a male Dorothy Thompson[15] who rushed down here to get the story on Yage in two weeks.

I took it again last night with the local *Brujo*. The effect can not be put into words. I will attempt to delineate as far as possible. There were about 6 Indians and myself sitting around outside on the edge of the jungle (I was well coated with citronella) drinking Yage or Ayahuasca as they call it here, no one talking or making any sort of noise. I experienced first a feeling of serene wisdom so that I was quite content to sit there indefinitely. What followed was indescribable. It was like possession by a *blue spirit*. (I could *paint* it if I could paint.) Blue purple. And definitely South Pacific, like Easter Island or Maori designs, a blue substance throughout my body, and an archaic grinning face. At the same time a tremendous sexual charge, but *heterosex*. This was not in any way unpleasant, but shortly I felt my jaws clamping tight, and convulsive tremors in arms and legs, and thought it prudent to take phenobarbital and Codeine. My sense of measure shot, I took 10 grains of phenobarbital and 3 grains of Codeine. Enough to put the late Phil White on his ass. Within minutes the tremors subsided, and all the Yage effects disappeared. I felt perfectly normal, and only a little sleepy, but now cold, and mosquitoes starting to bite and I wanted to go to bed. At once the witch doctor said (Mind you it was completely dark. He could not see me.), "Mister wants to go." I walked home, stopping off for coffee (with that amount of phenobarbital I should not have been in condition to walk at all), made some notes and went to bed 2 hours after taking the phenies. Obviously barbiturates

---

15. Dorothy Thompson, the journalist.

are the chemical antidote for Yage, and the two cancel out. I remember *now* that I experienced the blue invasion 1st time I took Yage, but not when I prepared it myself. I had forgotten this angle completely, I think owing to physiological amnesia produced by a terrific overdose.

I am going down river in a few days to see another witch doctor who has a tremendous local reputation. Like I say I am no longer so sure I know what the score is, but in any case I will not stay more than 2 weeks more. I am tired of fraternizing with cops and Army officers and priests and—ugh—Protestant missionaries, and governors, and such dull gentry. I want to be back in Mexico City and N.Y. I am definitely coming to N.Y. and soon. Next expedition I am going to spend my time among the Indians, and then *leave*. I am bringing back some Yage, of course, but I can't promise blue spirits. The plant should be fresh, and other leaves mixed in. The extracted alkaloid doesn't have no spirits. I will bring back some complete vines, and some extraction.

Love,
Bill

P.S. I have *worms*. What a disgusting condition.

[*Early July 1953*
Lima]

Dear Allen,

More notes aş they are in note-book, which is such a terrible mess I want to type the notes up and throw away the note-book.

These are notes at random in no order:

Esmeraldas: This is about the most God-awful, dirty, hot tropical town I was ever in. The inevitable Turk who buys and sells everything. He tried to cheat me on every purchase and I spent an hour arguing with this bastard. The Greek shipping agent with his dirty silk shirt and no shoes and his dirty ship that left Esmeraldas 7 hours late. Arriving in Manta, a shabby man in a sweater started opening my bags. I thought he was a brazen thief and gave him a shove. Turns out he was the Customs Inspector.

La Asia, a Chinese restaurant in Guayaquil, looks like an 1890 whore house and opium den. Holes eaten by termites in the floor. Dirty tasselled pink lamps, a rotting teak wood balcony.

Mocoa: The Governor thinks there is a pool of oil 80 miles across under the town. He thinks they are going to build a railroad terminal and an airport there. As a matter of fact the whole region is on the down grade. The rubber business is shot, the cocoa is eat up with broom rot. The land is poor and there is no way to get produce out. The dawdling psycophrenia [*sic*] of small town boosters. Like I should think some day soon boys will start climbing in through the transom and tunneling under the door. It seems impossible for small towners to ever look at the facts. Several times when I was drunk, I told someone brutally: "Look, there is no oil here. That's why Texas pulled out. They won't ever come back. I am not from the Texas Company or any other company." (One theory had me down as representative of Squibb [Pharmaceuticals]. They were about to have a Yage boom.) "Doc. Schultes talked to the Texas Geologists and he says there is no oil here. Understand?" But they couldn't believe me.

Tingo María: Comfortable, well-run hotel like a mountain resort. Cool climate, very high jungle. At dinner got bad case of stasis horrors. The feel of *location,* of being just where you are and nowhere else is unendurable. This feeling has been with me all over S.A. I think back on places like Puerto Assis, Puerto Umbria, ugh Mocoa, Esmeraldas, Manta. God I would hate to go back to any of these places. Especially I hate the whole Putumayo region.

A group of upper-class Peruvians in the hotel. Loud-mouthed bunch. Every few minutes one of them yells: "Senor *Pinto.*" This is Latin American humorous routine. Like they look at a dog and yell, "*Perro*" and everybody laughs. Simple-minded bastards.

Talked to a slightly crazed school teacher from California who chewed with her mouth open. The President arrived in Tingo Maria while I was there. Same thing happened to me in Colombia. Terrible nuisance. No dinner 'til nine o'clock and I made a scene with the waiter and walked a mile to town to eat a greasy meal there and walk back.

In Pucallpa there was a Naval Lieutenant, a furniture salesman and an old German who is planting African oil palms. This is a new business and everybody thinks they are going to get rich at it. I don't think so. Everything fails in this country: the rubber business is shot, the cocoa business is shot, the bottom fell out of Barbasco—this is an insecticide—I expect no sudden prosperity to result from the African oil palm. The old German had an interminable story about a treasure buried down Arequipa way. Forty tons of gold. I thought at first he was a swindler, concluded finally he was just a little touched, like everybody in this country. He had the treasure story from a character he cured of paralysis agitans who gave him the map in a twitch of gratitude. So the German went down there with mine finders and found where the treasure was. But everybody died so he couldn't get it out without help. Seems there is one of those curses on the deal. The old German spent his days typing out data on this alleged treasure, and chewed my ear off every meal.

Last five days in Pucallpa was a nightmare. I wanted to leave but was trapped there by impassable roads and rain. Everyone seemed on the point of disintegrating into his component parts. The Naval Lieutenant disintegrated into a silly queer and embarrassed me by goosing the waiter. The furniture salesman wanted to go in the cocaine business and get rich so he could live in Lima and drive a big fishtailed Cadillac. Oh God! People think all you

have to do is go in some shady business and you will be rich overnight. They don't realize that business, shady or legitimate, is the
same fucking headache.

They were driving me crazy with their silly talk and their stupid
Spanish jokes. I felt like Ruth amidst the alien corn. When they
said that English literature was very poor and American literature
didn't exist, I lost my temper and told them Spanish literature
belonged in the out-house. I was really shaking with rage and realized how the place was getting me down.

Met a Dane and took Yage with him, and he immediately vomited it up and avoided me after that. He evidently thought I had
attempted to poison him, and he was saved only by the prompt
reaction of his hygienic Nordic gut. I hate Danes. I never saw one
that wasn't bone dull. All their ideas are of a flatly practical nature.

Terrible bus trip back to Tingo María where I got drunk and
was helped to bed by the assistant truck driver. Hung up two days
in Huanaco. An awful dump. Spent my time wandering around
taking pictures, trying to get the bare dry mountains, the wind in
the white dusty poplar trees, the sad little parks with statues of
generals and cupids, and Indians lolling about with a special South
American abandon, chewing coca—the government sells it in controlled shops—and doing absolutely nothing. At five o'clock had
a few drinks in a Chinese restaurant where the owner picked his
teeth and went over his books. How sane they are and how little
they expect from life. He looked like junk to me but you can never
be sure with a Chinese. They are all basically junkies in outlook.
A lunatic came in the bar and went into a long incomprehensible
routine. He had the figure 17,000,000 dollars written on the back
of his shirt and turned around to show it to me. Then he went over
and harangued the owner. The owner sat there picking his teeth.
He showed neither contempt nor amusement nor sympathy. He
just sat there picking a molar and occasionally taking the tooth pick
out and looking at the end of it.

Passed through some of the highest towns in the world. They
have a curious, exotic Mongolian or Tibetan look. Horribly cold.

Back in Lima I met a boy and went with him to a dance place.
Right in the middle of this well-lighted non-queer dime and dance
joint, he put his hand on my cock. So I reciprocated and no one

paid it any mind. Then he tried to find something worth stealing in my pocket, but I had prudently hidden my money in my hat band. All this routine, you understand, completely good natured and without a trace of violence overt or potential. Finally we cut out together and took a cab and he embraced me and kissed me yet and went to sleep on my shoulder like an affectionate puppy, but insisted on getting out at his place.

Now you must understand this is average, *non-queer* Peruvian boy. They are the least character-armored people I have ever seen.[16] They shit or piss anywhere they feel like it. They have no inhibitions in expressing affection. They climb all over each other and hold hands. If they do go to bed with another male, and they all will for money, they seem to enjoy it. Homosexuality is simply a human *potential,* as is shown by almost unanimous incidence in prisons— and nothing human is foreign or shocking to a South American. I am speaking of the South American at best, a special race part Indian, part white, part God knows what. He is not, as one is apt to think at first, fundamentally an Oriental, nor does he belong to the West. He is something special, unlike anything else. He has been blocked from expression by the God-damned Spanish and the Catholic Church. What we need is a new Bolívar who will really get the job done. This is, I think, what the Colombian Civil War is basically about: the fundamental split between the South American Potential and the Repressive, Spanish, life-fearing character armadillos. I never felt myself so definitely on one side and unable to see any redeeming features in the other.

South America is mixture of strains, all necessary to realize the potential form. They need white blood as they know—Myth of White God—and what did they get but the lousiest white trash of the West, the fucking Spaniards. Still, they had the advantage of weakness. Never would have gotten the stodgy English out of here. They would have created that monstrosity known as a White Man's Country.

---

16. "Character armor" was the term Wilhelm Reich coined to describe defensive character traits, resistances that protected against pain at the price of restricting the capacity for pleasure.

Well that cleans the book out somewhat. I am going to buy a portable. Incidentally, it was that fucking Christer of a missionary who talked me into taking worm medicine. A horrible routine that ruined two days for me. It's one of those deals where it is a close thing between you and the worms but you have the edge being bigger . . . But sometimes children conk out on this terrible shit.

I am fixing to leave and will be out of here in three days at the latest.

Love,
Willy Lee

July 8, 1953
Lima

Dear Allen,

Start North in two days. So send no more mail here. I will see you in New York in a few weeks. Turned out I did not have worms. No there is no heat on me. I won't be tracking any fuzz into your pad. I am typing up some random notes to get them in some sort of order. So enclose same.

Tingo María:

Stuck here 'til tomorrow on bum steer. I was supposed to see a man about Yage and it turns out he moved away five years ago. This is a farming community with Yugoslav and Italian colonists and an American Experimental Agricultural Station—Point 4. As dull a crew of people as I ever set eye on. Farming towns are awful. Whatever gave me the idea I could ever be a farmer? This place gives me the stasis horrors. Suppose I should have to live here? Did you ever read H.G. Wells' *The Country of The Blind*? A great story about a man who could see in a country where everyone had been blind so many generations they had lost the concept of sight. He blows his top, saying: "But don't you understand? I can *see*."[17] These people lack something as necessary to me as food. No one in Tingo Maria could conceivably understand any of my routines. Only places don't give me stasis horrors are Mexico City, N.Y., and Lima. The Composite City of my Yage dream.

Pucallpa:

This is the pleasantest end of the road town I have seen in S.A. Terrible trip here in a car with two whoreish sisters who sprawled all over me throughout the 14 hour trip. A flicker of heterosex died of surfeit, too much of quite a bad thing. Peru is far and away better than Ecuador or Colombia. They do not have the small country inferiority complex nationalism. In Peru are *Pochos*, people

17. " 'You don't understand,' he cried in a voice that was meant to be great and resolute, and which broke. 'You are blind, and I can see. Leave me alone!' " In H. G. Wells, *Selected Short Stories* (Harmondsworth: Penguin, 1982), p. 138. That Wells located his Country of the Blind in Ecuador would not have been lost on Burroughs.

who don't like Peruvians. In Pucallpa alert intelligent personnel in shops and restaurants. In most small South American towns they never have what you want. If the place is hot, there are no cold drinks. A river town will stock no fish hooks. A place infested with mosquitos never heard of citronelle. There is something intentional in this, a determination to be stupid and jerk water, a negativistic hostility, a deep self depreciation. But Pucallpa has what you want. The hotel keeper introduced me to a missionary. What an awful crew they are, worse than the Catholics. He believes in Hell with burning sulphur, and him a grown man. Gawd. How simple-minded can you get. A local character contracted leprosy in the town of Contamana apparently from a leprous cook in the Pension Contam[in]atione. So this lousy Christer says he suspects the man had immoral relations with the cook and this is a judgment of God. I hope the Good Lord visits a few of the more gruesome local maladies on this bastard, like Brazilian Sore. As a Peruvian friend put it, "If you catch him in your nose it sure fall off." The missionary decided I was the Anti-Christ and will have no more to do with me.

Went with hotel manager to visit a local character who is supposed to know his Yage. This man turned out to be a fountain of bull shit. Told about a witch doctor who took Yage and vomited up a full growed viper, then ate the viper again. And when the witch doctor took Yage his spirits would come and shake the whole house.

Made connection with unassuming little witch doctor who prepared me some Yage. This was the first time I really dug the kick. It is not like weed or anything else in the world (though more like weed than anything else). It is the most powerful drug I have ever experienced. That is it produces the most complete derangement of the senses. You see everything from a special hallucinated view point. If I was a painter I could paint it. The substance of the body seems to change. I turned right into a nigger and then this blue spirit got to me and I was scared and took some codeine and Nembutal. Almost at once everything was back in prosaic focus. (This is perfect antidote for overdose and no one should ever take Yage without a barbiturate handy, as you can go in convulsions and conk right out.)

I took Yage five times after that. Amazing tolerance is acquired. After second dose I could drink with no ill effects the amount on which I vomited ten times in Colombia and came near going in convulsions.

Like I say it is like nothing else. This is not the chemical lift of C, the sexless, horribly sane stasis of junk, the vegetable nightmare of peyote, or the humorous silliness of weed. This is insane overwhelming rape of the senses. A few notes from Yage state:

The room took on the aspect of a near Eastern whore house with blue walls and red tasselled lamps. I feel myself change into a Negress complete with all the female facilities. Convulsions of lust accompanied by physical impotence. Now I am a Negro man fucking a Negress. My legs take on a well rounded Polynesian substance. Everything stirs with a peculiar furtive writhing life like a Van Gogh painting. Complete bisexuality is attained. You are man or woman alternately or at will. The room is Near Eastern and Polynesian at the same time, and yet in an undefined place you feel is familiar. I notice in lighter intoxication effect is Near East, the deeper the intoxication the more South Pacific. There is suggestion here of phylogenetic memory of a migration from Middle East to South America to South Pacific. I spoke of Yage spirits shaking the room. There is definite sense of space time travel that *seems* to shake the room. If I could only paint I could convey it all. This is not a sociable kick like weed. The only contact you want is sexual contact. I never experienced such sex kicks.

Now I have experimented with extractions, tinctures, dried preparations and they are all *nowhere*. I don't know whether I can bring any back in usable form. Seems only the fresh prepared vine and leaves have the real kick and it won't keep more than a few days. I will do my best. Need a chemist's. There is undoubtedly a volatile element involved because dried stuff has no kick, and the pure alkaloid Yageina or Harmine is pale replica. The essential is not there. So perhaps Yage is not a transportable kick. The vine grows from cuttings but would not grow anywhere in U.S. as climate is too cold. Green-house would be only possibility.

Yage is it. It is the drug really does what the others are supposed to do. This is the most complete negation possible of respectability. Imagine a small town bank president turning into a Negress and rushing to Nigger town in a frenzy to solicit sex from some Buck Nigra. He would never recover that preposterous condition known as self respect.

Well I will be seeing you real soon. I am in hurry to leave now.

Love,
Bill

P.S. Get rough with your little beast of a poet.[18] They're all alike, ingrates every one of them ingrates. Take it from an old queen, my dear.

It occurs to me that preliminary sickness of Yage is motion sickness of transport to Yage state. H. G. Wells in *The Time Machine* speaks of undescribable vertigo of space time travel. He is much underrated.

For God's sake don't leave New York now I am on my way there. That would be a hell of a reception.

18. The poet was Gregory Corso, whom Ginsberg had first met in the winter of 1950. By the summer of 1953, Corso had taken Ginsberg up on his commitment to support penniless poets, and had virtually moved in with him.

Hope you can decipher these insertions.

[*July 10, 1953*
Lima]

Dear Allen,

I can't dig this stuff. I boiled some down for transport and took it and no effect whatever except like I had took nembies, fell asleep before I could finish the cup. (Remember nembies are antidote for overdose.) The only answer is some volatile oil in the fresh leaves and fresh vine. I never got results from the Yage in pure form I prepared in Colombia. *But* the next day I get a delayed reaction, an hallucinated period, the illusion or actuality of telepathic contact.

For example in Colombia I walked into a café and looked at a boy and thought: "He is a liberal who will sell my gun for me." It turned out he was a liberal, did try to sell the gun and I finally gave it to him. Today I had a premonition like the first teasing chill of malaria, that I was in hot writing form. I had things to do. Those things that usually take up a lot of time like getting visas, plane tickets and checking with The Institute the scientific name of the other plant they cook with Yage (I have dried specimens). To my amazement I accomplished all these things in one hour. At the Institute who should I meet (not incidentally the man I was looking for) but a Botanist who is old friend of Doc Schultes. Then went to a café and began to write like I was taking dictation. Here it is:

Yage is space time travel. The room seems to shake and vibrate with motion. The blood and substance of many races, Negro, Polynesian, Mountain Mongol, Desert Nomad. Polyglot Near East, Indian, and new races as yet unconceived and unborn, combinations not yet realized, passes through your body. You make migrations, incredible journeys through jungles and deserts and mountains (stasis and death in closed mountain valleys where plants grow out of your cock and vast Crustaceans hatch inside you and grow and break the shell of your body), across the Pacific in an outrigger canoe to Easter Island. The Composite City, Near Eastern, Mongol,

South Pacific, South American where all Human Potentials are spread out in a vast silent Market.

Minarets, palms, mountains, jungle. A sluggish river jumping with vicious fish, vast weed grown parks where boys lie in the grass or play cryptic games. Not a locked door in the City. Anyone comes in your room anytime. The Chief of Police is a Chinese who picks his teeth and listens to denunciations presented by a lunatic. Every now and then the Chinese takes the tooth pick out his mouth and looks at the end of it. Hipsters with smooth, copper colored faces lounge in doorways twisting shrunk heads on gold chains, their eyes blank with an insect's unseeing calm.

Behind them, through the open door, tables and booths and bars, and rooms and kitchens, opium smokers, hasheesh, people eating, talking, bathing, shitting back into a haze of smoke and steam. And gaming tables where the games are played for incredible stakes. Never money. From time to time a player leaps up with despairing inhuman cries having lost his youth to an old man or become Latah to his opponent. (Latah is condition occurring in S.E. Asia. Otherwise normal, the Latah can not help doing what anyone tells him to do once his attention has been attracted by calling his name or touching him.) But there are higher stakes than youth or Latah. Games where only two players in the world know what the stakes are.

All houses in the city are joined. Houses of sod with high mountain Mongols blinking in smoky doorways; houses of bamboo and teak wood; houses of adobe and stone and red brick; South Pacific Maori houses; houses 100 feet long housing entire tribes; thatched houses, and houses of old boxes and corrugated iron where old men sit in rotting rags talking to themselves and cooking canned heat. No chromium, no red leather, *no glass bricks*. We got like a quota on Scandinavians. They have to undergo strict probationary period in filthiest quarter of the City and abstain for one year from washing.

Expeditions leave for unknown places with unknown purpose. Strangers arrive on rafts of old packing crates tied together with rotten rope; they stagger in out of the jungle their faces swollen by insect bites; they come down the mountain trail on cracked bleeding feet through the dusty, windy outskirts of the city where people shit in rows along adobe walls and vultures fight over fish heads; they drop down into the park in patched parachutes. They are escorted by a drunken cop to register in a vast public lavatory. The data taken down is then put on pegs to be used as toilet paper.

The cooking smells of all countries hang over the city, a haze of opium, hasheesh and the resinous red smoke of cooking Yage, smell of the jungle and salt water and the rotting river and dried excrement and sweat and genitals. High mountain flutes and jazz and bebop and one-stringed Mongol instruments and Gypsy xylophones, and Arabian bagpipes. The City is visited by epidemics of violence and the untended dead are eaten by vultures in the street. Funerals and cemeteries are not permitted.

Albinos blink in the sun, boys sit in trees languidly masturbating, people eaten with unknown diseases spit at passers-by and bite them, and throw lice and other vermin on them hoping to infect somebody. Whenever you get blackout drunk, you wake up with one of these diseased, faceless citizens in your bed who has spent all night exhausting his ingenuity trying to infect you. But no one knows how the diseases are transmitted or indeed if they are contagious.

Yes Yage is the final kick and you are not the same after you have taken it. I mean literally. How else explain the tolerance that seems to last indefinitely? With all other drugs—except junk—you start from scratch as soon as the drug is out of the system (36 hours at most). But my tolerance carried over 2 months from Colombia. I did not even vomit when I took Yage the first time in Pucallpa. How explain the sedative action of the extracted alkaloid? This requires a Chemist and extensive research.

Still cleaning out the note book:

Mocoa: They will bring on revolt like the hypochondriac brings on sickness by over defense. Their control is off in time.

Manta: Vultures eating a dead pig in a pool of rotten brown water.

Peru: I notice the Peruvian Army Officers are old time gentlemen. When our car got stuck, a truck load of soldiers with an officer came by. The officer approached me—not the chauffeur—and shook hands formally. He then supervised extraction of the car, shook hands again, got in his truck with his soldiers and drove away. Same thing happened in various other contacts with the Military. In Ecuador they have the manners of a cop.

South America does not force people to be deviants. You can be a queer, or a drug addict and still maintain position. Especially if you are educated and well mannered. There is deep respect here for education, and correct behavior in the sense of good manners. In the U.S. you have to be a deviant or die of boredom. Even a man like Oppenheimer is a deviant tolerated because of his usefulness.[19] Make no mistake *all* intellectuals are deviants in the U.S.

No attempt by the officers to put the private down, to humiliate him or establish a gulf. I have seen the same thing in treatment of prisoners. The guards drink coffee with them, joke with them, they feel no need to prove they are not like the prisoners. They know they are, and they don't care. South America has most uncowed prisoners I ever saw. Not that the guards are incapable of brutality. But the systematic sadism and humiliation that guards inflict, especially in Southern U.S. prisons, is not known here.

The normal Peruvians are all wise on subject of queerness. One day I met an Italian boy on the waterfront in Pucallpa. Queer but not obvious. He had a younger brother who was attractive in a loutish, sullen, brutal way. The boy said he had nothing to eat so I said, "Have a sandwich with me later in the Acapulco and bring your brother. Maybe he would like a sandwich too." He turned up without his brother, carrying a bible with an inscription from "His friend the Chief of Police in Contamana." The furniture salesman put his hand to the back of his head with an effeminate gesture and said. "And a very special friend, my dear. No?"

The Peruvians notice who you look at. If you look at boys they notice.

Pucallpa: Two boys sitting in a tree watching a whore walk by in her pink dress. How alive these boys are with a sweet masculine innocence.

Huanaco: This is a dreary place but not the complete hopelessness

---

19. J. Robert Oppenheimer, one of the fathers of the atom bomb, but whose postwar opposition to the hydrogen bomb was well known. In 1954, Oppenheimer was denied his government security clearance for, among other charges, "defects of character."

of a small town in Texas or Oklahoma or Ohio. You could get here boys and junk and, of course, C.

Last night I smelled weed in the Market. On my way day after tomorrow. Will bring back some of the extract but the virtue is not in it. You have to come to the jungle to get the real kick. But the vine would undoubtedly grow in Southern Mexico.

Love,
Willy Lee

[*August 3, 1953*
Mexico City]

Dear Allen,

Received copy of *Junkie* for which many thanks. I didn't mention before because I did not feel like talking about it, that I never heard from Marker after I left Mexico, though I wrote ten letters to his home address in Florida to be forwarded.

It seems he has disappeared under strange circumstances. I hope to find out something definite in next week or so before I leave here. Enclose more notes. I have been working ever since I got here sorting out notes and re-writing.

Narcotic Agent not so bad as I expected it would be.[20] He does not sound like an overly obnoxious character. How are sales? I will send along more notes. See you soon, best regards to Jack and Lucien.

As Ever,
Willy Lee.
Bill

---

20. Maurice Helbrandt's book, bound together with Burroughs' *Junkie*.

August 17 [*1953*]
Cobble Stone Gardens
Laura Lee Burroughs
Mortimer Burroughs
233 Phipps Plaza
Palm Beach, Florida

Dear Allen and Jack,

Back at home for brief visit. Will leave here for N.Y. in a week so stand by. Just wanted to let you know I am on the way. See you soon now. I have some business for the lawyer your brother.[21] A law-suit against the PAA Co. for fucking up my tourist card so I was ten days languishing in Colombia box subject to unspeakable indignities at the hands of degenerate guards. I have all the documents, a complete white book on this atrocity. We will sue for $25000 and settle for what we can get. Should be worth $1000 at least. So tell Louis to hold himself in readiness.

Love,
Willy Lee

---

21. Ginsberg's brother, Eugene Brooks. Referring to him below as Louis, Burroughs was confusing his name with that of Ginsberg's father.

Dec. 14 [1953]
General Steam Navigation Co., Ltd. of Greece
On board
T.S.S. Nea Hellas

Dear Jack,

In all my experience as a traveller I have never encountered such food and service and accommodations. Long greasy hairs in the scrambled eggs, no hot water, dirty state rooms, unwashed dishes. This is the crummiest line in the industry and 12 days yet. 3 days to go.

I had a dream someone hit Allen and he was lying on the couch at 206 East 7th [St.] with a bandage around his jaw.[22] Just mention it for the record.

I wrote Allen c/o Cook's in Mexico City. I suppose he has left N.Y. by now.[23] My address for next few weeks is c/o U.S. Consulate, Rome, Italy. Drop me a line.

As Ever,
Bill

---

22. Ginsberg had accommodated Burroughs for the past three months at his flat in New York.
23. After Burroughs' departure, Ginsberg traveled south; first to Palm Beach, where he stayed with Burroughs' parents, then to Havana, and on to Mexico for the New Year of 1954.

Dec. 24 [19]53
Rome

Dear Allen,

Reconciled with Alan [Ansen].[24] He is showing tonight.

As for Rome. In all my experience as a traveller I never see a more miserable place. I would rather be in Bogotá, yes even in Quito.

Finally found the baths. They have been closed. In all this town is no Turkish bath. Now you would think there would be bars like the San Remo etc., but such is not the case. I live in the Latin Quarter and I have ransacked this town. Properly speaking there are no bars in Rome. A Roman "bar" is a hole in the wall soda-and-ice-cream joint, no toilet and no place to sit down, with the door propped open or missing altogether, where you can gulp a drink with a cold, blue hand. It's cold here like N.Y. in Winter and you *never get warm*. There's no heat anywhere. *And* Rome is considerably more expensive than N.Y. Right now I am huddled in my room (wearing overcoat, of course. You never take off your overcoat in Rome) with a terrible cold, reading *The Invisible Man*.[25]

I plan to leave here the 28th and straight to Tangiers. Glad Kells did not come here on my account.

Love,
Bill

The hottest spot in Rome looks like that coffee joint I don't like next to the Remo (Rienzi's??). Some picture on the wall showing a bleak lack of talent, a few dreary dykes in sweat shirts, a sprinkle of ugly queers, and some characters with beards playing chess. A real cute waiter named "Chi Chi." However, since he is the son of the owner it looks like hands off.

Why did I ever leave Mexico?

---

24. Alan Ansen, onetime secretary to W. H. Auden, and a long-standing friend of Ginsberg's. In New York, Burroughs had made arrangements to meet Ansen in Rome.

25. H. G. Wells' novel.

1954

(From William Burroughs and Alan Ansen)

>Jan. 2, [19]54
>Rome.
>Saturday

Dear Allen,

Leaving Monday for Tangiers via Gibraltar. Will arrive with $50 to last me until Feb 1st.

The more I see of Rome the less I like it. Considerably more expensive than N.Y.C., cold like you never get warm because there is virtually no heat. No interest in this town at all.

I have made some contacts, and confirmed my impression that Rome was in a clean-up campaign. The Turkish baths have been closed. The heat is on junk, and the junkies of Rome are shivering sick in their traps. Alan [Ansen] was on the point of renting an apartment, but the landlord flipped when he heard I was going to flop on the couch for 3 days. So the deal fell through. Did you ever hear the like of that? Anyone comes in your trap even for *one night* has to be registered with the law. Colombia was freedom hall compared with this dump. And under no circumstances no matter how respectable can you have anyone who is not registered in the hotel up for a drink. Not for *10 minutes*. I am going to have something to say to that lying bastard Gore Vidal, and all these characters talking about how great Italy is and anything goes, and they got like a renaissance of culture. What a crock of shit! They can shove Italy all the way up. And incidentally I hear France is no better and twice as expensive. I am beginning to think there is no place like Mexico, and I wish to God I had gone with you to California. Well I will dig North Africa. Alan has been a little bit more happy here since he goes for Cathedrals and such, and can stand cold weather. Also he has negotiated several *affairs de coeur* in frigid doorways (average price $10 and pretty shoddy merchandise).

Let me hear from you. Alan sends buckets of love.

>As Ever,
>Love,
>Bill

Dear Allen,

No the price is only $3.20, but there may be extras if you suck in a buggy instead of a doorway. The fountains are wonderful (even old Cactus Boy melted at the sight of Trevi), and I feel that in spite of minor irritations Europe is just wonderful. Enjoy Yucatán and give my love to Neal.

Love,
Alan

P.S. After this week, I can never see a drugstore the same way again. Paregoric *is,* really, rather yummy.

Jan. 26 [1954]
Tangiers

Dear Allen,

I like Tangiers less all the time. No writers colony here or they keep theirselves hid some place. Everybody has both feet in your business; like some character I never see before says: "Your friend Ali is in the Socco Chico. Please give me one peseta." And the pay-off is I never get to lay Ali. No place to take him. You can't check into a cheap hotel here like in a civilized country. No they want inflated whore house prices when they see what the score is. And Ali is getting worried about his standing in the shoe shine set. (He is afraid someone might think I am scr--ing—careful about ob-scenity in the mails—him.) He thumps his little scrawny chest and says, "I am a man." Oh God! Such shit I could hear in Clay-ton, Mo.

Their lousy weed tears your throat out like it's cut with horse shit. And no more boot than corn silk. I try to connect for some O, and a citizen sells me some old dried up poppy pods. Well I will have a good look around since I am here. May change my mind. Would God I was back in Mexico. Or Peru.

What's all this old Moslem culture shit? One thing I have learned. I know what Arabs do all day and all night. They sit around smoking cut weed and playing some silly card game. And don't ever fall for this inscrutable oriental shit like Bowles puts down (that shameless faker).[1] They are just a gabby, gossipy simple-minded, lazy crew of citizens.

[Letter incomplete.]

---

1. One reason for Burroughs' interest in visiting Tangier had been his reading of Paul Bowles' Tangerine novel, Let It Come Down (1952) and The Sheltering Sky (London: John Lehmann, 1949; New York: New Directions, 1949).

Feb. 9, 1954
Tangiers
Morocco

Dear Allen,

Waiting for Kells to show. Expect him here momentarily. This town is left over from a boom. Hotels and bars empty. Vast, pink stucco apartment houses falling apart, not even finished. In a few years Arab families will move in with goats and chickens. I have a room in best district for 50¢ per day.[2] You can eat in native quarter for 20¢. But boys and sweet opium keep me broke. You can get a boy for $1 or even less, but the Aureomycin pro[phylactic]-coverage comes high. (Incidentally my ass seems to be working again.)

I have been doing some writing. Will send along samples when I locate a typewriter. This town seems to have several dimensions. I have experienced a series of Kafkian incidents that would certainly have sent Carl back to the nut house.[3] For example: I go to bed with an Arab in European clothes. Several days later in the rain (and loaded on hash. You eat it here with hot tea), I meet an Arab in native dress, and we repair to a Turkish bath. Now I am almost (but not quite) sure it is the same Arab. In any case I have not seen no. 1 again. When I walk down the street, Arabs I never see before greet me in a manner suggesting unspeakable familiarity (in past or future?). I told one of these Arabs, "Look, I don't like you and I don't know you. Scram." He just laughed and said, "I see you later, Mister." And I did in fact go to bed with him later, or at least I think it was the same one. It's like I been to bed with 3 Arabs since arrival, but I wonder if it isn't the same character in different clothes, and every time better behaved, cheaper, more

---

2. Burroughs took a room at No. 1, Calle de los Arcos, a tiny alleyway behind the Socco Chico in Tangier's medina.

3. Carl Solomon had been at the Columbia Presbyterian Psychiatric Institute at the time Ginsberg met him in 1949. In the spring of 1952, shortly after accepting *Junkie* for Ace Books, Solomon returned to Bellevue after a nervous breakdown.

respectful. (He has learned I can't be pushed beyond a certain point.) I *really* don't know for sure. Next time I'll notch one of his ears. [. . .]

Write to me c/o U.S. Legation, Tangiers. My best to Neal.

As Ever,
Love,
Bill

P.S. Paul Bowles is here, but kept in seclusion by an Arab boy who is insanely jealous, and given to the practice of black magic. May go on down to Dakar. There is a lot of work there.

March 1 [1954]
Tangiers

Dear Allen,

Tangiers is looking up. Meeting the local expatriates. Junkies, queers, drunks. About like Mexico. Most of them came from some place else for obvious reasons.

Sample Tangiers nocturne: Arrive in the Mar Chica, all-night bar where everybody goes after midnight. With me an Irish boy who left England after a spot of trouble, and a Portuguese who can't go home again. Both queer. Both ex-junkies. Both chippying with dollies (script not exactly necessary).[4] Both flat broke. The Portuguese wants me to invest in a pornographic picture enterprise, and also to go back in The Business. Proprietor of Mar Chica looks like 1890 ex–prize fighter, a bit fat, but still a man of great strength and exceedingly evil disposition. ·Beautiful Arab boy behind the bar. Languid animal grace, a bit sulky, charming smile. Every queer in Tangiers has propositioned him, but he won't play.

Two Lesbians who work on a smuggling ship drunk at a table. Spanish work-men, queers, British sailors.

Taylor (suspect to be a stool pigeon) seizes me and drags me to the bar, throwing an arm around my shoulders, and tightening his grip whenever I try to edge away. He gazes into my face putting down a sincere routine.

"Life is rotten here, Bill. Rotten. It's the end of the world, Tangiers. Don't you feel it, Bill? You've got to have some ideal, something to hang onto—where do you live, Bill?"

"Oh, uh near the Place de France."[5]

"Bill, you understand about money? What can I *do* Bill? Tell me, I'm disgusted." He clutches my arm. "I'm scared, Bill. Scared of the future, scared of life. You understand." He seems on the point of climbing in my lap like a child, convulsed by a hideous hunger for absolution. Actually I think he is not a stool-pigeon,

---

4. Dollies: Dolophine, i.e., methadone, a synthetic morphine substitute.
5. The Place de France, in the New Town of Tangier, was about a mile away from Burroughs' room inside the old medina.

but would like to be one. He just can't make the grade. Competition is keen. All the Arabs are pigeons (including the beautiful boy behind the bar). I never saw a face as wrong as Taylor's. The eyes pale blue, strained out of focus in the attempt to appear naïve and sincere. A horrible mouth—suggestion of hare-lip—that looks beat in with a hammer. Shabby clothes, whiney voice.

I disengage myself and sit down with the two Lesbians and the Irish boy. One of the Lesbians looks at me blearily like a Third Avenue Irish drunk.

"What does fuck you mean?"

"I don't know."

"Well fuck you anyway." She begins to cry and clutch the other Lesbian. "My child, my poor child. You're such an old drab."

Like you see Tangiers is almost too pat. No lower age limit on boys. An American I know keeps a 13 year old kid. "If they can walk I don't want them." Trouble is the Arabs are an awful-looking people.

I am hooked. Met a doctor's son, he need money, and the old man's script pad right there. Some stuff called Eukodol which is best junk kick I ever had.[6] Start Dolly cure in a few days now.

They got vicious, purple-assed baboons in the mountains a few miles out of town. (Paul Bowles was set upon by enraged baboons and forced to flee for his life.) I intend to organise baboon sticks from motorcycles. A sport geared to modern times.

Have done some work, but I feel dissatisfied with it. I have to find a completely new approach. Wasting too much time sitting around in cafés. I received your letter from Yucatán. Wyn is about due an accounting on royalties. You might drop him a line. Let me hear from you. Family spoke well of you.

As Ever,
Bill

---

6. Eukodal: dihydrohydroxycodeinone hydrochloride, manufactured by Merck, Darmstadt. An analgesic and hypnotic used as a morphine substitute.

March 12, 1954
Tangiers

Dear Neal,

What has happened to Allen? I received one letter from Yucatán and have heard nothing since then. My letters to Mexico City were returned unclaimed.

If he is there tell him to write me at once. If not do you know where he is? Please let me hear from you right away as I am quite worried. Is Jack with you?[7]

This town would please you. Weed absolutely legal, and you can smoke it anywhere.

Please write to me.

As Ever,
Bill Burroughs

c/o U.S. Legation
Tangiers
Morocco

---

7. In late January, Kerouac had hitchhiked from New York to see Cassady in San Jose. He waited until early March, hoping Ginsberg would rendezvous with him there on his return from Mexico as planned, gave up, and left for San Francisco.

April 7 [1954
Tangier]

Dear Allen,

I have written and rewritten this for you. So please answer.

Routines like habit. Without routines my life is chronic night-mare, gray horror of midwest suburb. (When I lived in St. Louis and drove home past the bare clay of subdivided lots, here and there houses set down on platforms of concrete in the mud, play-houses of children who look happy and healthy but empty horror and panic in clear gray-blue eyes, and when I drove by the subdivisions always felt impact in stomach of final loneliness and despair. This is part of Billy Bradshinkel story. I don't know whether it is parody or not.)

I have to have receiver for routine. If there is no one there to receive it, routine turns back on me ~~like homeless curse~~ and tears me apart, grows more and more insane (literal growth like cancer) and impossible, and fragmentary like berserk pin-ball machine and I am screaming: "Stop it! Stop it!"

Trying to write novel. Attempt to organize material is more painful than anything I ever experienced. Shooting every four hours. Some semi-synthetic stuff called Eukodol. God knows what kind of habit I am getting. When I kick this habit I expect fuses will blow out in my brain from overcharge and black sooty blood will run out eyes, ears and nose and staggering around the room acting out routines like Roman Emperor routine in a bloody sheet.

Notes on C:

When you shoot C in main-line—no other way of taking it gives the real C kick—there is a rush of pure pleasure to the head. Before you can clean the needle the pleasure dims. Ten minutes later you take another shot. No visceral pleasure, no satisfaction of need, no increase of enjoyment, no sense of well-being, no alteration or widening of perspective, C is electricity through the brain stimu-lating pleasure connections that can only be known with C. (As now scientists put long needles into the brain—brain has no feeling—and stimulate directly centers of pleasure and pain with electric current. Idea for science fiction, like a television set you attach electrodes to the brain and get broadcast of pure pleasure mixed with political indoctrination. Give that one to Bradbury.)[8] Once C channels are stimulated, there is urgent desire to restimulate and fear of falling from C high. The urgency last as long as C channels are activated—an hour or so. Then you forget it because it corresponds to no pleasure ordinarily experienced. ~~You never think, "How nice it would be to have a shot of C."~~ C is a specific substance, not a means to any other enjoyment. ~~It is the most autistic of all pleasures and the most destructive. When you want it you think of nothing else. Sex is no more on than with junk.~~ There is no withdrawal syndrome with C. It is literally all in the mind, hideous need of the brain, a need without body and without feeling, ~~an obsessed, earth-bound ghost need. Since it is not a need of the body it is a need without limits.~~ Reversal of natural direction of current which is from the viscera that feels to the brain that does not.

In C high, brain is berserk pinball machine flashing blue and pink connections in electric orgasm. (Science fiction note—C pleasure could be felt by a mechanical brain. First stirrings of autonomous activity.)

[*Letter incomplete.*]

8. The science fiction writer Ray Bradbury.

April 22 [1954
Tangier]

Dear Jack,

Having acted as official transmitter of letters for some time past it has been borne in upon me that you merit a completely independent communication.

Things here are so typically Tangiers—"My dear, *anything* can happen in Tangiers"—that it is positively sick-making. It seems there has been a junk beef about me—or at least a rumor to that effect, but another version is just a hoax on the part of certain parties to frighten me out of Tangiers. So Tony, the old Dutch man who runs this whore house I live in,[9] keeps casting me reproachful glances in the hall and saying: "Ach thirteen years and never before I haff such a thing in my house. And since two weeks are here in Tangiers two good English gentlemens I know since long times. With them I could make good business except my house is so watched at." However I am still his star boarder and he hesitates to evict me. Well the junk deal like blew over like there never was anything in it but Tanger bull shit if you ask me. Now the mother of my boy beefs to the fuzz and we have to meet like clandestine. It's degrading that's what. [. . .]

I am waiting for my boy now, and he is late and I am feeling very irritable.[10] Besides, Allen's behavior hasn't improved my disposition.

Now there is no reason why *you* can't answer my letters. So please write me as soon as you receive this if you have not already done so. ~~Get up off your rusty dusty like the song says.~~ It's like whether I will be here or not depends on what I hear from you and Allen. And I must hear something soon.

As Ever,
Bill

----

9. Anthony Reithorst, in whose house on Calle de los Arcos Burroughs had a room.
10. Burroughs' boy: Kiki, with whom he maintained a relationship for the next three years.

P.S. My boy just left, and I can now write with the philosophic serenity conveyed by an empty scrotum. Also have the Wisdom of the East under my belt in the streamlined form of four dolophine tablets. No script was necessary here until Brian Howard (old friend of Auden and Isherwood) burned the town down.[11] It was me introduced him to dollies, but I soon found I had reared up a Frankenstein. He sweeps into drug stores, "chemist shops" as he calls them, and says, "Give me four tubes of M. tablets quickly." He has decided that M. is after all more "amusing" than dolophine. "And you know, the strangest thing. I simply don't *feel* right in the morning until I've had my medicine." He always refers to it as his "medicine." Very gentle. Like some people got no class to them and go around saying: "I'm sick. I got the gapes. I'm yenning." Not Brian. He just says, "I needs my medicine."

Incidentally he has appeared in several of Evelyn Waugh's novels, and is very sweet when sober and has been quite a comfort to me.[12] I have really been terribly upset and hurt that Allen doesn't write to me and I need someone to talk to. Amazing how few people can pick up on what I say. In short most people are plain bone stupid, and right now I am in urgent need of routine receivers. Whenever I encounter the impasse of unrequited affection my only recourse is in routines. (Really meant for the loved one, to be sure, but in a pinch somebody else can be pressed into service.) And Brian really digs my routines. But he is leaving tomorrow, and I will be alone in this desert of beautiful boys who look at me with soft brown eyes like a puzzled deer. "What is the Americano talking

---

11. Brian Howard, born of American parents in Surrey and educated at Eton and Christ Church, Oxford (1926). A onetime figure of England's *jeunesse dorée*, Howard was rather tarnished by 1954. He spent a few months in Tangier, where he acquired a narcotic addiction to add to his tuberculosis. He committed suicide in January 1958.

12. Evelyn Waugh portrayed Howard as Ambrose Silk in *Put Out More Flags* and, with some license, as Anthony Blanche in *Brideshead Revisited*. In March 1954, Howard described Burroughs as "a nice, if slightly long-winded, ex-Harvard creature of forty who is endeavouring to cure himself of morphinomania by taking . . . Eukodal." (From a letter to John Banting, in *Brian Howard: Portrait of a Failure*, edited by Marie-Jaqueline Lancaster, London, 1968.)

about? Should I laugh now? Is he good for an extra 25 pesetas today?"

~~Allen's neglect will drive me to some extravagance of behavior. I don't know what I will do but it will be the terror of the earth.~~[13]

You must remonstrate with him. I didn't expect him to act like this (not a line in four months), and I didn't expect I would feel so deeply hurt if he did. That is rather a confused sentence and I think contains some sort of contradiction. What I mean is I did not think I was hooked on him like this. The withdrawal symptoms are worse than the Marker habit. One letter would fix me. So make it your business, if you are a real friend, to see that he writes me a fix. I am incapacitated. Can't write. Can't take interest in anything.

Kicking habit, by the way. Terrific hassle with my Portuguese Huncke.[14] I think he invented the story there was junk heat on me. He just this second came in with another version of the story, and when I pointed out the logical discrepancies in his communication he got furious . . . Like: "You Americans are too stupid to understand anything . . . I don't want to talk about it any more. It's too stupid." Uh huh. Europeans interpret American generosity as pure stupidity, and when they find out we have seen through their rather obvious maneuvers they are furious. Believe me, I have learned a lot about the Old World in the last few months and none of it is good. If Malaparte can make a fortune writing an anti-American book, I might could do the same thing writing an anti-European polemic.[15] Why not? Why should we stand around in awe of these chiseling bums simply because they are supposed to represent "culture." They are supposed to be mature, urbane, witty and all that crap. Actually they have no sense of humor whatever. For example this bastard, who says Americans are barbarians, his family is seven hundred years old, but he must endure our idiotic crudities. I gave

---

13. *King Lear*, act 2, scene 4, 275–77: "I will do such things— / What they are, yet I know not; but they shall be / The terrors of the earth."

14. Portuguese Huncke: called Eduardo, though renamed in Burroughs' routine Antonio the Portuguese Mooch (in *Interzone*).

15. Malaparte: pseudonym of Italian novelist Curzio Suckert. Burroughs was probably thinking of his novel *La Pelle*, translated as *The Skin* by David Moore (London: Alvin Redman, 1952).

him a barrage of routines tonight for our money. Now he suddenly sees he isn't going to get any more money, and how that continental charm goes up in smoke. The room was crackling with undischarged insults like an electric storm. Well he is leaving tomorrow. I forgot to say purpose of these maneuvers is to scare me out of Tangiers so I will take him to Spain where he desires to be. But I'm not about to take him to Spain or any place else.

Now Jack, if you are my boy, find out what the score is with Allen, and tell him he is hurting me and there is no reason for it. I haven't made any claims on him. I don't ask him to write every day. But he left me expecting a letter now for more than three months. In his last letter he said, "Write me to Mexico City." That letter came back unclaimed. In short I don't mind he doesn't write if he wants to feel completely free for a while, but he could have spared me all this hurt (which I am not playing up, which is worse than I describe it in my letters to him) by simply dropping me a line (as he apparently did to you) saying he would be out of touch for a while.

So if you have influence with him, exert same in my behalf. I need an Advocate who can reach The Court.

Jack, I am staying up tired, cooking my brains with tea, to write this so please answer promptly. It seems to me tonight I am always knocking myself out for my friends and they dismiss me as a vampire who tries to buy them with some gift, money, or routines, or cut off fingers. Even if lost my life in service of a friend, he would likely say: "Oh he is trying to buy me with his ugly old life."

Tell Allen I plead guilty to vampirism and other crimes against life. But I love him and nothing cancels love.

The scene with the Portuguese was wild. Would God I had a tape recorder. It took form of each disparaging the other's country, the insults getting more and more naked and personal. When I said Portugal was the Outhouse of Spain, the conversation reached its level of basic nastiness.

He hates me like Huncke because I have done so much for him, but do not really like him. His position is insufferable. He can't exploit me as if I was a sucker, and I can't fully accept him as a friend. I don't blame him for hating me.

Well I look forward to hear from you. And please remonstrate with Allen.

As Ever,
Bill

Cargo U.S. Legation
Tangiers, Morocco

P.S. No matter what Allen says I want to hear it, understand? If he says something that you know would hurt me, please don't keep it from me. I want to know. Nothing is worse than waiting like this day after day for a letter that doesn't come. Even Marker has written to me. ~~I can't stand it much longer~~.

This is serious, Jack. _DON'T LET ME DOWN._

May 2 [1954
Tangier]

Dear Neal,

I received letter from Allen dated April 9, and sent him some money in the form of traveller's checks. In his letter he said he was living on a finca (country estate) with a female archeologist.[16] All in all I can not think he is completely out of touch, and the return of your money may well have been simply a bureaucratic fuck-up. If he were in jail he would certainly have communicated with the U.S. Consul in Mérida, and his death would certainly have been reported by now since he seemingly has friends—the archeologist who is American, and the owner of the hotel in Chiapas.

All in all I am inclined to think everything is quite O.K.

But there is some cause for worry to be sure. I think I had best write to his father, and ask him, if he has not had word recently, to check through U.S. Consul in Mérida, or through the Embassy in Mexico City. You always check through your consulate, never direct with Mexican officials.

I will write his father today. Meanwhile write me at once if anything develops.[17] I will look into the books you mention.

As Ever,
Love,
Bill

c/o U.S. Legation
Tangiers, Morocco

---

16. In Chiapas, Ginsberg had met Karena Shields, whose cocoa finca was deep in the forest in the region of Xibalba. Shields had played Jane in early Tarzan movies, had studied Mayan history, and was the author of several papers and the book *Three in the Jungle* (New York: Harcourt Brace, 1944).

17. April 23, 1954, Cassady to Ginsberg: "I'm writing a note to US Embassy, Mex City . . . and one to Bill Bourghs [*sic*] in Tangiers and for godsake allen, write him, I get practically daily letters from him wailing your desertion of him, he's desperate, believe me." (In *As Ever*, p. 178.)

May 4, 1954
address, cargo: U.S. Legation
Tangiers, Morocco

Dear Jack,

I hear from Neal that you are back in New York. What did you do about that deluge of letters I sent you to be relayed to Allen? If you still have them, hang onto them, since the Chiapas address is no longer sure, and I do not wish such personal letters subject to be opened and read.

Both Neal and I are extremely worried about Allen. Neal wired Allen some money at Allen's urgent request the 6th of April. This money was returned to Neal unclaimed, and Neal has heard nothing since.

I received a letter dated the 9th of April in which Allen mentioned he was waiting on money from Neal. I immediately sent a telegram to my parents asking them to send Allen thirty dollars in traveller's checks, and to withhold this amount from my next month's allowance. I have heard nothing from Allen since the letter dated the 9th. All in all I am afraid he may be in serious difficulty, perhaps held incommunicado in jail. To stupid people, he *looks* like a communist. Allen said there was mounting tension and anti-American feeling in the area, and he urgently wanted to leave as soon as he could get the money.

Neal seemingly has no idea what to do, talks about sending letter to police chief of Chiapas. Good God! So I sent a letter to Allen's father urging him to contact the Protection Dept. of the U.S. Embassy in Mexico City, and ask them to check on Allen's whereabouts and welfare. I also sent letter to Lucien, he should check with UP friends in Mexico City.

If I was in U.S. I would go to Mexico at once and find out what is wrong. I wish you would follow through, get in touch with Allen's brother, with Lucien, and let me know what you find out. If someone gets in jail in one of those remote districts, only pressure from above can get them out.

So *please* point out to Allen's brother the *necessity* of *immediate* and *vigorous* action (that is unless they have assurance Allen is all right). When someone is waiting for money they urgently need, and that money comes back "unclaimed," it looks very bad indeed. So for God's sake don't lose any time. If you don't know how to contact Allen's brother, contact his father. He may not have taken action on my letter, or he may not realize how serious the situation might be. ~~For example, I know of an American who was shot by a high Mexican politician and the whole thing was hushed up.~~ I am relying on you, Jack. Please do everything you can and do it right away.

I don't know what I would do if anything happened to Allen. I guess you have seen the letters I wrote to him and have some idea as to how much he means to me. So, Jack, if you are my boy please help me now. And please write me what you find out.

As Ever,
Love,
Bill

P.S. Allen's last address, in case you don't know, is:

Hotel Arturo Huy
Salto De Agua
Chiapas, Mexico

May 11 [1954
Tangier]

Dear Allen,

I arranged with an Englishman who is broke he should keep
my clothes, bring me food, and dole out dollies for ten days. I am
paying him fifty dollars. His name is Gifford.[18] He seems to be a
fairly right guy. I was shooting every two hours. There are no
sanatoriums here so this is the only way to arrange cure. This is
second day and pretty rough. Yesterday I stole clothes from other
boarder, sneaked out, and bought some Eukodol ampules and glut-
ted myself. Gifford found out about it, confiscated the remaining
ampules, and now the other boarder locks his door when he goes
out, and Gifford also took my money. So I am really stuck now.
I wish you were administering this cure. Gifford, he's a hard man.
No use trying to coax an extra ampule out of him.

"By God," he says, "I'm being paid to do it and I'm going to
do it right."

He just brought in a long letter from you from Chiapas. Sorry
you didn't get the money I had sent. I did my best. I am afraid I
made rather a fuss about your "disappearance," but Neal did write
me he was sure you were either in jail or dead by a mule path.[19]

I will send along two more letters. You haven't seen anything
yet. There were even some letters I *destroyed* as too extreme.

I just thought of a scheme to lure an Arab into my room. (Easy
enough. They are always knocking on the window.) And get his

18. Eric Gifford. Former civil servant, model for Burroughs' routine "Leif the
Unlucky," in *Naked Lunch* (pp. 181–82, in the "interzone" section). See "the saga
of Eric the Unlucky" in letter of July 3, 1954. After a career of spectacular failure,
Gifford went on to write a weekly social column in the *Tangier Gazette*.
19. Allen Ginsberg to Neal Cassady, Salto de Agua, May 12, 1954: "Bill is all
taken care of . . . He just never got my letters & began imagining all sorts of
things. He sure is lonely or imagines himself such and I guess it drives him off
the road at times . . . In some respects situation quite horrible you know, a kind
of evil which in other situations I would not dream of putting up with or being
cause or object of; in this case not really dangerous since Bill ultimately sane
somehow & anyway I do not believe in black magic." (In *As Ever*, p. 179.)

clothes on pretext I have to go out and get money and all my clothes are in the laundry.

This would be a good place to build a house. You can get a lot for about $250. And building material is cheap.

Enclose beginning of novel. Glad to see we coincide on idea you should come here or anyhow we travel together somewhere. I am pretty fed up with travelling alone, and never meet any routine receivers and it is a bore without you. Well, we will talk further on this matter.

Love,
Bill

P.S. Note material in novel from letters.

May 24 [1954]
Tangiers

Dear Jack,

Allen is all right and probably in Mexico City by now en route to Frisco. Thank God he is O.K. I don't know what I would do without him.

As always you go direct to basics of situation: "If I love Allen why don't I return and live with him?" You are right. I will, unless he can arrange to come here very soon. One basic fact I learn on this trip is how much I need the few friends I have. So far as companionship goes, I can't live off the country. There are only a few people in the world I want to see.

As you know I picked up on Yoga many years ago. Tibetan Buddhism, and Zen you should look into.[20] Also Tao. Skip Confucius. He is sententious old bore. Most of his sayings are about on the "Confucius say" level. My present orientation is diametrically opposed [to], therefore perhaps progression from, Buddhism. I say we are here in *human form* to learn by the *human* hieroglyphs of love and suffering. There is no intensity of love or feeling that does not involve the risk of crippling hurt. It is a duty to take this risk, to love and feel without defense or reserve. I speak only for myself. Your needs may be different. However, I am dubious of the wisdom of side-stepping sex. Of course women have poison juices I always say.

What are you writing? I have been working on a novel. Enclose a dream routine derived from your dream of the iron racks and the tremendous, overcrowded cities of the future.[21] This is definitely hope and along the lines of faith I have come by in last few months, a conversion like. I *know* that the forces of spontaneous, emergent

---

20. While staying with Cassady in February, Kerouac had found Dwight Goddard's *A Buddhist Bible* in the San Jose library, and began to study Buddhism seriously.

21. Routine entitled "Dream of the City by William Lee." Four pages long, the text begins, "This is one of the worst habits I ever kicked . . ." Titled by Ginsberg "Iron Wrack Dream." (Published in *Interzone*.)

Life are stronger than the forces of evil, repression and death, and that the forces of death will destroy themselves.

What is new with Lucien? I may see you in New York fairly soon. Enclose routine about purple-assed baboons, and Tangier miscellanea.

Love,
Bill.

[*June 16, 1954*
Tangier]

Dear Allen,

There is an end-of-the-world feeling in Tangiers, with its glut of nylon shirts, Swiss watches, Scotch and sex and opiates sold across the counter. Something sinister in complete *laissez faire*. And the new police chief up there on the hill accumulating dossiers. I suspect him of unspeakable fetishistic practices with his files.

When the druggist sells me my daily box of Eukodol ampules he smirks like I had picked up the bait to a trap. The whole town is a trap and some day it will close. Not snap shut but close slowly. We will see it closing, but there will be no escape, no place to go.

Allen, I never had a habit like this before. Shooting every *two hours*. Maybe it is the Eukodol, which is semisynthetic. Trust the Germans to concoct some really evil shit. It acts direct on nerve centers. This stuff is more like coke than morphine. A shot of Eukodol hits the head first with a rush of pleasure. Ten minutes later you want another shot. Between shots you are just killing time. I can't control this stuff any more than I can control the use of coke. Morphine controls itself, like eating. When you are loaded on M. you don't want another shot any more than you want to eat on a full stomach.

From taking so many shots I have an open sore where I can slide the needle right into a vein. The sore stays open like a red, festering mouth, swollen and obscene. [. . .]

Eukodol is banned in U.S. like heroin. As you know, heroin is eight times stronger than morphine. No reason why scientists couldn't develop junk eight times or a hundred times stronger than heroin. Junk you would get a habit on one shot and be hung up for life. If you don't get your shot of Super Plus Square Root H every two hours, you die in convulsions of over-sensitivity, flashes of pleasure intensify to acute agony in a fraction of a second. [*Letter incomplete: see note p. 443*]

June 24 [*1954*
Tangier]

Dear Allen,

I always like keep a letter to you on the stove and put in miscellaneous ideas, a sort of running diary.

I've been thinking about routine as art form, and what distinguishes it from other forms. One thing, it is not *completely symbolic,* that is, it is subject to shlup over into "real" action at any time (like cutting off finger joint and so forth). In a sense the whole Nazi movement was a great, humorless, evil *routine* on Hitler's part. Do you dig me? I am not sure I dig myself. And some pansy shit is going to start talking about *living* his art.

Last night went with Kells [Elvins] to extraordinary Arab restaurant that looked like remodelled bus station. Bare, galvanised iron roof. A huge banana palm growing in this barn-like or hangar-like room with tables scattered here and there. Served by a snotty Arab queen who was barely courteous when we ordered two plates and one portion of Cous Cous. An Arab stew of chicken, nuts, raisins, and corn meal. Delicious. I was tea high and never got suck (leave error) taste kicks. We had just been in Dean's Bar, where I encountered barrage of hostility. Brion Gysin was there and wanted to cut me, but I am learning the practices of this dreary tribe.[22] I never saw him, he never got a chance to cut me. Dean wanted not to serve me, rolling his eyes in disapproval, but there was Kells, a good customer. (Dean has heard that I am a dope fiend. More than that, he instinctively feels me as danger, far out, an ill omen.) So I sat there, loaded on tea savoring their impotent disapproval, rolling it on my tongue with glass of good, dry sherry.

---

22. Brion Gysin: Burroughs had first encountered Gysin at an exhibition of his paintings in the Hotel Rembrandt, late January 1954. They did not become friends until after leaving Tangier.

Dean: of ambiguous origin, ran one of Tangier's two most popular expatriate bars, a tiny place between the Place de France and the Grand Socco. Marek Kohn, in his book *Dope Girls: Birth of the London Drug Underground* (London: Lawrence & Wishart, 1992), suggests that Dean was "London Dope Girl" Donald Kimful. Kohn's source for this identification is Gerald Hamilton via Robin Maugham.

Really cutting down on junk and sooo sexy. Kiki coming to-night. [. . .] [*One or more pages of the letter are missing.*]

Got letter from my Portuguese Huncke. They are locking his grandmother out of her iron lung for non-payment of rent. The finance co. is repossessing his wife's artificial kidney. Up his with a grapefruit. I am really toughening up on mooches. Bastards who wouldn't give *anything,* to me most of all not. That's mooch psychology—they most specially wouldn't help people who helped them. Well I've subsidized my last mooch. From here on out all my money I need for myself, my few friends, and the few people, like Kiki and Angelo, who have been right with me.[23]

Most secure form of security is friends who would help you *unconditionally.* You know so long as I have anything, you have part of it. So long as I have a place to stay, so do you. That is really something can't be bought, Allen. Yes, I like to hear you *say* it means same thing to you, and you are glad I do feel that way about you.

Let's get on with this novel. Maybe the real novel is letters to you.

Love,
Bill

Original I got caught short with.[24] Sending this along. I figure to send you like one page per day.

23. Angelo Porcayo [sp.?], a Mexican boy who had a long-standing affair with Burroughs, 1951–1952.
24. I.e., the copy Ginsberg received was a carbon.

July 3 [1954
Tangier]

Dear Allen,

I am really ill. Pain and swelling in the joints. I ask the Captain[25] what it could be . . . "Oh," he says, "I *hope* it isn't a bone fell."

"A what?"

"An infection of the bone. See that scar? I had the same thing once and they had to cut down and scrape off the bone . . . Of course maybe it isn't that at all. Maybe it's just nothing and then *on the other hand* it may be arthritis or God knows what awful thing!"

"I never had arthritis or anything like that."

"Well there's always a first time . . . Oh it's probably nothing . . . But then you never can tell."

So here I am sick and broke and Kells left for Madrid this morning. Hope to God I don't get laid up here. I want to get out of Tangiers. Would like to go straight to Denmark.[26] Unless I can get a job in Madrid. But this place drags me like a sea anchor. Just took a short walk to see if I could find someone to talk to and give me a lift. Two people looked the other way quickly. I don't like either one of them in any case. Then I met Eric [Gifford] who is one of those people pursued by almost incredible bad luck. I don't feel up to recounting the saga of Eric the Unlucky, beyond to say he is 50, no job, no money, no prospects, an eighty-year-old mother to support . . . Tangiers is full of people like that, sort of washed up here. The sight of him brought me down the rest of the way. No use telling myself this is nothing. Pain worse by the minute. And Kells would have to leave *exactly* when I need him. Eric has a hard luck story worth three of that, like the time he got septicemia from an abdominal abscess and they put him in a Syrian hospital

25. David Woolman, who was Burroughs' next-door neighbor in three different houses in Tangier. An ex–Air Force officer from Indiana, Woolman wrote two columns in the *Moroccan Courier,* and later, under the anagrammatic pseudonym Lawdom Vaidon, was the author of *Tangier: A Different Way* (Metuchen, N.J., and London: Scarecrow Press, 1977).

26. Elvins was now living in Rome, married to his third wife, the Danish film actress Mimi Heinrich, and traveling with her to Copenhagen.

. . . ~~He was delirious and just got moved into the military hospital~~ ~~with hours to spare. But that was when he was working for Civil~~ ~~Service and had connections~~ . . . And the Greek surgeon goofed and sewed up a live monkey in him—and he was gang fucked by the Arab attendants . . . Or the self-righteous English doctor who gave him an enema of hot sulphuric acid for the clap . . . Or the German Practitioner who removed his appendix with an old, rusty can opener and tin shears: "The germ theory is a nonsense." Flushed with success ~~and canned heat~~ he then began snipping and cutting out everything in sight. "The human body is most inefficient machine. Filled up vit unnecessitated parts . . . You can get by with von kidney, vy have two? Yes dot is a kidney. The inside parts should not be so close in together crowded. They need *Lebensraum* like der Vaterland . . ." This German cat practices something he calls technological medicine. This has got worse while I wrote the letter. Now I can hardly move. Kiki. is here. If I am not better tomorrow, will see if I can score for a good croaker. Tangiers is known for its bad doctors . . . Kiki comes on more affectionate all the time . . . a real sweet kid. He is helping me get my clothes off.

I can just barely make it around the room, my ankle hurts so. I must see a doctor tomorrow. What a bum kick to die in this awful place! You're one of the few people I would want around me if I was dying. That is a special compliment. Will write in morning again how I feel.

Morning, still can't walk or just barely. Will try and get a croaker here. Send this letter via the Captain.

Love,
Bill

P.S. What gives with Neal's spiritualism? You never mentioned it.[27]

---

27. Both the Cassadys had recently become followers of Edgar Cayce, taking up his theories of reincarnation and karma. When Kerouac stayed with them in February, he found their obsession tiresome, dubbing Neal "Billy Graham in a suit" (letter to Ginsberg, March 1954, quoted by Gerald Nicosia in *Memory Babe: A Critical Biography of Jack Kerouac* [New York: Grove Press, 1983], p. 457). Neal's adherence to Cayce was one reason Kerouac had turned to Buddhism.

July 15 [1954]
Thursday
[Tangier]

Dear Allen,

Still confined to my room and sleep most of the time.

I am completely unproductive. Haven't written a word. Feel deep heaviness and lassitude, like I have been five minutes writing these few lines. In fact decided to go back to sleep and finish letter later.

The doctor was just here. Heart O.K. Secondary infection in the right ankle which will have to be punctured and drained. How tiresome. Now I have to prepare a hot poultice for my ankle and the thought of it exhausts me. I will wait until tomorrow when Kiki comes and he will do it.

Friday Morning, July 16

The doctor came today and tapped my ankle, drawing out a jigger glass full of pus. This is a secondary infection which will necessitate a course of penicillin. The rheumatism is seemingly cured. I can consider myself very lucky in that I left an acute attack of rheumatic fever for a week without treatment and suffered no damage to the heart. Many people are invalided for life by such an attack, which leads me to observe that I do generally have good luck in matters of basic importance.

Just sent Kiki to the Embassy, and he brought back a long letter from you which has roused me from this lethargy. I think your suggestion of writing after receiving a letter is a good one and will tend to avoid confusion, and to come closer to the ideal of letter writing, which is to communicate with someone not there. I will follow this practice in the future.

With your letter I receive a note (Regular mail. She used to write air mail. Now I'm not worth an air mail stamp. There should be a special abject class of mail that costs almost nothing, but is subject to get there a year late if it gets there, to be opened and read and commented on by anyone who handles it; in short to every delay and indignity.) from that idiotic agent who is supposed to be handling *Junkie* in England. She says: "We have now received letter . . . making clear that you have signed contract with Ace Books that they shall have the sole right to dispose of foreign rights." I quote from the answer I am writing her: "You will recall I offered to send you a copy of my contract with Ace Books. Had you accepted this offer and read the contract the present misunderstanding would have been avoided."

It seems to me, Allen, that the so-called practical people, agents, publishers, lawyers and so forth are being overtaken by a form of psychotic stupidity. Obviously the first step would have been to ascertain whether the rights were already reserved through examining the contract with Ace Books and communicating with Ace Books. But this woman, when I offered to send her a copy of the contract, said it was not necessary since "Everything is now quite clear." On the basis of what facts this condition of lucidity had been predicated I was unable to surmise. I decided it was one of those mysteries of the business world that we dreamers can not hope to grasp. [. . .]

And Phyllis Jackson losing Jack's manuscript.[28] What is wrong with these people? If I ever launch a commercial enterprise I shall stipulate only those without business experience need apply for work. I would not care to struggle with a staff of idiots.

Now your letter: I'm going to experiment. I just lit up, and will say it like it comes pops. Just took three drags of the righteous gage, man, twenty-three skidoo the joint is jumping . . .

Your aphorisms about love are . . . That is, I concur wholeheartedly. [. . .] Observation has convinced me that salvation lies not in receiving love but in giving it. A persistent and disastrously mistaken goal is expressed in the formula: "I will be saved if some one loves me." In short I agree with what you say. However, I am puzzled to know how much of this is to be regarded as general

---

28. Phyllis Jackson was John Clellon Holmes's literary agent at MCA, to whom Kerouac had sent his manuscripts of *On the Road*, *Doctor Sax*, and *Maggie Cassidy* in late 1952. For a time, *On the Road* had been missing.

observation on the Phenomena (Oh God! Am I going to start refering to love as The Phenomena? Sounds like some great man's arch and rather nauseous private letters.)[29] [. . .][30]

Tibetan Buddhism is extremely interesting. Dig it if you have not done so. I had some mystic experiences and convictions when I was practicing Yoga. That was 15 years ago. Before I knew you. My final decision was that Yoga is no solution for a Westerner and I disapprove of all practice of Neo-Buhudsim. (Spell it different every time and maybe it will spell itself right. I went to a progressive school where we never learned to spell.) Yoga should be practiced, yes, but not as final, a solution, but rather as we study history and comparative cultures. The metaphysics of Jiu-Jitsu is interesting, and derives from Zen. If there is Jiu-Jitsu club in Frisco, join.[31] It is worthwhile and one of the best forms of exercise, because it is predicated on relaxation rather than straining. I am anxious to read all the material on Cayce, and will do so. But that must wait.

My ankle is still swollen. The doctor says some restriction of movement may persist, may in fact be permanent. The thing was unfortunately neglected. However the fever and infection are seemingly cured. Thanks for your offer of medicines. Tangiers seems pretty well supplied with the latest products. Unlike Greece where, according to Kells, there is difficulty procuring the most common drugs. It occurs to me diagnosing could be done very well by a thinking machine. You feed in the symptoms and out come all possible conditions that could produce that syndrome. For example, Doctor Perone never thought of rheumatic fever because the rheumatic symptoms were hardly perceptible. Thinking back now, I recall joint pain at that time.

I have written to Kerouac asking for those addresses in Paris. If I get them I will likely go from here to Paris—boat to Marseille skipping Spain—in next two weeks. For intellectual stimulation

29. These two paragraphs were heavily crossed out on the original letter manuscript. They were, however, used, almost verbatim, in a retype made by Burroughs in November 1955, as part of INTERZONE'S "Chapter 2: Lee's Letters and Journals."
30. Typescript is missing pp. 3, 4, and 5 here.
31. After leaving Mexico, Ginsberg had gone to stay with the Cassadys in San Jose.

Tangiers is nowhere. There are a few writers here, mostly friends of Bowles, who seemingly want nothing to do with me. It has occurred to me that Bowles perhaps wishes to avoid contact with me because of my narcotic associations, fearing possible hassles with customs inspection and authorities in general if he is known to be on familiar terms with me—guilt by association.[32] I don't know. But Tangiers is a small place and he has quite pointedly avoided me. He and Brion Gysin, a painter, and an assortment of other painters and writers. In short, the intelligentsia of Tangiers has put me in Coventry. [. . .]

[Letter incomplete.]

---

32. Burroughs had first met Bowles in late April, discussing his *Junkie* contract, very briefly—Bowles was ill at the time. There is nothing to confirm Burroughs' reading of Bowles's disinterest, but his intuition regarding Bowles's nervous attitude to the authorities is on target.

[*Aug. 18, 1954*
Tangier]

Dear Jack,

Thanks for your letter providing me with Paris addresses. I wrote a note to Bob Burford identifying myself, and asking would he be in Paris, since I wanted to see him.[33] No answer. Perhaps he is no longer at that address. I have generally received a cool reception in Europe and Tangiers. The one time I met Paul Bowles he evinced no cordiality. Since then he has made no effort to follow up the acquaintance. (Under the circumstances it is his place to make advances once he knows that I am here and who I am). He invites the dreariest queens in Tangiers to tea, but has never invited me, which, seeing how small the town is, amounts to a deliberate affront. Perhaps he has some idea that trouble might result from knowing anyone associated with narcotics. Since Tennessee Williams and [Truman] Capote etc. are friends of Bowles I, of course, don't meet them when they come here.

So far as I am concerned, ready to go home, but every line I have contacted so far is booked solid until October. Have several travel agencies working on the deal, but it doesn't look good. I wanted to travel with you to Frisco, joining Allen and Neal to work on R[ail] Roads or something to save money so I can make expedition to S.A. jungles. Well I will make it as soon as I can.

Kiki has confiscated all my clothes and intends to cure me of the habit. I also have various new, substitute preparations prescribed me by a good, German Jewish, refugee doctor. So I have hopes of success with Kiki here to care for me, and to provide the appropriate amenities when I start coming off in my pants (I have no pants)— spontaneous orgasms being one of the few agreeable features of the withdrawal syndrome. And not limited to single orgasm, one can continue, with adolescent ardor, through three or four climaxes. Usually you are too weak to go out and find a "love object" as the analysts call them. (When you are coming off the junk, I mean,

---

33. Kerouac had met Bob Burford in Denver in 1947. Burford had gone to Paris in 1949, and was now an editor of the magazine *New Story*.

you don't feel up to looking around for sex.) Sounds so passionless, like, "I found a pretty hot 'object' last night." I find myself getting jealous of Kiki—he is besieged by importunate queens. In fact I am downright involved, up to my neck in Maya.[34] He is a sweet kid, and it is so pleasant to loll about in the afternoon smoking tea, sleeping and having sex with no hurry, running leisurely hands over his lean, hard body, and finally we doze off, all wrapped around each other, into the delicious sleep of a hot afternoon in a cool, darkened room, a sleep that is different from any other sleep, a twilight in which I savour, with a voluptuous floating sensation, the state of sleep, feeling the nearness of Kiki's young body, the sweet, imperceptible, drawing together in sleep, leg inching over leg, arm encompassing body, hips hitching closer, stiffening organs reaching out to touch warm flesh.

Jack, I would think twice before giving up sex.[35] It's a basic kick and when it's good as it can be it's *good*. Sounds like literary marriage of Gertrude Stein and Hemingway. It just occurred to me: Paul Bowles is *not* a prissy queen. I mean he is not the type to be upset by the *idea* of dope. It may well be that he is himself engaged in some kind of illegal currency operations—like many solid citizens of Tangiers—and does not want anybody tracking heat into his trap. Especially not the least suspicion of junk trafficking. You can readily see why a currency dealer, in slightly illegal currency transactions and transport, would shun like poison anyone to whose garments clings the leprous taint of narcotics. He is, allowing that my hypothesis is correct, of course, imputing to me the condition of a trafficker which, at the present time, I quite sincerely want no part of. I do not have time or inclination for such activities, charged with a risk I am no longer willing to incur because it threatens to interfere with pursuits such as writing and exploration, that really interest me. In fact so far as *any* criminal activities are concerned, unless we are all forced underground, I am no longer interested.

I can't help but feeling that you are going too far with your

---

34. Maya: from Hindu philosophy, meaning "illusion."
35. Kerouac had taken an oath of chastity along with one of temperance, the latter demanded by his doctors after a bout of his recurrent phlebitis. Kerouac's study and practice of Buddhism had led to his renunciation of sex that April, as indicated in Burroughs' letter of May 24.

absolute chastity. Besides, masturbation is *not* chastity, it is just a way of sidestepping the issue without even approaching the solution. Remember, Jack, I studied and practiced Buddhism (in my usual sloppy way to be sure). The conclusion I arrived at, and I make no claims to speak from a state of enlightenment, but merely to have attempted the journey, as always with inadequate equipment and knowledge (like one of my South American expeditions), falling into every possible accident and error, losing my gear and my way, shivering in cosmic winds on a bare mountain slope above life-line, chilled to the blood-making marrow with final despair of aloneness: What am I doing here a broken eccentric? A Bowery Evangelist, reading books on Theosophy in the public library (an old tin trunk full of notes in my cold water East Side flat), imagining myself a Secret World Controller in Telepathic Contact with Tibetan Adepts . . . Could I ever *see* the merciless, cold *facts* on some Winter night, sitting in the operation room white glare of a cafeteria—NO SMOKING PLEASE—*See the facts and myself,* an old man with the wasted years behind, and what ahead having seen The Facts? A trunk full of notes to dump in a Henry St. lot? . . . So my conclusion was that Buddhism is only for the West to *study* as *history,* that is it is a subject for *understanding,* and Yoga can profitably be practiced to that end. But it is not, for the West, *An Answer,* not *A Solution.* We must learn by acting, experiencing, and living; that is, above all, by *Love* and by *Suffering.* A man who uses Buddhism or any other instrument to remove love from his being in order to avoid suffering, has committed, in my mind, a sacrilege comparable to castration. You were given the power to love in order to use it, no matter what pain it may cause you. Buddhism frequently amounts to a form of psychic junk . . . I may add that I have seen nothing from those California Vedantists but a lot of horse shit, and I denounce them without cavil, as a pack of pathetic frauds.[36] Convinced of their own line to be sure, thereby adding self-deception to their other failings. In short, a sorry bunch of psychic retreaters from the dubious human journey. Because if there is one thing I feel sure of it is this: That human life has *direction.* Even if we accept

---

36. Vedantists: i.e., followers of philosophies based on the Hindu Vedas.

some Spenglerian Cycle routine, the cycle never comes back to exactly the same place, nor does it ever exactly repeat itself.[37]

Well, about enough of that. I am about to become a long-winded German with some philosophy about the direction of life arising from the potentials inherent in the cellular structure of the human time-space traveller. When the potentials of any species are exhausted, the species becomes static (like all animals, reptiles and other so-called lower forms of life). What distinguished Man from all other species is that he *can not become static*. "*Er muss streben oder untergehen*" (quotation is from myself in character of German Philosopher)—"He must continue to develop or perish." This is going to run to five tremendous volumes. What I mean is the California Buddhists are trying to sit on the sidelines and there *are* no sidelines. Whether you like it or not, you are committed to the human endeavour. I can not ally myself with such a purely negative goal as avoidance of suffering. Suffering is a chance you have to take by the fact of being alive. I repeat, *Buddhism is not for the West.* We must evolve our own solutions. If you don't enjoy sex, try an analyst. Some of them are good. I'd like to have a go with a Reichian myself. You might find yourself caught up in some tremendous D.H. Lawrence affair with a woman, orgasms together and all that.

Well, enough of abstract subjects. I am having serious difficulties with my novel. I tell you the novel form is completely inadequate to express what I have to say. I don't know if I can find a form. I am very gloomy as to prospects of publication. And I'm not like you, Jack. I need an audience. Of course, a small audience. But still I need publication for development. A writer can be ruined by too much or too little success. Looking at your letter again, I am dubious of finding any of these people since Burford does not reply (he may yet). Like I say, whole European trip has been unsuccessful. I have met no one anywhere. I feel myself out of place and unwanted wherever I go. So I am dubious of Paris. It is very expensive. If I

37. Oswald Spengler, author of *The Decline of the West,* translated by Charles Francis Atkinson, 2 volumes (Munich: C. H. Becksche, 1922; London: Allen & Unwin, 1928), whose apocalyptic prophecy of historical change and cultural entropy formed a cornerstone of the Beat sense of history. Burroughs introduced Ginsberg to the book in 1944. Kerouac was already familiar with it.

didn't make contact with anybody, and this trip has been filled with such fantastic twists of ill luck, from the moment I stepped on that awful, dirty, Greek boat. The signs just ain't right

Like here I have nobody to talk to except Kiki. Some artist and writer colony! Oh yes, there are two people who think I am a character I should be in television. Kiki is slowly denuding me of my clothes. He enjoys them so much and I care so little. What sort of character is Burford and where do you know him from and how well? If he received my note and did not answer, it is in the way of being a definite slight unless he is extremely careless and Bohemian. I simply said I had been given his name by my old friend Jack Kerouac, and wondered would he be in Paris at this time, even intimated I might make a side trip to see him if he was going to be there, as is indeed the truth. My Paris trip hinges on whether I will find anyone there. I also mentioned I was the author of *JUNKIE*, and had some unpublished work he might be interested to see. Well, I don't feel like running up to an expensive town just for a look see. After all I want to have my ass operated on when I get back to N.Y. and I can't be throwing money around. The way things look now, I don't see Paris as a good idea. All boats on North line booked solid. It costs me $70 from here to Paris . . . I will likely stay here unless Burford shows an inclination to roll out the carpet, or at least an old beat rug. Are these people all dating back to your period of favor with that bastard Giroux? If so they might all regard me with a decidedly dim view . . .[38]

As Ever,
Bill

38. Robert Giroux was the editor at Harcourt Brace who had accepted Kerouac's first novel, *The Town and The City*. Kerouac disliked Giroux's editorial changes and blamed him for the book's limited commercial success. In 1952, Giroux had rejected *On the Road*. When Burroughs did meet with Bob Burford, in New York at the end of September, Burford was "knocked out" by *Junkie*, but took a decidedly dim view of Burroughs himself.

August 26 [1954
Tangier]

Dear Allen,

I have made definite reservation to leave on the Italian Line Sept. 7 from Gibraltar. Paris is out. No $ to go there. No reply from Burford. No way out by North route until mid-October.

The following is transcript from earlier letter which will show a definite progression and change of attitude:

Most definitive reason to stay here is Kiki. Lately I want him with me all the time. I found out last night that I love him. He comes in late last night. I had been sleeping, still drowsy, not digging exactly what he says. Suddenly I realize he is describing in ghastly detail the designs he proposes to have tattooed on the beautiful, copper-brown skin of his chest, and shoulders and arms. I run my hands over it by the hour while he purrs in sleep like a contented cat.

So I had hysterics, cried and kissed and begged him not to do it. "It's like you were going to put a plug in your lip, or a ring in your nose, or knock out your front teeth to put in gold teeth—" (Some of the Arabs do this)—"It's a desecration!" He was finally impressed by my intensity. I gave him my last sport coat, and my other pair of pants (I have nothing left now but my combat jacket, one pair of slacks, and that odd sort of costume jewelry cheap brown coat from the chic-est shop on Worth Ave. in Palm Beach), and ten $ I could ill-afford, to *promise* me *never* to have himself tattooed. I was shocked into an awareness that in a way I love him. Now I know I should not allow myself to be emotionally involved. He doesn't understand and looks at me in bewilderment when I embrace him with special intensity.

It is exasperating. I can't really get near him. I feel all-out attempt to do so would be disastrous for me. I know I should let matters rest in status of liaison, fond of him in an off-hand way, but no involvements, and no risk of hurt. But it's so dull like that. I notice the sex is much more enjoyable since I feel some variety of love for him.

I am deeply distressed to hear of your difficulties with Neal, especially since they sound like the sort of thing nothing can be done about, a cul-de-sac of the soul.[39] I only wish I was on the spot to render what aid and comfort I could give you. It seems to me you deliberately demand the impossible in love. Couldn't you be happy, for example, with someone like Kiki? (His brows are *not* *bushy,* just copious, but in a perfectly symmetrical, straight-line arrangement. It's an Indian characteristic, and don't know where from, but Kiki looks like a South American Indian.) Sweet and affectionate, but indubitably masculine? Of course he is never going to fall madly in love with *you.* That's obvious. Incidentally, Kiki isn't always sweet by any means. He can be sulky, and sometimes he shocks me with tirades of abuse. At such times find myself faced by a hostile stranger. Once he reduced me to tears.—I have always a fear with anyone I love that they really hate me and I will suddenly be confronted with their hate. Kiki always says afterwards he was only joking.

I know exactly how you feel about Neal preferring to play chess with some square rather than spend an evening with you who not only love him, but have so much to teach him, and to offer in line of straight entertainment.[40] I had exactly same experience with Marker who was chess player. I don't mean that chess is the point. The point is they don't dig anything *special* about you. Or is it they *do* dig it and don't want it? Fear and/or hate it?

Know anything about chess? It can be a virtual life work, and what is it to absorb all a man's thought and energy? A waste and complete escape from reality on any level. It is not creation. It is not even a real game, and if the theory of chess is ever fully understood it will cease to exist . . . I hope we can take an apartment together when I get there. I mean perhaps you would be better off if you moved out under present set-up. I am not just speaking from self-interest here, but thinking of you.

---

39. Ginsberg's situation in San Jose with the Cassadys and their children was not conducive to his fantasy of renewing his love affair with Neal, whose feelings toward him had in any case cooled.
40. When he wasn't attending Cayce meetings or chasing women, Neal frustrated Ginsberg by playing endless games of chess with his neighbor, Dick Woods.

I rewrote the story about the car wreck with Jack Anderson.[41] I think it is quite good in present form, one of the most nearly perfect things I have done. I think it may be publishable, and send along two versions, one cut for magazine consumption, the other containing a profane anecdote perhaps as well omitted. The symbol of the car interior, conveying illusion of security while hurtling towards inevitable disaster, is central. I have four alternative phrasings which I submit for your judgement. I have worked over it so much I can't judge. I choose number four for magazine version. Please try and sell this story some place, as I think it is saleable.

Love,
Bill

P.S. Kiki was here and hurt me so I am quivering all over. Oh, he'll come around all right because of the $. It hurts me to know that is the reason, at the same time glad I have that advantage. A complete shambles of feeling . . . I simply can't take these deals lightly: if I do, it's no more than masturbation; if I don't, I get hurt like this. One learns nothing by experience but caution, if you *want* to learn that. I don't, because that way you defeat yourself, removing the pleasure with the pain so the whole maneuver is pointless. I was just trying to sell you a deal like Kiki. Now I don't know. I am sick of being wise and Mahatma-ish about love, when it just looks to me like a ghastly mess with only one consistent pattern: hurt and frustration. All this talk about how it is never wasted and you will get it all back one day, a good fairy is stashing it away some place and it is drawing interest and will all roll in with your Social Security payments. I am just writing along to put off the misery I will feel when I stop writing. I know it's there waiting for me . . . Doesn't he think he went too far walking out—

[*Letter incomplete.*]

---

41. Set in St. Louis, 1940, this story appears to have been first written in Mexico in 1952, then again in New York in 1953, and was originally titled "The Hot Rod." It was finally published in *Interzone* as "Driving Lesson."

Sept. 3 [1954
Tangier]

Dear Jack,

Arrive in New York Sept. 16, 8 am., on *Saturnia,* Italian Line. That's a rough hour, but may not be accurate. I sure would like you to meet me at the boat if you can make it. I don't have your phone number, and don't know where I will be staying in New York. If we miss at boat, I will be in San Remo at 5 pm. on the 16th. I plan to have my ass operated on in New York, then to Florida for a short visit. After Florida to join Allen in Frisco. Yes he wrote me about he had been throwed out of the Cassady house.[42] Hardly surprising. You know how women are. Come on broad-minded and understanding . . . I knew a woman in Chi, a German, said she was emancipated and didn't mind her husband going with other women until he did it, then she attacked him with a carving knife, called the cops and attempted suicide. Well I guess Carolyn has what she wants, now. What every U.S. bitch of them wants. A man all to herself with no pernicious friends hanging about.

I have not the slightest interest or desire to go to Calif. The whole State is police ridden. They have special laws on sex, junk, and every other manifestation of life. The only reason I am going there is to be with Allen. You read my letters. You know what the score is. If he decides to stay in Frisco, that is where I have to go. Seems I can't make it without him. I learn that during past six months we are separate.

I hope you decide to come with me to Frisco. We could all work there for a few months and save money, then go to Mexico together. We will talk it over in New York.

I am not so all fired anxious to meet Bowles. It's just that he stands for what there isn't anything better than in places like Tanger, Capri, etc. I wanted to meet what there was here to meet. But they seem to have scented my being different and excluded me, just as all squares instinctively do. And these people, Bowles, Tennessee

---

42. One afternoon in August, Carolyn had found Ginsberg in bed with Neal and, not surprisingly, escorted him out. She drove him from San Jose to Berkeley.

Williams, Capote, are just as square as the St. Louis Country Club set I was raised with, and they sensed I was different and never accepted me as one of them. Like I say, Bowles and company are just as rigidly conventional and frightened of deviants. But I am not self-sufficient. I need audience for my routines. Buddha doesn't help me a bit. I'm bored and lonely. Of course I know Bowles and company nowhere, but there is no one else here.

Well I will see you on the 16th. My best to Kells if he is still there.

Now Allen is talking about making it with a chick, and I am really upset and worried.[43] If I get out to Frisco and he is making it with a chick I might as well turn around and start back. You know how U.S. chicks are. They want it all. It would be the end of my relation with Allen. At this point I couldn't stand to be around him all the time with no sex. It would be too much strain on me.

As Ever,
Bill

---

43. In San Francisco, Ginsberg had met and fallen in love with Sheila Williams Boucher. He was living with Sheila and her infant son in an apartment on Nob Hill, earning $250 a month with the market research firm Towne-Oller. This romance clearly threatened Burroughs more than Allen's infatuation with Neal Cassady.

[*Beginning of letter missing*]

[*Early Oct. 1954*
New York]

Wednesday Night

Operation completed. Ritchie was supposed to show with supplies at noon.[44] He didn't show. I have never suffered anything to compare with the next 6 hours. Finally rolling around biting the bed and beating on the wall, and so wrung a shot of demerol out of the nurse. I don't know what I would have done without a shot. It was *literally* intolerable. Then Ritchie shows. So I was cheated out of the fix of a lifetime, it would have been pure relief. Instead I am half fixed with demerol, and miss a vein, so I don't feel the fix as such, but I am fixed now. Jack was supposed to be here, but he hasn't showed. I must get out of here tomorrow no matter what. This looks like the worst infestation of the Chinaman I ever contracted. Milwaukee and all Wisc[onsin] is legalizing junkies. They get a permit like Mexico. I hope this splendid idea spreads. If I could only buy codeineetas kicking would be a cinch. But here you buy H or nothing. No dollies around anymore. The Feds have cracked down on the dolly writers. Georgia and Walter had some dollies to kick with, and the Feds came and confiscated them. They don't *want* anyone to kick. I will go to Florida and the family doctor will give me a cure. Be in Frisco in 2–3 weeks. Couldn't hurry it much anyway as I must live very quietly until the operation heals. It would be nowhere for you to have a semi-invalid around.

Thursday Night

Out of the hospital.[45] Jack didn't show or call so I can only contact him now by mail. Sometimes he seems to lack ordinary ego-orienting sense. It wouldn't *occur* to him to call the hospital. (I had a phone in my room.) I am still shaky and bleeding, but the op-

---

44. Ritchie: an old-time junk friend dating back to when Burroughs first began to use narcotics.
45. Burroughs stayed at the St. George Hotel, Brooklyn.

eration a complete success. Doc says reason for failure of previous operation was it did not remove those growths which are cause of narrow rectum. From here on I will be equipped with a functioning ass. I got the nurses pretty well trained before I left, and they brought me demerol without argument, having seen my horrible and completely genuine exhibition of bed-biting.

Why do you say my "stringent requirements" of love are exasperating and idiotic? I still read your letter over from time to time.[46] Went to bed knowing somehow I would have a Dream. Woke up about 3 o'clock and took a small shot. Woke up now at 7. Tremendous dream. I will write it down here: I have returned to North Africa *several years ago*. Meet a fatuous fairy who pounces on every word with obscene double entendre. Beneath this camp, I can feel incredible evil. He clings to me, moves into a house with me. I feel sick like some loathesome insect was clinging to my body. In the street we meet two Lesbians who say, "Hello Boys," recognizing Fairy-Lesbian status. A horrible, dead, ritual greeting from which I turn in retching disgust. (This perfect for ballet.) The Fairy gives me my mail he picked up at the Embassy. *Every letter has been opened,* and they are all jumbled together, typewritten pages, so *I can't tell whose letter it is.* I keep shuffling the pages looking for *the end of the letter* and a signature. I never find it.

I walk out along a dry, white road. There is danger here. A dry, brown, vibrating in the air, like insect wings rubbing together. I pass a village of people sleeping, living under mounds—about 2 feet high—of black cloth stitched on wire frames. I am back in the town. The vibrating is everywhere now, horrible, dry, lifeless. Not a *sound* exactly; a *frequency,* a wave length.

The vibrating comes from a Tower-like structure. A Holy Man is causing it. He has a black face. He demands more money from the townspeople. His opponents are two Arabs, the only people I

---

46. Kerouac had told what he termed "a kind white lie" to Burroughs, to the effect that Ginsberg secretly shared Burroughs' desire for a sexual relationship. Ginsberg, appalled by Kerouac's deception, had then written "a severe formal reject letter to Bill" spelling out the facts. Kerouac sought to make amends by appealing for "a return to Beat Generation 1947 confessions and honesties." (Kerouac to Ginsberg, October 26, 1954, Ginsberg Collection, Columbia University.)

have seen who look alive. One is a vigorous man in his forties, the other a Boy. I am immediately attracted to the boy. I approach them and ask: "How much will you give me to kill the Holy Man?" We haggle about price, but both know money is not the point. I am bragging foolishly to the Boy of my marksmanship, and "I don't mind using a knife either." He looks at me and laughs, *understanding everything*. They give me a note to a gun store where I will be issued a rifle. I start into the town. A Friend comes with me. He says the Holy Man is *right,* we must *accept him*. I am about to tell him about the gun, but say instead: "I won't tell you any of my plans."

He says: "No, don't tell me. I would tell Him. *You little fool!* He knows about your silly plan!!" He shouts this with great passion, seizing my arm. "Can't I make you understand, it's hopeless!"

"That—" (I am about to say the gun plan and check myself) "is only camp. My real plan he doesn't know because I don't know it yet. *It's life! He* can't predict Life, only death."

"He can predict it."

"You're wrong! Wrong! I don't want to see you again for all eternity!"

I run into the town and hide from the Friend in a florist shop under a case of flowers. He comes and stands there like at my coffin, wringing his hands and crying and begging me to give up the idea. I am crying too, the tears falling into dry, yellow dust. But I won't give up.

Will attempt to enlarge on this dream. May provide frame-work for novel. The Friend, so far as I can recall, was Rex Weisenberger, whom I haven't seen in years, a converted Catholic.[47] He owes me $10 which I could use—well that indicates—I was thinking yesterday I could use that $10 I sent you—the Friend is you too. Funny, I thought it *wasn't* you at all, but Rex, and the first thing I think of is the $10. In the dream the Friend looked like Rex who disap-

---

47. Rex Weisenberger: a friend from St. Louis, with whom Burroughs had traveled to Europe in 1934.

John Kelly: he went to Yale with Weisenberger and had converted him to Catholicism.

peared ten years ago. I have heard he is living in Japan, having *left his money to Mrs. Kelly,* John Kelly's mother who has plenty money of her own. Well, want to mail this,

Love,
Bill

Write me: 202 Sanford Ave., Palm Beach, Florida.

Oct. 13 [1954]
Cobble Stone Gardens
Laura Lee Burroughs
Mortimer Burroughs
233 Phipps Plaza
Palm Beach, Florida

Dear Allen,

Set-up looks worse all the time. Doubtful if I can raise return fare to Tanger. They keep asking me why the Hell I came back to U.S. in the first place.

Marker in Miami looking for a job. I am going down there today to see him. Guess I better start looking too.

Understand I forgive you the letter, but for the record I still think there was a lot to forgive. Especially wish you had changed your mind about sharing pad etc., before I left Tanger. In that case I would still be there and not faced by present beat situation. Well maybe *you* have some suggestions as to what I should do now. Only thing I can think of is to go in the Business with Ritchie or start boosting. It isn't just I don't want to work. There aren't any jobs I can get. Well I will look anyway. Maybe I can blackmail them into sending me back to Tanger. They don't want me sitting around Palm Beach, that's for sure, and the hotel (they insist no room in the house, my bed having been removed to make way for a television set) is $5 per day. Well, *a ver*. But not to mince words, I *did* come back to U.S. to see you. Just wanted to be sure you knew that, and to put you in cognizance of my generally altered situation, like I can't be shifting around any more.

Don't mean to come on sour, but this is a beat set-up,

Love,
Bill

Palm Beach
Nov. 12, [19]54
202 Sanford Ave.

Friday

Dear Allen,

Thanks for letter. I am still suffering from P.G. weekend with Bette Jones.[48] Never knew anything to hang on like this. Never again will I kick on the street.

Scheduled to sail Sat. Nov. 20. Sorry I can't meet you in N.Y. Another month here would unseat my reason.

Been reading everything I can find on the Amazon. I am convinced The Lost Inca City is a fact. Independent accounts place it in same approximate area (where Faucett disappeared, and still most dangerous spot in the Amazon Basin.[49] Hostile Indians, etc.). Seemingly it was inhabited by light-skinned Inca descendants in 1900, is probably empty now, but loaded with gold. As soon as I can save the $ I am going to have a look.

Sure, I am agreeable to make any changes in MS. However I am exceedingly uncreative just now on account of my junk trouble. What a relief it will be to get back to Tangiers. If you shift to N.Y. I will be seeing you soon, either in N.Y. or Europe. Everything you tell me about Frisco sounds like U.S. Inferno. Have you dug Brubeck etc., new telepathic jazz? I didn't realize 'til this past month how awful America is. God what a fate to live here! (N.Y., of course, is not America.)

I heard from Alan [Ansen]. He was caught by a servant *in flagrante* and thrown out of his apartment. Italy still sounds like a

---

48. Betty Jones: a friend of Burroughs and Marker around the Bounty, Mexico City, 1951 (at that time lately separated from her husband, Glenn). Shortly before this letter, Burroughs and Marker paid a memorably opiated visit to her in Hollywood, Florida.
49. Colonel Percy Harrison Fawcett, the famous explorer and source of Conan Doyle's novel *The Lost World*. Fawcett set off in 1925 to find Atlantis in the Río Xingu area of Amazonian Brazil and was never heard of again.

bad deal to me. Address is c/o American Express, Venice, Italy. Will be curious to hear what Rexroth says.[50]

Sat.

Still sick. If I was anywhere else could taper off with codeine or demerol. But I have already burned the town down on P.G.

If you run into anybody wants to look for The Lost City and all that Inca gold, and can put up a few thousand $, let me know.

Love,
Bill

---

50. The poet Kenneth Rexroth was then a reader for New Directions. Ginsberg, resuming his role as literary agent, had shown him some of Burroughs' routines, including "Roosevelt After Inauguration." Rexroth was not amused, and Burroughs wrote to Ginsberg, December 6: "It's not supposed to be *accurate*. Does he think it has anything to do with *Roosevelt?* His remarks seem to me completely inapplicable."

Dec. 7, 1954
Tanger

Dear Jack,

Just a line to tell you I am back in the Promised Land flowing with junk and boys. The trip was rough, but by sheer will power I managed to sleep straight through to Gibraltar, waking up only to eat occasionally. Been spending 15–20 hours a day in bed with Kiki catching up on my back screwing. He is really a treasure, my dear. So sweet and affectionate but at the same time indubitably male.

The town is wide open as always and no holes barred. Haw Haw. I am back with The Dutchman. He runs a nice clean whore house. If I had someone to go in with me I would rent a house in the Native Quarter. A big, three bedroom, bath, kitchen and living room goes for $20 per month, smaller houses for $10. It would be ideal if you and Al would come here and we all take a house together, pay about $7 per month each, and cooking in we could live for just about nothing.

I sat down seriously to write a best-seller Book of the Month Club job on Tanger. So here is what comes out first sentence:

"The only native in Interzone who is neither queer nor available is Andrew Keif's chauffeur, which is not an affectation on Keif's part but a useful pretext to break off relations with anyone he doesn't want to see: 'You made a pass at Aracknid last night. I can't have you to the house again.' (People are always blacking out in the Zone whether they drink or not. No one knows for sure what he did last night.)

"Aracknid is the worst driver in the Zone. On one occasion he ran down a pregnant woman in from the mountains with a load of charcoal on her back, and she miscarriaged a bloody, dead baby on the street, and Keif got out and sat on the curb stirring the blood with a stick while the police questioned Aracknid and finally arrested the woman."[51]

---

51. These paragraphs were used nearly verbatim as the opening lines of the "interzone" section of *Naked Lunch* (pp. 177–78).

I can just see that serialized in *Cosmopolitan* or *Good Housekeeping*. I mean it's hopeless, Jack. I can't write in a popular vein. Well I wish you would save some money and come here. Any news on *On The Road?* Any news with the junkie set? Write soon.

Love,
Bill

P.S. Andrew Keif is Paul Bowles, of course.

Dec. 13, 1954
Tangiers

Dear Allen,

I always have so much I want to say to you, that a letter is major operation. Never get it all said, either. I wish you could make it here.

I am downright incapacitated without a typewriter, but have written 1st chapter of a novel in which I will incorporate all my routines and scattered notes. Scene is Tangiers, which I call Interzone. Did I write you anything about novel in progress? Starts with a deal to import and sell "a load of K.Y. made of genuine whale drek in the South Atlantic, currently quarantined by the Board of Health in Tierra del Fuego." (Whale drek is what remains after they get finished cooking down a whale. A rotten, stinking, fishy mess you can smell for miles. No use has been found for it.)

As you gather, in my most extreme line. I am going to attempt a complete work. I am afraid it will be unpublishable as "*costumbre*."[52]

Did I tell you about my Merchant Marine papers? The application came back from Washington with a notation in Civil Service code, whereupon they gave me a form to fill out. "Are you or have you ever been addicted to, etc." They were very nice about it all, patting me on the shoulder. The application has to go back to Washington again. It looks hopeless.

The drug store here is packing me in. They have sold me 10 boxes to kick on, and Kiki is doling them out according to a schedule. This is a lucky break. I was compulsively taking larger doses at shorter intervals, and experiencing paranoid kicks. For example, a group of Arabs walk by and I distinctly hear them say: "William Burroughs," and it seems everyone I pass in cafés is looking at me, laughing and commenting. At the same time I *experience* these hallucinations, I *know* they are paranoid reactions caused by the drug so I am not alarmed; that is I *know* they are not real. A curious state, simultaneous insight and hallucination.

---

52. *Costumbre:* i.e., as usual.

If there is any possibility of publishing *Naked Lunch* I have some notes on cocaine that belong in it, but in the *Junk* section.[53] I don't know as it's a good idea to drop *Junk* (you will recall I put some of the material from *Queer* back into *Junk*). Well, use your judgment. I am up to my neck in this new work right now plus kicking habit. Besides I don't have a complete MS. In fact I have hardly any of *Queer*. I still think Roosevelt skit is funny. Sounds to me like Rexroth just doesn't dig what a routine is. You don't study Zen and then write a scholarly routine for Chrissakes! Routines are completely spontaneous and proceed from whatever fragmentary knowledge you have. In fact a routine is by nature fragmentary, inaccurate. There is no such thing as an exhaustive routine, nor does the scholarly-type mind run to routines.

Well I must close now. Must get to work on my new novel. This writing in long-hand is extremely exhausting. Please write,

Love,
Bill

P.S. When I was home I fell into a disgusting state of stagnation, ate and slept to excess. A horrible thing was happening to me. I was getting *fat*. An inch of nasty, soft flesh, marring my flat stomach I have always been so proud of. And I felt terrible. No energy, no life. It would literally *kill* me to live in U.S., except maybe in Frisco or N.Y. I could make it.

Now I feel alert and charged with energy, and my gut is once again hard and flat.

It's like I can't breathe in the U.S., especially in suburban communities. Palm Beach is a real horror. No slums, no dirt, no poverty. God what a fate to live there! No wonder men die young in U.S. and women outlive them and batten on their insurance. The U.S. simply does not provide sustenance for a man. He gets fat, and his vitality drains away, and he dies from spiritual malnutrition. It is significant that in other cultures (like Islam, for example), men

---

53. At this time, Burroughs conceived *Naked Lunch* (a title he credited to Kerouac) as a tripartite work consisting of "Junk," "Queer," and "Yage." His "new work," much of which would eventually be published under that title, was therefore considered as separate from the collective trilogy.

live as long or longer than women, while in U.S. statistics show women outlive men by a wide margin.

So I am counting my blessings in Tangiers. Awful thought occurs to me. Suppose I am like preserved in junk and will get fat if and when I get off it? What a dilemma! I would probably sacrifice everything to my narcissism and preserve my flat stomach at any cost.

Glimpsed a new *dimension* of sex: Sex mixed with routines and laughter, the unmalicious, unstrained, *pure* laughter that accompanies a good routine, laughter that gives a moment's freedom from the cautious, nagging, aging, frightened, flesh. How angelic such an affair could be! (Note that sex and laughter are considered incompatible. You are supposed to take sex seriously. Imagine a Reichian's reaction to my laughing sex kick! But it is the nature of laughter to recognize no bounds.)

I am strangled with routines, drowning in routines and nobody to receive. I was about to throw myself at Paul Bowles' feet, Last Chance Bowles so to speak, when he took off for Ceylon with all his entourage: His dungaree-wearing Lizzie wife,[54] and his talented boy friend, Ahmed Yacoubi the painter.[55] (The young man I protected with counter magic against a vile attempt by a rival. Both young, good-looking in a greasy sort of way, well uh proportioned, willing to oblige either sex, with a facility for melting old, rich bitches . . . Well, like I say *rivals* right down the line. You dig? So here I am way off the subject doing a mambo with Miss Green and is she ever in the slot tonight! And in this number the Rejection Dance, the Anti-Sex that mambo basically is, finds graphic representation. The man turns towards the woman with a hard-on that subsides as he digs her. The sex organs are artificial, huge papier maché constructions. As the dance progresses they become more and more realistic until we get to the real thing. The woman does

---

54. Jane Bowles, whose sexual orientation was well known in Tangier, was an author of repute in her own right, though her creative talent had become increasingly blocked.

55. Ahmed Yacoubi, born in Fez, 1931, was a *f'qih* (healer), and had been a self-taught painter when Bowles first met him in 1950. Yacoubi's paintings had by now been exhibited in New York, Madrid, and Tangier. He died in New York in the early 1980s of a brain tumor.

a mocking dance showing her cunt and her ass in rapid, whirling succession as if to say "it's all one to you the Eternal Pederast." He polishes his nails on his erection in parody of sulky, male indifference, etc.

Infinite possibilities. A tremendous Ballet of Rejection Desecration and Repression of Life. If successful would be unbearably depressing, unless I can produce a rebuttal. Well I will think on it. Whole idea just came to me this second.)

Like I was saying the rival makes an attempt by means of witchcraft on Yacoubi's talent, and I am moved to intervene with counter magic and the attempt is turned back on the attempter. Funny thing is Yacoubi is seriously convinced that my intervention was efficacious, because the following day there is an article in local press describing the rival's work as "a poor imitation of Yacoubi."

Well Bowles has gone with all his retinue. I do wish I had somebody to *talk* to.

Dec. 30, 1954
[Tangier]

Dear Allen,

Enclose first chapter of current novel. Reading it over I get an impression of something very sinister just under the surface, but I don't know what it is. Just a feeling. The second chapter covers some material I wrote before, some of which you must have seen. From there on I have no plans. Will let the book write itself.

I will work over the S.A. letters, and let you know about alterations. Suspending work on novel to give all my time to the letters. The magazine sounds great.[56] I only hope nothing fucks it up. You can count on me to help out any way possible.

Love,
Bill

P.S. What's this about Rexroth saying Auden says Jack is a genius but ruined by his friends? Jack wrote me that. Also Auden say I am a genius too.

Jack sounds paranoid. The cops caught up with him and served non-support warrant.[57] He says he has imitators in Frisco owing to your lack of discretion. What's this about you have a boy in Frisco?[58]

---

56. "I guess Al told you about this idea to publish our work, yours, his and mine in a Frisco magazine called *Crazy Lights*." (Burroughs to Kerouac, ca. January 21, 1955, Kerouac Collection, Columbia University.)

57. Kerouac was still denying paternity of his daughter, Janet. In mid-January, he appeared in domestic relations court, but his lawyer—Eugene Brooks—convinced the judge to suspend the case.

58. In December, Ginsberg had met twenty-one-year-old Peter Orlovsky.

1955

Jan. 6, [19]55, Tangiers
Start anyplace you want.
Start in the middle and read your way out.
In short, start anywhere.

Dear Allen,

Enclose some random notes plus what I have done on the S.A. letters. I have written a new introduction to Yage quest which I think is much better and prepares for following action.

Reading over a bit I wrote on Miami stop-over, I think it is good and should be included. I enclose same. It comes immediately after the new introduction. If you don't like it, however, omit.

I have just conceived, at this second, the way to achieve my work, solving the contradictions raised by dissipation of energy in fragmentary, unconnected projects. I will simply transcribe Lee's impressions . . . The fragmentary quality of my work is *inherent* in the method and will resolve itself so far as necessary. Tanger novel will be Lee's impressions of Tanger, discarding novelist pretext of dealing directly with his characters and situations. *I include the author in the novel.* I feel guilty even writing this letter when I should be up to my balls in the work. But "nothing is lost" . . . (A horrible vision of suffocating under the accumulated shit and piss and nail clippings and eyelashes and snot excreted by my soul and body, backing up like atomic waste: "Go *get* lost for Chrissakes.") I already made a novel outa letters. I can always tuck one in somewheres, bung up a hole with it, you know.

A strange, ill-omened incident. The other night I was standing in a bar. A man touched my arm. I made him immediately, and as it seems correctly, for Law. He asked if I was Max Gustav. I said "no," naturally. Then he showed a picture in a passport to the bartender. He said the picture looked like me and that was why he asked. I could not see any resemblance. Today I read they have found Max Gustav dead, apparently from overdose of veronal, in a ditch somewhere. Like I say, it's a bad sign, especially since I don't look anything like the late Max.

I am working through the letters making small alterations here and there. Mostly cross-outs of material that seems dull or nothing to the purpose. I may try to work in my dream of the Iron Wracks, and the ex-pug, you remember?[1] Also Penal Colony dream could be included.

I will send along alterations when I get them all finished.

Love,
Bill

P.S. If you can see your way clear, would greatly appreciate a little money. I am really hung up this month what with moving into another flat, and various other expenses.[2]

Eight hour stop-over in Miami. I stood in the door of Walgreen's feeling the air-conditioned chill hit my wet shirt back as the door opened and closed. I did not see The Thief, The Junkie, The Queer, The Dying Man. No face stood out sharp and distinct in the flash bulb of urgency. These faces were out of focus, a sun-tanned anonymous blur, moving to random doom and meets of juxtaposition without contact.

A man stopped on the corner. With a little gold knife he was nicking a cigar. Thick, shiny, black hairs criss-crossed a huge diamond on his finger. The man was tall and fat, his eyes a very pale, dead gray.

Miami is an inorganic *chambre de passe*. A masseur with sun-bleached blue eyes, sad, hopeless testicles drooping to his knees, rolls the Fat Man into cabinet baths and oil rubs and high colonics. Now he pops out of a Speed up Sun Tan Toaster ready for the main event. A sponge rubber, vibrating mannequin is wheeled in on an operating table. Wired for sound, she is singing soft and husky, choking with sex. The Fat Man shifts his cigar. His pale eyes sweat. "Sweet kid," he says. Aided by the masseur, he rolls onto the girl with a fluid plop. "O.K. George. Throw the switch."

---

1. Ex-pug: former pugilist [?]
2. In January, Burroughs moved out of his room at Calle de los Arcos, into more spacious accommodation rented from Jim Wylie, higher up in the medina.

You decide about this, Al. It doesn't contribute to *Yage Quest*. I mean it's completely incidental, and I don't know if it justifies its existence. Please decide. Remember it is very difficult for me or anyone to judge his own work exactly. Inserting this also breaks continuity of journey from Mexico to S.A. and back to Mexico.

Jan. 9, 1955
Tangiers

Dear Allen,
[. . .]
   Really, it is exasperating to sit helpless like in a nightmare while these life-hating character armadillos jeopardize the very ground under our feet and the air we breathe. Thirty more explosions and we've had it, and nobody shows any indication of curtailing their precious experiments.[3]

Love,
Bill

P.S. It must be Hell to live subject to continual annoyances from presumptuous cops. I can't understand how the cops got all out of hand in America. Since I feel so strongly that the law has no ethical right to interfere with me or anyone, such annoyances evoke in me intense reactions of hostility, so that my peace of mind is fucked up. In Calif. I could get six months for scars on my arm. One of my reasons for preferring to live outside the U.S. is so I won't be wasting time reacting against cops and the interfering society they represent. I do not object to cops in their legit function of maintaining order like here in Tanger. Living here you feel no weight of disapproving "others," no "they," no *Society*, consequently no resentment.

---

3. Aboveground nuclear testing was taking place at the time.

Jan. 12, 1955
Tanger

Dear Allen,

I need you so much your absence causes me, at times, acute pain. I don't mean sexually. I mean in connection with my writing. I think I am at the point of jumping in the lake instead of skirting the edges, and feel a great need for your help at this critical juncture. In fact I think we might even be able to collaborate on this novel.

Here is from the blurb jacket of the novel. Getting a bit previous, I admit. The theme just came to me in the form of this blurb:

"Suppose you knew the power to start an atomic war lay in the hands of a few scientists who were bent on destroying the world? That is the terrifying question posed by this searching novel."

"The book grabs you by the throat." Says L. Marland, distinguished critic. "It leaps in bed with you, and performs unmentionable acts. Then it thrusts a long cold needle deep into your spine and gives you an injection of ice water. That is the only way I know to express the feeling of fear that reaches out of these pages. Behind the humor, the routines, the parody (some of it a bit heavy-handed to be sure), you glimpse a dead-end despair, a bleak landscape of rubble under the spreading black cloud of a final bomb.

"The desperate struggle of a handful of men— 'Strangers' with no status, no place, no power under the present system —with the forces and emissaries of Destruction has the immediacy of a barroom fight, the kick to the groin, the broken beer bottle thrust at the eye.

"This book is a must for anyone who would understand the sick soul, sick unto death, of the atomic age."

So that's the novel of which I sent you the first chapter . . . I can work in all my routines, all the material I have written so far on Tanger that is scattered through a hundred letters to you.

When I don't have inspiration for the novel, I busy myself with hack work. I am writing an article on Tanger . . . Perhaps *New*

Yorker: "Letter From Tanger."[4] Will send along in a few days. You should be able to sell it. After that will write an article on Yage, possibly a short book with photos. I have some very fine pictures of me and the Yage vine taken by Doc Schultes. He sent me these photos when I was in Florida with no accompanying note. I wrote a thank-you letter, sent a specimen of the plant used to potentiate Yage that I collected in Peru (hitherto, the other ingredients *were not known,* so it is a matter of some importance) for the collection at the Harvard Botanical Museum, and a Christmas card. No word. I guess he read my book, and it was more than his conservative Boston soul could stand. Too bad. He was a great help to me, and a very nice person. It always hurts to lose a friend. Why must people be so silly? I wonder what specific facet of my character alienated him? A queer? A "common thief"? A dope peddler? In future expeditions and the dealings with squares involved, I shall prepare a complete camouflage. Too bad I don't have some kind of degree in anthropology or something.

You should have all the Yage corrections now, except the final version and end to the Yage City and Bar section. Please keep me posted constantly. Sometimes I wish I had come to Frisco.

Love,
Bill

P.S. Really a drag not to have anybody here I can talk to about writing or anything else of fundamental interest to me.

---

4. This almost certainly refers to the text later published as "International Zone," in *Interzone.*

No idea what the date is
Jan. 21, [*19*]55 Tangiers[5]

Dear Allen,

Why don't you write to me? The typewriter is fucked again, and so far to carry it to be fixed; it is heavy desk model.

I am suffering from a profound depression, the worst of my life. I have a complete conviction that I can't write any more, that my talent, such as it is, has given out, and sit for hours looking at a blank page, and there is no one I can talk to. I shouldn't be here hung up on Eukodol. Of course take more on account of depression . . . I should have gone to Frisco. If you could have borne with me a little longer . . .

I don't know what is wrong with me, but it is bad. Every idea I get on my novel seems ridiculous, like this atomic deal. And everything I write disgusts me. Some fucking German came here and committed suicide, so now it's RX for everything, even goof balls . . . such a bore. The druggist goes out and gets my script while I wait.

There was a Danish boy around town a few weeks ago. He was here last year and ran out of money, and I helped him out, but this time I figure it's too much. And such a dreary *déjà-vu*, exactly the same set-up. So I tell him go get yourself repatriated. So the Danish Consul sends him home on a Danish ship which sank with all hands in the North Sea. Don't know why I mention it. It's very uninteresting. He gave me an alarm clock just before he went away, which keeps very poor (not even appropriate) time.[6] The other mooch preyed on me last year, the Portu-

---

5. Unlike the top line, the date is not written in Burroughs' own hand— presumably added by Ginsberg on receipt.

6. The ship was almost certainly the *Gerda Toft,* which sank off the Frisian Islands on December 23, 1954. In *The Soft Machine* (Grove 1966, 1992 edition): "He gave me an alarm clock ran for a year after his death. Leif repatriated by the Danish. Freight boat out of Casa for Copenhagen sank off England with all hands" (p. 10). Also mentioned as Leif the Dane in *Port of Saints* (p. 111, Calder and Blue Wind editions, 1980).

guese, is rumored to be dead too, of unknown causes in Madrid.[7]

I really feel *awful*. A feeling of complete desolation. This typewriter is impossible.

Love,
Bill

P.S. I did not receive copy of Yage City section. Have had no word from you in the past 3 weeks or so.

Just looking over what I wrote last night. It is terrible. I wrote an article on Tangiers but it depresses me to see it even. It is so flatly an *article* like anybody could have written. I will send it along, however, when I get around to making a few corrections. Maybe you can sell it some place. I don't know.

I have my own house now. Can't get up energy to clean it, and live here in slowly accumulating dirt and disorder.

Maybe I will feel a little better when I get my shotgun and kill something. It has taken me all this while to get a permit.

---

7. In the "atrophied preface" section of *Naked Lunch:* " 'Taxi boys waiting for a pickup,' Eduardo said and died of an overdose in Madrid . . ." (p. 234).

Feb. 7, 195[5]
Tangiers

Dear Allen,

Here is my latest attempt to write something saleable. All day I had been finding pretexts to avoid work, reading magazines, making fudge, cleaning my shot-gun, washing the dishes, going to bed with Kiki, tying the garbage up in neat parcels and putting it out for the collector (if you put it out in a waste basket or any container, they will steal the container every time. I was going to chain a bucket to my doorstep but it's like too much trouble. So I put it out in packages), buying food for dinner, picking up a junk script. So finally I say: "Now you must work," and smoke some tea and sit down and out it comes all in one piece like a glob of spit:[8]

"The incredibly obscene, thinly disguised references and situations that slip by in Grade B Movies; the double entendres, perversion, sadism of popular songs; poltergeist knockings and mutterings of America's putrefying unconscious, boils that swell until they burst with a fart noise as if the body had put out an auxiliary ass hole with a stupid, belligerent Bronx cheer.

"Did I ever tell you about the man who taught his ass hole to talk? His whole abdomen would move up and down, you dig, farting out the words. It was unlike anything I ever heard (being a decent girl and don't you forget it, Mister). 'Some people think just because they take a girl to dinner at Dysentery Dave's Ox Ball House, they can go and get physical.' 'This is Jaundice Johnnies' Second Run V. (Viscera) Room, my Dear.' (I am cutting a long portion on second-run reject liver that doesn't pass the inspector because of live worms etc. A whole section on parasitic worms.)

"This ass talk had a sort of gut frequency. It hit you right down there like you gotta go. You know when the old colon gives you the elbow and it feels sorta cold inside, and you know all you have to do is turn loose? Well this talking hit you right down there, a bubbly, thick, stagnate sound, a sound you could *smell*.

---

8. For the following, compare *Naked Lunch*, pp. 131–35, in the "ordinary men and women" section.

"This man worked for a carnival, you dig, and to start with it was like a novelty ventriloquist act. Real funny, too, at first. He had a number he called 'The Better 'Ole' that was a scream, I tell you. I forget most of it but it was clever. Like, 'Oh I say, are you still down there old thing?'

" 'Nah! I had to go relieve myself.'

"After a while the ass started talking on its own. He would go in without anything prepared and his ass would ad lib and toss the gags back at him every time.

"Then it developed sort of teeth-like little, raspy, incurving hooks and started eating. He thought this was cute at first and built an act around it, but the ass hole would eat its way through his pants and start talking on the street, shouting out it wanted equal rights. It would get drunk, too, and have crying jags, nobody loved it and it wanted to be kissed same as any other mouth. Finally it talked all the time day and night, you could hear him for blocks screaming at it to shut up, and beating it with his fist, and sticking candles up it, but nothing did any good and the ass hole said to him: 'It's you who will shut up in the end. Not me. Because we don't need you around here any more. I can talk and eat *and* shit.'

"After that he began waking up in the morning with a transparent jelly like a tadpole's tail all over his mouth. This jelly was what the scientists call Un-D.T.—Undifferentiated Tissue—which could grow into any kind of flesh on the human body. He would tear it off his mouth and the pieces would stick to his hands like burning gasoline jelly and grow there, grow anywhere on him a glob of it fell. So finally his mouth sealed over, and the whole head would have amputated spontaneous (did you know there is a condition occurs in parts of Africa and only among Negroes where the little toe amputates spontaneously?) except for the *eyes* you dig? That's one thing the ass hole *couldn't* do was see. It needed the eyes. But nerve connections were blocked and infiltrated and atrophied so the brain couldn't give orders any more. It was trapped in the skull, sealed off. For a while you could see the silent, helpless suffering of the brain behind the eyes, then finally the brain must have died, because the eyes *went out* and there was no more feeling in them than a crab's eye on the end of a stalk.

"So what I started to talk about was the sex that passes the censor, squeezes through *between* bureaus, because there's always a space *between,* in popular songs and Grade B movies, as giving away the basic American rottenness, spurting out like breaking boils, throwing out globs of that Un-D.T. to fall anywhere and grow into some degenerate cancerous life form, reproducing a hideous, random image. Some would be entirely made of penis-like erectile tissue, others viscera barely covered over with skin, clusters of 3 and 4 eyes together, criss-cross of mouths, and ass holes, human parts shaken around and poured out any way they fell.

"The end result of complete cellular representation is cancer. Democracy is cancerous, and bureaus are its cancer. A bureau takes root anywhere in the state, turns malignant like the Narcotic Bureau, and grows and grows, always reproducing more of its own kind, until it chokes the host if not controlled or excised. Bureaus cannot live without a host being·true parasitic organisms. (A Cooperative on the other hand *can* live without the state. That is the road to follow. The building up of independent units to meet *needs* of the people who participate in the functioning of the unit. A bureau functions on opposite principle of *inventing needs* to justify its existence, but the *need must always come first.*) Bureaucracy is wrong as a cancer, a turning away from the human evolutionary direction of infinite potentials and differentiation and independent spontaneous action, to the complete parasitism of a virus—(It is thought that the virus is a degeneration from more complex life form. It may at one time have been capable of independent life. Now has fallen to the borderline between living and dead matter. It can exhibit living qualities only in a host, by *using the life of another.*)—the renunciation of life itself, a *falling* towards inorganic, inflexible machine, towards dead matter.

"Bureaus die when the structure of the state collapses. They are as helpless and unfit for independent existence as a displaced tapeworm, or a virus that has killed the host.

"In Timbuctu I once saw an Arab boy who could play the flute with his ass, and the fairies told me he was really an individual in bed. He could play a tune up and down the organ hitting the most erogenously sensitive spots, which are different on everyone, of course. Every lover had his special theme song which was perfect for him and rose to his climax. The boy was a great artist when it came to improvising new combines and special climaxes, some of them notes in the unknown, tie-ups of seeming discords that would suddenly break through each other and crash together with a stunning, hot sweet impact."

This is my saleable product. Do you dig what happens? It's almost like automatic writing produced by a hostile, independent entity who is saying in effect, "I will write what I please." At the same time when I try to pressure myself into organizing production, to impose some form on material, or even to follow a line (like continuation of novel), the effort catapults me into a sort of madness where only the most extreme material is available to me. What a disaster to lose my typewriter, and no possibility of buying one this month. My financial position slides inexorably. I started off this month in debt and in hock until I absolutely couldn't have promoted another centavo. I am afraid to count—will do that Monday morning—but I think I have $60 left. That's $2 per day for this month. Wouldn't be so bad if I didn't need junk. I spend $2 per day on junk alone. And I give Kiki 50¢ per day pocket money, and I have to feed him. He found work for three weeks, but the job gave out. His mother is sick and she can't work so he has to support her. My 50¢ goes, usually, to his mother. Then he will want another 50¢ to see a football game or a movie. Well enough of all this dreary ledger so inexorably in the red. [. . .]

I have started writing a Chandler-style, straight, action story about some super Heroin you can get a habit on one shot with it or something similar. I'm not even sure yet. But it starts out 2 detectives come to arrest me. I know I am to be used in experiments with this drug. (They don't know this.) To save myself I kill them both. That is where I am now. On the lam. Waiting to score for ½ ounce of junk to hide out with, the alarm is going out right now; to every precinct, every prowl car, etc., etc. Don't ask me what is going to happen I just don't know. May turn allegorical or even sur-realist. A ver.[9]

I read interesting case. England. 2 naval Lieutenants. Good friends. Drinking. One hits a shot glass every time at six feet with

---

9. This narrative became the "hauser and o'brien" episode in *Naked Lunch*.

his pistol. The other picks up a hat and holds it in his hand, and says "shoot it." The Lieutenant shot a hole in it. Later on the 2nd party puts the hat on his head and says, "Now try it." Then, at a distance of six feet, the Lt. in the first part takes *careful aim at the very top of the hat* and fires (there were witnesses) hitting his friend in the head. Friend may live, though. I am amazed by exact similarities. I am quite a good shot and accustomed to handle guns. I aimed *carefully at distance of 6 feet for the very top of the glass*. Do you know the story of Mike Fink? He'd been shooting shot glasses off the bar all afternoon. Finally a young friend of his put a shot glass on his head and Mike missed and killed the boy. The bartender did not believe it was an accident because Mike was known as a good shot. He got his own gun and shot Fink dead. (Another case in Durango, Mexico. Politico in whore house tried to shoot glass off whore's head. Killed her.)

I mean there is something odd here. The Lt. saying just like me "But how *could* I miss at that distance?" I don't understand it. May yet attempt a story or some account of Joan's death. I suspect my reluctance is not all because I think it would be in bad taste to write about it. I think I am *afraid*. Not exactly to discover unconscious intent. It's more complex, more basic and more horrible, as if the brain *drew* the bullet toward it. Did I tell you Kells' dream the night of Joan's death? This was before he knew, of course. I was cooking something in a pot, and he asked what I was cooking and I said "Brains!" and opened the pot showing "what looked like a lot of white worms." I forgot to ask him how I looked, general atmosphere etc.

To summarize, I pass along one of my specialized bits of wisdom like "always use poultry shears to cut off fingers": "*Never* participate in active or passive role in *any* shooting things off of, or near one, or knife throwing or *anything similar* and, if a bystander, always try to stop it."

I told you of horrible, nightmare depression and anxiety I had that whole day, so that I asked myself continually: "What in God's name is the matter with me?" One more point. The idea of shooting a glass off her head had *never entered my mind,* consciously, until, out of the blue so far as I can recall—I was very drunk, of course —I said: "It's about time for our William Tell act . . . Put a glass on your head, Joan." Nothing led up to the idea. From then on I was concentrating on aiming for the *very top of the glass*. Note all these *precautions* as though *I had to do it* like the original William Tell. Why, instead of being so careful, not give up the idea? Why indeed? In my present state of mind I am afraid to go too deep into this matter.

By the time it takes for you to receive this letter and answer it, I will be most urgently in need of money. (Sorry, just find I already mentioned this.) But please try to send me some. The loss of my typewriter was a real disaster. I don't want to lose my camera. I am going on a budget and will do my best to make it so I don't get in debt again . . .

Love,
Bill

P.S. Personal check is O.K. as I know someone here with bank account. Don't bother with those international money orders as they take 3 weeks to clear. Cashier's check preferable if not too much trouble.

Feb. 12, 1955
Tanger

Dear Jack,

I am now settled in my own house in the Native Quarter which is so close to Paul Bowles' house I could lean out the window and spit on his roof if I was a long range spitter and I wanted to spit there. Bowles is in Ceylon. A friend of mine rents the house and I got access to Bowles' books.[10]

Last month I ran out of money and was 36 hours without food or junk, and sold my typewriter. I wrote Allen to send along some of the money he owes me because I need it urgently. Once I get behind like this it takes something extra to put me back on even keel.

Doing a lot of work, but none of it satisfies me. It was a disaster for me to lose my typewriter. I hate to work in long-hand. I have been attempting something similar to your sketch method.[11] That is I write what I see and feel right now trying to arrive at some absolute, direct transmission of *fact* on all levels.

"Sitting in front of the Café Central in the Spring like rainy sunshine. Sick. Waiting for my Eukodol. A boy walks by and I turn my head, following his loins like a lizard turns its head to follow the course of an ant."

---

10. Bowles's house was a few yards from the Place Amrah, just below the Kasbah; the "friend" renting his house was probably Eric Gifford. Burroughs' house was situated on the other side of Amrah and a little higher up. Burroughs' phrasing here reworks Hemingway's "A Natural History of the Dead": ". . . and a hole in back you could put your fist in, if it were a small fist and you wanted to put it there . . ." In Ernest Hemingway, *Winner Take Nothing* (London: Granada, 1977), p. 126.

11. When staying with Burroughs in Mexico City, Kerouac had described his sketch method in a letter to Ginsberg (May 18, 1952, Ginsberg Collection, Columbia University). In the fall of 1953, at Ginsberg's and Burroughs' request, and again in the latter's company, Kerouac elaborated his method into the statement, "Essentials of Spontaneous Prose." Compare *Naked Lunch*, p. 221, in the "atrophied preface" section: "There is only one thing a writer can write about: *what is in front of his senses at the moment of writing . . .*"

Skit on Paul and Jane Bowles. I call him Andrew Keif and her Miggles Keif:

"Miggles looked up at her husband. She sniffed sharply:

" 'Have you been rolling in carrion again?' She demanded. (Ever see a dog roll in carrion? Well, they do it though they know they shouldn't.)

" 'Yes,' he said slowly and complacently, 'I have. *But,* believe it or not, I've been rolling in a dead *woman!* That's a good sign don't you think?' Like many homosexuals, Keif decided, periodically, that he wanted to be "cured" and lead a "normal life." To this end he had been analyzed by a Freudian, a member of the Washington group, a Horneyite (he chicly avoided Jungians and Adlerians),[12] and finally by a female Reichian who attached electrodes to his penis, stuck an orgone sprayer up his ass, urging him, at the same time, to relax and let the "orgasm reflex" take over. The result was a dislocated spinal disc which required prolonged chiropractic treatment. He decided to let his woman desiring maleness suffer inside him and emerge when it was ready."

Flashback to tremendous scene in Mexico. He has found a huge centipede under a stone: "His whole body was jerking in uncontrollable spasms. The current ran up his spine, a penetration unspeakably vile and delicious, to burst in his brain like a white hot, searing rocket. He doubled forward, fell on his knees in an attitude of passionate worship. 'Now! Now! Now!' The words broke from his thin lips in an ascending scream. He flung out his hands, every tendon white with strain, and seized the hideous creature. With a terrible cry he tore it in two. The severed centipede squirming horribly in his grip, its claws digging into his flesh, yellow and green juices running down his arms, he cried out again and again as he tore the centipede to pieces and rubbed the pieces on his chest. Slowly the bloody, soiled hands went slack, an overwhelming torpor settled in his limbs, his eyes closed and he fell on his side and slept till sundown."

My novel is taking shape. Scientists have discovered an anti-dream drug that will excise the intuitive, empathizing, symbolizing, myth- and art-creating faculties . . . We—a few counter con-

---

12. Sigmund Freud, Karen Horney, Carl G. Jung, Alfred Adler.

spirators—are trying to obtain and destroy the formula. So there will be a lot of shooting, violence etc. In fact one beginning I kill two cops who have come to arrest me because I know I am slated to be used as guinea pig in experiments with the anti-dream drug. The two cops think it is just routine pick-up of a junky. "I snapped two quick shots into Hauser's belly where his vest had pulled up showing an inch of white shirt . . . O'Brien was clawing at his shoulder holster, his hands stiff with panic . . . I shot him in his high, red forehead about an inch below the white hair line."[13]

How are things with you? Any line on Allen's magazine deal? If you write him, let him know I am living on one skimpy meal a day. Sample menu: fried apple peel and a piece of Spanish bacon —which is mostly fat—bread with no butter and tea with no milk. In short I need money! Best to Lu and Cessa.[14]

As Ever,
Bill

---

13. Compare *Naked Lunch*, pp. 212–13, in the "hauser and o'brien" section.
14. Cessa: Lucien Carr's wife, Francesca Von Hartz.

Feb. 19 [19]55
Tangier

Dear Allen,

Heartfelt thanks for the check, which arrived dramatically as the Embassy was closing its doors, and saved my camera . . . That morning Alan Ansen had surprised me most agreeably by sending a check for 5000 lira—about $15. (I had mentioned my financial condition, but had not asked, or even hinted, that he send me anything.) Imagine the shock of disappointment (6 cents, 2 shots, and half a loaf of stale bread constituted my total assets) when the bank told me this type check is only negotiable in Italy. I tried to borrow money. Those that would lend it don't have any, and those that have won't lend. Not centavo one could I promote. My only recourse is to sell the camera. I take it to a Hindu shop-keeper who says, "Come back in 2 hours and I will give you my price." He won't do business on the spot. So I rush to Embassy on the chance of letter from you, and there is your check. Jerk my camera back from disgruntled Hindu.

I am living now on strict budget, and should be able to avoid such acute crisisi (plural of crisis) in future. I was able to cash that personal check because I have a friend with a bank account. Otherwise I would have to wait weeks for it to clear. Money can also be sent by American Express checks made out to me. American Express could explain this method. Cost is nominal. International money orders take about 3 weeks to clear. So either personal checks or American Express is best method. American Express preferable if not too much trouble, as this friend might renege on cashing checks for me.

The novel is taking shape. Something even more evil than atomic destruction is the theme—namely an anti-dream drug which destroys the symbolizing, myth-making, intuitive, empathizing, telepathic faculty in man, so that his behavior can be controlled and predicted by the scientific methods that have proved so useful in the physical sciences. In short this drug eliminates the disturbing factor of spontaneous, unpredictable life from the human equation. I have spoken of the increased sensitivity to dream-like, nostalgic impressions that is conveyed by light junk-sickness. This is point of departure for creation of anti-dream drug. Novel treats of vast Kafkian conspiracies, malevolent telepathic broadcast stations, the basic conflict between the East—representing spontaneous, emergent life, and the West—representing control from without, character armor, death . . . But it is difficult to know what side anyone is working on, especially yourself. Agents continually infiltrate to work on other side and discredit by excess of zeal; more accurately, agents rarely know which side they are working on.

At the same time Scientists are working on the anti-dream drug, dream situations are breaking through into three-dimensional reality, and drugs have been discovered to increase symbolizing and telepathic powers so that any deviant threatens The Controllers, who seemingly have every advantage since they have precisely the means of Control on three-dimensional level (Police, Armies, Atom bombs, poison gas etc.), but this great mass of armor suffocates them like over-armored dinosaurs. (However, the outcome is left in doubt.) [. . .][15]

I wasn't using the right approach with you? So that's it! Well that can be remedied. I will eat wheat germ oil, exercise and think Positive Thoughts until I crackle with vigor leaving a faint odor of ozone in my wake. When we meet again, I will fix you with a glittering hawk glance, and, without a word, sweep you into my potent arms. Disregarding your coy protests, I will have my way with you on the spot. Seriously, Allen, what I want and look for is relation of equals with courage and nobility as prerequisites, preferably against backdrop of romantic adventure. Unfortunately, in our culture, adventure·is almost synonymous with crime, hence fantasies of committing crime for loved one. South America offers adventure without crime, hence my desire to make expedition with you. In short, self-pity and dependence set-up is not what I want; if I sometimes fall into it, I do so because what I do want I can't get. Committing crime for beloved, incidentally, is not as proof of devotion so much as demonstration of courage and nobility. "None but the brave deserves the fair."[16] Well, *basta* (enough).

---

15. Letter manuscript missing pp. 2–4.
16. Dryden, *Alexander's Feast*.

Your boy was indeed traumatized.[17] At what age did this occur? Did he remember it or was memory brought out in analysis? Is he really satisfied now with chicks? You said he was 22? That seems rather late to be *discovering* the cunt. Why can't you take a photo of him? You have that 35 mm camera, do you not?

I appreciate your critical notes on my work. They have been very helpful to me. I guess all writers suffer from fear of losing their talent, because talent is something that seems to come from outside, that you have no control over.

Too bad the magazine deal fell through.

There is a hip American bull fighter in town name of Tuck Porter.[18] Nice stud. He make pod but not junk. Knows Stanley Gould.[19] Spent 3 years in Mexico. Also met woman who was in Peru and knows about Yage (but never tried it). Enclose some old odds and ends. One illustrating romantic adolescent concept of queer love. (It was too gooey on re-reading. I censored it.)

When I get next month's allowance I will try to buy a typewriter. A new portable here costs $50. Second-hand machines run $25–$35. I am pretty well in the clear now. Haven't run up any debts this month. Next few days will be pretty lean, but I'll make it. Must close now and get this in the mail. Thanks again for life-saving check.

Love,
Bill

P.S. Glad you liked finger story. I will send along article when I get typewriter.[20]

---

17. Your boy: i.e., Peter Orlovsky.
18. Porter Tuck, known as *El Rubio de Boston*.
19. Stanley Gould was one of the jazz crowd that Kerouac met in Greenwich Village, 1953, dubbed "subterraneans" by Ginsberg.
20. In January, Burroughs had sent copies of his routine "The Finger" to both Kerouac and Ginsberg. By "article" he probably meant his "Letter From Tangier" piece.

April 20 [1955]
Tanger

Dear Allen,

Miss Green always accentuates prevailing mood. Depends which way you are leaning. I'm too precarious to venture a date with her, though she's always around the house to accommodate visitors. I received $5 check for which many thanks.

Trying to kick. Seems hopeless. I didn't get back on when I came back to Tanger. I never was off. All those weeks in Florida and another week on the boat and I hit Tanger sick. I should have gone to Lexington for the winter season. Now I have to quit or find some place where junk is cheaper—I can't control this Eukodol. Not that it's so great. It always leaves you feeling not quite fixed, like you need a little more. A shot of Eukodol is like a hot bath that isn't *quite* hot enough, if you dig me. But this not knowing where next shot is coming from—I am living on the level of an Australian Aborigine. I spend all my money on junk and don't eat right. Considering a shift to Near East, Beirut, which is said to flow with junk like the Promised Land.

Woke up last night at 3 am. with a character in mind who is writing "a great, gloomy, soul-searing homosexual novel. 600 pages of heartache and loneliness and frustration." Title: *Ignorant Armies* from "Dover Beach."[21]

"Swept with confused alarms of struggle and flight

Where ignorant armies clash by night."

The hero Adrian Scudder: "His face had the look of a super-imposed photo, reflecting a fractured spirit that could never love man or woman with complete sincerity or wholeness; yet driven, by an overwhelming passion, to change fact, and make *this* love real. Usually he selected someone who could not or would not reciprocate, enabling him to shift (cautiously, like one who tests uncertain ice, though in this case the danger was not that the ice should give way, but that it might hold his weight), the burden of failure onto the partner. The recipients of his dubious affections

---

21. By Matthew Arnold.

often felt the necessity of declaring neutrality, feeling themselves surrounded by a struggle of great, dark purposes, but not in direct danger, only liable to be caught in line of fire, because basically they were outsiders . . . Adrian was the last of a strange, archaic clan, or, perhaps, the first. In any case he was without context, of no class and no place."

And that terrific last scene where Adrian puts his head in a gas oven after killing Mark, and vomits and shits (Kitchen gas often causes vomiting and uncontrollable diarrhea. I recall years ago in Chicago I helped the landlady break down the door where a woman was trying to kill herself with gas. She had shit all over herself. [. . .]) and finally tries to get out just as he is losing consciousness: "Seized with the panic of one buried alive, he tried to sit straight up through the jagged metal of the stove. Pinwheels of pain careened through his head, setting off a fresh paroxysm of nausea. He saw a high wall and a little metal door, and he knew he must somehow get through the door, get the door open and get out through the door . . . No, he had not been allowed to slip away like one who leaves a dull party early with a few negligent handshakes, and the meaning[ful] look across the room to the one he will see later, perhaps . . . It was as if all the incarnate demons of his cautious, aging, frightened flesh, that he had tormented so long and with such cool malice, had mustered at the door of death to pelt him with filth, trip him, and finally kick him through the door, unwilling, whimpering, soiling himself like a frightened ape."

By God, Allen, that's purple as a baboon's ass! Why do I always parody? Neither in life nor in writing can I achieve complete sincerity—like Adrian of the novel—*except* in parody and moments of profound discouragement [. . .][22]

I have introduced some new characters into the novel: A man given to surrealist puns and practical jokes. Someone asks (an Englishman, of course) for a fag (cigarette in English slang case you don't know), and he produces, from under a great black cloak, a screaming, swishing fruit, who goes jabbering and swishing off

22. Letter manuscript missing pp. 3–4.

stage . . . He is in a bad restaurant (with pretensions to be good), as I was the other night and complained about the meat and they said, "Oh it must be good, it comes from a good butcher shop" (not *looking* at it, you dig). Faced by this contingency, my boy lets out a great cry, and in comes a trope? troup, well *group*, of great, filthy, snorting hogs and he feeds them his plate. (Did you ever hear anyone call hogs? They give this weird, long cry and the hogs come running and grunting with anticipation from incredible distances. The pig is by no means a stupid animal.) This character also keeps a purple-assed baboon on a lead, sometimes whipping the animal through a crowded café. (On the other hand I think I will have a blind man with a seeing-eye baboon. Which do you think is best?)

I sympathize with all your feelings of depression, beatness: "We have seen the best of our time." You at least can make a living, and perhaps a very good living. It wouldn't surprise me if you achieved a considerable degree of success in the way of a high paying job. I'm absolutely nowhere so far as a job goes in U.S. Only hope lies in the jungles of S.A., or conceivably writing a book that will sell. Now that seems about as likely as winning the lottery. [. . .] I am hoarding demerol and Paracodina (Codeine tablets *á la Mexicaine* which are available here—but only sporadically. Supply is uncertain.) in a new attempt to kick. Despite new restrictions Tangier is still fantastic by U.S. standards. Imagine buying demerol in shootable ampules right across the counter. In fact the druggist called it to my attention. I am famous all over town, and the druggists bring out the best they can sell without RX when I walk in, saying, "Bueno . . . fuerte." "Good . . . strong." They are shameless, and always try to overcharge, but how much pleasanter than the sour, puritanical shits in U.S. drug stores. In N.Y. I had a script for codeine tablets. I give it to this old fuck and his *pince-nez* falls off. Then he calls the doctor (but can't find him in), asks questions, finally refuses to fill the script without talking to the doctor. *Codeine!!* Here plain codeine, ¹⁄₁₀ the U.S. price, has written on the tube: *No script necessary for sale.*

I have no companionship here since Alan went back to Venice. I told you about Charles Gallagher who is writing a history of

Morocco for Ford Foundation?[23] Very charming, and a brilliant linguist. He says "Ghazil" can mean almost anything. Unfortunately he is gone to Rabat to be with the Archives, but will return in the Summer. It is really a deprivation to be without intelligent conversation. I evolve concepts, but no one to communicate with. Well enough, I am getting garrulous.

Love,
Bill

---

23. Charles Frederick Gallagher later wrote *The United States and North Africa: Morocco, Algeria, and Tunisia* (Cambridge, Mass.: Harvard University Press, 1963).

June 9 [1955
Tangier]

Dear Jack,

Sorry to be remiss about writing. I was 2 weeks in a clinic taking the cure. Lost 30 pounds. It's like too much trouble to do anything now. This time I intend to stay cured. I don't ever want to see any more junk.

I read *City City* in the clinic, and was able to forget my sickness for a while[24]—I only got *2 shots* in the whole nightmare 2 weeks I was in there. I am still very weak like convalescing from a long period of great sickness . . .

One thing about *City*; you must concentrate on specific characters and situations involving them. No doubt you intend to do so, and what you sent me was introductory. I found so many of my own kicks, control through broadcasts of feeling, etc. I want to see the rest of it as you get it done.

Allen is replaced by an IBM machine.[25] (Machines can do all office work better than people. Why hire fallible filing clerks when a machine can do it all quicker, better, and cheaper?) I can see the boss watching Allen work. "That man works with machine-like precision—machine-like? . . . Mmm."

Now that I am free I intend to do some travelling. I want to see all of Morocco, Spain, and possibly the Near East. But I am leery of the Near East since all that O might lead to a relapse, and I want to stay off from here on out. If I don't make it now I never will.

---

24. Kerouac's "cityCityCITY" was later published in *The Moderns: An Anthology of New Writing in America,* edited by Leroi Jones (New York: Corinth Books, 1963). When Kerouac mailed a draft to Burroughs in May, he introduced it as "the story that I think we should collaborate on, for a full novel, making the first truly literarily valuable book written by two men . . . William Lee and Jean-Louis." (May 1955, Ginsberg Collection, Columbia University.)

25. On May 1, Ginsberg had lost his job when Towne-Oller closed down their San Francisco office. The computerization of his job had been Ginsberg's own idea.

I hear your jazz story is in New Writing.[26] Congratulations. We have all been a long time without publication.

Bowles is back from India, but I have not met him.

This isn't much of a letter, but like I say I am really lassitudinous. Just writing to let you know I'm still alive after a fashion,

As Ever,
Bill

---

26. "Jazz of the Beat Generation," an amalgam of passages from *On the Road* and *Visions of Cody*, had appeared under the name Jean Louis in *New World Writing* that April. It was Kerouac's first publication in five years.

July 5 [*1955*
Tangier]

Dear Allen,

I have been too discouraged and disgusted to write. The trouble was I left the hospital half sick. Two weeks is not long enough for me to kick now. I used to kick in ten days.

Even so I probably would have made it except I came down with an excruciatingly painful neuralgia in the back. I thought I had kidney stones. I never experienced such pain. That finished me, and I relapsed into demerol which is really evil shit. After that awful cure it is really heartbreaking to find myself hooked again. But I am more determined than ever to quit. Even if I have to take the whole cure over. This time I'm going to succeed. If I don't kick now I never will . . . I wish you were here. I am so disgusted with my prevaricating—always some excuse for one last box—I have been buying absolutely the last box of demerol ampules every day for the past 3 weeks. Such a dreary display of weakness. At the same time I want to be rid of junk more than I ever wanted anything. So tomorrow I will shift to codeine, and try a rapid reduction. If I don't make it I will return to the clinic. Everyone thinks it's hopeless . . . I would gladly go to jail for a month and kick cold.

Maybe I will have Kiki take my clothes away and dole out the codeineetas. But I've done that so many times before. Well I hope I can report definite success in next letter. I enclose royalty report from those bastards. As you see they have *subtracted* current earnings instead of adding. A Freudian slip. See what you can do. They owe me $57.

I have met Paul Bowles, by the way. Very nice. In fact there are quite a few people of interest around now.

I will write in more detail later on. Want to get this in the mail.

Love,
Bill

P.S. You might send the royalty report to your brother and ask him to call them. But handle it anyway you see fit. There is no use for me to write to Wyn. He never pays any mind to my letters, and obviously harbors a deep personal dislike for me.

August 10, 1955
Tanger

Dear Allen,

[. . .]

Ominous occurrence here. For some time past I have become acquainted, much against my will, with a local "eccentric."[27] This citizen, an Arab, first approached me when I was strolling on the boulevard, hailed me as "his dear friend" and asked me for 50¢. I replied, with some asperity, that I was not his dear friend, that I had never seen him before in my life, and would not give him peseta one. Since then I run into him from time to time. His communications are progressively more cryptic; obviously he has built up an elaborate delusional system in which the U.S. Embassy is the root of all evil. I am an agent, a creature of the Embassy. I decide he is insane, probably dangerous. (An uninhibited paranoid is always a bad deal.) I cut the interviews as short as possible, holding myself always on the alert, ready to kick him in the stomach, arm myself with a bottle or a chair, at the first hostile move. But he makes no hostile moves in my direction. In fact there is something curiously sweet about him, a strange, sinister jocularity, as if we knew each other from somewhere, and his words referred to private jokes from this period of intimacy.

On Monday, August 1, he ran Amok with a razor-sharp butcher knife in the main drag, killed 5 people, and wounded 4, was finally cornered by the police, shot in the stomach and captured.[28] He will recover, and, unless he can prove insanity, will be shot—the form of execution obtaining here, but very rarely invoked. I wonder if he would have attacked me? I missed him by 10 minutes. The whole town is still hysterical. They shut the shops and rush inside barricading the door if anyone is seen running on the street.

The trip to West Africa never came off. They don't have the money yet. I have decided, in any case, not to go, as they are engaged in *the most dangerous* contraband operation—taking illegal

---

27. Abdelkrim Ben Abdeslam, a/k/a Mernissi, a pie vendor in the Socco Grande.
28. The *Tangier Gazette* reported four dead. The amok made the London *Times*.

diamonds *out of* W. Africa. It is five years to be found in possession of unregistered diamonds in this area. It is worse than dope. (They might hide the diamonds in my state room, or otherwise throw the bust into my lap.) In any case they are evil citizens, quite capable of throwing me over the side. They are lushed from wake up to pass out, they live and eat like dirty animals. All things considered, in the words of J. B. Myers: "Include me out."[29]

I have not heard from Alan Ansen in 2 months, though he owes me a letter. Writing him today.

Perhaps we could arrange like I wait here until you arrive next year, we do Africa and Europe together, *then* make S.A. expedition. What do you think? I mean, of course, if we can get squared away financial. I certainly want someone with me who is with it. So much more angles are turned up travelling like that than alone. On the other hand, bad or indifferent company is an active detriment. I take on no excess baggage of boring or grating characters, not even if they put up the money. It's not worth it. Such personnel would ruin the trip, fuck up relations with the Indians, etc. Nor will I tolerate any prissy, prudish scientists. This is an anything goes deal, the realization of a wild routine. No sea anchors need apply.

I wrote you how much I was impressed by the poem on Joan's tomb. In fact the impression was so sharp as to be quite painful.[30]

Please let me know how your plans shape up. What will you do when your compensation expires?[31] Back to N.Y.? What became of Neal's third ball?[32] Disappeared I hope. Which letter of mine did Neal groan when he read?

Love,
Bill

---

29. Actually one of Samuel Goldwyn's bon mots, but it is interesting that Burroughs was apparently thinking of the New York art critic and curator John Bernard Myers.
30. "Dream Record: June 8 1955" in *Reality Sandwiches*, pp. 48–49.
31. Since May Ginsberg had been receiving thirty dollars per week in unemployment benefits, which were due to run out in October.
32. Cassady was suffering from an abdominal hernia.

Sept. 21, 1955
Tanger

Dear Allen,

Received your two letters. I am sorry to be remiss about answering. I have been so involved in attempts and preparations to evict the Chinaman once and for all. Have tentatively arranged to take a cure here. I am going in a clinic and stay there until I am completely cured. One month at least, probably two. In any case I need a period in which I will be isolated and without distraction, to organize my novel. I intend to give all my time to work during the period of cure.

Some nights ago I got hold of some ampoules, each containing ⅙ grain of dolophine and ¹⁄₁₀₀ grain of hyoscine. Now ¹⁄₁₀₀ gr. of that awful shit is already a lot, but I thought the dolophine would offset it and shot 6 ampoules in the main line.

The ex-Captain found me sitting stark naked in the hall on the toilet seat (which I had wrenched from its moorings), playing in a bucket of water and singing *Deep in The Heart of Texas,* at the same time complaining, in clearly enunciated tones, of the high cost of living—"It all goes into razor blades." And I attempted to go out in the street naked at 2 A.M.—What a horrible nightmare if I had succeeded and came to myself wandering around the Native Quarter naked. I tore up my sheets and threw bottles all over the floor looking for something, I did not say what. Naturally Dave and the Old Dutch Auntie who runs this whorehouse were alarmed, thinking my state was permanent. They were vastly relieved to see me the following morning, fully dressed and in my right mind. I could only remember snatches of what had happened, but I do remember wondering why people were looking at me so strangely and talking in such tiresome, soothing voices. I concluded they were crazy or drunk, and told Tony he was stinking drunk.

I have read over your poem many times, and think it is one of the best things you have done. How is your book coming?[33] I am

33. The "poem" probably refers to "Dream Record" again, and the "book" either to *Empty Mirror,* which Ginsberg had been hoping Lawrence Ferlinghetti would

on pretty good terms with Paul Bowles now, but still don't know him well enough to ask his opinion on a MS.

This character who makes it with son and daughter sounds rather engaging. What are your plans for the next year? I heard from Jack in Mexico City. Dave [Tercerero] is dead.[34] I wrote Garver why the Hell didn't he go to the Far East or to Persia where they got like *opium shops,* and get what he wants instead of subsisting on a miserable diet of codeine pills. The man has no gumption left. It is too much for him to get on a boat or a plane—almost as cheap now. You can fly from Tanger to N.Y. for $300. Those places are too "far away" though from what I can't understand. Also they are vaguely dangerous. With his income and his one-track mind, I would be on my way to Teheran or Hong Kong tomorrow. That's what I would do if I intended to stay on junk. I would go somewhere I could get the real stuff cheap and legal.

Your moment of illumination very interesting, especially the flowers.[35]

In your place I would take a firm stand with Peter's brother and his appetite.[36] Sounds to me like he needs a boot in the ass figuratively and literally. I mean why kowtow to an obnoxious young punk? My love to Jack if he has arrived. I hope to enter clinic in 2 days.

Love,
Bill

---

publish, or to "Howl," the first part of which he had just written and shown to an enthusiastic Ferlinghetti.

34. Kerouac had arrived in Mexico City in early August, where he fell in love with Garver's junk connection, Old Dave's widow, Esperanza Villanueva, whom Kerouac had first met three years earlier. Changing her name from "hope" to "sadness," he was inspired to write Part 1 of *Tristessa.* Kerouac also composed 242 choruses of *Mexico City Blues,* before leaving for San Francisco on September 9.

35. Probably refers to Ginsberg's poem "Transcription of Organ Music," written September 8. Burroughs appears to misquote the line "animal heads of the flowers" in his letter of October 21.

36. Lafcadio Orlovsky, who emptied the icebox as fast as Ginsberg could fill it.

[Beginning of letter missing]

[Oct. 6, 1955
Tangier]

I have a short story written in long-hand which I will type and send along. Will also do an article on Yage. But most important I want to do some definite work on my novel about Interzone. If I can really concentrate on that I have a chance to kick this habit. But I never felt less creative.

Why do you take all this crap from Peter's punk brother? People are better off if they don't get all they want to eat. It's been proved with rats.

The Arabs are more and more hostile and insolent, and sullen and insufferable. Just now a kid rapped on my window and asked me for a cigarette. I told him to shove off, and he continued banging on the window until I picked up a cane and started out the door. I would have hit him with the cane if I caught him. I hate these people and their cowardly, snivelling, stupid, hostility. Another trick they have is putting banana peels on the door step.

Oct. 7 [1955]

I just went to see the woman in a strange Kafkian bureau built into a massive stone arch. I have passed it every day and never noticed the office was there: Office of Social Assistance it is called. Within ten minutes she had conjured up a doctor who will treat me, and procured me a room in the Jewish Hospital. Private room where I can use my typewriter, for $2 per day! I am going to stay there until I am cured. At least a month, more likely two. Checking in tomorrow morning. I can hardly believe it. Hope there is no last minute slip up. My introduction to this woman came about through an old English mooch and drunk. For the past five months I have been giving him a little money several times a week. Everybody told me it was a waste of money but I persisted. Like a fairy story, what?

The dollar is going up like a beautiful bird.

Strange, vivid junk-sick dreams lately, permeated with a feeling of nostalgia and loss. Well, now I have two months to do nothing but write. I will see what I can accomplish. One reason I want to make the S.A. expedition is it will give me something definite to write about. Any news of Jack? Please write to me.

Love,
Bill

P.S. Finally bought a typewriter. Brand new for $46. A real bargain.

No telling what I will do after my cure. Figure to make up for lost time, and I never want to see any more junk.

The Yage article might sell. I have those photos to go with it you know.

And maybe in two months I'll have something to show a publisher on the novel. We will see.

Maybe I will go East overland right on around the world and come to see you from the East.

Once I get off junk, anything is possible.

You really should dig South America. More interesting than Africa or Europe. I will dig up the money some way. I might even write something that will sell. The prospect of cure has given me a concentration of energy I haven't had for months.

I should have been your first affair instead of that fucking sea captain.[37]

The English mooch who got me in touch with this woman is blossoming out in new clothes and all manner of schemes to make a fortune. Who knows but what I may get in on something good? I am already paid back for the money I gave him and the meals and drinks I bought, by this introduction. I had tried two doctors, every hospital and clinic in town, and finally gave up. It seemed like no hospital or clinic would accept a case of addiction. Then Leslie [Eggleston] (that's his name, I say rather superfluously; that reminds me once with Marker *in medias res* he said, "This does seem rather superfluous") told me to go see this woman and gave me a note to her. Tangiers has more people without money stranded than any place I ever saw, but no one had ever heard of this woman, who

---

37. Ginsberg's first sexual encounter had been with a forty-year-old sailor in the Seamen's Institute in New York City in 1945.

doles out all manner of assistance to any inhabitant of Tanger regardless of nationality. I could have got the treatment free most likely but I didn't want any delay. Besides, the price is so low.

Well, Love again and Good Bye for Now.

Write to Legation. Kiki will pick up my mail there and bring it to me.

Bill

[*Beginning of letter missing*]

[*Oct. 10, 1955*
Tangier]

Well, I must get busy, realize something from this horrible, stagnant period of cure.

The only thing to do with junk sickness, like pain, is to plunge right into the middle of it. I have never succeeded in doing this. Certainly there is no question of quitting or backsliding this time.

I enclose the story I wrote about Terry who was killed by the lion. I don't like it too much. I am not cut out to write anything so separate from myself. Well, see if you can peddle it somewhere. You are my agent. We both need the money. I am raising you to 20 percent. Can't think up a title for the story. Not good with titles. I don't expect to write anything like this again. Like I say it isn't my sort of thing, but since it was done, I am typing it and sending along. So see what you can do. Did you ever try anywhere with the finger story? I keep reading over the poems you sent. Like I say this last batch seems to me better than anything you have done. I will go into detail in next letter.

Possible titles for story: Death in Another Country; "You Gotta Have Something Special"; Tiger Ted.

I realize you probably want to dig Europe and Africa before S.A. I wish you would come on over here. When I get out of here I will see what I can do to expedite matters. There are people here who support themselves teaching English, piece-work journalism, translation, etc. Of course you can count on me for all the help I can give you. With no Chinaman to support, I could get by on half present income. If you could once get here, you would be O.K., and you could get here for $160 from N.Y. via the Homeland Line. Come to think, it's much more to the point you come here than I should go to Frisco, where I don't especially desire to be. We will think further on it. I have even considered building a house here. Still, I feel my real destiny lies in Mexico and S.A. When I get home-sick it is always for Mexico City. That is home to me. I think of the little park in front of the Penitentiary where I used to get off the bus every Monday to sign my bond at 9 am., and the whole beauty of Mexico City in the early morning.[38] But look. If I could raise money enough for your fare here, would you come? It strikes me you are not doing anything special now in Frisco, and have no real prospects. Plenty time to think about it. I will be in hock for another month at least. More like two.

I can't think of any reason why you shouldn't come on here right away. I may start some business here when I get out, and could give you a job. Or we might put out a magazine. It is time we should see each other again. I think there is no possibility of any basic incompatibility, or any irreconcilable divergence of interests. Such difficulties exist only in the imagination of both of us, and have no bearing on the realities of our relationship. I mean a real misunderstanding is not possible, could only be the result of an error on the part of one or the other. If we should see each other this would immediately be clear. I can not exactly make this clear in words because exactly what I am referring to is understanding on a non-verbal basis. That is why there has been so much misunderstanding in our exchange of letters. For example: Do I want, need, to sleep with you? Don't know. Couldn't know without seeing you.

These are created difficulties that would not arise, false dichotomies. On the level of non-verbal understanding, such impasses are not possible.

When we see each other again, it will be like no time before. So how can either of us predict, or lay down conditions?

We must not attempt to do so, but trust in our ability to communicate and understand on the basis of an actual situation.

I have been waiting three days for Kiki to come and take this letter. That is why I keep adding to it. I can't understand what is keeping him. I enclose some additional work on the Yage City bar section—do you have a copy of it?—I am filling in the past.

Writing now causes me an almost unbearable pain. This is connected with my need for you, which is probably not a sexual need at all, but something even more basic. I wonder if we could collaborate? So many questions that I can't answer until I see you.

---

38. Burroughs was referring to his bail bond, and to the period, after September 1951, when he was awaiting trial.

Still no Kiki to take this letter. Where is the little beast? Perhaps sick again. He knows I don't approve of sickness. Have been working all day on Interzone Novel. Horrible mess of long-hand notes to straighten out, plus all those letters to go through. A veritable labor of Hercules. Reading over my letters to you, I am impressed by my reasonableness, and readiness to come to any sort of terms. Can't see why they should have upset you. It is extremely painful trying to weld all this scattered material into some sort of coherent pattern. But I have made a start. Will send along chapter when I finish one. You have first chapter.

Kiki is here so I will give him this letter. Working on novel all day. It is terribly painful. *There is no art in the act of writing.* As Kells said: "You are too essentially active to be a writer."

Love,
Bill

Benchimol Hosp.[39]
Tangers
Oct. 21, 1955

Letter B[40]
(Written before I got your letter)

Dear Allen,

Letter A is the beginning of Chapter II of Interzone novel. Chapter II is almost complete. About 40 pages. I will send along in next week or so.

Still getting 40 Mg. shot of dolophine every 4 hours. (That = about 1 grain of M.) Only half-way comfortable cure I ever took. It will take about two months. When I leave here I will be completely off, able to drink and function *sans* junk.

Chapter II is: *Selections from Lee's Letters and Journals*. With this gimmick I can use all letters including love letters, fragmentary material, anything. Of course I am not using anywhere near all the letters. I will often sort through 100 pages to concoct 1 page. Funny though how the letters hang together. I figure to use one sentence and it pulls a whole page along with it. The selection is difficult, and, of course, tentative. (I have letters from past year, and longhand notes of past six months.) This is a first draft, a sort of framework. I plan to alternate chapters of Letter and Journal Selections, with straight narrative chapters like Chapter 1. May end up relegating the Letter and Journal chapters to an appendix. We will see. In next two months I should have enough completed to show a publisher, if there is a publisher who will look at it. The selection

---

39. Benchimol Hospital, founded by Haim and Donna Benchimol, is situated a mile or so southwest of the medina, on Avenue Menéndez y Pelayo. Among its rooms is one called Salle Salvador Hassan, a name subsequently used in *Naked Lunch*.

40. The majority of the existing manuscript of "Letter A," dated October 20, appears in *Interzone*, pp. 124–30. Of the rest, one part reproduces the Sargasso section of "Letter C," and another is the Diplomat routine as used in *Naked Lunch*, pp. 62–64, in "the black meat" section.

chapters form a sort of mosaic with the cryptic significance of juxtaposition, like objects abandoned in a hotel drawer, a form of still life.

Reading over my letters, I have thought a lot about you. By all means you should come here as soon as possible. As regards my feeling for you at present time, don't worry about it. Personally, I'm not a bit alarmed about that. But it is much better deal you come here than I should go to Frisco. The U.S. is no place for me. I need a place with more room, more leeway.

My mind is turning to crime lately. "Strange things I have in heart that will to hand."[41] Of all crimes, blackmail must be the most artistically satisfying, I mean The Moment of Truth when you see his front, his will to resist, collapse. That must be real tasty. I mention this angle in Chapter II.

This writing is more painful than anything I ever did. Parentheses pounce on me and tear me apart. I have no control over what I write, which is as it should be. I feel like the St. Anthony of Hieronymus Bosch or however his name goes.

I have book of Klee's work and writing. Terrific. The pictures are literally alive. Have Genet's *Journal of a Thief* in English, and have read it over many times.[42] I think he is the greatest living writer of prose. Dig this—He is being fucked by a big Negro in the Sante Prison: "I shall be crushed by his darkness which will gradually dilute me. With my mouth open, I shall know he is in a torpor, held in that dark axis by his steel pivot. I shall gaze over the world with that clear gaze the eagle loaned to Ganymede." The translation is not bad except for the dialogue. He translates into outmoded U.S. slang. I mean nobody now talks like this: "I'll drill somebody for just a little loose cash." Terrible. Why not leave the French argot and explain meaning?

Reading over your poems and letters: The following lines strike me from *Siesta in Xbalba:* "That register indifferent greeting across

41. "Strange things I have in head, that will to hand, / Which must be acted, ere they may be scann'd." *Macbeth*, act 3, scene 4, 139–40.
42. Bernard Frechtman's translation of Jean Genet's *Journal du voleur* was published by Olympia Press in April 1954.

time." . . . "Vanished out of the fading grip of stone hands." . . .
The whole stanza beginning: "Time's slow wall overtopping etc."
is superb. "Like burning, screaming lawyers" HMMM . . . One
line shockingly bad: "And had I money" . . . . [43] The poem as a
whole very good, but cannot compare, *as a unified piece of work,*
with your *Strophes,* which is really all in one piece and to my mind
the best thing you have done. [44] I do not single out lines, because
it is all excellent. I believe I already wrote you that the poem on
Joan's grave gave me a very distinct shock—because of personal
associations—almost unpleasantly intense. The poem is certainly a
success.

Your mystic moment with "the glistening animal aspect of
the flowers" reminds me of Yage intoxication. So does the
work of Klee. One of his pictures entitled "Indiscretion," is exact
copy of what I saw high on Yage in Pucallpa when I closed my
eyes. [45]

[. . .]

A good selection of people in Tangiers now: Dave Lamont,
young Canadian painter who comes to see me every day; Chris
Wanklyn, Canadian writer; Paul and Jane Bowles quite accessible
these days; Charles Gallagher, extremely intelligent and witty, writing history of Morocco on Ford Foundation; Viscount des Iles, a
brilliant linguist and student of the occult; Peter Mayne, who wrote
The Alleys of Marrakesh. [46] In short, plenty people around now. I

43. "Siesta in Xbalba," published in *Reality Sandwiches.* The line Burroughs disliked reads: "And had I mules and money . . ."

44. *Strophes:* i.e., "Howl." Ginsberg had titled the second draft of Part 1
"Strophes."

45. Burroughs was undoubtedly referring to his visions as recounted in his letters
of June 18 and July 8, 1953. In *An Approach to Paul Klee* (Phoenix House: London,
1956) Nika Hulton offers this gloss of 'Indiscretion' (1935): "To understand it one
must (as with all his pictures) follow the line—in this case by following the coils
to the ghostly face on the right. The minute lines, so usual in Klee's style, give
depth and volume to the coils. The title 'Indiscretion' is one very well adapted to
the composition. Can one not imagine words swelling out of all proportion and
changing in meaning and sense?" (p. 64).

46. Peter Mayne, born in England, 1908. *The Alleys of Marrakesh* (London: John
Murray, 1953) was reprinted under the title *A Year in Marrakesh.*

hope you can make it here real soon. Love to Neal and Jack if he
is there,

Love,
Bill

P.S. Like very much *At Sunset* and *Her Engagement*.
The Wallace Stevens poem is real great. The best thing he has
done. I never liked him before.[47]

---

47. The titles of two lost Ginsberg poems. The Stevens poem was probably
"Lebensweisheitspeilerei."

Benchimol Hosp.
Tanger
Oct. 23, 1955

Letter C

Dear Allen and Jack,

Kiki just brought me your letter—no date on it. Now, Al, I'd cut off my right nut to see you, may I fall down and be paralysed and my prick fall off, but I don't want to give you the impression I'm like on my way to Frisco, because it ain't necessarily so like a lot of things you're liable to read in my letters. To begin with I got no loot. I wrote you from the withdrawal doldrums. Actually, Tangiers is looking up—What I mean to say is I don't know what the fuck I will do when I get out of here and that is a pact, I mean a fact. There's a war here I want to dig, also *Perganum harmala* which is same thing as Yage used by Berbers, also Barrio Chino of Barcelona that Genet writes about,[48] and the rest of Spain for which I feel an affinity; may make overland trip to Persia with Charles Gallagher. May visit Ansen in Venice, would like to dig Yugoslavia, and the queer monasteries of Greece . . . Also figure to start at one end of Interzone and screw my way through to the other. I am tired of monogamy with Kiki. Dryden speaks of the Golden Age, "Ere one to one was cursedly confined."[49] Let's get on back to that Golden Age. Like the song say, "A boy's will is the wind's will"[50] . . . Besides which my mind is seething with ideas to make a $—some of them not exactly legit. The Nice Night Nurse just gave me a bang and it is hitting me right in the gut, a soft, sweet blow. I call her "The Nice Night Nurse" to distinguish her from the bitch who gave me a shot of plain water a few nights back. I suspect her to be a schmecker but it's hard to tell with women and

---

48. "The Barrio Chino was, at the time, a kind of haunt thronged less with Spaniards than with foreigners, all of them down-and-out bums." (*The Thief's Journal*, p. 18.)

49. "Absalom and Achitophel," line 4.

50. Longfellow: "A boy's will is the wind's will / And the thoughts of youth are long, long thoughts"—from "My Lost Youth."

Chinamen. Anyhoo I don't want her ministering to me no more.

(Just went to the head again. Still locked. Locked for six solid hours. I think they are using it as an operating room.) I am getting sexy, come three times last night. The Italian school is just opposite, and I stand for hours watching the boys with my 8-power field glasses. Curious feeling of projecting myself, like I was standing over there with the boys, invisible earthbound ghost, torn with disembodied lust. They wear shorts, and I can see the goose pimples on their legs in the chill of the morning, count the hairs. Did I ever tell you about the time Marv and I paid two Arab kids sixty cents to watch them screw each other—we demanded semen too, no half-assed screwing. So I asked Marv: "Do you think they will do it?" and he says: "I think so. They are hungry." They did it. Made me feel sorta like a dirty old man . . . [51] Frisco sounds like kicks and I would love to dig all of you, I mean you, Allen, and Jack, you, and sweet Neal . . . Your letter thawed out my bleak, wind-swept psyche. At times lately I come on downright mean. Jump all over the Arab servants. I am the most unpopular patient in this malodorous trap. Talk about hospital smell . . . You ain't had it till you sniff a Spanish hospital . . . You all shame me with your Buddhistic love and sweetness, torn as I am by winds of violence and discord . . . This violence has nothing to do with you, Allen.

Glad to hear you are getting some $ on your work. No one deserves it more. What is the HOWL Allen read? The reading sounds really great.[52] Wish I could have been there. So I should bring Kiki with me? I'll find plenty young boys around there? Come now, Allen, what's this you're hinting at? Who are these important people who are mad at me? Dirty VIPs. It's about time you wised up to Trilling.[53] He's a type can't and won't do you any good anyway. He's got no orgones, no *mana,* no charge to him. Just soaks up your charge to keep the battery of his brain turning out crap for the *Partisan Review.* Publishing in those obituary pages is really the kiss of death, the very fuck of death. That pornography

---

51. Compare this paragraph with *Naked Lunch,* p. 59, in the "black meat" section.
52. At San Francisco's Six Gallery on October 13, Ginsberg, cheered on by Kerouac, followed readings by poets Philip Lamantia, Michael McClure, and Philip Whalen with his premiere performance of the first part of "Howl."
53. Lionel Trilling, Ginsberg's former English professor at Columbia.

reads real nice. I'd like to see it all. Now look, sweetheart, you are my agent so see what you can do with this Interzone deal. You will have about a hundred pages in next two months. Twenty percent . . . But I have wandered off the point, out of contact, fallen into a great gray gap between parentheses . . . Sit back and look blankly at the letter. No I can't neither be no fucking monk . . . Really I am dubious of the Land of the Free, not over-keen to walkabout long Stateside in those great boy-less spaces . . . but *quien sabe?* I may decide on Frisco. Of course, if I latched onto some gelt, I would sure come to visit en route to South America . . .

Your letter has a warming, heartening, relaxing effect on me . . . Yes I would like to see old Garver again before he dies. Tell Neal from me to drop the bang tails. You can't beat it. Dream hunches are *not supposed to be used that way*. You understand, Neal? You know what horse is going to win, but you *can not use that knowledge to make money*. Don't try. It's like fighting a ghost antagonist who can hit you but you can't hit him. Drop it. Forget it. Keep your money . . .[54]

I am progressing towards complete lack of caution and restraint. Nothing must be allowed to dilute my routines. I know I used to be shy about approaching boys, for example, but I can not remember why exactly. The centers of inhibition are atrophied, occluded like an eel's ass on The Way to Sargasso—good book title. You know about eels? When they reach full maturity, they leave the streams and ponds of Europe travelling downstream to the sea, then cross the Atlantic Ocean to the Sargasso Sea—near Bermuda— where they mate and die. During this perilous journey they stop eating and their ass holes seal over. The young eels start back for the fresh water ponds and streams of Europe. Say that's better than *Ignorant Armies* ("Dover Beach" by Arnold) as a title for my Interzone novel:

Meet Me in Sargasso, I'll See You in Sargasso, The Sargasso Trail. Death opens the door of his old green pickup and says to The

54. Neal did not forget it, and the results were disastrous. That November he persuaded his girlfriend, Natalie Jackson, to forge Carolyn Cassady's signature on $10,000 worth of bonds, in order to win a fortune with her racetrack system. He blew all the money, and Natalie, guilt-ridden, committed suicide on November 30.

Hitchhiker: "You look occluded, friend. Going straight through to Sargasso?"

Ticket for Sargasso, Meet in Sargasso, On the Road to Sargasso. What I want to convey, though, is the *inner* pull towards Sargasso: *Sargasso Yen, Sargasso Time, Sargasso Kicks, The Sargasso Blues.* I can't get it. This is all trivial, doesn't convey those eels wiggling across fields at night in the wet grass to find the next pond or stream, thousands dying on the way . . . If I ever buy a boat, I will call it *The Sargasso . . . Sargasso Junction, Change for Sargasso, Sargasso Transfer, Sargasso Detour. Basta.* Do you know about lampreys? When they mate they tear each other with their suction cups so that they always die afterwards. Either a prey to other fish, or to virginal lampreys, or infiltrated by fungus.

Some of this letter I am transcribing into Letter A which is the beginning of Chapter II. Material often overlaps. You are free to choose, add, subtract, rearrange if you find a potential publisher. This is Sat., and the letter can't go off before Monday. I will be adding to it. May come up with *the* Sargasso title. So thanks for your letter and goodbye for now . . . See you in Sargasso . . . One of the Sargasso titles might do for my story about Tiger Ted . . .

Love,
Bill

Yesterday I took a walk on the outskirts of town. Environs of the Zone are wildly beautiful. Low hills with great variety of trees, flowering vines and shrubs, great, red sandstone cliffs topped with curiously stylized, Japanese-looking pine trees, fall to the sea. What a place for a house on top of those cliffs!

I used to complain I lacked material to write about. Mother of God! Now I'm swamped with material. I could write 50 pages on that walk, which was a mystical vision comparable to your East Harlem Revelations. That letter where I come on sorta whiney, like: "Tangiers has nothing for me and it's all your fault I'm here anyhoo." . . . Well, Al, 'taint necessarily so. Beginning to dig Arab kicks. It takes time. You must let them seep into you . . . Well like I say, could write a book on that walk. Instead I will select one moment:

I went in an Arab café for a glass of mint tea. One room 15 by 15, a few tables and chairs, a raised platform covered with mats stretched across one end of the room where the Arabs sit with their shoes off playing cards and smoking kif, the inevitable picture of Ben Youssef, The Deposed Sultan[55]—You see his undistinguished pan everywhere like those pictures of my fran Roosevelt[56]—pictures of Mecca done in the hideous light pinks and blues of religious objects, profoundly vulgar like the final decadent phase of Aztec mosaics—Pawing through this appalling mass of notes and letters, looking for something, I run across one of your old letters, Al, and the following jumps out at me: "Don't be depressed. There's too much to do." And that *is* a fact. So much I am flipping. You're a fucking genius, Al . . .

I draw some dirty looks from a table of Arabs and stare at them till they drop their eyes and fumble with kif pipes. If they insist to make something out of it, I'd as soon die now as anytime. It is as Allah wills. Here on the red tile floor of this café, with a knife in my kidney, you dig one of them slipped around behind me. I always carry a knife myself, and I would get the best price I could in the blood and flesh of my opponents. I'm not one to turn the other kidney. The metaphysic of interpersonal combat: Zen Buddhist straightaheadedness applied to fencing and knife fighting; Jiu-Jitsu principle of "winning by giving in" and "Turning your opponent's strength against him," various techniques of knife fighting, a knife fight as a mystic contest, a discipline like Yoga—You must eliminate fear and anger—and see the fight as impersonal process. Like primitive drawing depicts parts of an animal the artist can not see —spinal column, heart, stomach—though he knows they are there. See *Arts of the South Seas* by Ralph Linton[57]—so the knife fighter

55. Sultan Sidi Mohammed Ben Youssef, who had been on the throne since 1927, had angered the French by his support for Moroccan nationalism, and in August 1953 they flew him into exile, first to Corsica, then to Madagascar. The French installed his cousin, Sidi Mohammed Ben Moulay Arafa el Alaoui, in his place. Most Moroccans continued to regard Ben Youssef as their legitimate ruler.

56. Franklin D. Roosevelt always began his speeches: "My friends . . ."

57. Ralph Linton and Paul S. Wingert, *Arts of the South Seas* (New York: Simon & Schuster, 1946).

sees the inner organs of his opponent—heart, liver, stomach, neck veins—that he is attempting to externalize and delineate with his knife. Or you can conceive it as cool and cerebral as chess, a game involving the barter of pain and blood in which you try to get for your boy, your golden body, the best deal possible. Jiu-Jitsu proverb: You give your muscles—Let him knock you around—You take his bones. In knife fight you must be ready to give without hesitating your left arm and your face. You take a liver, a stomach, a carotid artery . . .

Not that I ever look for or want any kind of a fight, and a man has to be out of line to seek a fight with me—It almost never happens—The knife-fight potential was simply one facet of that moment sitting in the café looking out at hill opposite, stylized pine trees on top arranged with the economy of a Chinese print against blue sky in the tingling, clear, classic, Mediterranean air . . . I was completely alive in the moment, not saving myself, not waiting for anything or anybody. "I have told no one to wait."[58] This is it right now . . . Some French writer said: "Only those who love life do not fear death."

So don't ever worry about your boy Willy Lee, Al. I quote from one of your letters: "You lose sight of life, lose vigor, become dependent and listless, become a drag, sink, lose blood, junk up, crawl off threatening to die." Sounds like advertisement describing the victim of a sluggish colon. "And then I took Ma Lee's Orgone Yeast! WOW!"

Actually I am so independent, so fucking far out, I am subject to float away like a balloon . . .

Today's walk was different. More incident, less revelation. Actual fight in another café. Minor fracas. Hitting each other with their heavy rubber-soled sandals. No knives, no broken glasses, no blood. Nothing tasty. The proprietor, a young kid, left when the fight started . . . The fight just suddenly stopped for no reason. Well that's Africa, son . . . The proprietor came back with another kid, walking with arms around each other's ribs,

---

58. T.S. Eliot's translation of St. John Perse's poem *Anabase,* section 5 (first edition, 1931; revised, London: Faber & Faber, 1959).

and gave me a dazzling smile when I got up to pay for my tea . . .

On the walk I was thinking: All complete swish fairies should be killed, not as traitors to the cause of queerness, but for selling out the human race to the forces of negation and death. Kill the nanny beater too:

"Let petty kings the names of parties know
Where 'er I come I kill both friend and foe."[59]

How do you know when a man is "complete fairy" . . . *"De carne tumefacta y pensamiento in mundo Maricas de los ciudades . . . Madres de lodo, enemigos sin sueño del Amor, Que dais a los muchachos gotas de sucia muerte con amargo veneno."* Garcia Lorca, "Ode to Walt Whitman." Translates: "You fucking fairies of the cities"—He has just said he don't object to queers as such—"with rotten flesh and filthy thoughts. Mother of mud, sleepless enemies of love, who give to boys drops of dirty death with bitter venom." Hear! Hear! . . . They *never* would be missed . . . And how do you know anybody is in that class? *They* know. They are self-condemned. You can see it in their eyes. A judge in Interzone who will listen to no evidence, doesn't want to know what a man is accused of. He just looks into his eyes and acquits or passes sentence . . . Complete lack of quantitative orientation leads to a sort of divine madness. So be it.

Saw an Arab boy incredibly delicate and fragile, wrists like thin brown sticks . . .

When you see Eddie Woods[60] give him my love and ask what he hears from Marker. I don't hear from him in six months.

Well I gotta get back to Interzone novel. Imshay Allah—God Willing—I complete Chapter II today and start on narrative chapters. I tell you, sifting through those letters and notes for usable

---

59. "Others may boast a single man to kill; / But I, the blood of thousands, daily spill. / Let petty Kings the names of Parties know; / Where e'er I come, I slay both friend and foe." From act 5 of *The Rehearsal* by George Villiers, the Second Duke of Buckingham (1628–1687). The play parodied contemporary heroic drama, including Dryden's *The Conquest of Granada by the Spaniards,* which the quoted lines, indirectly, echo.

60. Eddie Woods, Jr., whom Burroughs knew in Mexico in 1951, was then in the San Francisco Bay area.

material is a labor of Hercules. Two weeks I am hung up on this selection chapter. Every time I try to terminate it, another routine pounces on me. I will keep a sort of diary of my cure. I mean the above is my page for today. Maybe I should be a columnist yet. Sell me to a newspaper, Al. You're my agent.

Nov. 1, 1955
[Tangier]

Dear Jack & Al,

Arab Café: Sat down and had three words, just three long words, with Miss Green . . . Really I never knew That One to come on so wild anyplace else, I mean not with such wild kicks . . . I've known her to get more *physical* other places, but that was in another country and besides . . . Watching a glass of mint tea on a bamboo mat in the sun, the steam blown back into the glass top like smoke from a chimney. It seemed to have some special significance like an object spotted in a movie. I was thinking like a book you read which also has pictures and accompanying music. Of course couldn't approximate life itself which is seen, heard, felt, experienced on many different levels and dimensions . . . I didn't need Miss Green to tell me that, I mean what a *bore* she can be.

Some Arabs at a table. I am sitting there watching the cup of tea. It is unthinkable they should molest me. Suppose they do? And suddenly they have seized me, and preparing to castrate me? It can't happen . . . must be a dream . . . In Interzone it might or might not be a dream, and which way it falls might be in the balance while I watch this tea glass in the sun . . . The meaning of Interzone, its space-time location is at a point where three-dimensional fact merges into dream, and dreams erupt into the real world . . . ~~The very exaggeration of routines is intended to create this feeling.~~ In Interzone dreams can kill—Like Bangutot[61]—and solid objects and persons can be unreal as dreams . . . For example Lee could be in Interzone, after killing the two detectives, and for various dream reasons, neither the law nor The Others could touch him directly. Similarly, it looks easy to assassinate the Spanish Politico, but as The Boy told Lee: "It's not as easy as it looks. He's well protected . . ."

"You mean secret police . . ."

---

61. In "the market" section of *Naked Lunch:* "Bang-utot, literally 'attempting to get up and groaning . . .' Death occurring in the course of a nightmare . . . The condition occurs in males of S.E. Asiatic extraction . . ." (p. 71).

"Oh there will be secret police, of course . . . No I didn't imply you were stupid enough to need worry about *them* . . . What I mean is a very different kind of protection."

All letters off today. Will probably be sending along something every 5 days or so.

Love,
Bill

[*Nov.*] *2, 1955*
[Tangier]

Dear Jack and Allen,

Tanger is the prognostic pulse of the world, like a dream extending from past into the future, a frontier between dream and reality—the "reality" of both called into question.

No one here is what they seem on the surface. Take my last doctor, Dr. Appfel from Strasbourg. The best physician in Tanger; seems at first sight a typical European intellectual—(He asked me if I thought schedule feeding had any bearing on drug addiction. Real sharp you dig)—passes himself off as Anti-Nazi, Jewish refugee, says he is a doctor first, not a business man. Radiates high class Jewish honesty·. . . The first hint I get that all is not kosher with Appfel is in that other clinic where he come near killing me with his fucking cold turkey sleep cure . . . I gave him $4 and wrote out a telegram to send my parents asking for more money. Next day I asked if he sent the telegram and he said yes but did not bother to give me a receipt, that is he didn't bother for the good reason that there was no receipt. Dr Appfel never sent the telegram. He kept the money. It seemed so out of character I put it out of my mind, almost believing I had made a mistake . . . Then I began to notice other little things. Like his bill was out of line by about $30. I paid what I thought reasonable, and he never said any more about it. In short, he had simply given me a large bill hoping I would pay it and say nothing. Instead I said nothing and didn't pay it. I paid half . . . "God!" It hit me suddenly leaving his office. "An Arab trick! Ask outrageous price and settle for half!" Later I found out he was no Anti-Nazi refugee, but a Collaborator who got out of Strasbourg just ahead of the French Partisans . . . Withal, he is still the best physician in Tanger.

"Oh *him*," the gossip chorus says. "Notorious collaborator, my dear, *and* he's, well, *queer* for money."

So what does he do with the money. Addict? Uhuh, not with that careful, anal face, without a trace of oral impulsiveness. No junky, no lush he. Boys? No, the queens would have smelled him out, bitched him out years ago. But not the maddest gossip in Tanger, not even paranoid bitch on wheels Brion Gysin, ever said Appfel was queer. Women? Uh-uh. He looks like he "gets that over with" about once every two weeks. Besides, the chorus of Old Women in the Porte Tea Room cover that entrance.

There are two potentials. No. 1: He is a modern miser—He's not the type to fill a bathtub with gold coins and roll around on them naked—No, I mean a Security Miser who keeps his family on starvation rations—(funny, you can tell by looking at him he has no appreciation for food, would set a tasteless table)—has safe deposit boxes in Switzerland, Uruguay, New York, Sydney, and Santiago, containing assorted currency, gold, diamonds, heroin and antibiotics.

No. 2: He is a gambler. Now gambling is the one vice that does not thrive in Tanger. There is no casino, and the sub rosa joints are pretty tight. But I see him as gambling in Exchange, deals to buy Swedish Kronen with Abyssinian Turds in Hong Kong and re-sell in Uruguay . . . He keeps charts and tables and graphs and there is a ticker in his room, so he wakes up [in] the morning with the room full of tape, he fell asleep over his charts and forgot to shut it off again. In short, any gambling he did must be thoroughly anal. He's another character for my Interzone Hospital. The mad doctor Benway who is oral type (operating with a can opener and tin snips, massaging patient's heart with a vacuum cup, toilet cleaner:

"We croakers gotta have know-how and make-do," he explains to his appalled assistant.

Nurse: "I'm afraid she's gone, doctor."

Benway: Peeling off his gloves, "Well it's all in the day's work.").

And Dr. Anker who is insane oral exchange gambler, stealing gold fillings out of the patient's mouth on the operating table, and performing other acts of incredible meanness . . . This hospital has funeral rites in the patio, cremations, exposure to vultures, a cemetery adjoining. There is a Hospital Official who does nothing but console relatives, professional mourners and funeral impresarios hang about the entrance soliciting the patients and visitors . . . Now

I must stop writing *about* this novel, and start writing the novel itself. Of course these letters about what I intend to do, help to clarify my own mind . . .

A family of Europeans has moved in next to me bag and baggage. The old lady is having an operation, that is she has had it if you ask me, and her daughter has moved in with her to see she gets proper looked after. The two rooms share one wash basin in the hall. So the daughter empties her mother's piss in it, and beefs when I wash a jacked-off-in handkerchief. Imagine! God knows what or who they are. There are innumerable relatives, one of whom wears as glasses those gadgets jewellers use to look at diamonds. I think he's a diamond cutter on the skids. The man who fucked up the Throckmorton diamond and was drummed out of the Industry . . . Dope peddlers from Aleppo? Slunk traffickers from Buenos Aires? I.D.B.s (Illegal Diamond Buyers) from Johannesburg? Unethical Slave Traders from Italian Somaliland? Collaborators at the very least . . . [62] Like Appfel they are Jewish but not kosher. They've got that lamster look . . . And always beefing about my typewriter. You should dig the daughter. Hair dyed blonde, nice surface manners, and hard as a diamond drill.

So like I say, I will not be writing so many letters, but putting everything in Interzone novel. I've got 2 more pages of this letter in long-hand but *it must wait* . . .

Love,
Bill

---

62. Compare this passage with *Naked Lunch*, pp. 56–57, in the "black meat" section.

1956

Feb. 17, 1956
Tanger

Dear Allen,

The way things break lately it's like there was a vast, Kafkian conspiracy to prevent me from ever getting off junk. At the beginning of the month I almost had money to get to England. I wrote for more, asking them to cable it. Ten days later they cable me $100, but by then I am almost $100 in debt to the ex-Captain who lives next door—not only dishonest but impractical to leave without paying him. So I telegraph I need $100 more. That was a week ago, and no answer to my telegram. Meanwhile the $100 is half gone, there isn't another boat till the 20th, and by then this $100 is all gone, and even another $100 isn't enough to get me to England. I mean the way they feed me $ a little bit at a time, I never have enough to move. And then they say, "Money is so short now we want to be sure it isn't wasted," while doling it out in such a way I have no alternative but to waste it.

The shipment of dolophine arrived finally, but now is running low again. Not only do I have a habit, but a synthetic habit which is hardest to kick, most harmful to the health, and the least enjoyable. And I am never sure from one day to the next of my supply—though it is never cut off long enough for me to switch to codeine. All in all I have fallen into a state of chronic depression and hopelessness. All I can do is sit here day after day shivering and contracted over my stinking little kerosene stove waiting for money.

Trouble in Tangier lately. A friend of mine waylaid and stabbed in the back for no reason, not even robbery.[1] (In the lung. He will be all right.) The old Dutch pimp who runs the place where I used to live set upon by five Arabs and beaten to a pulp. An Argentinian queer severely beaten by a gang of youths. I will try to pick up a pistol some place. It's really getting to a point where you need one.

---

1. Burroughs' friend: the Canadian writer Christopher Wanklyn, a longtime resident of Morocco.

I am typing up one version of the Yage article in what I hope will be acceptable form. I will send this on to you together with the Tanger article which is completed and typed.

Terrible weather here. Cold and wet and windy.

Love,
Bill

Sun. Feb. 26, 1956
Tangers

Dear Allen,

Still in condition of biostasis, waiting on money to reach England. I will definitely get away when my $200 comes next week.

I just experienced indescribable, nightmare flash of physical helplessness: wherever I go and whatever I do, I am always in the straitjacket of junk, unable to move a finger to free myself, like I was paralyzed by an anaesthetic, and suddenly realized that my will had no power to move my body. I keep dozing off into dreams or structural presentations of thought.

President Eisenhower is a junkie, but can't take it directly because of his position, so he gets his junk kicks through me.[2] He doesn't have to be with me, but from time to time we have to make contact, and I recharge him. These contacts look, to the casual observer, like homosexual practices, but looking closer one observes that the excitement is not sexual, and the climax is the separation when the recharge is completed, not union or any counterfeit or symbol of union. The erect penises are brought in contact—at least we used that method in the beginning, but contact points wear out just like veins. Now I sometimes have to slip my penis under his left eyelid. Of course I can always give him an osmosis recharge—which corresponds to a skin shot—but that is admitting defeat. An O.R.—Osmosis Recharge—will put the President in a bad mood for weeks and might well result in Atomic Shambles. For the President pays a high price for the Oblique Habit. A whole spectrum of subjective horror, silent protoplasmic agonies, bone frenzies, is known only to the man with an Oblique Habit. Tensions build up, pure energy without emotional content finally tears through the body, throwing him about like a man in contact with high-tension wires. Sometimes, if his charge connection is cut off cold, the Oblique Addict falls into such violent, electric convulsions that his bones shake loose, and he dies with the skeleton straining

2. Compare the following routine with *Naked Lunch*, pp. 67–68, in the "black meat" section.

to climb out of his unendurable flesh. The Oblique Addict has sacrificed all control. He is helpless as a child in the womb.

The relation between an O.A. (Oblique Addict) and his R.C. (Recharge Connection—often jokingly referred to as his RX) is so intense that they can only endure each other's company for brief and infrequent intervals (I mean aside from the R.M.—Recharge Meets—when all personal contact is eclipsed by the recharge process).

Conversation piece. Two elegant pansies in excruciatingly chic apartment. John Hohnsbeen's dream apartment.[3]

P.1: (Bursting into the room), "My dear, you'll never guess what I've got . . . Lab reports just in . . . Leprosy!"

P.2: "How *Medieval* of you!"

P.1: "I'm having a black cloak designed by Antoine. Absolutely authentic. And I shall carry a bell . . ."

P.2: "Oh they'll most likely arrest you before anything really picturesque develops . . . Everything is curable these days . . . If only we could have a real, old, corny plague . . . You know, corpses sprawled sexily about the street . . . those *boy* corpses, dungarees tight over the basket, lying there so helpless, so *young* . . . For Gawd's sake, Myrtle bring a basin for me to drool in . . . And mixed with the smell of decay and death there was another smell seeping through the bolted doors, the shuttered windows: the sharp, acrid smell of fear . . . I suppose I'm a hopeless romantic . . ."

P.1: "One thing I do ask of you, of all my dear friends—God rot the silly bitches—leave us have no mealy-mouthed blather about 'Hansens Disease.' "[4]

Character for novel: rich, queer leper who is not supposed to frequent Turkish Baths or swimming pools. They keep a plainclothes man on him at all times, and he is always trying to shake his shadow so he can get to a Turkish Bath for "a spot of good, unclean fun." I think he's English but not sure yet. Can't see him good on account of the steam.

---

3. John Hohnsbeen: an art student when Burroughs knew him in New York, 1948. He shared a building with a group of Columbia intellectuals at Forty-fifth Street and Tenth Avenue.

4. Hansen's Disease: so called after Armauer Hansen, the Norwegian physician who, in 1868, identified the bacillus that caused leprosy.

"You've no idea the money I save," he says. "When I show the little beasts my card—all God's lepers got cards with their finger-prints, photograph, and number. I managed to wangle number 69. It took some doing—they generally bolt without even thinking about *fluss*."[5]

This letter is the only writing I have done in a week now. In the gray Limbo of junk I seem to depend on you as my only point of reference, in fact the only strong emotional contact I have left. Well, Imshah Allah (with Allah's endorsement) I will be out of this sneak preview of Hell by this time next week. Telegram from home that $200 is on the way. As soon as I get my hands on it, I take the next plane out of here.

Tanger. Monday, Feb. 27, 1956:

I expect my getaway money this week. Probably this afternoon or tomorrow. Then the plane for London. (There is a plane every morning that gets in London about 2 o'clock of the same afternoon.) So hold up any communications until I write you from England. I haven't heard from you in some weeks, and hope you are at the same address and receiving my letters. [. . .] Before I leave here I will send you the Tanger article, and one version of the Yage article which I am typing up as neatly and accurately as I can.

If I don't make it in England, I am coming back Stateside and give myself up in Lexington. I simply will not travel with this Chinaman any longer. Taking so much I keep going on the nod. Last night I woke up with someone squeezing my hand. It was my own other hand. Or I fall half asleep reading something and the words change or take on a curious dream significance as if I was reading code. Obsessed with codes lately. Like a man contracts a series of illnesses which spell out a message. Or he gets message from subsidiary personality by farting in Morse code. (Needless to say such obvious devices as automatic writing would never get by the Censor.)

I believe I wrote you the natives are getting uppity. [. . .] Time for some counter-terrorism, seems to me. The police are quite

---

5. *Fluss:* "money" in Arabic.

worthless, the Arab police now quite openly taking sides against Europeans or Americans in any *contretemps*. A number of queers got notes warning them to leave town, and signed "The Red Hand." (No note for me.) As usual Puritanism and Nationalism come on together in a most disagreeable mélange.

Degenerate spectacle: I just hit a vein (not easy these days. I don't got many veins left). So I kissed the vein, calling it "my sweet little needle sucker," and talked baby talk to it.

Did you read about the five missionaries killed by the Auca Indians in Ecuador? I'd like to try contacting the Auca. Nobody has succeeded in making contact with them. Might drop kegs of paregoric from a plane until they all got a habit. See myself surrounded by sick Auca: "You make medicine heap quick!" They found some films on the dead missionaries. You see they contacted one group of Auca and thought they were in. Their last radio message was: "A group of Auca we haven't seen before has just arrived." The pictures show them as a fine-looking people, completely naked. As for the missionaries, it's no loss. I've met them in S.A. and they are a perfect plague. Telling the Indians they shouldn't chew cocaine or take Yage or drink their home-made liquor, they should put on clothes. I mean all the old missionary crap. And such stupid, ignorant, ugly-looking people. I hate them. And they teach the Indians to sing their ugly, Protestant hymns. The father of one of the dead missionaries (they were all killed with spears, by the way, except one who was killed with one of the machetes they had given to the Indians) remarked rather enigmatically on learning of his son's death: "God doesn't make any mistakes."

That picture you sent of the cops in women's clothes, I had already seen in the local Spanish paper here. It has quite good news coverage, but like all Spanish papers, completely controlled by the Franco government, the virtues of which they are continually editorializing. Enclose a picture I drew. I just started doodling, with no idea as to what I intended to draw, and it just took shape and seems to have a sort of life, and I call it "The Blind Mouth." (When I was a child I thought you saw with your mouth. I remember distinctly my brother telling me no, with the eyes, and I closed my eyes and found out it was true and my theory was wrong.)

312

I still haven't written to Jack. Must do so.

Gag for Milton Berle: Feller say I reckon Christ got Mary's immaculate cherry on the way out.

Love,
Bill

March 14, 1956
[Tangier]

Dear Allen,

Just got your letter of Feb. 26. My father writes I should wait here until he makes arrangements with a sanitarium in England. I am inclined to go on and see if I can't arrange to get free treatment. (The thing to do nowadays is to get one's snout in the public trough.) I am only deterred by the possibility of being hung up in London *sans* junk and *sans* sanitarium. I know they license addicts in England, but don't know whether that applies to foreigners. There is an English doctor here who might be able to give me the info. Right off-hand it seems rather unlikely they would welcome alien junkies with open arms and immediate junk permits. But *quién sabe?* Trying to decide whether to go on now or wait, I have fallen into a sort of *folie de doute,* waiting for a sign to make up my mind. God knows I don't want my father to spend an unnecessary cent on the deal. It all comes out of my pocket one way or another. Also I want to get away from this horrible, synthetic shit.

I had not seen any of this material before. It was not in the first copy you sent me. I don't wonder the poem is causing a stir.[6] Like I say it seems to me definitely the best thing you have done as a sustained whole. The "I'm With You in Rockland" section excellent and very moving. I like especially the stanza that contains "starry spangled shock of mercy."

I just fell asleep for a moment and had a flash of dream: a policeman on a bicycle, screaming with shrill lust, following a boy down a long, dusty road in Mexico. In the distance is a river with trees growing along the banks, and on the other side of the river a town.

Moloch stanzas excellent. Where do they fit in exactly? Be sure to send me copy of the whole poem as soon as you get copy. It is finished now and ready for publication by Crazy Lights??[7] This

---

6. The poem was "Howl." The Rockland stanzas formed Part 3, Moloch Part 2.
7. Ferlinghetti's City Lights Books published *Howl and Other Poems* in the Pocket Poet Series that August.

poem is undoubtedly the best thing you have done; also, it seems to me, the end of one line of development. I am wondering where you will go from here.

Long dream about you last night. Seems we were in the Foreign Legion together, but the Legion seemed to be in Russia. I asked you how long we had been in, and you said: "A year and a half." And I groaned thinking of the three and a half years we still had to go . . .

I enclose some routines, and a slightly amended version of the Monster Birth routine, which might do for *Black Mountain*.[8] I think maybe a routine and the Yage Dream, including Meet Café, might be better. Say The Baboon Huntsmen routine and the Yage Dream. But do whatever you think best. Perhaps the first chapter of Interzone . . . Please, Allen, you decide. Well I want to get this in the mail,

Love,
Bill

8. *Black Mountain Review*, no. 7, published material under the title "From *Naked Lunch*, Book III: In Search of Yage," and under the pseudonym William Lee. Although this was the Autumn 1957 issue, it did not appear until spring 1958.

April 16, 1956
Tanger

Dear Allen,

At last I have travelling orders. I move out Tuesday to contact a Doctor MacClay in London, one of those incredibly English addresses—Queen's Gate Place. So it looks like I will see some action at last. Just after I wrote you, I received $500 from my father to clean up debts and go to England. And there is plenty medicine in the *farmacias,* so I can make a comfortable, leisurely exit, and not hitting the town sick with $10 capital.

Perhaps all the delay and the failures of the past two years were necessary to show me exactly how nowhere junk is, and I can't use it if I want to do anything else. And no more of this "one shot" routine. In a word no more junk any kind ever.

[. . .] I have nothing of interest to say, just want to let you know I am on my way at last. Want to get this in mail before I leave,

Love,
Bill

Write to this address:
May 8, 1956
44 Egerton Gardens
London S.W.3
England

Dear Allen,

I still feel terrible. Sleep maybe 1, 2 hours at dawn. I can walk for miles and come in stumbling with fatigue but I can't sleep. The thought of sex with anyone gives me the horrors . . . Last night went to a ghastly queer party where I was pawed and propositioned by a 50-year-old, Liberal M.P. I told him: "I couldn't sleep with Ganymede now, let alone you."[9]

There has been no backsliding. No codeine, no paregoric, no nothing. Not even a sleeping pill. This time I'll make it if it kills me.

Where are you and what are you doing and when are you coming to Europe? I am torn to pieces with restlessness. The Amazon expedition is becoming an obsession with me. Of course I could easily kill a few months in Spain, Italy, and Tanger. But please let me know what the exact score is with you.

Do you have Seymour Wyse's address or any London addresses?[10] If so please send along. Did you send the Wyn money to Tanger?

The cure itself was awful. From 30 grains of M per day to 0 in 7 days. But I had a real croaker, interested in Yage, Mayan archaeology, every conceivable subject, and would often come to see me at 2 A.M. and stay till 5 since he knew I couldn't sleep.[11] Please write.

Love,
Bill.

---

9. See letter of December 8, 1957.
10. Seymour Wyse, who went to Horace Mann School with Kerouac, 1940, and was a figure in the jazz scene, then running a music shop in London.
11. The "croaker" was Dr. John Yerbury Dent, author of *Anxiety and Its Treatment* (London: John Murray, 1941; 1947, 1955) and a pioneer in the use of apomorphine to treat addiction.

May 15, 1956
44 Egerton Gardens
London S.W.3

Dear Allen,

Just received your long letter. This should reach you in plenty of time.

I am amazed and delighted to hear of your fabulous job.[12] Would God I could get one. May try the U.S. construction companies in Spain. Publishing news is good. I have given up the idea of making money from my writing so I'm not concerned about that. Creeley can publish anything he wants for any amount or nothing.[13] Like I say, I don't care about the gelt angle.

I am completely recovered now, very active, able to drink. Still no interest in sex. I am physically able you dig, just not innarested. When I look at a boy nothing happens. Ratty lot of boys they got here anyhoo. Maybe when I come around to it, I want women. Maybe. London drags me like a sea anchor. I want to see bright blue sky with vultures in it. A vulture in London would be an Addams cartoon. But I won't leave until I dig what's here. Dropped Seymour [Wyse] a line. Hope to see him. Don't worry about chipping. I know the score now. I can't take one shot or paregoric or codeine or demerol or junk in any form. Not now or ever. If I ever have to take some for intense pain, the withdrawal syndrome can be headed off with several injections of Apomorphine. The doctor has given me 3 tubes of apomorphine to keep with me at all times. Addiction to apomorphine is impossible. It's nothing you take for kicks.

During early withdrawal vivid nightmares when I could sleep. Sample:[14] North Africa, ten (?) years from now. A vast rubbish heap. Blue sky and hot sun. Smell of hunger and death. Smoke of petrol fires in the distance. Dave Lamont walking beside me car-

---

12. In May, Ginsberg had joined the USNS *Pvt. Joseph F. Merrell* as a yeoman-storekeeper with a yearly salary of $5,040.
13. The poet Robert Creeley was then editing *Black Mountain Review*.
14. Compare the following passage with *Naked Lunch*, p. 234, in the "atrophied preface" section.

rying a can of gasoline. He is actually 26. In the dream he looks sixty, any age, and I know I look the same. We meet five Arabs. I see the eyes of the Arab in front and say to Dave: "Throw the petrol on them and light it! It's our only chance." Two Arabs down, covered with burning petrol (petrol is English word for gasoline, *not kerosene*. I got in habit of using it). Other Arabs running up. We won't make it. My leg is covered with petrol. My leg is part of the dump heap. When I try to move it, broken bottles and tin cans and rusty wire cut into the flesh. Someone screaming in my ear.

One of a series of dreams in which I am a minority in a vast, hostile country. Finally comparative security through Public Works, complicated locks and channels and harbors and markets all synchronized with physiological calendars. In short, the Natives can't use the Works without us. If they could understand the Works, they would not be hostile. Some day they will maybe. But that's hundreds of years away now. Now they must use the Works and put up with us or die. An extremist party wants to destroy the Works, and kill us, even if they do die. The Natives and The Work Guards (who form a separate power group) keep the extremists in line. Burning them to death when they catch them.

I just got letter from friend in Tanger. Another Arab ran Amok and cut up six Europeans. Curious fact is this: The Arabs put the snatch on him and were getting ready to burn him alive when the police intervened.

I can't tell you how glad I am that you are coming around to accept your Harlem experience, rejecting Trilling etc. I have felt for years that this is right for you.

I can't write any more now. I am still very restless and it is a great trouble to sit down and write anything.

Love,
Bill

June 18, 1956
Venice

Dear Allen,

I wrote twice to your ship address.[15] Hope the FBI didn't intercept. I'll say it again. London is about the most God-awful place I was ever in. Barker is a bore.[16] I never want to see England again except maybe Doc Elks on business and Dr. Dent. Seymour [Wyse] stood me up three times. He should look me up somewhere, sometime, and I'll do as much for him. I did give Barker your MS., but did not see him again to get reaction.

Venice is perhaps the greatest place I ever see. Such a cornucopia of available young ass. I mean, too much. Since the cure I been sexy as an eighteen-year-old and healthy as a rat. Row or operate gondola for 2 or three hours every day. Also swim. Rest of the time chasing after the *ragazzis*. Difficult to get any work done here. However I am planning a nightmare tour of Europe entitled THE GRAND TOUR—(HELL IS WHERE YOUR ASS IS), of which I enclose beginning of Scandinavian chapter. This was inspired by a Swede I met at party, a cured alcoholic who told me in Sweden drug addicts are chained—chained yet—to the bed and left there until cured—or dead. I begin to suspect that all is not well behind that hygienic Scandinavian facade.

Alan is writing you. Incidentally I got country drunk in Peggy Guggenheim's palazzo, in consequence forever banished from her premises.[17] In fact I have managed to alienate quite a number of people by my drunken behavior which can, I realize, be rather difficult to take. Well, I'm not a bit alarmed about that. One thing

---

15. Possibly refers to a new ship, the USNS *Sgt. Jack J. Pendleton*, that Ginsberg joined at about this time, and which would take him to the Arctic Circle via several West Coast ports.

16. George Barker, the English poet, whom T. S. Eliot had published with Faber & Faber in the 1930s. He disapproved of the Beat writers.

17. At a cocktail party for the British consul, Ansen had told a very drunk Burroughs that it was customary to greet Guggenheim by kissing her hand. Guggenheim overheard Burroughs' reply: "I will be glad to kiss her cunt if that is the custom."

is sure, I'm really off the junk now, but would like to pick up on some weed. They got like a connection in Padua, an old bitch in a tenement that sells black market cigarettes. Looks like set for Italian movie or [John] Horne Burns novel.

Interesting about your mother's improvement.[18] I have thought a great deal about Schizophrenia (S in the trade).[19] Convinced that it is as much a disease of disturbed metabolism as diabetes. In my opinion psychological treatment is not only worthless but absolutely contra-indicated, certainly while the disease process is in operation. I have revised my earlier theory which I outlined to you (anxiety produces adrenalin which produces histamine, both H and A break down into the S substance—recently isolated from the blood of S's—which in turn produces more H and A). The S substance must be produced by the body for an excellent biological reason, perhaps to *counteract* the metabolic products of anxiety. Now I have frequently observed that there are no psychotic junkies, at least not when on the junk. (Patient of Dent who was in nut house for alcoholism complicated by psychosis—undiagnosed. He was violent and hallucinating. So they gave him morphine, he became addicted and was discharged from the hospital cured of alcoholism and psychosis, but on the junk. Then some croaker gave him demerol to get him off morphine and he came to Dr. Dent with a demerol habit—one of the worst if you ask me, and I'm the man who should know—So Dent makes with the apomorphine treatment (note apomorphine as back-brain stimulant and general regulator of disturbed metabolism), and when I meet this character he is fully dressed and in his right mind, cured of demerol, alcoholism and psychosis.) Now fix yourself on this: the terminal state of addiction is quite similar to the terminal state of S. Complete destruction of affect, withdrawal etc. I used to spend six hours looking at my shoe. Seymour knows heroin addict who spends his whole life in bed, even shits there when he shits if he shits. But here is crucial difference between deteriorated S and terminal addict (by a terminal addict I mean one who gets all he wants). The T.A. will get up off his piles on the double if his junk is cut. With suitable

18. In fact, Naomi Ginsberg had died on June 9, 1956.
19. Burroughs spells the term "Psyzophrenia," and uses the initial "P."

withdrawal treatment he will be his normal pre-junk self in a month. His sickness *is* H. Possibly S is quite similar. If the body produced its own H until tolerance and withdrawal syndrome was established and then continued to produce it to prevent withdrawal syndrome, we would have analogy of S process as I tentatively see it. So I say give S's H for some months until addiction is established, then a withdrawal treatment with apomorphine. If that doesn't work, try giving LSD—S sub.—and maybe the body getting it from outside will stop producing, and the S substance can be withdrawn like junk. I tell you, with a free hand I could get all the S's out on the street collecting unemployment compensation.

The family is making tiresome sounds like things are tough and I should get a job. Investigating possibilities of work in Spain and Casablanca. *A ver.* I had letter from Jack. I will write him presently. The $70 went to London, but will be forwarded here.

P.S. I am 42 but feel like eighteen. Also act that way.

Will send first chapter of HELL IS WHERE YOUR ASS IS later. Enclose instead latest routine.

Address: c/o U.S. Consulate

Venice, Italy.

S is probably a drug psychosis, the drug being produced by the body.

I always told you Trilling was a shit.

July 26, 1956
Venice
Cargo U.S. Consulate

Dear Bill,

After taking the cure for my drug habit in London, I am staying with Alan Ansen in Venice. This time there will be no relapse.

My plans are extremely fluid. Financial reverses force me to consider possibilities of employment (my novels are grown un-publishably obscene). I am prepared to accept any job from bank president to lavatory attendant outside the U.S.A. But lavatory attendant sinecures are hard to come by these days. I got several irons in the fire: deal to manage a delicatessen in Casablanca, start a haberdashery in Abyssinia, collaborate on a pharmacology of narcotic drugs in London, construction projects in Spain, teaching school in Pakistan. And there is always the possibility of finding a live one to finance Amazon expeditions I have in prospect. Ten-tatively, I will be here until about the 15th of next month, then proceed to Vienna for a few weeks, then South through Italy to Libya—Tripoli—arriving there middle Sept. Spend winter in Libya. On the other hand, if I get a green light from Casa may leave immediately and be in Tanger to welcome you.

Tanger loses its international status as of Oct. 1.[20] You should not miss seeing it before then. If I am not there proceed to the Socco Chico and ask for Tony Reithorst. He can fix you up with the young amenities. A friend of mine, name of Dave Woolman, is still in Tanger. Hotel Muniria—a good place for you to stay. Anything goes there. And cheap. If the Hotel Muniria is not existing now—many changes in past few months—you will always find Dave, Tony, and anybody else who is hanging on, in the Café Central, Socco Chico. Ask the waiters or anybody looks like he speaks English. It's an informal place. You can't miss. Tanger is extremely cheap. You should pay less than one dollar for your hotel. Excellent meals from sixty cents. Visit the Mar Chica after 12 pm.

Venice is real great, but not cheap, no work here. Besides it's

---

20. The international zone of Tangier was actually abolished on October 29, 1956.

not exactly for me. There is something unreal about the place. It lacks depth, nuance and horror. Mexico City, Tanger more my sort of thing. Please write me what your plans are, how long you will stay in Europe etc. I am sure we can arrange to connect some place.

As Ever,
Bill

P.S. Do you know Ilse's present address?[21] I was unable to locate her the last time I was in New York, thought maybe she is back in Europe. If so would like to contact her.

[. . .]

Alan sends his regards.

---

21. Ilse Herzfeld Klapper, Burroughs' first wife.

Sept. 16, 1956
Tanger, Morocco

Dear Allen,

Just got your letter so will expect you and entourage January. 'Tis I'll be here in sunshine or in shadow like the song say (unless they are giving me the hard toe).[22] There is no town like Tanger town. The place relaxes me so I am subject to dissolve. I can spend three hours looking at the bay with my mouth open like a Kentucky Mountain Boy. Man, I don't *need* junk. Speaking of which, I never feel the slightest temptation. I think junkies relapse because they are not *metabolically* cured by the usual methods of treatment. Dent's apomorphine method could dispose of the whole problem.

This you gotta hear: There is a Holy Man around town who tells fortunes in his spare time from being a Holy Man. So an English woman consults the old fuck and he tells her: "Lady, you want to get my potent virtue from the living source," hauling out the living source. "Lunch on it, sister, and do yourself some good. I'm giving you the chance extraordinary." The routines some citizens put down.

I never been so horny in my life as right lately. Like yesterday I had two hour set-to with Nimún, my latest heart-throb—that's a way of putting it. So today I should be thinking about higher things. So what I do all afternoon? Lounge about in my wine-colored, Czechoslovakian Poplin pajamas devising Rube Goldberg sex contraptions: like an ingenious assortment of rocking chairs and sofas that rock back and forth and sideways, not to mention Ma Lee's Special: the rocking swivel chair guaranteed to run up casualties among the Saturday night lush trade; vibrating mattresses, innaresting hammocks, facilities in scenic railways and stunting planes; currently working on an arrangement involving aqualungs and a blood-temperature swimming pool with artificial waves.

Spot of landlady bother. She tells me to slack off on the Arab visitors. So me and Dave [Woolman], the Walter Winchell of Tan-

---

22. The song: "Oh Danny Boy."

ger, have found us the original anything goes joint.[23] Run by 2 retired junky whores from Saigon. On the ground floor will be Dave, myself, and Eric [Gifford] the Public School Man (Eton '26), who conspired with a male hustler to forge a stolen traveller check. The boy brought the deal to me first and I told him, "I should felonize myself for $25?? What you think I am, a crook? Take that business to Eric." So they got by with it I hope. You never know. The mills of American Express grind slow but they grind exceeding fine. One of these days a man in a grey flannel suit (the bastards come on elegant these days, making so much money) is likely to tap Eric on the shoulder and say: "Are you Eric Trevor-Orme-Smith-Creighton also known as 'El Chinche' (The Bed Bug)?" Anyhoo we three occupy the ground floor with our rooms opening on the garden and have a private entrance: "You can be *free* here, you understand?" the old whore says to me, digging me in the ribs. The houseboy is a Spanish queer, good-looking in a depraved sort of way. I don't often use the word, but no other word gets this job done: that boy has one of the most degenerate faces I ever saw. When you hear one of the whores screaming "Joselito! Joselito!" you know Joselito is laying one of the clients again. Eric throws a fuck into him when he gets caught short. So it's like a goodly crowd is there you might say.

A strange thing happened this morning. I was doing my special abdominal exercises I learned from a citizen named Hornibrook in London who learned them from the Fiji Islanders near as I can make out. So suddenly a wave of sex come over me and I have a spontaneous orgasm stap my vitals. Now a spontaneous, waking orgasm is a rare occurrence even in adolescence. Only one I ever experienced before was in the orgone accumulator I made in Texas. And another thing. I find my eyes straying towards the fair sex. (It's the new frisson, dearie . . . Women are downright piquant.) You hear about these old characters find out they are queer at fifty, maybe I'm about to make with the switcheroo. What are these strange feelings that come over me when I look at a young cunt's little tits sticking out so cute? Could it be that?? No! No! He thrust the thought from him in horror. He stumbled out into the street with the girl's mock-

23. The Hotel Mouniria, at 1, calle Magallanes.

ing laughter lingering in his ears, laughter that seemed to say, "Who you think you're kidding with the queer act? I know you, baby." Well it is as Allah wills . . .

I am writing now a straight continuation of Interzone. If you are going to be around a bit I will send along the second chapter when I get it finished which will be very soon. Maybe I can publish with Obelisk Press in Paris.[24] Alan didn't say anything to me about this deal to publish *Naked Lunch* in Paris. Well, *a ver, a ver*. If you have copy of *Times* article on *Howl,* I would love to see it. What issue? We get it here eventually in the American Library.[25]

My best to Jack, Neal, Corso. I will write Jack in Mexico.

They got like half-assed gondolas I row around every day. Physical exercise, the contracting and relaxing of muscles, is for me an exquisite sensual pleasure. So many things give me pleasure, walking around town, sitting in a café. I have no compulsion to write or to do anything except when I am possessed by routines, which can happen any time. A lot of the time I just sit blank and narcotized letting sensations flow through me. I have a feeling that I might turn into somebody else, that I am losing my outlines. A curious illusion I get lately when I am a little lushed and swing on Miss Green's unnatural tit, I feel that there is another person present. I mean like the last time I laid Ahmed—He is being the most "sincere" (advertising agency argot for somebody all out on the make) male hustler in Greater Tanger and is sensational, uninhibited sex. The things that boy thinks up to do—So I feel there is like a Third Man in the room. Not disapproving or anything. Just there. At times I feel myself on the verge of something incredible, like I will meet myself on the way out. This extra person kick has happened several times. And I don't really need Miss Green any more.

The English boy was talking about suicide, life not worth living.

24. Obelisk Press: Burroughs meant Olympia Press, set up in 1953 by Maurice Girodias, the son of Jack Kahane who had run Obelisk before the war. Both Parisian presses were committed to publishing English-language authors, such as Henry Miller and Lawrence Durrell, whose work was considered too explicit for mainstream publishers.

25. On September 2, 1956, the *New York Times* featured a major article by Richard Eberhart, entitled "West Coast Rhythms," that focused favorably on Ginsberg's "Howl."

This seems incredible to me. I think I must be very happy. I got like a Revelation but can't verbalize it. Let me know when you are going etc.

                                        Love,
                                        Bill

P.S. Address Cargo U.S. Consulate
     Tanger, Morocco.
     The Legation has moved to Rabat.[26]

---

26. When the American legation moved to Rabat in June 1956 and was upgraded to embassy status, the United States retained only a diplomatic agent in Tangier. Later a new American consulate was built.

Oct. 13, 1956
[Tangier]

Dear Allen,

I don't see our roles reversed exactly but expanded and altered on both sides. I have entered a period of change more drastic than adolescence or early childhood. I live in a constant state of routine. I am getting so far out one day I won't come back at all. I can't take time to go into all my mystic experiences which I have whenever I walk out the door. There is something special about Tanger. It is the only place when I am there I don't want to be any place else. No stasis horrors here. And the beauty of this town that consists in changing combinations. Venice is beautiful, but it never changes. It is a dream congealed in stone. And it is someone else's dream. The final effect is to me nightmarish—Example: sky supersonic, orgone blue, warm wind, a stone stairway leading up to the Old Town. Coming down the stairs a very dark Arab boy with a light purple shirt.

I get average of ten very attractive propositions a day. My latest number is Spanish, 16, with a smile that hits you right in the nuts. I mean that pure, uncut boy stuff, that young male innocence . . . American boys are not innocent because they lack experience. Innocence is inseparable from depravity . . . You can lay him when you get here. Everyone else has . . . That child innocence, but what technique and virtuosity. Oh la la. Now I got myself agitated. Must have him today instead of tomorrow. Incidentally, the one reason I get so many propositions is I am being the most eligible queer in Greater Tanger. Everyone knows how generous I was with Kiki. And I got a rep for being a perfect gentleman in every sense of the word.

I work when I can sit still long enough or when I get time out from fucking. Actually Interzone has taken complete shape. If I only had a tape recorder I could finish it in a month. Enclose selections which will indicate where I am. Finale is they set off a new atom bomb at the Fourth of July celebration and destroy the world . . . Getting quite friendly with Paul Bowles. He is really a charming person . . . New quarters are superb. My room opens onto a garden. No maids to bother me. A private entrance on a quiet street . . . I don't see how anyone could be happier than I am right now. I mean this is it. I am not saving myself for anything. I hope to God I don't have to leave Tanger. Of course the South of Spain is terrific. They are all Republicans, even the fuzz . . . The old folks sit in the kitchen drinking wine while you lay their boy in the bedroom. Nice, informal atmosphere, you dig . . . I mean I won't exactly be withering on the vine if I do have to leave. But Tanger is my dream town. I did have a dream ten years ago of coming into a harbor and knowing that this was the place where I desired to be . . . Just the other day, rowing around in the harbor I recognised it as my dream bay.[27]

I wish you would come on here before you fritter away your loot. By all means bring Jack and Peter [Orlovsky]. I assure you I will not be jealous. In fact jealousy is one of the emotions of which I am no longer capable . . . Self-pity is also impossible for me. You know what is wrong with it? Self-pity is a symptom of a divided ego, split into a pitied and a pitier. If your ego is intact you *can't* pity yourself. I discovered this in a state of complete despair a few days ago . . . I woke up one morning to find that my ass and environs was a bright purple red color—overtook by my nemesis you might say . . . So after a session with medical books in the Red Cross, I was *convinced* I had that awful virus venereal disease —Lymphogranuloma—where your ass turns purple and seals up, only deigning to emit an occasional purulent discharge . . . [28] I went home and dosed myself with antibiotics—that disease is difficult to cure though Aureomycin has proved effective in some cases. Then I began to cry and roll around biting my knuckles in complete despair. Despair unifies the ego. Self-pity is impossible. Did you know that tears rid the body of poisonous wastes like sweat or urine? In jaundice your tears are bright yellow. In short, grief or despair causes metabolic poisons to accumulate. The old idea that someone who is greatly afflicted must cry or die has a sound met-

27. By an odd coincidence, Paul Bowles attributed his residence in Tangier to a dream of the city he had at about the same time as Burroughs suggests he had his own dream. See Bowles's autobiography, *Without Stopping* (New York: Putnam's, 1972), p. 274.
28. Compare *Naked Lunch*, pp. 41–42, in the "Benway" section.

abolic basis. Anyhoo I never seen anyone take on the way I did for hours and hours, repeating over and over "Take it away. Take it away." So the next day I go to the doctor, he takes a look and purses his lips and says: "Yes you have rather a severe case of ringworm . . . athletes foot . . ." Then he looked at me over his glasses and smiles discreetly. "And there seems to have been a certain amount of uh chafing."

So I used Mycoctin [sic] and my ass is no longer purple. Seems to me I got my despair revelations at bargain basement price. I mean the self-pity insight was only one angle. Another was I found out how emphatically I disapprove of stealing or any criminal activities. I mean criminal not illegal, whether performed by criminals or by police or by anybody. That is crimes against property and person of others. Brain-washing, thought control, etc., is the vilest form of crime against the person of another. There is no greater disaster than the confusion of ethics and legality. It is the curse of the Western World, the substitution of law—that is, force—for instinctive feeling for others. Once this is done, on the one hand anything legal is right and such monstrosities as Nazism and Communism are loosed on the world; on the other hand anything you can get by with is all right too, which is the lesser, because self-limiting, evil of ordinary criminality. Only America could have set up such a perversion as the concept that the good are dull and the wicked charming. Al Capp says: "Good is better than evil because it is nicer."[29] I say it's better because it's more interesting. Evil is dull, about as glamorous as a cancer. And evil men are dull—as I am sure Himmler was dull. But I doubt if I could ever have learned this in the States. And I used to admire gangsters. Good God. I remember seeing in the paper those gangsters who conspired to throw acid in Reisel's [sic] face and thinking quite spontaneously, "What a bunch of shits they are."[30]

Well I was never one to beat around inna bush. I mean enough of this silly lovemaking, take off your clothes . . . Al, I am a fucking saint, that is I been fucked by the Holy Ghost and knocked up with

---

29. Al Capp: American cartoonist who created "Li'l Abner."
30. Victor Riesel was a New York labor columnist who exposed organized crime inside the unions, and was attacked and blinded as a result.

the Immaculate Woid . . . I'm the third coming, me, and don't know if I can do it again . . . So stand by for the Revelation . . .[31]

Christ? That cheap mountebank, that bush-leaguer. You think I'd demean myself to commit a miracle? That's what Christ shoulda said onna cross when the citizens said, "Make with a miracle and save your own ass." He shoulda said, "I wouldn't demean myself. The show must go on." He always was one to miss a cue . . .

I recall when we was doing an Impersonation act in Sodom and that is one cheap town. Strictly from hunger. Well this citizen, this fuckin' Philistine who wandered in from Podunk Baal or some place, calls me a fuckin' fruit right onna floor . . . And I said to him, "Three thousand years in show business and I always keep my nose clean . . . Besides I don't hafta take any shit off any uncircumcised cock sucker." Like I say, miracles is the cheapest trick inna industry. Some people got no class to them. That one shoulda stood in carny. "Step right up Marks and Marquesses and bring the little Marks too, good for young and old, man and beast, the one and only legit Son Of Man will cure a young boy's clap with one hand—by contact alone folks—create marijuana with the other whilst walking on water and squirtin' wine out his ass . . . Now don't crowd too close. You are subject to be irradiated by the sheer charge of this character . . ."

Buddha? A notorious metabolic junky. Makes his own you dig. In India, where they got no sense of time, The Man is often a month late. "Now let me see, is that the second or third monsoon? I got like a meet in Ketchupore about more or less."

So you dig these junkies settin' around in the lotus posture waitin' on the Man.

So Buddha says: "I don't hafta take this sound. I'll by God metabolize my own junk."

"Man, you can't do that. The revenooers will swarm all over you."

"No they won't. I got a gimmick, see? I'm a fuckin' Holy Man as of now on out."

"Jeez, Boss, what an angle."

---

31. A version of the following appears, introduced as "The Prophet's Hour," in *Naked Lunch*, pp. 113–16, in the "market" section.

"Now some citizens when they make with the New Religion really wig . . . No class to them. Besides they is subject to be lynched because who wants somebody hanging around being better'n other folks? 'What you want to do, Jack, give people a bad time?' So we gotta play it cool, you dig, cool . . . We got a take-it-or-leave-it proposition here folks. We aren't shoving anything up your soul, unlike certain cheap characters who shall be nameless and are nowhere. These frantic citizens don't know how to come on."

Mohammed? Are you kiddin'? He was dreamed up by the Mecca Chamber of Commerce. An Egyptian ad man onna skids from the sauce wrote the continuity . . .

"I'll have one more, Gus. Then I'll by God go home and receive a Surah. Wait till the morning edition hits the Souks. I'm blasting Amalgamated wide open."

"Give 'em Hell, Kid, I'm in your corner."

"Gus, when the roll is called up yonder you'll be there if I hafta louse up the universe . . . I won't forget you Gussie. I won't forget what you done for me . . ."

"*Wait* a minute . . . Wait a *minute*. That'll be ten clams . . . in cash."

Confucius . . . Who he?

Lao Tze . . . They scratch him already . . .

So now we got the place cleaned up a bit, I'm gonna make with the Living Word . . .

Everybody in this fuckin' curved universe and anybody say it's not curved is blaspheming The Immaculate Fact and the first prophet of Fact, Einstein—one of my stooges you dig . . . Everybody and everything is in this universe together. If one explodes we all explode. That Thermodynamic drag brings everybody down . . . Fuck your nabor. He may like it. And I want you fellows to control your most basest instinct which is the yen to control, coerce, violate, invade, annihilate, by any means whatsoever, anybody else's physical or psychical person . . . Anybody wants to go climb into someone else and take over is no better than a fuckin' control addict. He should kick his noisome habit instead of skulking around with his bare ass hanging out lousing up the universe. Be it known that such nameless ass holes will suffer a painful doom.

And remember, when the control yen rips through your bones like a great black wind, you have connected for Pure Evil . . . Not the glamorous bitch, but the cancerous, rotting Drag who says, "I have nothing to offer but my sores." So when you feel that yen, brother, and everybody in the industry must feel it, and say "How can I make it without the stuff?" I say open The Door and the whole universe will rush in with The Immaculate Fix . . . and you will look The Man straight in his disks—power pushers don't need eyes—and say, "Gimpy take up thy shit and walk.[32] Go on the nod and dream of a square universe. I stand with THE FACTS."

I mean enough of these gooey Saints with that look of pathic dismay as if they were being fucked and pretending not to pay it any mind. He who denies himself will shit sure deny others. Leave us have no more square saints . . . Get a typewriter whyncha? This letter is like a Mayan codice. Neither of you write good anyhoo. It reads like the Drunken Newscaster . . . [33] Remember? . . . At last a sentence I can read . . .

Yes Peter, I live on a hill overlooking the bay in the most beautiful city in the world or at least it's always young and fair to me . . . You got cockroaches. Well I wake up this morning with rat shit on my sheets . . . I am subject to be took advantage of by rats . . . When I lived in the other house I usta get my exercise killing rats with a cane in the patio . . . the bastards eat babies you dig, so I put them to the sword or whatever . . . No compromise with the unbelieving pricks. Now I haven't issued a Surah on cockroaches yet since there are none here. You boys will just have to piece out the odds without a, you know, The Last Word on roaches . . . Want to talk to you about the nut house, schizophrenia being like one of my hobbies you might say, and I got theories about it like I got about most everything. Don't be responsible

---

32. Gimpy: someone who is lame, needing a "gimp stick."
33. "Fade-out to a New York recording studio, 1953 . . . Jerry Newman played me a tape called *The Drunken Newscaster,* made by scrambling news broadcasts. I cannot recall the words at this distance but I remember laughing until I fell on the floor." (Burroughs, *The Third Mind,* p. 89.) In 1944, Newman's style of comic cuts had inspired the alternative title *And the Hippos Were Boiled in Their Tanks* for the novel Burroughs and Kerouac wrote together. Now it fitted the fragmentary routines Burroughs was writing. Later it would coincide with his cut-up methods.

Peter . . . That sentence sounds like you was applying for a position
. . . You know the routines citizens put down, like, "I am a young
man with clean habits. I don't juice and I don't mainline" . . . If
what's on my mind is on your mind you must be kid simple. If
so, you are coming to the right place. Now look here, don't worry
about my sensitiveness. There'll be no Indian rope trick put down.
Nobody disappears in Tanger. Now look I feel a Surah coming on
the subject of roaches . . . I mean you gotta draw the line someplace.
Like I should go around with a purple ass I don't want to kill them
cute little ringworms already. They has committed an unspeakable
crime in violating my person without so much as a by your leave
. . . Germs got no class to them. And the evilest of them all are
the virus . . . So bone lazy they aren't even hardly alive yet. Fuckin'
transitional bastards . . . So I say cockroaches can live for all I care
but not in my quarters. I didn't send for no cockroaches. They is
invading my privacy and I by God won't stand still for it. The
prophet has yacked . . . I'm off to this restaurant where all
the waiters and the cook are Arabian Fruits who keep feeling up
the clientele. Sign over the bar: "Employee must wash hands after
goosing the clients."

Enclose samples of Interzone. This is first rough draft. I have
written about fifty pages . . . A boy last night and another this
noon . . . I am declaring a two day sex Lent,

Bless you My Children
Love from
Pop Lee Your Friendly Prophet
Bill

DON'T GO TO MEXICO . . . COME RIGHT HERE RIGHT
NOW WHILE YOU HAVE THE LOOT. TANGER IS THE
PLACE. WHY WAIT . . . ???[34]

---

34. Ginsberg, Corso, and Peter and Lafcadio Orlovsky were planning to visit
Kerouac, who had been in Mexico City since late September. They arrived in
early November.

Oct. 29, 1956
Tanger

Dear Allen,

Pick out whatever you like for *Cambridge Review,* and bring MS. with you when you come. I really got the juice up on Interzone and it will be finished by Xmas. I am working at least four hours a day. Possible finale: Anal technician pulls the switch that blows up the world: "They'll hear this fart on Jupiter."

This town really has the *jihad* jitters—*jihad* means the wholesale slaughter by every Moslem of every unbeliever. Yesterday I am sitting in the Socco and suddenly people start running and all the shop-keepers are slamming down the steel shutters of their shops —I plan to market an automatic shop closer whereby you press a button and your shutter falls like a guillotine—and everybody in the cafés drops their drink and leaps inside and the waiters are closing the doors. So at this point about thirty little children carrying the Moroccan flag troop through the Socco . . . A few days ago we had a general strike.[35] Everything closed, restaurants, drug stores, no cars allowed on the street. About four pm. I am out with my Spanish kid trying to score for a bottle of cognac, and everybody says, "No! Go away! Don't you know there's a strike on?" and slams the door. About this time such a racket breaks out like I never hear and I can see thousands of Arabs marching down the Boulevard yelling. So I cut by police headquarters, where about a hundred young Arabs are yelling at the cops, who have barricaded themselves inside. What had happened, this idiot Frenchman climbed into a tree and harangued the crowd: "How dare you say anything against La France." Fortunately, the police succeeded in rescuing him, and they had him locked in the station. On the Boulevard I dig about 20,000 Arabs, mostly teenagers, yelling, *"Fuera Français!"* ("Out with the French!") and jumping around and laughing . . . So nothing happened. Tell Jack not to worry about a thing.

---

35. On October 23, 1956, the Moroccan Traders Union syndicate called a sympathy strike to protest at recent French actions in Algeria. There was no violence in Tangier itself.

As to my house, it is one room and one bed generally cluttered up with Spanish boys. The sexual mores here unlike anything you can imagine. So long as I go with Spanish boys, it is like having a girl in the U.S. I mean you feel yourself at one with the society. No one disapproves or says anything. Whereas to walk around town with an Arab boy would be unthinkable at this point. You would be insulted, stared at, spit at, and the boy would be subject to reprisals. You dig no one cares what the unbelievers do among themselves. I have a strange feeling here of being outside any social context. I have never known any place so relaxing. The possibility of an all-out riot is like a tonic, like ozone in air: "Here surely is a song for men like wind in an iron tree"—*Anabasis* more or less.[36] I have no nostalgia for the old days in Morocco, which I never saw. Right now is for me.

My disregard of social forms is approaching psychosis. Drinking with some very stuffy English people on their yacht and someone says something about someone tied to a buoy, and I say, "Tied to a boy? Lucky chap," and sit there doubled over with laughing, completely knocked out by my own wit. I can assure you no one else thought it was a bit funny. Now when they see me they get a *sauve qui peut* look and take off on the double, probably thinking, "Here comes that dangerous old fruit." So about two weeks ago I am having tea with Paul Bowles and he is entertaining this grim, rich American woman. So I was talking about Yage, knocked out on gage and lush, and she says, "How long does it take to rot you?" and I said: "Lady you should live so long," and she left the room. So I thought that finishes me with Bowles but nothing of the sort. He had been amused apparently. And I have seen him twice since, and dig him like I never dig anyone that quick before. Our minds similar, telepathy flows like water. I mean there is something portentously familiar about him, like a revelation. I also borrowed and read his book which I think very good.[37] Unfortunately he is leaving

---

36. "Surely a history for men, a song of strength for men, like a shudder from afar of space shaking an iron tree!" (T. S. Eliot's translation of St. John Perse's poem, section 6.)

37. Bowles's book would probably have been his novel *The Spider's House* (New York: Random House, 1955).

for Ceylon in a few days. He will be back here in February I think, so you will probably see him.

Yes I have typewriter which I own, and a good one. These Black Mountain cats sound like too much of rather a bad thing.[38] You shouldn't be put off base by those puerile tactics. It's one of the oldest routines in the Industry. I mean distracting, or rather engaging your attention with one hand while he hits you with the other. The counterpunch? I could suggest a dozen. Like say: "Of course the only writing now is in scientific journals," and read him something about the use of anti-hemoglobin treatment in the control of multiple degenerative granuloma. Further rules: Never answer him directly, never ask what he means, just nod as if everything he was saying was rather obvious and tiresome, and talk always to someone on one side of or behind him, and then fall into long silences as if listening carefully to this invisible person, nodding at intervals you dig, and interjecting like, "Well I wouldn't go that far. At least not yet," or, "You *can* say that again, but it's uncalled for really." You dig you are discussing him with this phantom cat he has apparently brought with him into the room . . . I can't explain all this. It's like the sight of someone about to flip or someone full of paranoid hate excites me. I want to see what will happen if they really wig. I want to crack them wide open and feed on the wonderful soft stuff that will ooze out. When an Arab looks at me with insane hate, I hope maybe he will come apart for me, I can see the bare bones of human process spill right out under the Moroccan blue sky . . . You see a paranoid has to have the other half, that is he must have complementary fear or hate. If I could get him to leap on me without I feel any answering fear or hate, he might crack wide open and God knows what would crawl out. Kicks, man, kicks . . . I mean it's like a yen. "~~We were the first that ever burst into that silent sea.~~"[39] . . . Jack must not

_____
38. Black Mountain College, near Asheville, North Carolina, where the poets Charles Olson, Robert Creeley, Robert Duncan, and others taught. Some ex-students from the college had intimidated Orlovsky, against a background of increasing poetic factionalism.
39. Quotation (heavily crossed out in manuscript) is from Coleridge's *The Rime of the Ancient Mariner,* lines 105–6.

be afraid of Arabs. I am in a position to officially abolish fear.

The chaos in Morocco is beautiful. Arab hipsters are developing in Casablanca, and a vast underworld. The police drive around in jeeps machine-gunning each other . . . Where does Rexroth get off at, he has been attacked by juvenile delinquents inna soda fountain already? I mean he had no business to go in a soda fountain. Anyhoo it sounds like an old maid story to me. [40]

This letter is like for you and Jack and Peter. Now listen. I will have the prologue of Interzone, which is about fifty pages, complete in a few weeks. Should I send you a copy? And if so where? What I am writing now supersedes, in fact makes obsolete, anything I have written hitherto. Write me on this point. I am really writing Interzone now, not writing about it . . .

Enclose picture of Spanish boy who has quit his job and left home and moved in with me. Not, my dear, an unmixed blessing. The chorus of guides and queens in the Socco has passed it along: "Tell Willy The Junk he is asking for it shacking with that Spanish kid who is always in hassles with the fuzz." This kid has been arrested many times for such offences as playing ball in the street, breaking windows with his slingshot, and hitting his girl friend in public and two teeth fall out already—loose anyhoo I think, and she is just making capital of her pyorrhea, four out of five get it before forty like the ad man say . . . I mean I'm a creative artist, I gotta have some privacy instead of which boys is crawling all over me at any hour at all.

I got a great idea. A number called the Jihad Jitters . . . Start is we hear riot noises in the distance. Ever hear it? It's terrific . . . You wouldn't believe such noises could result from humans, all sorts of strange yips. Then the sound of shop shutters slamming down. Then the vocal comes on. You dig various characters who got the Jihad Jitters.

---

40. Kenneth Rexroth, who initially sponsored Ginsberg and helped to stage the Six Gallery reading, had begun to resent the Beat invasion from the East Coast. Drunken behavior by Ginsberg and Kerouac antagonized Rexroth further.

Like first comes on this fag:

> "The Istiqlal[41] hates me,
> The guides all berates me,
> I'm nobody's sweetheart now.
> I got the Jihad jitters,
> I mean scared of those critters,
> They's a-coming for to disembowel me."

Then comes on this English contrabandist:

> "I just wanna make a buck
> So now I gotta duck,
> and leave my bundle stand inna bank?
> I'll stay and take my chances
> With the bloody fucking nances,
> Jihad you can't jitter me."

Now comes on a retired Colonel:

> "I've been through this before
> From Belfast to Singapore
> And I jolly well know the old score
> A native's like a horse
> Respectin' only force . . .
> So call out The Queen's Sixty Ninth."

And now a Syrian Greek who peddles second-hand condoms in the souks and does a spot of feelthy tattooing on the side.

> "You boys all know me
> The friendly little gee,
> Who keeps the bugs offen your meat
> And where'd you be without the rubber
> When you don't wanta club her
> You gotta enough events as it is?"

---

41. The Istiqlal, founded in 1943, was the principal Moroccan nationalist party. Banned in Morocco itself, the Istiqlal's leaders operated relatively openly in Tangier because of its international status.

Well you dig other types too. I'll have to give it thought. So finally all the voices together mixed with the riot noises like: "Can't you see the Lady doesn't *want* that knife? Wait here, honey face, I'm going to call the manager."

"Roy! That old nigger is lookin' at me so nasty!"

"How dare you throw gasoline on me. I'm going to call a cop." (Alt: "How dare you stick a knife up my ass? I'll . . . I'll, why I'll call a cop.")

"I say, these blighters don't look like members to me?"

And the music will be Arab, jazz, strains of the Marseillaise, old Berber tunes, etc . . . Really, rioting must be the greatest, like snap, *wow.* I mean I dug it watching them Arabs jumping around yelling and laughing, and they laugh in serious riots. We laugh when anxiety is aroused and then abruptly relieved. Now a riot is, for the participants a classical anxiety situation: that is the complete surrender of control to the id. But this surrender is condoned: laughter.

I was looking at this Wildeblood book *Against the Law*—he was one of the people convicted with Lord Montague [*sic*] of homosex practices.[42] These English . . . The prosecutor keeps saying like, "These citizens been consorting with their social inferiors. I suspect them to be fairies." See an upper-class Englishman with a lamp: "Looking for an inferior . . . Like a spot of fun you know."

I have purchased a machete. If they stage a *jihad* I'm gonna wrap myself in a dirty sheet and rush out to do some jihading of my own, like, "I comma Luigi. I killa everybody." I say it's nothing but a half-assed *jihad* that confines itself to Unbelievers: "Let petty kings the names of parties know / Where'ere I come I kill both friend and foe." Like there's this awful queer guide here, name of Charly, who keeps insulting poor Dave Woolman on the street, saying: "Just wait. We're going to take care of you fucking American queers." So comes the *jihad,* I will scream, "Death to the queers!" and rush up and cut Charly's head off. And I will shit sure

---

42. Peter Wildeblood, *Against the Law* (London: Weidenfeld & Nicolson, 1955). Wildeblood, then diplomatic correspondent for the London *Daily Mail*, was tried in 1954 together with Lord Edward Montagu and Michael Pitt-Rivers. They were sentenced to twelve to eighteen months. The book recounts the case as a frame-up, part of an English antihomosexuality campaign resulting from American governmental pressure.

avail myself of the next *jihad* to take care of the nabor's dog, the bastard is barking all night. I mean them suicidal Black Mountain boys should dig Islam already. What a beautiful way to commit suicide, to get yourself torn in pieces by Arabs. Like snap, *wow*. A few suggestions: Rush into a mosque, pour a pail of garbage on the floor, then make with a hog call—to coincide of course with the call to prayer—Whereupon a herd of hogs you have posted nearby rush into the mosque grunting and squealing . . . Go to Mecca and piss on the Black Stone. Overpower the Muezzin—the gee who makes the prayer call—put on a hog suit and make with the prayer call. Well the possibilities are unlimited.

I hereby declares the all-out massacre of everybody by everybody else. Let it Be . . . I mean we will have J DAY once a year. All police protection suspended from the world. All frontiers open . . . No firearms. Just knives and clubs and brass knuckles and any other devices short of explosives.

Perhaps come the *Jihad* I will have to yell, "Death to the American queers!" and cut off Dave Woolman's head. It's a cheap baboon trick. When a baboon is attacked by a stronger baboon he leads an attack on a weaker baboon, and who am I to deny our glorious Simian heritage? I am working on a divine invention: A boy who disappears as soon as I come, leaving a smell of burning leaves and a sound effect of distant train whistles . . .

New character for Interzone. This international bore who comes on with, "Of course the only writing worth considering is in scientific and technical journals," and reads interminable articles to his guests. Of course he concocts them himself and they mean absolutely nothing. Well after a while he burns a town down, and tours the world in search of victims, prowling through ocean liners and hotel lobbies with his briefcase of periodicals and journals and reports from nonexistent conferences.

I had to have one of those father-son talks with my boy this morning, you know: "Now sit down son I want to talk to you. Now I've had a lot of expenses lately. Of course I've always tried to give you every advantage, but it's time you took a little responsibility . . . After all I'm not made of money." So he hangs his head and says, "*¿Tu estás tan enfadado conmigo?*" "You are so angry with me?"

Group of old queens telling each other the cute things their boy said. "So my boy said he could become an American because he has blond hair." "So when I tried to fuck him he said, 'Morocco for the Moroccans.' "

Love,
Bill

Dec. 20, 1956
Tanger

Dear Allen,

You apparently did not receive letter I send to D.F. with picture of Paco, this Spanish kid wind up buggin' me like I throw him out already. One thing I love in the Arabs, when the job is done they put on their tents and silently steal away, unlike some Spanish citizens who want to take off their coat and throw it in a corner, stay all night and stay a little longer.[43] What with Jack, he afraid??? When you gotta go, you gotta go and as Allah will. Maybe you better not tell him how three Arabs follow me back to my pad a few nights back, and one produce a shiv at least a foot long, at sight of which I am expect to swoon or cream in my dry goods. So I haul out my blade which opens with a series of ominous clicks and it got six inches, Gertie . . . advance in knife-fighter's crouch as illustrate inna Commando Tactics—left hand out to parry—and my would-be assailants take to their heels. They run about fifty feet and see I am not yelling copper on them—though there wasn't a cop I should yell one—So they burst out laughing and one of them comes back and mooch a dime off me which I give him at arm's length, gracious as one can be with knife in hand . . . Now I am not about to be uprooted from Tanger, and I think you will find it ideal for a place to take it cool and organize MS. It's cheap, there are characters enough to dig, unlimited boys . . . So I suggest you stay here until early Spring when we can all make Paris—which is cold and miserable and expensive now—fuel oil shortage, you know. I talk to this Spade Hipster name of Carl Latimore, "Rocky", who knows everyone in the Village. I understand he used to push and now has plenty loot seems as how, well he just made Paris and say, "Man, it really is *nowhere*." I mean when we get MS. organized,

---

43. References are to Longfellow's "The Day is Done": "The cares that infest the day / Shall fold their tents, like the Arabs, / And as silently steal away," and to a then popular American song by Bob Wills and the Texas Playboys: "Stay All Night and Stay a Little Longer."

we make it . . . Morocco is really great and I know you will like it, and the Arabs are not to compare with American counterparts for viciousness, and it is sheer Provincialism to be afraid of them as if they was something special, sinister and Eastern and un-American. I met Americans in Tripoli who were afraid to venture into the Native Quarter after two years' residence. I went there every night . . .

The Sultan keeps exhorting his subjects to respect the lives and property of resident foreigners . . . And a military court is trying those responsible for the Meknes atrocities.[44] Several death sentences so far. Opposed as I am to capital punishment, I can not but feel that the practice of throwing gasoline on passers-by and burning them to death should be rather firmly discouraged. Meknes has always been a trouble spot and a long way from Tanger in every sense. Nor would I hesitate to go there if I had a mind to, or anywhere else in Morocco.

Garver's *ménage* sounds perfectly ghastly.[45] If I were him I would go to England, where you can get H on RX. They figure an addict has a right to junk like a diabetic to his insulin . . . Inconceivable that I should get back on junk . . .

What's with you? You wig already and remove your dry goods inna public hall??[46] For the Love of Jesus, that cheap ham, don't bring Gregory. If anything bugs me it's these people complain about the sanitation. Such citizens should stand in Sweden. Doctor Dent is publishing an article I wrote in the January issue of *British Journal of Addiction* . . . [47] He is one of the really great people I meet in last three years, the other being Paul Bowles. Don't recall I ever meet

---

44. An accidental machine-gun discharge by Arab policemen of the Al-Glaoui faction in Meknes led to riots in which several Portuguese nationals were killed.
45. Garver was living in Mexico City with Dave Tercerero's widow, Esperanza Villanueva, and a Yucatecan they called "the Black Bastard."
46. Before going to Mexico, in late October Ginsberg had given a performance of "Howl" at a reading organized by Lawrence Lipton in Los Angeles. There Ginsberg took his statement of poetic nakedness to its literal conclusion.
47. Burroughs' "Letter from a Master Addict to Dangerous Drugs" appeared in vol. 53, no. 2, issue of Dent's magazine, in January 1957. It was the first publication of anything by Burroughs since *Junkie*.

anyone I dug so quick as Bowles. Well, he has gone to Ceylon but will return in June . . . My regards to Lucien, Jack, Peter, the whole Village.

Porter Tuck the bullfighting hipster just passed through *en route* to N.Y. You might dig him, he will be waiter in Pablo's Spanish restaurant on East Fifties or Sixties, and will no doubt hang out in San Remo or Joe's Lunch Room, he not a junker but digs charge and friend of Stanley Gould.[48] His last goring put him off the bull-fight kick, he come near to die with a *cornada* in the lung . . .

I will send along about 100 pages of Interzone, it is coming so fast I can't hardly get it down, and shakes me like a great black wind through the bones . . .[49]

Of course we can all make a trip to Spain if you get tired of Tanger, which I doubt you will want to leave soon. Or we could dig Southern Morocco, which is great in the Winter, or Portugal which I never see . . . But I repeat, this fear of Arabs is utterly groundless. They are certainly much less sinister than Mexicans.

I can't get the MS. organized in time to send it, and no point to send fragments, it is all like in one piece and must be dug as a continuum. By the time you get here it should be about half finished, though I have no way to know how long it will be, except I will know when it is done. Like a dictation I am getting it. More Meknes death sentences today. The Istiqlal say: "Order must be maintained. Cooperation with European Colonists is matter of life and death for Morocco. We promise protection to resident foreigners. Those who leave Morocco from fear are committing a grave error." And that is the Nationalist Party speaking.

Merry Xmas, Love
Bill

Keep me informed on sailing date. No visa needed for Tanger to date, but yes for Southern Morocco.

---

48. Charge: i.e., marijuana.
49. Phrase from St. John Perse, *Anabasis*.

1957

No Moslem or anyone else who has glimpsed the truth of God can ever again pity himself *under any circumstance*. There is *one misfortune: Not to know God.*

Jan. 23, 1957
[Tangier]

Dear Allen,

Glad to hear from you at last. I will say it again and say it slow. TANGER IS AS SAFE AS ANY TOWN I EVER LIVE IN. *I* feel a chill of fear and horror at thought of the random, drunken violence stalking the streets and bars and parks and subways of America. Tanger incomparably safer than Mexico City. ARABS ARE NOT VIOLENT . . . In all my time here I know of only three people robbed—late and drunk. In no case did the Arabs harm them beyond taking the gelt. They do *not attack people for kicks or fight for kicks like Americans.* Riots are the accumulated, just resentment of a people subjected to outrageous brutalities by the French cops used to strew blood and teeth over a city block in the Southern Zone. There hasn't been a riot in Tanger since 1952, when one European was killed.[1] A riot at this time is very unlikely anywhere in Morocco and above all here. The Sultan has shown exemplary severity in punishing the Meknes rioters and thereby serving notice that such behavior is in no way officially approved or condoned . . . So for Christ sake tell Jack to stop this nonsense.

Interzone is coming like dictation, I can't keep up with it. I will send along what is done so far. Read in any order. It makes no difference . . . My religious conversion now complete. I am neither a Moslem nor a Christian, but I owe a great debt to Islam and could never have made my connection with God ANYWHERE EXCEPT HERE. And I realize how much of Islam I have absorbed by osmosis without spitting a word of their appalling language. I will get to

---

1. According to Woolman, in *Tangier: A Different Way*, the riot of March 30, 1952, left over 100 wounded and 18 Moroccan dead. Taking place on the fortieth anniversary of the Treaty of Fez, which had led to the internationalization of Tangier, this incident was regarded as a turning point in the city's history.

that when I have a free moment. Now hardly time out to eat and fuck . . .

I have never even glimpsed peace of mind before I learn the real meaning of "It is As Allah Wills." Relax, you make it or you don't, and since realizing that, whatever I want comes to me. If I want a boy, he knocks on my door, etc. I can't go into all this, and [it's] all in the MS. What's with Lucien? He need more Islam to him. We all do and Jack especially. As one of the Meknes rioters say when they shot him, "*Skikut*"[2]—"It is written" . . . And remember, "God is as close to you as the vein in your neck"—Koran . . .

Now I must get the MS. in what shape I can to send. If you can, please have copy made and bring one with you, but leave one at least in N.Y. It would be disastrous if I lost it as impossible to reproduce—often I do not know what I wrote last night till I read it over—the whole thing is a dream . . . Incidentally the most obscene thing I ever read. I will enclose some with this letter and send the rest separate cover. By the time you get here I expect will have written another hundred pages supersede present material. Love to all and you more than anybody.

Love,
Bill

P.S. Latest is you need visa for Tanger, unless they change mind again. Apply Moroccan Legation, N.Y. No doubt you *could* get in without one, but get one if possible. In case of fuckup at boat. (You take ferry from Gib. to Tanger and I will meet you in Tanger.)

Address here
in case we miss at boat:
Villa Mouniria
1 Calle Magallanes
(Corner Calle Cook and Magallanes.)

---

2. Burroughs usually renders this Arab word as "*Mektoub.*"

Jan. 28, 1957
[Tangier]

Dear Allen,

The MS. you have seen by now—I sent it in four separate envelopes—is just preliminaries, Golden Glove kid stuff. Now my power's really coming and I am subject to write something downright dirty. I am building an orgone accumulator to rest up in and recharge myself. Also careful to row every day. A man of my caliber has to watch himself.

Now the latest is you don't need a visa—now you see it now you don't. Well, ask at Moroccan Legation in New York if such exists, if not don't give it a thought. Ask around the Village if anyone knows this cat Rocky Latimore, a big spade is here in Tanger and it couldn't happen to a nicer guy. Interpol has him down as an international pusher of the white shit. We got this gossipy Chief of Security tell things in strictest confidence to the local Walter Winchell, writes a gossip column for *The Minaret* and live next door to me.[3] It could only happen in Tanger. And check with Wyn bastards sons of bitches.

Tell Jack that Paul Bowles, who is very much afraid of violence, live twenty years in Morocco and wouldn't live anywhere else, is afraid of Mexico—where he spent a year. I really love Tanger and never feel like this about any other place. Such beauty, but more than that it's like the dream, the other dimension, is always breaking through. There is for example this square American kid here who says, "I heard it was dangerous here but I never felt safer. Somehow I like it here better than any place." In fact we got quite a colony now of Americans on the lam from those black tornados sweep the land of the free and suck all the meaning and beauty—the two are synonymous and no one knows what beauty is until he knows the

---

3. Colonel Gerald Richardson, C.M.G., O.B.E., ex–Scotland Yard, had been the zone's *Chef de la Sureté* since March 1955. Richardson wrote an account of his time in Tangier in *Crime Zone* (London: John Lang, 1959), where he describes Burroughs as "Morphine Minnie" who "got up to some strange tricks."

Walter Winchell: i.e., Dave Woolman, who wrote a gossip column for the *Moroccan Courier*.

truth of God—out of life . . . We got for example an ex-cop, and ex–school teacher female have the affair of her life with a horrid Arab pimp disliked by everyone who know him. "Not a viler man in the Northern Zone than old Ali." And a refugee from South Africa—Johannesburg must be one of the blighted spots of the universe. And a hipster from Frisco, and Rocky, in short the town really comes on these days . . . Alan Ansen will be here in March. Paul Bowles returns in May, I think. Yes I know Jane Bowles but she is not exactly one of my fans. Not on bad terms you understand, just don't click exactly.

Now Allen, leave us have no more dilatory and come on here right away. It is important. I will meet you at the Gibraltar ferry, the *Mons Calpe,* and beat the fucking guides off you. They are the curse of Tanger, tell the tourists it's dangerous here to go any place without a guide. But they got this Union, it's not healthy to buck them and *The Minaret* is scared shitless to run an editorial on these foul abuses. My address here in case of fuck-up at the ferry is: Hotel Mouniria, Calle Magallanes, no. 1, corner Calle Cook and Magallanes.

Love,
Bill

31 Jan. 1957
Tanger

Dear Allen,

This is about the last letter can reach you if you plan to leave on or about the 8th. I have already sent the MS. Find I have almost complete copy here, so if there is not time to have a copy made and you can leave it to advantage with someone, do so by all means. I am writing straight ahead and have another thirty, forty pages complete already. I mean the MS. I sent is definitely work-in-progress.

Beautiful weather here. Incidentally I have been hitting the *majoun* pretty heavy of late—that is hash you take with hot tea. All the etiology of my homosex and practically everything spill right out of me. Quotes from last night *majoun* high: "So what's holding him up?—homosex orientation—Some old tired synapse pattern won't go to its long home like it's supposed. There must be an answer, I need the answering service. I think I can arrange but it will be expensive. Modern Oedipus." This give me an out already, I can put down the old whore and hump some young Crete gash heat my toga like the dry goods of Nexus, you might say Nexus had the rag on.[4] So the liz fuck this boy with a joke prick explode inside and blow his guts out at navel and the liz roll on the floor laughing:

"Oh! Oh! Give me ribs of steel!"

And this glumph stick his proboscis up your nose while you sleep and suck out your brains, every morning you wake up with another center gone.

A jug of paregoric and thou under the swamp cypress of East Texas, sweet screams of burning Nigger drift in on the warm Spring wind fan our hot bodies like a Nubian slave. How obliging can you get?

The Sheriff frame every good-looking boy in the County say, "Guess I'll have to hang some cunt for the new frisson," he hang

---

4. Most of the following appears in Burroughs' "Word" manuscript, as published in *Interzone*, pp. 150–51.

this cute little corn-fed thing her tits come to attention squirt milk in the sheriff's eyes blind him like a spitting cobra. "Oh land's sake!" say the sheriff, "I shoulda never hang a woman. A man can only come off second best, he tangle ass holes with a gash. Weell, I guess I can see with my mouth from here on in. Heh heh." So the sheriff have glass eyes made up with feelthy pictures built in. "Look me in the eye son and see what's on my mind." Her cunt click open like a switchblade. Don't offend with innocence, you need Life Boy soap, body smells of life a nasty odor stink in the nose of a decent American woman.

Come in at the door after the delouse treatment. Don't give the angels halo lice.

See you soon. Look when you get to Gib. best deal is to fly here. It don't cost much more than the ferry, less trouble with customs and spare me the trouble of horrible scenes with the guides think I am out to steal a live one . . . Weel that's a suggestion . . .

Love,
Bill

Feb. 1

Look to see you. Don't go and die on me as the whore say to the cardiac case, haw haw.

Feb. 14, 1957
[Tangier]

Dear Allen,

I was disappointed you delay. Please don't miss the Feb. 22 boat. Since sending MS. have written about fifty pages more, wilder than what you have. This is almost automatic writing. I often sit high on hash for as long as six hours typing at top speed.

I have been involved in an unfortunate affair here, gave the final fillip to my reputation. I am now known around town as of all things a Nanny beater. It all happened like this. Fade out. Somerset Maugham takes the continuity.

"Five no trumps," and other bridge table noises. So there they were gathered around a bridge table in the upstairs lobby of the Hotel Cecil, as disreputable a quartet as ever spewed out the public schools of England. Tony G.—two forgery convictions, Colonel P.—he always leaves under a cloud before his juggled accounts stand revealed, B.—old queen, and Lester—ditto.

So the Colonel send for his money sealed in envelope, takes out some and hands the envelope back to B., manager of the Hotel. B. puts the envelope on a shelf behind him, meaning to return it later to the safe. So when he gets around to return it, it's not there. Now anyone at the table could have done it and the waiter (whose nationality was never determined) subsequently fired for theft . . . The hotel denied responsibility . . . The envelope allegedly contained $500 . . .

So some weeks later I have a few drinks with the Colonel and Paul Lund the English gangster,[5] and Tony G.—he says his reputation had suffered, as if it could—so one thing leads to another:

"They can't do this to our old friend the Colonel."

"Bunch of fucking nances."

---

5. Paul Lund, born 1914 in Birmingham, England, to a Danish father. Like Burroughs, he arrived in Tangier in January 1954. Lund was on the run from a career of robberies; he had served time in Dartmoor, occupied Oscar Wilde's old cell in Reading Gaol, and spent 1955 in an Italian jail for cigarette smuggling. Lund inspired Rupert Croft-Cooke to write his portrait, *Smiling Damned Villain: The True Story of Paul Axel Lund* (London: Secker & Warburg, 1959).

"Let's go down there and take the place apart. Show them what can happen if they don't pay up."

"Drinks and dinner on me boys," says the Colonel.

So I get in my Grade B ham actor groove and outdo everybody, they is hanging on my coat-tail. "For Christ sake, Bill, play it cool." And me yelling across the bar. "Hey Gertie. Give us another round."

Very funny I thought. But Richardson—head of security—interpreted this merry prank of middle-aged cut-ups as plain extortion. The Colonel has been asked to leave Tanger—turns out he has a really bad record every place he goes and a notorious international heterosexual, drummed out of the Tanger Country Club for pinching young girls on the ass . . . And we are all under a cloud, and everybody cray-fishing around. "I didn't mean nothing. Just had a few drinks is all." And that phony bastard Tony G. went down and got a statement from B., he "just happened to be there." (It was his idea actually.) And took it to Richardson . . .

The Colonel, thank God, is leaving day after tomorrow. Meanwhile he has printed up a manifesto regarding "certain unspeakable conditions obtaining in the Hotel Cecil, where a huge beetle galloped across my bed, not to mention the spectacle of the manager kissing the Norwegian Barman in the corridors, which I personally found nauseating." And plans to give mimeographed copies to Arab street boys distribute through the cafés of Tanger. I don't figure to be around when it happens.

I am attenuating my relations with Lund and company. Too much of rather a bad thing. And as for the Colonel, in the words of the Immortal Bard: "Old man I know thee not."[6]

Please Allen, don't delay any more. Just as well you did not arrive a month ago, because I needed to work out my method alone. Now I am badly in need of advice, editing, collaboration. You see Alan showed my prologue to someone in Paris. Olympia Press may be interested. They want to see as much as I can send in finished form, but will not be able to give it attention till the beginning of April. It is hard for me to evaluate this material. Some

---

6. *Henry IV, Part 2*, act 5, scene 5, 48–49: "I know thee not, old man. Fall to thy prayers. / How ill white hairs become a fool and jester!"

of it obviously should be omitted and the whole put in some sort of order, but I keep writing more and no time to revise. I wonder how collaboration would work out. I think might be terrific. As you see I am running more and more to prose poems and no straight narrative in over a month. I must take it as it comes . . . Now listen, when you get here if I am not there to meet you at the dock—those Yugoslav boats subject to arrive at any hour—get in a taxi WITH NO GUIDE. Bastards!! Sons of bitches! and come to HOTEL MOUNIRIA, CORNER CALLE COOK and MAGAL-LANES. Love,

Bill

March 25, 1957
Cargo U.S. Consulate
Tanger, Morocco

Dear Bill,

I have been back in Tanger since September. Wrote once to Ibiza, but I guess you already left at that time. I would like very much to see you, and plan to hit Europe in another month more or less. Allen Ginsberg and Jack Kerouac are here.[7] I would be very interested to hear the details of the business deal you speak of. My writing does not show indications of yielding even approximate support.

Please let me hear from you. You remember Alan Ansen? He lives in Venice . . . Cargo American Express. However he is coming here to visit April 8th, and we may all return with him to Italy. Plans are unformed as usual. However I feel sure we can arrange to meet soon. Are you often in France? I am planning to go there this Spring or Summer to see about possibilities of publishing my latest opus which is too much, it seems, even for Olympia Press. Frechtman, the man who translated *Our Lady of the Flowers,* is interested in what he has seen but say publication extremely difficult.[8] Please write me in detail what you are doing and what your plans are. Hope to see you soon.

As Ever,
Bill Burroughs

---

7. Having borrowed $200 from Ginsberg, Kerouac set sail for Tangier on February 15. Ginsberg—and Orlovsky—arrived in March. They stayed on after Kerouac left on April 5 for brief trips to Paris and London, and did not leave Tangier until June, when they set off for Madrid, Barcelona, Venice, and finally Paris.

8. Frechtman's translation of Genet's *Notre-Dame des Fleurs* was published by Olympia Press in their Traveller's Companion Series in April 1957. Kerouac later wrote: "NO ONE wants anything to do with it [the *Naked Lunch* manuscript] not even Bernard Frechtman (translator of Genet) to whom I took it in my rucksack in Paris . . . only Alan Ansen and Ginsberg believe in it (and me) and worked with Bill on it after I left." (Kerouac to John Clellon Holmes, June 23, 1957, in *The Beat Journey,* edited by Arthur and Kit Knight, California, Pa., 1978.)

June 15, 1957
[Tangier]

Dear Allen,

Forwarding various letters. We are now finished with the MS. and it looks good. Alan is going back to Venice in next few days.

Had a letter from Wolberg. Very nice letter. Not much new around town. Corpse of indeterminate nationality fished out of the bay, revolver bullet in back of the head. The boys went back to Paris unconsummate and intact. At least I managed to head off Operation Milk Sugar.

I will definitely take off at the end of this month. Can't drink at all. On the wagon. Feel O.K. otherwise. Most sinister news bulletin I ever read in the paper today. The only forms of life that mutate favorably under radiation are the smallest, namely the viruses. Flash. Centipedes a hundred feet long eaten by viruses big as bed bugs under a gray sky of fall-out . . .

My best to Peter . . . See you in Barcelona . . .[9]

Love,
Bill

P.S. Addresses of queer and/or hip bars in Madrid:
Rincón Ordobez . . . Calle Huertas
La Panuelita . . . Calle Jardines
Bar Tanger . . . Calle Echegarraz
Calle Echegarraz many other bars
Bar Calle Jardines . . . *Echacaráy*
Metro Station Plaza Mayor—for Pot ask for the Fat Woman

---

9. By the time Burroughs reached Spain, Ginsberg and Orlovsky had left for Venice, where they arrived on July 1.

July 18, 1957
London

Dear Alan,

Went once to the Prado for half an hour. Spent most of my time in Madrid lying in a curtained room. I am definitely ill. Don't know the precise nature of the illness yet pending a series of tests. Meanwhile can't drink even a glass of wine. London is dull as ever. I have no definite plans, beyond ascertaining the nature of illness.

I wish someone would take five minutes out to send along the MS.—leaving "Word" aside for the moment and ending MS. with "Market" section.[10] After all, it takes long enough to locate a publisher without unnecessary delays. I am sending along amended version of "Word" cut down to thirty pages. But I think will split it up and scatter through the other sections. In any case most the rest of MS. can be sent out as is. There will always be time for additional changes.

It was hardly in the cards that Peggy Guggenheim should find Peter and Allen congenial.[11] However, it does seem to me she is being a bit unreasonable to move in admittedly Bohemian circles and simultaneously demand conventional behavior.

London dull as ever of course. May make a trip to Copenhagen, dependent on state of health and Kells' report.[12] He will be here in a few days . . .

As Ever,
Bill

---

10. "Word" was the largest section of the manuscript. Most of "Word" was not used in *Naked Lunch*, and remained unpublished for over twenty years; see *Interzone*. The "Market" section of the manuscript corresponds largely to the "market" and "ordinary men and women" sections of *Naked Lunch*.

11. Ansen must have reported to Burroughs that Guggenheim was put off by a sweaty, playful, towel-throwing incident that erupted between Ginsberg and Orlovsky while she was visiting them at Ansen's Venice apartment.

12. Kells Elvins and his wife, Mimi, lived in Copenhagen.

July 30, 1957
Copenhagen

Dear Alan,

Here in Freelandt. I walk in a bar and get the eye from this beautiful boy, last night being day of arrival. So we have a few drinks and I say something about "going back to my hotel." So he says: "You mean both of us go back there?" And I say: "That's the general idea." He says: "Do you want to?" And I say: "Yes," and he say: "No, I can't," long pause, "I have a wife." I don't dig it at all. Why does he first pin it down like that, then refuse and then lie? "Calling Doctor Benway. You are wanted in reconditioning."

Sandwich bars, workman in overalls listening to classic music on the radio. No one talks. On the other hand, no one can talk longer and with less point than a Dane once you get his blood up.

London is by all odds the evilest place I have ever been in, a vast Kafkian maze of frustrating agencies. A Turkish Bath there beats anything I ever see for nightmarish horror. Like one of the more undesirable naborhoods of the *Inferno,* my dear. Incidentally nothing wrong with liver. It was a mild atypical hepatitis like I thought from the jump. So I could have spared myself that little sojourn in Hell. Did pick up some valuable bits of info from Dent. The LSD6 people are clamring up. I don't think their letters were lost. More likely not answered.[13] They won't even talk to Dent. I know a trick or two would make the blighters talk soon enough. "You vill answer my questions now, Doctor Elk" (heavy Russian accent).

Really I can hardly be expected to sympathize with your boy problems, coming from the land of fifteen-dollar tarts, and have a feeling things aren't going to be brilliant here either. I have not had a piece of ass since leaving Tanger. It's absolutely intolerable, since I refuse to masturbate. I don't seem to make any time without Pimp Hunger.

---

13. A few days later, Burroughs finally received an "evasive" reply from a Dr. Tait of Dumfries, Scotland.

Well I will see what can be done here and in Hamburg. Expect to reach Paris by October.

Love to all and kiss Guggenheim for me you know where.

Allen-Peter, Sorry to hear you are not clicking *chez* Guggenheim. She is strictly a Queen Bee. I thought might be worthwhile sending along copy of MS., or at least "Benway" and "Market," to the American agent for submit to New Directions or New Writing or something. See you in Paris which I hope has more innarest than what I see already.

Love,
Bill

P.S. Write cargo American Express . . . Further research has confirmed my original impression that Copenhagen is not the Promised Land. In fact I haven't been able to do any good here to date. Stuck until more money arrives. Very expensive here. I really don't know what the fuck I will do. May cut back through Paris in another two weeks; if that is as nowhere as every other place I see this trip, will return to Tangiers. Seems to be the only place a man can score for any ass . . . Well, plans are completely tentative. Two weeks is a long time and anything can happen. Lots of jazz here which sounds incredibly dead and tenuous, separate from all the tension and horror that gave rise to it.

August 20, 1957
Copenhagen

Dear Allen,

I can not see breaking with Tanger before I find something better. Since leave there have not seen anything remotely comparable from any point of view. And I have learned this for sure: *I don't want to do any more travelling.* I am dead sick of living out of suitcases, shopping around in bars for dull conversation, and lousy lays at exorbitant prices. The only procedure is to pick some place, go there and stay at least three months. I am slowly narrowing down the earth by process of elimination. At least I have crossed out Scandinavia this trip, as I did Libya and whole Near East during my last bout of inconvenient, expensive, and totally unrewarding travel. However I can not say that present trip has been lost on a connoisseur of horror. Scandinavia exceeds my most ghastly imaginations. Freelandt in the "Benway" section was underdrawn. Curious that I should have known without ever having been here that the place is a series of bars along a canal. You did not see that section which I later dropped. And the R.C. is actually running full blast here, grinding out every variety of dull lunatic, and not a few INDs.[14] This is the police state without police, which is scene of my latest opus of which will soon send along the first chapter. Danes are at once bone dull and completely insane.

Most important omission in "Benway" section as I check over it: Page 14, sixteen lines down: "I noticed that all my homosexual patients manifested strong unconscious heterosex drives." Now this sentence has been omitted, which is whole point and basis of Benway's subsequent experiments in the deliberate induction of homosexuality in healthy subjects: "And all my heterosexual patients manifested strong unconscious homosex tendencies."

About plans. Like I say, do not feel like a trek across Europe at

---

14. R.C. = Reconditioning Center; INDs = Irreversible Neural Damage. See *Naked Lunch,* "Benway" section. P. 14 of the manuscript equates with *Naked Lunch,* p. 36.

great personal expense to Vienna.[15] *Not* particularly cheap, very crowded in the Summer and boys very much an unknown quantity. DON'T GO TO ISTANBUL. I have it from those who been there, *nowhere*. Expensive, much police surveillance—they don't like any foreigners, you need a permit for everything. No ass he or she. Incidentally the whole fucking town is in condition of rebuilding, vibrating with air hammers, bulldozers popping out all over, wreckers uncovering fixing junkies, etc. A nightmare I tell you. And if there is any place in Europe does not welcome Bohemian visitors, this is it. You have been warned. Now Athens is possible. Cheap at least, and I think well stocked with boys. You might want to settle there instead of in Paris. I hear on all sides hair-raising stories of the Paris prices. No rooms, etc. You might find it difficult to settle there. What seems to me indicated is this: You get settled and I will visit you later on. I have a lot of work pending that I must be settled to do. And for a cheap, satisfactory place to work I certainly do not know of any place like Tanger. My financial situation is bad. I have run over allowance, must settle down and recoup. For this, Paris is about the last place. So I would strongly advise a look at Greece. Life on the Greek islands is as cheap as any place in the world. [. . .] If you are settled there—or in Paris— then I will come for a visit of a few months or even shift residence. The point is I don't want to travel any more at this point, and want to be very sure of any move I make. I have spent enough money to no purpose and been in enough places I wanted to get out of with all possible speed. Let me know what you think.

Love,
Bill

---

15. By the end of August, Ginsberg was en route from Naples to Paris via Vienna and Munich.

August 28, 1957
Copenhagen

Dear Allen,

I can't cover in this letter the developments of the past week except in bare outline.

I have always felt that the MS. to date was in a sense notes for a novel rather than the novel itself. This novel is now taking shape faster than I can write it down. I made no mistake to come here. Only Scandinavia could have catalysed the Great Work, and no other place could be the background. Briefly, the novel concerns addiction and an addicting virus that is passed from one person to another in sexual contacts. The virus only passes from man to man or woman to woman, which is why Benway is turning out homosexuals on assembly-line basis. Real theme of the novel is Desecration of the Human Image by the control addicts who are putting out the virus. As Lola la Chata, Mexico City pusher, said: "Selling is more of a habit than using." I can't go into more detail now, too busy. It's like concepts I have in larval form for years are all falling into a pattern. This is correlated with my experience here. Everytime I reach impasse, something happens to show me the way. Sleep with boy the other night and whole new angle comes to me in a dream. A Danish cockteaser gave me essential character.

So plans are in complete state of flux. I hesitate to leave this source of inspiration. I want to see the Northern Lights, and the blighted town in Sweden that produced Urjohn.[16] Did you dig how much he looked like junk? The shabbiness, neglect of person, grey invisible quality and the depression of sexuality?

On the other hand I am out of tea and want to get back to Tanger, and I am short of money. In brief, don't know. But I can't see that Paris would give me anything at this juncture. In Tanger is tea and cheap living and I can settle down to work. There is a lot of straight work to do. Whole sections of "Word" and other parts of present MS. are to be incorporated into present work. This

---

16. Urjohn was a Swede in Tangier; Burroughs had taken a photograph of him and sent it to Ginsberg.

in no way changes present arrangements for seeking publishers on MS. as is. This present novel will mean at least three, four, six months intensive work. My feeling is, looking over MS., that many parts of it are publishable as is—"Benway," "Market," "Voices," "County Clerk"[17]—but that it does not hang together as a whole . . . So it boils down to this: If I meet you in Paris next week or two my stay there will be brief. Most likely. I am completely in the hands of Allah or whatever you want to call it. *Paris is the last thing I need for this work.* If you are going to *settle* in Paris, I could join you there after I have completed at least a first draft, say around Xmas. So tentatively will work and dig Scandinavia next two weeks, then head back for Tangier via Paris. Love to meet you there but I will be *in transit*. There is also possibility I may be hung up here longer. I don't know, but this is the way it looks right now . . .

P.S. Doing all right with the boys but they are expensive and not the greatest as lays. Love to everyone. Please write me at once.

Love,
Bill

P.S. I mean don't plan on my staying in Paris now. It's not in My Line.

P.S. I feel very definitely that the amended version of "Word" is preferable. It contains many essential changes as well as cuts. I think important it should be submitted with the longer version to any prospective publishers or agents.

---

17. Two thirds of "Voices" was used for *Naked Lunch*, most in the opening, some in the final section.

Sept. 20, 1957
Tanger

Dear Allen,

Back in same room. Relief to unpack, organize my life, and get started on enormous volume of work I have pending. It would have been out of the question for me to wait in Paris, living out of suitcases in some lousy hotel, no place to work, spending a lot of money on bars, boredom and frustration. Paris looked pretty nowhere to me.[18]

As regards MS., I think any attempt at chronological arrangement extremely ill-advised. To my way of thinking *Queer* and letters have no place in present work. It is not at all important how anybody gets from one place to another. Entirely too much space is wasted in this transporting one's characters here and there which, with the aid of American Express, they are able to do for themselves. The MS. in present form does not hold together as a novel for the simple reason that it is not a novel. It is a number of connected—by theme—but separate short pieces. My feeling is that it will eventually grow into several novels all interlocking and taking place simultaneously in a *majoun* dream. But I do not see organization as a *problem*. The gap between present work, that is last year or so, and work before that is such that I can not consider the previous material as really pertinent, and trying to fit it in according to any schema could only result in vitiating the work.

At present I am working on Benway and Scandinavia angles, also developing a theory of morphine addiction. [. . .] Incidentally, this theory resulted from necessities of the novel. That is, scientific theories and novel are inseparable. What I am evolving is a general theory of addiction which expands into a world picture with concepts of good and evil.

Poor Kiki was murdered last week in Madrid by that shit of a Cuban singer. Seems the frantic old fruit found Kiki with a girl and stabbed him in heart with a kitchen knife. Then he attacked

---

18. Ten days earlier, Burroughs had made an eight-hour stopover in Paris, which was long enough to find the prices too high.

the girl, but the nabors rushed in and the Cuban took off, but was shortly afterwards detained by the Civil Guard.

One of Alan's ex-boys, a pathetic character nobody wanted because he was ugly, went to France and murdered a cab driver. When the police came to arrest him he shot himself.

[. . .] The town is jumping with ex-junkies and active junkies. Someone named Harold Mensky, who knows all the NYC crowd, just left. Carlos Fiore is in Paris with Marlon Brando.[19]

Jane Bowles has flipped completely and in sanitarium in England. Paul just went to see her.[20]

Write what your plans are. Like I say, don't know how you will dig Paris. They tell me it is quite impossible to find an apartment there. And I can't think of a place less suited for someone with very little money.

I was not aware that Auden had seen any of present work.[21] Give my best to Gilmore. Sorry I can't dig him in Paris. Best to Peter. Write me soon.

Love,
Bill

P.S. I don't see where there is any confusion in MS. if regarded as separate pieces connected by an interweaving of theme and characters.

---

19. Carlos Fiore was one of Burroughs' "customers" in Greenwich Village in 1946; he later was an assistant to Brando.
20. Jane Bowles had suffered a serious stroke on April 4, 1957. In early September, in a state of severe depression, she went to the Radcliffe Infirmary, Oxford, and from there to Saint Andrew's, a psychiatric hospital in Northampton. Paul, accompanied by Ahmed Yacoubi, had just left to join her there.
21. In August, Ginsberg had visited Auden on the island of Ischia, and may have shown him part of the Burroughs manuscript he helped to type up in Tangier.

[*Oct. 8, 1957*
Tangier]

Dear Allen,

I am sending along my General Theory of Addiction. This is essential to understanding of the work I am doing now. In fact novel in progress is illustration of this theory. I have sent a copy to Wolberg and another copy to Dent. Could you please send this copy along to the agent after reading it. *It belongs with the Benway section of Interzone,* as postscript to theories on morphine and schizophrenia . . . I can't take time to bring you up to date on the novel. There are about a hundred pages of notes and fragments. The point is the novel illustrates this theory. Like I start developing the theory and take off on long *majoun* parentheses which is the novel. For example there is a section about the wanderings of adolescent queer hipster through the jungles and mountains of South America, really looking for the fecund green CUNT in the middle of S.A., and disappears like Colonel Fawcett so we never know did he find the cunt or not. There is a huge Surrealist amusement park modeled on the Tivoli in Copenhagen. There is a country—Sweden—hooked on the addicting virus. A final War of the Sexes. There is Benway creating male and female queers with Enzyme Therapy. A monster plastic surgeon who remade Johny Yenn's face . . . etc. Don't have time to go into it.

I feel myself closer and closer to resolution of my queerness which would involve a solution of that illness. For such it is, a horrible sickness. At least in my case. I have just experienced emergence of my non-queer persona as a separate personality. This started in London where in dream I came into room to see myself not a child but adolescent, looking at me with hate. So I said, "I don't seem to be exactly welcome," and he say: "Not welcome!!! I hate you!" And with good reason too. Suppose you had kept a non-queer young boy in a strait-jacket of flesh twenty five years subject to continual queer acts and talk? Would he love you? I think not. Anyhoo, I'm getting to know the kid, and we get on better. I tell him he can take over anytime, but there is somebody else in this deal not yet fully accounted for and the kid's not up to deal with him, so I hafta stay around for the present. Actually, of course the kid and all the rest of us have to arrange a *merger. A ver.*

Real wild kicks lately. I am utterly convinced of the accuracy of my theory. Oh forgot. I read this book in Sweden, and as soon as I read the part I quote in theory, I have this flash and say: "Morphine must act on the cell receptors." So between trains in Paris, I make my usual line for a medical book-store and read in *Year Book of Medicine:* Doc Isbell of Lexington has suggested that morphine acts on the cell receptors and that an excitant forms inside the cells. Well, that takes some of the uniqueness out of my theory, at the same time plenty left to make it worth sending around. But what I mean is, it shows I am in THE GROOVE, and my theories are not a lot of paranoid vaporings. You may be sure of one thing, young man. *On medical subjects I am seldom if ever wrong.*

Now what's with this Hank Wertha deal? I got three pages and can whip up a general scheme of action which will occupy about ten pages or so. If he wants to see a more detailed script, O.K., but I don't want to be wasting my time writing onna spec., you dig? I got a lot to do now and I am getting so restless I can hardly sit down even. Write and give me the news. Bernard [Frechtman] went back to Paris I think. Did I tell you Carlos Fiore was there? I saw the reviews of Jack's novel.[22] They seemed favorable on the whole, except *Sat. Review.*

Will send the Theory along to Paris in a few days. Keep me informed. Love to Peter. Peter, go and see Doctor Wolberg when you get to N.Y. Doctor Lewis Wolberg. His advice will be good.[23]

Love,
Bill

P.S. Amsterdam sounds all right. Any boys?[24]

---

22. *On the Road* had been published in September 1957.
23. Peter Orlovsky had heard from his mother that Lafcadio had become violently disturbed—mental problems plagued the Orlovsky family—and Peter tried, without immediate success, to raise the return fare to New York.
24. Ginsberg and Orlovsky had been visiting Gregory Corso in Amsterdam, before returning, with him, to Paris.

Did I tell you about the rat who was conditioned to be queer by the shock and cold water treatment every time he makes a move at a female? He says: "Mine is the love that dare not squeak its name."

Oct. 19, 1957
Tanger, Morocco

Dear Allen,

I now have a schema that includes all the material of Interzone in novel form—most of Interzone is introduced as a long junk-sick night of reminiscences and what happened to so and so. There will be at least another hundred pages of new material which I think is, at its best, better than anything I have done. Material from *Queer, Yage,* etc. does not belong in this novel, except maybe pieces here and there. It's a colossal job anyway. You see I have about three novel themes running at once and merging together. I hope to have all done by Christmas with intensive work. Does the agent have the abbreviated form of "Word"? I think that the cuts were essential and this abbreviated form is now official, I declare it. Too much material vitiates the effect.

The Theory of Addiction is essential. I will introduce it in another place, or it can go in the Benway section. You see there is another long Benway section in current novel. I have about three chapters complete and in more or less final form, which I can send along to you or to the agent. The schema is now clear in its entirety and comprises a sort of queer *Inferno.* In fact I have introduced a vast Turkish Bath under the whole CITY—you can enter by manholes or subway entrances, cellars, etc.

The Theory of Addiction is, incidentally, correct, in essentials. I received a letter from Wolberg, quote . . . "Particularly interesting is your theory about cancer and schizophrenia. I have made no study of this, but telephoned a friend who works for a large mental institution. He said the incidence of cancer among schizophrenics is appreciably lower than among non-schizophrenics." The importance of this one fact is immeasurable. My theory contains the key to addiction, cancer, and schizophrenia. I have not yet heard from Doctor Dent.

Enclose epitaph on Kiki. Also few quotes from current work:

"A boy walked by and looked at Carl with calm, clear young eyes. Carl followed the young figure down the tree-lined walk past the Greek wrestlers and the discus thrower with aching sadness. Train whistles, smell of burning leaves, harmonica music. Two boys masturbate each other in swimming pool change cubicle—smell of chlorine on the hard, young flesh.

"Carl was running down a wooden corridor in a curious green light. Steam puffs up through knot holes and cracks in the floor, which is hot under his bare feet. Sound effects of Turkish Bath steam room: bestial nuzzlings, whimpers, groans, sucking and farting noises. He opens a green door into The Room. In a corner of the room he sees himself lying on a straw pallet. Dust drifts across the floor littered with dried excrement and crumpled shit-stained pages of bright color comics. The window is boarded up.

"Outside a dry husking sound and a terrible dry heat. The body is eaten to the bone with sores of rancid lust, the brand of untouchable vileness on the face. Slowly the thing moves to show its purple, suppurating ass-hole, with little transparent crabs crawling in and out. The thing is gibbering and whimpering in some vile phantom embrace. The abdomen swells to a great pink egg covered with veins. Inside, something black, legs and claws stirring.

"Benway: 'The broken spirits of a thousand boys whimper through my dreams, sad as the erect wooden phallus on the grave of dying peoples, plaintive as leaves in the wind, howler monkeys across great brown river in jungle twilight, whisper through my sleep, scurry like mice, bat wings, something in the room, stir of animal presence, somewhere, something.

" 'Let me out. Let me out.' I can hear their boy images scream through the flesh. Always boy crying inside and the sullen averted boys' eyes and those who still love me, and say: 'What have you done to me? Why did you do it? WHY??' "

Incidentally, I know the "why" now. But that is getting ahead of the story. In short, I am ready to deliver a complete novel in a few months.

My best to Gregory. He complains about Paris concierges. Concierges, my boys, are bad by nature.

Love to Peter.

Love,
Bill

The work involved in this novel is tremendous. I really have to curb routines and give time to routine correlating, editing and typing of material, which keeps coming like I can never catch up. But the schema becomes always clearer. Benway is emerging as a figure comparable to the Grand Inquisitor in *Brothers Karamazov*.

Oct. 28, 1957
[Tangier]

Dear Allen,

Enclose a section of the narrative. This narrative will run for a hundred pages or so, connecting up all the Interzone material, possibly some of the other material. But I never know whether something will fit in or not until it fits into the narrative as an organic part of the structure. That is I will not drag anything in, and can not say ahead of time what will be included and what left out. In a sense the action occurs in a superimposed place which is South America, U.S.A., Tanger and Scandinavia, and the characters wander back and forth from one place to another. That is a Turkish Bath in Sweden may open into a South American jungle . . . the shift from schizophrenia to addiction takes a character from one *place* to another. Actually, of course, there is only one main character: Benway and Carl (who is now wandering all over the Amazon Basin—I hope to have this S.A. section in order in another week or so) and Lee are, of course, one person. I find the whole is developing into a saga of lost innocence, The Fall, with some kinda redemption through knowledge of basic life processes. If anyone finds this form confusing, it is because they are accustomed to the historical novel form, which is a three-dimensional chronology of events happening to someone already, for purposes of the novel, dead. That is the usual novel *has happened*. This novel *is happening*.

The only way I can write narrative is to get right outside my body and experience it. This can be exhausting and at times dangerous. One cannot be sure of redemption . . .

[. . .]

I will send along the sections as they are finished. Love to Peter, Gregory. Where is Gilmore?

Love,
Bill

Nov. 10, 1957
[Tangier]

Dear Allen,

I have not heard from you in a month . . . Are you receiving the material I send??? I sent three sections of MS.: *Kiki Epitaph, General Theory of Addiction,* and *Carl Peterson section.* Did you receive this material?? What about Wertha? Any news from Frechtman, or the N.Y. agent??

[. . .]

I do nothing but work. . . . Given up liquor entirely. Writing the narrative now, which comes in great hunks faster than I can get it down. Changes in my psyche are profound and basic. I feel myself not the same person. I am about ready to leave Tanger. I really can't seem to interest myself in boys any more. Love to all.

Love,
Bill

Nov. 26, 1957
Tanger

Dear Allen,

Answered Feldman's letter, saying go ahead and use my true name.[25] It has nothing to lose.

The narrative section takes all my time. I see no one, don't drink. Nothing but weed and work all day. It is not a question of fitting this narrative material into Interzone. Interzone will be fitted into the narrative. As I write I will suddenly realize that a piece from Interzone belongs here. For example, "blue movies" goes into a South American Sodom section which I have just completed . . . "Word" fits into a junk-sick subway ride. "Benway" into my Freelandt section. I will mention in passing, the forces of evil are represented by a Scandinavian tycoon head of Trak Inc., who control the Sex Utilities of most of the world. That is they can disconnect your orgones and leave you strictly from impotence . . . In short I am beginning to see now where I have been going all along. It's beginning to look like a modern *Inferno*.

The narrative will consist of an American section, a long South American section—of which I have completed about sixty pages—a section in Scandinavia and the Interzone sections, with switches back and forth between them, when, for example, the same point is reached in Scandinavia and South America . . . I will send along one short section which is complete in itself, might do for Paul Carroll.[26] If you think so, please send it along to him. If not, I will make another selection. Since Olympia has rejected MS. in present form, there is no hassle there. I don't know when the whole thing will be complete. It is a tremendous job. For example, the short section I will send you as soon as typed up, took me a full week of solid work. And always new material to be incorporated.

---

25. Gene Feldman coedited, with Max Gartenberg, *The Beat Generation and the Angry Young Men* (New York: Citadel Press, 1958), and included an excerpt from *Junkie* entitled "My First Days on Junk." Despite Burroughs' comment, the pseudonym William Lee was still used.
26. Paul Carroll was then the poetry editor of the *Chicago Review*.

Tanger is completely dead. Bowles not here. See absolutely nobody.

Have reached a point where I don't seem to want boys any more, can't make it. Must have some cunt. I was never supposed to be queer at all. The whole original trauma is out now. Such horror in bringing it out I was afraid my heart would stop. Did get a severe intracostal neuralgia and sciatica. Expect me more or less in Paris by New year . . . Nothing holds me in Tanger except it is convenient place to work. Otherwise sick of it and everybody in it, especially B. B., who is now going with eight-year-old Arabs and it is really disgusting, pre-pubescent gooks prowling about the house looking to rush in and steal something. And he says gaily, "Oh, it's just that I feel *inadequate* with older people," and *laughs*. The stupid bastard is in the middle of a particularly undesirable section of Hell and *doesn't even know it*. "I just feel *inadequate*. He, he, he." I mean, too much . . .

Please give my best to Gregory and Peter. I think I wrote you about how my theory has been, in many respects, confirmed. Early research in Germany has already established that addiction lessens psychosis. I mean they already tried it . . . So why don't they go on with it? No, can't make addicts. Take out their brains with an apple corer, but recoil in horror from a safe and curable condition.

Love,
Bill

Tanger . . . *Dec. 4, 1957*

Dear Jack,

Congratulations on your success.[27] I wish you would send me a copy of your book, but don't send it here unless it can reach me before the first of the year. I am leaving Tangiers probably forever. There is a strange malady here which destroys your sex desire—I think an atypical form of virus hepatitis . . . God knows how many atypical virus strains may follow in the wake of atomic experiments—Paul Lund has it, I have had it twice. I know at least ten cases around town. It goes away when you leave Tanger. This is no fable. I have checked and rechecked. Besides, I am sick of boys anyhoo and about to switch to cunt.

I have been working up to ten hours per day on a narrative which includes and incorporates all the material in Interzone . . . There is a section in Scandinavia, one in U.S.A., and one in South America, and one in Interzone all linked up back and forth—like a character enters a Turkish Bath in Sweden and comes out in South America. Incidentally, I have cut "Word" down to twenty pages . . . Much better this way . . . I will send along when I get typed up. Tremendous amount of work but I do nothing else. No sex, on the wagon, see nobody. Just work and smoke a little *kif*.

I enclose two sample sections which stand alone. One is from new U.S.A. section, the other from South American section. Will give you idea and may be saleable. They look good from here. I plan to join Allen in Paris around the first of the year, or maybe move to Spain, but out of this blighted area in any case. May hit New York next Spring or Summer. Best to Lucien and thank him for sending along the book copies. I will write him separate letter. I really don't have ten minutes from the time I get up . . . All the best. See you soon I hope.

As Ever.
Bill

---

27. The appearance of *On the Road* had attracted enormous publicity and a barrage of contract offers for Kerouac's unpublished manuscripts, new books, and film rights.

Dec. 8 [*1957*
Tangier]

Dear Allen,

Enclose two short pieces [. . .] Don't know if suitable for the Chicago outfit—if not let me know what sort of an item they would be likely to want.[28]

Alan is here since a few days, currently suffering from a cold. It looks like I am really getting ready to move out of here come the month's end. Nothing new around here. Paul and Jane are back from England, and Jane is better but far from well. Poor Ahmed Yacoubi is in jail for leaving Morocco with his case (involving the fourteen year old German boy) pending . . .[29] Brion Gysin has opened the *Thousand and One Nights* with troop of sorry dancing boys, all with ferret faces and narrow shoulders and bad teeth, looking rather like a bowling team from Newark.[30] Alan Ansen reports he was regally entertained by Lord F., that silly old peer who made an attempt on my person on one nasty occasion. Here I am still junk sick just after the cure, and the last thing I wanted was some lecherous old peer rutting about on me . . . Weak-minded old man. I mean it's like Angus Wilson invites one to tea and makes indecent proposals.[31] Too horrid.

---

28. Chicago outfit: i.e., the *Chicago Review*.

29. In September, Yacoubi had gone to England with Paul Bowles for an exhibition of his paintings at the Hanover Gallery, organized partly by Francis Bacon. Yacoubi's arrest in June 1957, and subsequent rearrest in late November, concerned Moroccan politics as much as it did morality.

30. Gysin had first opened the 1001 Nights restaurant in early 1954 as a showcase for the Master Musicians of Jajouka, in a wing of the Menebhi palace on the Marshan, not far from Tangier's Kasbah. In the aftermath of Moroccan independence (November 6, 1955), at the suggestion of John and Mary Cooke, he closed it in summer 1956. After returning from Algeria in summer 1957, Gysin reopened the restaurant at the same address, but was forced to sell it to the Cookes before the end of the year.

31. Angus Wilson, the English novelist, author of *Hemlock and After* (1952) and *Anglo-Saxon Attitudes* (1956).

Well I have been working, and have at least a hundred pages of new material complete. Will see what kind of narrative I can concoct. I had a letter from Jack . . . Seems in good shape . . . Alan sends love to all, and I likewise,

Love,
Bill

1958

Jan. 9, 1958
[Tangier]

Dear Allen,

By all means hang onto the room. I will be along shortly. Delayed by illness and inertia . . . Must absolutely get out of here for my health. The place is plague-ridden—some obscure virus, probably Ardmore's disease—see current *Time* . . . [1]

Regards to all in Paris and see you very soon. I will probably leave here within the next three or four days. Will telegraph time of arrival if I can find out what it will be.[2]

Alan fine . . . Not much new around here.

Love,
Bill

---

1. The January 6, 1958, issue of *Time* magazine carried an article about the outbreak of a mysterious viral disease among airmen at Ardmore Air Force Base in southern Oklahoma.
2. Burroughs reached Paris by plane on Thursday, January 16, 1958.

Feb. 16, 1958
[Paris]

Dear Allen,

Yes, received the checks for which many thanks—still don't have my check from Tanger. I wrote a letter to Consul Konya finally . . . Meanwhile family sent me some money here, so paid the rent.

Letter from Alan . . . He and Gregory are getting along very well again now that the junk is gone . . . Gregory also making time *chez* Guggenheim. She gave him a wrist-watch. He confessed prison. I mean she gave him the watch after he confessed prison. I wonder if Gregory was actually ever in jail???[3]

[. . .]

I am about half hooked on paregoric, which is unlimited here . . . We are not a bit alarmed about that . . . Intend to make experimental use of it in analysis.[4] If you can find Wikler's book on opiate addiction, buy it . . . University of Illinois Press . . . [5] Write when to expect you back . . . [6] Weather here is phenomenal, warm like Spring.

Alan and Gregory and Guggenheim may go onto Greece . . . It's great I tell you, great . . . [. . .]

Bad news from Tanger . . . Paul and Jane took off for Portugal.

---

3. In exchange for Corso's big leather German coat, Burroughs and Ginsberg had paid his fare to Venice. He left on January 21, taking a parcel of junk for Ansen, which never reached him. Corso had served time in the Tombs, Bellevue, and three years in Clinton Prison, Dannemora. He also had a long-standing obsession with wristwatches.

4. According to Ginsberg, Burroughs had come to Paris "not to claim me but visit me now & also see an analyst to clear up psychoanalytic blocks left etc.," and Burroughs "made arrangements to see [Dr. Schlumberger] twice a week at $10 per." (January 20 and 28, 1958, to Orlovsky, in *Straight Hearts' Delight*, pp. 125, 134.)

5. Abraham Wikler, *Opiate Addiction: Psychological and Neurophysiological Aspects in Relation to Clinical Problems* (Springfield, Illinois: Thomas, 1953).

6. At the end of January, Ginsberg visited England, returning to Paris the third week of February. After making another trip to England, he finally left Paris for New York on July 17.

It seems there was danger of involvement . . . Poor Ahmed had lost all his front teeth from police beatings . . . This is from Francis Bacon . . . Pasapoga closed down.[7]

See you soon,

Love,
Bill

---

7. Burroughs had been introduced to the English painter Francis Bacon by Paul Bowles. The Pasapoga was a bar on rue de Fez, run by Dowell Jones, an aging Welshman with a glass eye.

April 18, 1958
9 Rue Git Le Coeur
Paris 6, France

Dear Mr. Ferlinghetti,

Regards selections from my MS., which is not easy to find one's way around in, I offer the following suggestions:[8] The whole last section entitled *WORD* to be ignored, since I have finally cooked same down to three pages which herewith enclose, and suggest this be the beginning and the title be *Have You Seen Pantapon Rose?* . . . Omit *Andrew Keif and KY Scandal* which is beginning of MS . . . In *Voices,* which is section II, start on page three: "When I was on the junk I minded my junky business" etc., to end of that section. *County Clerk* omit if you want to follow a straight, coherent junk line . . . Omit *Interzone U, Islam Inc. A.J.'s Ball* and *Hassan's Rumpus Room.* Include *Hospital* (except for the Mickey Spillane part in the middle).[9] Include *Benway* (except for the theoretical part on addiction and schizophrenia). Include *The Technical Psychiatry Conference,* and take whatever you want from *The Market* . . .

Now that's one way of doing it, holds together in some sort of coherent line. Of course, you may have different ideas. It could be presented as a series of unrelated, short pieces. All I mean is the arrangement I suggest is more or less all in one piece. Also have avoided the more obscene sections which would involve difficulties of a legal nature . . .

Well, only a suggestion,

Sincerely,
William Burroughs

---

8. Burroughs enclosed a 200-page manuscript, titled "Interzone," for City Lights to consider. Apart from the "Word" section and a different sequence, the material was largely the same as the published text of *Naked Lunch.* Ferlinghetti rejected it.

9. The "hauser and o'brien" section was formerly part of "hospital" and followed the line: "Quite possible to develop a drug so habit-forming that one shot would cause lifelong addiction." (*Naked Lunch,* p. 65.)

July 20, 1958
9 Rue Git Le Coeur
Paris 6, France

Dear Paul,

Denver is about the last place I would expect you to be. You mean the show is put on in Denver?[10]

I am stuck in Paris until early Nov.—tentatively—at which time I may go to India. I have a friend here who has travelled all through the Far East. He says Bangkok and Japan nowhere. Both Americanized. Only place untouched by Western influence is India. He is going back there to live in Nov. and I will very probably go along. He plans to rent a house in Calcutta. From what he tells me about India, it sounds like your sort of thing. Perhaps you will consider joining us?? Jack Stern—that's his name—is far and away the most interesting person I have met in Paris.[11] We have a lot in common. Both graduates of Harvard and junk. He reports tea situation in India is fantastic.

Chicago Review is completely sold on my work, publishing it in sections. One is already out—Spring 1958. Another will appear next issue. Editor says he will publish all I send him.[12] Trouble is, no gelt.

Dave Woolman writes Tanger not much changed, but I would not consider returning there to live under present circumstances. He says the State Dept. took Jane's passport. This seems preposterous. I can't conceive anyone less political . . .

---

10. Bowles had written the score for the opera *Yerma,* based on García Lorca's play, and after rehearsals in New York, he went with the cast to Denver. The opera was premiered at the University of Colorado on July 29, 1958.

11. Jacques Stern, polio victim, writer, bibliophile, and addict from a wealthy French Jewish family, whom Burroughs had met through Gregory Corso that spring. Stern is mentioned by name in the first edition of *Naked Lunch* (p. 55), though the reference (crediting him with the "Heavy Fluid" concept) was deleted for all subsequent editions, (*cf.* p. 54 in the Grove Press, 1992, edition).

12. Irving Rosenthal, then a graduate student at the University of Chicago, was editor of *Chicago Review.*

Have you any plans for permanent residence? Please let me hear from you soon again,

As Ever,
Bill B.

[*July 1958*
Paris]

Dear Allen,

I read Mrs. Kerouac's letter. Evidently she intercepted your letter to Jack.[13] The woman is mad. She thinks she can scare you out of ever contacting him again by all this nonsense about the FBI.

A stupid, small-minded vindictive peasant, incapable of a generous thought or feeling. I mean she is really evil in her small way. In your place I would show Jack the letter. If he is content to be treated like a child and let his mother open his mail and tell him who to see and correspond with, he is a lost cause.

More bad news. Neal got five years to life.[14] Bob LaVigne writes that the judge accompanied his sentence by a stream of insults.[15] Neal bore himself with complete dignity and composure and kept his temper.

Stern is in the hospital taking a half-assed cure with demerol, his doctor not knowing from nothing about apomorphine or much of anything else looks like. I am going to put up a sign on the door: *Ginsberg Doesn't Live Here Anymore.* That fucking Arab woke me up at three A.M., and at eight A.M. somebody came around looking for "friends from Oxford" . . .

Otherwise, nothing new.

Love,
Bill

---

13. Mrs. Kerouac had written to Ginsberg after reading one of his letters to Jack. Because she put only six cents postage on it the letter was sent by sea, so that by the time it reached Paris, Ginsberg had left and Burroughs opened it for him. (See also following letter.)

14. Neal Cassady had been arrested in April 1958, having supplied marijuana to several undercover agents of the San Francisco Police Narcotic Division. He was sentenced on June 14, transferred to San Quentin on July 4, and served exactly two years.

15. Robert LaVigne, the painter through whom Ginsberg had first met Orlovsky in San Francisco in December 1954.

July 24 [*1958*
Paris]

Dear Allen,

I herewith forward Jack's weak and cowardly letter. Like some cat explaining to former friend how he "can't have him to the house anymore because of the little woman don't like Jews, and after all I am out of 'all that' now . . . Not that we can't meet now and then (not too often) for a glass of beer someplace maybe, etc." Weak and cowardly. "And of course you understand I can't help out with Neal or Julius.[16] After all, why should I involve myself. Must consider Mother first. She is easily upset, you know, and I *did warn* him after all." And a *Catholic*-Buddhist yet. My God! She really has him sewed up like an incision. And for whip cream and a Maraschino cherry this rot about "wise-man Uncle Sam," at a moment when bungling, criminal stupidity is losing America the last shred of respect and love throughout the world. Meanwhile Mrs. Kerouac continues to shower on you and me her psychotically obscene letters writhing with a sick hate enough to make a man puke. "You is not fit to be talked to as a human being, you and your dirty books and dirty mind and dirty dope. Don't you ever mention Jack's name again in your filthy writings." Etc. I burnt her last letter in the bidet, and advised her that I would not forward any more of her letters to you, but destroy them *unopened* . . .

I am writing this letter *to you*. Please do *not* show it to Jack. *No useful purpose would be served*. However, you *can* tell him from me that no one can achieve the fence-straddle he attempts. No one can simultaneously stand behind those filthy letters of Mrs. Kerouac and be in any meaningful sense a friend of the person to whom those letters were addressed. Jack has reaped fame and money telling Neal's story, recording his conversation, representing himself as Neal's life-long friend. Maybe the fuzz got onto Neal through Jack's book. In any case he has sold Neal's blood and made money. Now he will not lift a dollar to help. I don't see it, Allen.

---

16. Julius Orlovsky, who had been in Central Islip mental hospital for several years.

And isn't it just like her to send along her poison letters with inadequate postage?

Well, enough of Jack. You must make up your mind as [to] what you want to do. Stern is in the clear now but hooked of course.[17] So am I still. But I have a stock-pile of apomorphine and plan to take off in a week or so for Spain. My analyst is taking August and first two weeks of Sept. off.[18] I am getting along well with Stern's wife.[19] I think she is a really nice person, and I have come to like her very much.

I have great novel idea . . . The period in human history when there were many species of homo. Perhaps the most beautiful did not survive. This idea I can only realize if I get the *vision* to realize it. I see now great swamps and deserts, sad meaningless lemurs. Hideous, carnivorous baboons. Human potentials in a larval state . . . I may not be able to do it. Don't know. Just got the idea yesterday. Analysis is coming to a head. No doubt now: I witnessed a miscarriage, by Mary the evil governess, and the results were burned in the furnace in my presence.[20] That is the "murder."

Stern leaves in a few days for yacht cruise. Stern laid $150 on Gregory. I hope that kicking will reverse my liver trouble and restore me to state of pristine health I enjoyed after cure with Dent. That is one reason have not been in hurry to kick. I want a *basic cellular turn-over, you dig.*

Write to me soon.

Love,
Bill

Gregory is having bomb poem printed up to be sent to U.S.[21]

P.S. I guess that about covers my position. Gregory wrote a letter to Jack which he decided not to send. I repeat, *don't show Jack this*

---

17. Jacques Stern had been facing narcotics heat.

18. Analyst: Dr. Schlumberger.

19. Stern's American-born wife, Dini.

20. Mary Evans, the Welsh nanny who looked after Burroughs as a child.

21. Corso's "Bomb" was published in *The Happy Birthday of Death* (New York: New Directions, 1960).

letter. No use feeding his paranoia like, "I just want to be a peaceful dove and everyone is against me, etc." What in effect he wants is to be a Nazi and keep his Jewish friends at the same time. In most basic terms he does not *love* his mother, he is *shit scared* of her, tries to separate himself from the whole complex via unenlightened Buddhism (Buddhism without psychoanalytic insight is only a treadmill of anxiety, delimited circles) and now joins with her in such an intellectually disreputable bastard as *Catholic* Buddhism . . . And the one possible out for him—psychoanalysis—he rejects as "decadent, European, Jewish, Anti-American." Oh God, it's hopeless! He seems to forget all your hours of work getting his manuscripts before publishers, agents, etc . . . I don't like this reference to shit mouth Julius, nor the way he shrugs off the horrible injustice of Neal's imprisonment. All he wants is *security for himself*. A weakling, no, a coward who cannot be trusted under any pressure. He doesn't want *his* name mentioned. What about *your* name and *Neal's* and *mine* in his books?? This P.S. is written a day after the letter. More I think about it, the *less* I think of him, and the less desire I have to have to see any more of him. Well, enough.

Tanger
Aug. 25, 1958

Dear Allen,

Analyst on vacation—I have come here to rest and escape the interruptions of Paris. I am going to ruthlessly eliminate, or at least thin, the ranks of visitors on my return.

Tanger is finished. The Ouab days are upon us.[22] Many a queen has been dragged shrieking from the Parade, the Socco Chico, and lodged in the local box where sixty Sons of Sodom now languish. Dave Woolman has been up for questioning, ditto Croft-Cooke, ditto Joseph.[23] Dexter Allen, Dave [Woolman], are leaving tomorrow.[24] Tony [Reithorst] has fled to Malaga. The boys, many beaten to a pulp, have spilled a list of hundreds. I may even be on it. There is always the warning of a preliminary interrogation which means "get out now." Well, I am all packed and could walk out of here in 2 minutes.

Working on varied projects. No time to go into. Write soon. I will be here until the 10th more or less—Must work now. Ahmed Yacoubi cowers in his room paralysed with fear. This is really it. The End. I never come back here any more.

India roll out your carpets—

Love
Bill

---

22. "The Ouab days were the five days left over at the year's end in Mayan calendar. All bad luck of the year was concentrated in the Ouab Days." (Gloss given by Burroughs in letter to Irving Rosenthal, July 20, 1960 [Ginsberg Collection, Columbia University]. *Cf. Naked Lunch,* p. 233, in the "atrophied preface" section.)
23. Rupert Croft-Cooke, the author, a frequent visitor to Tangier, and Joseph, his Hindu Secretary.
24. Dexter Allen, author of a collection of poems, *Ghazal* (Los Angeles, 1953), and the novel *Jaguar and the Golden Stag* (New York: Coward-McCann, 1954).

(from Gregory Corso and William Burroughs)

[*Sept. 28, 1958*
Paris]

Get Don Allen[25] & Kerouac
to contribute $$

Dear Allen,

Bill and I are set on doing a magazine, INTERPOL, "the poet is becoming a policeman"—and our content will be of the most sordid, vile, vulgar, oozing, seeping slime imaginable. We only want the most disgusting far-outness. For first issue Bill has in mind: Bowles (his most disgusting); Tennessee Williams (his most); and your bubbling, gooey cocaine writing; and Stern's most humiliating, and Kerouac's most maudlin, etc. So we are determined to do this because like Bill says, we're policemen and we can't help doing such things, it ain't our faults. So we decided to make you co-editor of suggestion and fund-raising; it will be your task (thus to insure this historic venture) to collect the most hideous of material, and money, lots of money; go to Don Allen, Kerouac, everybody, and demand they send Bill Burroughs money for this ghoulish enterprise. We, Bill and I, are confident that you won't fail us. To encourage you in your quest for funds, I will tell you what we plan for our format: first an editorial, by either Bill or me or both. In it we will inform our readers that the thing this week is Palfium, or that one needs a prescription now for Diosan in Spain—kind of junk news, etc. Also we will review books, books written by junkies, fiends, cross-eyed imbeciles, huge-footed oafs, etc. We will praise and hail and laud all kinds of bile, and put down, pan, condemn all kinds of respectability and whiteness.

So please aid us. I will write to Ansen and Ferl[inghetti] and Stern, and you to Phipps,[26] Don Allen, Kerouac, etc. Good luck:

---

25. Donald Allen, editor at Grove Press.
26. Harry Phipps, from Palm Beach, a wealthy young patron of the Beats whom Kerouac and Corso had met in Paris, and who later died of an amphetamine overdose in New York, aged thirty.

in your hand you have Bill's golden rod of vile to burn a path on the pavements of untrodded history. All will be blue pus and green eggs. Lo! Onward! For onward is gawking scum of Interpol! Beware those who get on Interpol's blacklist! Bill is going in his room, I'm crankling in mine. Beware! Interpol is born! Aruuuuugggggh!

[Gregory Corso]

When the Human Image is threatened, The Poet dictates forms of survival. Dream police of poetry protect us from The Human Virus. The human virus can now be isolated and treated. This is the work of The New POLICE-POET.

The virus must be traced with radioactive images before it crystallizes in cancer, blood, stone and money of the world nightmare surface. The Nightmare of last night is the soggy toast of this morning's breakfast. This is latest revelation and way of action . . .

As regard your nitrous oxide experiences:[27] Yes, I have had similar insights. In fact I have visions now practically constant . . .

So-called solid reality is only crystallized dream. It can be undreamed. There is nothing stronger than dream, because dreams are forms of THE LAW.

Bill

27. The painkilling gas administered to Ginsberg by his dentist had given him a vision of reality as a comic illusion, inspiring Ginsberg to write the poem "Laughing Gas" (published in Kaddish).

Oct. 10 [1958]
Paris

Dear Allen,

Sorry to be remiss. So much has happened on basic levels I can't cover it all, like ten years pass since I see you. When I think back to my arrival in Paris last year, the image of myself at that time is remote as an image from childhood. More so actually. Analysis is coming to spectacular climaxes. I am completely dissatisfied with all the work I have done in writing and with the whole medium. Unless I can reach a point where my writing has the danger and immediate urgency of bull-fighting it is nowhere, and I must look for another way.

Brion Gysin living next door. He used to run *The 1001 Nights* in Tanger. He has undergone similar conversion to mine and doing GREAT painting. I mean great in the old sense, not jive talk great. I know great work when I see it in any medium. I see in his painting the psychic landscape of my own work. He is doing in painting what I try to do in writing. He regards his painting as a hole in the texture of the so-called "reality," through which he is exploring an actual place existing in outer space. That is, he moves into the painting and through it, his life and sanity at stake when he paints. Needless to say no dealer will touch his work. It is unlike anything I ever saw. When you see it, your thought process stops dead and *satori* opens up in front of you. What [Francis] Bacon hopes to do, Gysin has done repeatedly.

I must simply eliminate all visitors and give all my time to work. I find that I simply can not stand contact with others on the usual meaningless level.

I have also found the way to beat withdrawal. I just go right through the depression and out the other side. So many extraordinary experiences lately. Of course life is literally a dream, or rather the projection of a dream. That is why political action fails, just as attempts to coerce neurosis with so-called will-power always fail. But the whole existing system can be *dreamed away* if we get enough people dreaming on the Gysin level. There is nothing can stop the power of a real dream. I mean this literally. You know, I can dream money into my pocket. I can dream up H and O. Yesterday morning, sick, flat broke (Jack Stern in England taking the cure), I mean it looked like time to throw in the towel. So I just dreamed of junk and Bernard [Frechtman] wanders in and lays a huge piece of O on me. Someone else practically insisted on lending me ten thousand Francs. An H connection showed up . . . And this has happened repeatedly.

But I still can't get a line on writing . . . Sending all old work to [Irving] Rosenthal. Best to Jack, Peter, etc.,

Love,
Bill

Oct. 19, 1958
London, England

Dear Paul,

This writing finds me in London, taking the cure with a junkie friend.[28] Since Doctor Dent only takes two patients at a time, there are no alcoholics about to lower the tone of the establishment.

As to the advisability of your returning to Tanger, it is for the Clouded Crystal Ball Dept.:

I have it from Paul Lund, who allegedly read it in *ESPAÑA*, that you were officially expelled from the Sherifian Empire, no reason given by Rabat. Others deny that such a notice appeared. [Charles] Gallagher has it straight from *Securité* that you can return at any time. Brion Gysin, surprisingly, thinks you could return without danger . . . So??

General situation not overly alarming. Bent Anderson indeed languishes in the Casbah, but that could happen to a man of his caliber in any country. Dave Woolman, when he was called for questioning, spilled on everybody in town. Dexter Allen fled at my urgent, and not altogether disinterested, warnings. As it turned out I did us both a favor, whereas I had only intended to benefit myself, since the police were around looking for him two days later. Tony Dutch fled to Holland. Eric [Gifford] still unmolested. For myself, never passed a quieter and pleasanter month, eating *majoun* and working. Ahmed [Yacoubi] is looking well and not worried. I finally told him I could not listen to any more rambling and utterly incomprehensible accounts about Maurice—whoever he may be— and The Paul, as he calls you, concerning things left in the apartment, etc. I have no idea what he was talking about, and the more he talked the less I knew.

Brion Gysin is living in the hotel next to mine and we are getting along at last.

He has produced, in the last three months, some amazing work. I don't know painting, but I do know great **work** when I see it in

---

28. Jacques Stern had paid Burroughs' way to London, where they rented a flat at 2 Mansfield Street.

any medium. And this is great work. Needless to say no dealer will look at it because they never see anything like it before. Appalling what small-minded people control the money side of painting. They sound worse than publishers.

Naked Lunch is being published piecemeal in *The Chicago Review*.[29] Rosenthal, the editor of *Chicago Review*, is the only editor who really understands what I am doing. I don't know if Jay Laughlin has seen the MS. or not.[30]

I will be here for a few weeks then back to Paris. Address: Cargo American Express, London. Please let me hear from you. I was sorry to hear about Jane.[31] Please give her my best regards. Hope to see you someplace soon . . .

As Ever,
Bill B.

---

29. After the spring issue of *Chicago Review*, the autumn one had published another excerpt from *Naked Lunch* that October.
30. James Laughlin, editor at New Directions.
31. While Paul was in Denver with the cast of *Yerma*, on October 1, Jane entered the Cornell Medical Center in White Plains, New York, where she suffered several seizures.

1959

Jan. 2, 1959
Paris

Dear Allen,

I have been slow writing because events of last month complex and fantastic to point where coverage is difficult. Like covering events of ten crowded years.

The para-normal occurrences thick and fast. I enclose latest productions which cover this period and reflect the phenomena observed: I saw Stern lose about seven pounds in ten minutes when he took a shot after being off a week. (That flesh you gain back when you kick is soft and ectoplasmic at first, and it melts *literally* at touch of junk). On another occasion he felt my touch on his arm across six feet of space . . . After writing the "Fats Terminal" section, I saw Fats' face in an amber bead Brion Gysin showed me from magic, Arab necklace . . . (Monster virus forms frozen in amber, looking for a way out *and in* you might say.) Once I looked in mirror and saw my hands completely inhuman, thick, black-pink, fibrous, long white tendrils growing from the curiously abbreviated finger-tips as if the finger had been cut off to make way for tendrils . . . And Jerry,[1] who was sitting across the room, said: "My God, Bill! What's wrong with your hands???"

"My hands?" I said innocently.

"They are all thick and pink and something white growing out the fingers."

Many people have commented on my growing invisibility . . . So the material is a catalogue of actual events.

Above are only a few high-lights. I suddenly began writing in word forms, of which enclose samples, and also have done illustrations for the material. I am at the beginning in this medium.

Gregory will tell you about the ball and Brion and the coffin etc.[2]

---

1. Jerry Wallace, a twenty-year-old boy from Kansas, in Paris at the time.
2. From a magic shop, Burroughs had bought a key chain with a small stainless steel ball on the end. Gysin claimed to see an image of Tangier in the ball, and when Burroughs looked he saw the same vision, of a Moslem funeral. The mirror-gazing experience had also been initiated by Gysin.

I know that I am in a very dangerous place, but point of no return is way back yonder.

Above to be read upside down and backward.[3] They are *alive*, these forms like living organisms.

Love to Peter, Jack, Lucien.

Love,
Bill

P.S. Might try *Evergreen* or *New Directions* with this material.[4]

---

3. "Above" referring to forty-nine Gysin-style calligraphic swirls (seven lines of seven figures, marked, upside down, "Top" and "Bottom" in reverse of page direction), of the sort drawn by Burroughs for the dust jacket of the Olympia Press edition of *Naked Lunch*. A following page consists of nine lines of either seven or eight similar glyphs.
4. *Evergreen Review*, the magazine of Grove Press, since 1957.

Jan. 17, 1959
9 Rue Git-Le-Coeur
Paris 6

Dear Brion,

Thanks for your letter. I will write PB at once. I visited Jacques Stern in London. He is having visions *sans* ball and also saw the coffin in the library independent, before receiving my account of events. So everybody agrees there is a coffin in the library—rather an odd place for a coffin I'd say. Is this the Faubourg Saint Germain? In the *library?*

As for myself, I have taken to painting lately, seemingly at the end of verbal communication : . .

I had planned to start South about the middle of next month. Hitting Ciotat and dig your pictures, then on to Tanger or Ceuta or some warm place.[5] So keep me informed as to your plans . . .

Gregory writes he needs DEATH poem which you have. Will you please send to Gregory Corso, Cargo Allen Ginsberg, 170 East 2nd Street, NYC, Apt. 16.

Oh, strange thing about my painting. Only Arab themes emerge. Did you receive my Christmas card?

By all means a Tanger conference is indicated . . .

Please keep me informed. I am waiting to see your pictures.

As for me, I am ready to move any direction after middle of next month more or less, that is any South direction.

As Ever,
Bill B

P.S. The calligraphs always emerge upside down.[6]

---

5. La Ciotat: a coastal village between Marseilles and Toulon with a long tradition as an artist colony. Gysin had traveled there around New Year's, returning to Paris the second week of February. Ceuta: the Spanish enclave just east of Tangier.
6. There are two rows of calligraphs at the foot of the page, marked "Bottom" and "Top."

Jan. 17, 1959
9 Rue Git Le Coeur
Paris 6, France

Dear Paul,

If I have not written it was partly owing to your constant shifts of address—for example, sent a card to the Morris Agency.[7] Hear you are in London, and now back in Tanger.

I am planning to move South in another month, possibly stopping over to see Brion en route . . .

The *Chicago Review* folded out from under me.[8] Also I was denounced in *The Nation* as an international homo and all around sex fiend . . . Reminds me of old-time Junky talking about the Uptown citizens come down to The Village, he is trying to hustle for the price of an H cap: "Jesus, Bill, sex orgies they want yet."

Looks like *NAKED LUNCH* is finished. As to whether it will ever be published in complete form, I have no idea at this point. Complications and the manuscript scattered all over U.S. and Europe.

What is the news in Tanger? Like I say, I plan to go there myself in next month or so. Not definite yet. Is Jane with you? If so give her my best regards. Hope to see you very soon. .

As Ever,
Bill B.

---

7. William Morris Agency, in New York.
8. The appearance of Burroughs' material in the Autumn 1958 issue had provoked an outcry by Chicago *Daily News* columnist Jack Mabley, leading to the suppression of the winter issue by university authorities.

Feb. 20, 1959
9 Rue Git-Le-Coeur
Paris 6, France

Dear Paul,

Thanks for your letter. I will be in Tanger from mid-March to July more or less—this is tentative like any plans I make—Hope to see you there.

Brion is here in Paris. Unfortunately down with appendicitis and must undergo operation. He is doing great work, better all the time. [. . .]

There seems to be possibility of publishing expurgated version of *Naked Lunch* in U.S. Various publishers have shown interest after the phenomenal publicity accorded Allen and Gregory on their late reading tour to Chicago.[9]

I hear from Mexico that two hundred resident Americans have been deported for variety of reasons or for no reason at all, and prices up. All in all, any ideas I had of returning there are definitely cancelled.

Brion sends his best . . .

As Ever,
Bill Burroughs

---

9. In January 1959, Ginsberg, Corso, and Orlovsky did benefit readings and held press conferences in support of Rosenthal and Carroll, who had resigned as editors of *Chicago Review* and planned to launch their own magazine to publish the suppressed material. The activities were featured in *Time* and *Life* magazines.

April 2, 1959
c/o U.S. Consulate
Tanger, Maroc

Dear Allen,

My arrival poorly timed. Tanger rocked by another *cause celebre* in which I am involved owing to series of unfortunate conjunctures. Briefly: Capt. Stevens, the Master of the jinxed vessel *Amphitrite*[10] currently impounded in Gibraltar pending litigation, was busted in the Socco Chico copping for ½ kilo of O from The Old Black Connection. (Both held incommunicado). After usual processing by fuzz, Old Black Joe[11] spills, involving Lund and another "American with glasses." (Flashback: About six months ago I thought of pushing a little Moroccan tea in Paris, and wrote Lund a letter asking if he could make delivery on "Moroccan Leather Goods." I subsequently dropped the project.) This letter, for some as yet undisclosed reason, Capt. Stevens had in his possession at the time of his arrest. So the fuzz can only conclude that I am Paris O outlet. So now they know my name and Paris address. They shake Paul's trap down and find some old manuscripts I left behind, and wade through a suitcase full of my vilest pornography looking for "evidence." (They must figure hanging has code significance.) Evidently they are not aware of my presence here (or at least they have not been around for that 8 am. visit.) Well, I am keeping my nose clean and they can look at my drawings any time.

The drag in all this—puts me on top of check-list in France and likely U.S. In any case I would not take anything back to France now. That would be asking for it à la Shell.[12] Oh, and the fuzz has a letter I sent to Shell from London in which I say something to

10. Clive Stevenson was both captain and owner of the three-masted topsail schooner.

11. Old Black Joe: Reference is to the nineteenth-century "Negro dialect" song of the same name by Stephen Foster.

12. Mack Shell Thomas, a Texan friend who had been arrested in Texas earlier in the year for possession of heroin. In Burroughs' letter to Ginsberg and Corso, February 12, 1959 (Ginsberg Collection, Columbia University): "Imagine that idiot going back with a saxophone and loud clothes . . . A *saxophone!!!* My God,

effect: "Pooling our knowledge could be of great benefit to both parties." I can see myself taking shape in their 12 year[-old] minds as "the evil, perverted brain behind international narcotic ring, the agents of which pretend to be poets and painters to cover their sinister operations." It's all so tiresome. I mean, such a *bore*.

The actual facts are infinitely more sensational. It is difficult to put in words the visions that I experience lately. (Sudden wave of activity since the beginning of Ramadan. I noticed in Paris like—"Things picking up the last few days, since . . . since . . . *Ramadan, of course!*")

A few pin-points: underwater medium, strange enclosed spheres moving through it. I am in one of these spheres. Beautiful pink and black landscapes, people of black, flexible metal, people covered with green—brown—red—fuzz. Live, flying saucers like flat fish full of black fuzz.

But something new has been added since I arrive here, something that I am not always sure I can handle. (Last night sleep with the light on.) This is *physical pressures* on my person, like I was *pushed* away from the ball. Things *move* in my hands. I can not describe the sensation—I am not pushed with hands—It is like a new dimension of gravity.

Well, I will not turn back (even if I could): "Let it come down—"[13]

Seems I never think about sex—So don't know if I am interested in man or woman or both or neither. I think neither. Just can't dig the natives on this planet—certainly the analysis has, with a slow scalpel of fact, cancelled my sado-masochist visa to Sodom. I wonder if any but the completely innocent can enter without a S-M Visa? I don't know. Brion in Marrakesh. Have not yet seen Jane Bowles. My drawings are only way I can illustrate what is hap-

---

how fucking stupid can a man get . . ." He served five years in prison. Thomas wrote poetry and had published a novel about his childhood, entitled *Gumbo*. In 1965, Grove Press published his prison memoirs, *The Total Beast*.

13. The first murderer's reply to Banquo in *Macbeth*, act 3, scene 3, which was also the title Paul Bowles had used for his Tangier-set novel. Burroughs may have been thinking also of Bowles's *The Sheltering Sky*, whose last section is prefaced with this quote from Franz Kafka: "From a certain point onward there is no longer any turning back. That is the point that must be reached."

pening. Some of these are positively alive. Will send along a few samples.

Love,
Bill

P.S. Enclose clipping from *Herald Tribune*—please save—which bears out my theory on addiction, schizophrenia and cancer. I suggested giving cancer patients a habit and then withdrawing junk, since during withdrawal, *"substances similar to LSD 6 are released in the body."* I suggest that: "LSD 6 and related substances *may have direct anti-cancerous action,* but the physiological state that produces these substances in the body is probably the real curative agent."

That was 3 years ago. I sent theory to Wolberg. Nobody pays it any mind. Now they get around to using LSD 6 . . .

Stupid swine! When will they learn to let those do the thinking that have been blessed by God with the necessary equipment?

If the theory is published in Benway section of *Naked Lunch,* this fact should be included in a note. Please pass along to Rosenthal.

Love to All.

Love, Bill

April 21, 1959
Paris
9 Rue Git-Le-Coeur

Dear Allen,

Just to let you know I am in Paris. Did I tell you about the O scandal? Yes, of course I did—Memory all shot these days.

Return U.S. probably end of June. Lund and his stupid cohorts really fucked up my vacation. How can I relax with the fuzz looking for me, and have to hide even kif out of the room—They searched Paul again—I was there by accident and, miraculously, no passport check of my person, not to mention the 5 grams of O in my pocket at the time. Stevens still in and might as well make himself comfortable.

Good to be back in Paris. Alan Ansen came back here with me via the Pacquet Boat. I hate boat-trips and travel generally. Found out you can buy Diosan in France—just another name is all you need to know. No word from Stern—Looks like he is out of my picture. Too bad. Not many like that from mystic stand-point—And Shell gone.

I am speaking of objective and demonstrable phenomena, not vague Huncke skin pickings.

For example, there is a phenomenon, a magnetic attraction between the ball and magnifying mirror which moves the ball *every time under any circumstances*. The LSD6 bit should show you I know what I am doing, and know evidence when I see it. (Alan Ansen has confirmed, by repeated observation, the magnetic phenomena of which I speak.)

Thanks for *Big Table* issue—Looks great.[14] See any more of Jerry?[15] He says you don't dig his latest writing—It looks good to me—and he has offer from publisher and New Directions on basis of small excerpt in Daniel's little magazine, D.F., which folded after

14. *Big Table* no. 1, published in March, included "Ten Episodes from *Naked Lunch*." The Chicago post office impounded copies of the magazine, which only increased media interest in the States and focused Girodias's attention on the desirability of publishing Burroughs' novel.
15. Jerry Wallace.

one issue[16]—I mean looks like good writing for what that is worth—Myself wonder if any writing now has much *raison d'être*. Brion doing great work. Back in Paris soon.

My health is terrible which makes kicking difficult—No future plans—Tanger out as place of residence until *L'affaire Stevens* settles, and in any case fading into just another town. All the Spanish boys got the toe. Not that I care for myself, but it is sad, the whole place now is sad and deserted.

I seem to have reached the end of the line on drawing. No more—Writing, I dabble around—Write a few pages and lose interest—I wrote a letter to the man who is experimenting with LSD6 for cancer—See if I can get some info out of him—

Love to Gregory, Peter, Jack *et al,*

Love,
Bill

16. Daniel F.: a young Frenchman and friend of Jerry Wallace.

May 18, 1959
9 Rue Git-Le-Coeur
Paris 6, France

Dear Allen,

Bowles has nothing to worry about. No general heat. Is specific for O.

Glad to hear you are doing well. I have written the family for boat-gelt. Plan to leave here late June. Yes, I wrote Rosenthal. Doubt if advance will come through in time. Could use it in N.Y.C. in any case.

Alan [Ansen] back in Venice. Heat on tea here like I never see it— I mean nothing, nowhere. Stern in complete seclusion. Answers no letters—at least none of mine. Says the presence of people is painful to him. I think Gysin is afraid of me as notorious carrier of Black Fuzz, bad luck and death. Of the three mystics I had hoped to form nucleus and get something definite and useable via cross-fertilization —Shell, Gysin, and Stern—and then there were none. I continue to see visions and experience strange currents of energy, but the Key— the one piece that could make it useable—Stern had part of it, and so did Shell (Gysin more a catalyst or medium in strict sense): "You can look anywhere, no good, *no bueno*—hustling myself—"

Tea-less and healthless. I weigh about 120 pounds. But one thing I know for sure now like I know any fact: so-called "death" is not final, though a powerful lobby or interest block presumes to know what Life and Death is, and give out with their bulletins of "scientific" horseshit—*I know what I have seen, being strictly from Missouri.*[17]

Enclose late[st] drawing. To really dig these drawings you must be tea high, then you will suddenly *see*. Love to Peter.

Love,
Bill

P.S. May call on you for money if family is short.

---

17. Missouri: the "Show Me State."

June 8, 1959
9 Rue Git Le Coeur
Paris, France

Dear Allen,

Thanks a lot for the loot, but it looks like I won't need it after all. Stern is back and has invited me to spend a month with him on his yacht. In consequence I will be about a month late in return to U.S. Needless to say it is not a taste for high living that persuades me to accept his invitation. Stern has discovered an abbreviated form of psychotherapy—never longer than two weeks—which he will show me during the trip which is a work trip for both of us you dig.

I do not have time to go into all the fantastic details. Briefly, Stern fell and broke his leg in London. He went to Dent's nursing home to take cure at same time. After a week there he came down with a severe sinus headache. The pain spread to his spine and his whole body until he was screaming with pain. Dent came and: "First time I ever saw him when he really did not know what to do." So he starts shooting in heroin a grain at a time. Twelve grains in two hours and the pain was not alleviated. (No other doctor in the world would ever inject that amount of heroin. There is no question that he saved Jack's life.) Two nurses holding him down, he bit a piece of wood right in two. Then went into complete state of catatonia. This lasted two days. They called in a shock specialist who said the obvious: that the catatonia was physiological escape mechanism from the pain, which would otherwise have precipitated shock and death . . . They gave him one shock and he came out of the catatonia and began writing. Wrote a novel in nine days—I have seen part of it.[18] It is great, I mean *great*, not jive talk great. This is not only my opinion. I have talked with the translator of French edition, Faber and Faber in London is publishing it in English.[19] Three plays, poetry, etc.

There were four psycho cases in the home and he discovered a

---

18. Jacques Stern's novel: *Fluke*, privately published by Stern.
19. This was a Stern fantasy. Publication by Faber & Faber never happened.

method of treatment which he calls functional therapy. All of them are out now and cured. These were people who had been in and out of mental hospitals for years. So far, I do not know the details of this therapy since he wants to *show* me rather than *tell* me.

As for Jack's writing, I think it is better by far than mine or Kerouac's or yours or Gregory's or anyone I can think of. There is no doubt about it, he is a *great writer*. I think the greatest writer of our time . . . Remember that this is only the beginning.

The change in him since the pain is startling. But difficult to pin down. He used to give off emanations of death, now he gives off life. But he lives in constant danger. In last week 2 serious accidents. Ran his Bentley into a concrete island at 130 miles per hour, flipped over twice end over end, right side up and not a scratch on him or the car.[20] (I would have been with him except was too tired. Might not have been so lucky.) Fell down marble stair-case and broke a tooth. Not to mention overdose of sleeping pills and some poison shit that came near to kill him—I had to confiscate it finally . . . Full of scopolamine—Never a dull moment around Jack, like center of a storm.

I don't know how long before we will leave for the yacht, which is in Monte Carlo—expect in the next week or so. Will keep you posted and hang onto the loot you sent. Thanks again. Love to Peter.

Love,
Bill

P.S. Jack says he is not a member of The Beat Generation, and does not wish to be so typed, which is why he hesitates to publish in *Big Table*.

Needless to say the pain and all circumstances surrounding it are absolutely without medical precedent or explanation. Dent says he never saw anything as horrible.

---

20. Burroughs later learned that the entire Stern–Dr. Dent story was fictitious. The wrecked Bentley story is also unconfirmable. In *The Soft Machine* (Grove 1966, 1992 edition): "I had this terrible accident in a car a Bentley it was" (p. 70).

[*Late July 1959*
Paris]

Dear Allen,

Don't know where to send this since you are probably in process of leaving S.F.

I am sure the deal I made with Olympia was the best deal I could have made.[21] I saw Jack fucking around five years with American publishers. And no book is ever out less than a year from date of acceptance in U.S. scene. Of course the two pornographic sections—"Hassan's Rumpus Room" and "A.J.'s Annual Party"—are in, and very important part of the whole structure.

I had exactly ten days to prepare the MS. for the printers. Pressure welded the whole book together into a real organic continuity which it never had before. The book will be out this week. Realize that in the last month I have edited the entire MS., corrected the galley-proofs, and the final proofs, and designed a cover, and the book is rolling off the presses right now. I don't make mistakes. Not any more I don't. This was a unique opportunity. Selling to a U.S. publisher is now going to be easier—all I have to do is jerk out 2 chapters which are right together. In short, I can prepare the MS. for American or English markets in five minutes. I will send you a copy, which I should have like I say in a few more days.

We do not feature masochism this season in Hell, psychic or any other kind. Complete power and confidence has broken through at last, though it has been gathering since my original revelations of two years ago. You completely misunderstand about Stern. I am immune to his tantrums. All I mean is he can do certain things better than I can. For one thing, he is a great writer. There was no break or anything between us. He just went to sell the boat, which he had intended anyway after the trip. But he got a cash offer.[22] Meanwhile I have been making such incredible discoveries

---

21. Girodias, who had approached Burroughs in early June concerning publication, gave him an $800 advance. *Naked Lunch* appeared in the Olympia Traveller's Companion Series, no. 76, late July, in an edition of 5,000 copies, soon followed by a reprint of another 5,000.
22. In fact, the cash offer was pure fiction. There was no boat in Monte Carlo.

in the line of psychic exploration, I may well be ahead of him by now. You dig in this area, superiority of knowledge (and I *was not speaking* of any other, absolute and therefore non-existent *superiority*) shifts from one person to another in a matter of days or even hours. What is happening now is that I literally turn into someone else, not a human creature but man-like: He wears some sort of green uniform. The face is full of black boiling fuzz and what most people would call evil—silly word. I have been seeing him for some time in the mirror. This is nothing, of course. But when other people start seeing him without being briefed or influenced in any way, then something is really there. So far, Brion has seen him (or it). And so has Stern. But Stern left at the wrong time, since it is just in last few weeks that he comes through so clear that people stare at me in restaurants. Enclosed picture will give you some idea.

Oh, I got busted the other day. Eight am. tap tap tap. They had an order for my arrest issued April 9th. I wonder who grassed? Spent a horrible junk-sick day in vast Kafkian building while they typed out forms and took my picture, and when they went to develop the picture there was nothing on the plate . . . Not for nothing am I known as "The Invisible Man." Three tries and two hours before they got a picture. The machine was broken or something. Twelve hours I was in the fucking joint . . . All they were looking for was pot. Didn't even mention the word junk. They found some hash . . .

As to immediate plans, I am staying to launch the book. My pictures are also attracting attention, and I may have an exhibit. Also, Girodias is putting out a review on freedom and control in widest sense—just up my alley, you dig—and wants me to contribute and participate, and there is possibility of *Naked Lunch* being dramatized in London. All in all, it smells like real money.

I forgot—some big French outfit is translating the book (Gallimard).[23] Girodias has the English language rights, of which he gets one third.

So I must come back to U.S. to see the family. Probably within

---

23. Girodias's brother, Eric Kahane, did the translation, though Gallimard's publication of *Le Festin nu* did not appear until 1964, and then under several interdictions that made the book available only under the counter.

the next two months. So will tentatively meet you in N.Y. Difficult to make plans with so many things breaking at once . . . *But I am not going to India without seeing my family first.* Love to Peter. Love

Bill

P.S. Fact is I have become a megalomaniac, but with one essential difference and advantage. I have been outside. I have come up from the area of total humiliation and failure, climbed up cell by cell with a million set-backs and debacles. I don't figure to go back—(And no one can stand still. Precisely the most dangerous thing in this world or any other—and what I have SEEN in the past six months has convinced me that there are literally billions of other worlds. How could people ever have been so limited as to think otherwise?? The most dangerous thing to do is to STAND STILL. And no one can do it actually. You are going up or you are going down. And I know the down area. I came from there.) I am going on up. What I am putting down on paper now is *literally* what is happening to me as I move forward. This is no land of the imagination. It is real as a table (which, seen from the four dimension point of time, is, of course, a phantom). And dangerous in a most literal sense.

I enclose sample beginning of sequel to *Naked Lunch*. I don't know where it is going or what will happen. It is straight exploration like Gysin's paintings, to which it is intimately connected. We are doing precisely the same thing in different mediums. The Soul Crackers who move BETWEEN layers of light and shadow and color I saw first in his pictures (and my own of course).

9 Git-le-Coeur
Paris VIe.
August 24, [1959]

Dear Allen,

Sorry to be slow in answering your letter in regard to *Naked Lunch*. Have been in bed the last week with the cure.

When I wrote to you last week I was not in possession of all the facts. After several enlightening talks with Girodias, I have decided to let him handle the whole contract bit.

The reason for this is U.S. income tax. He has devised a method to avoid the U.S. taxes on American sales by transfer funds to branch office in Switzerland, thus reducing the tax—if there is enough money to raise tax questions—from 90% to 10%. Girodias thinks we are going to make that kind of money. I must establish foreign residence—this and other matters to be arranged.

I appreciate, God knows, your efforts and those of Irving [Rosenthal]. The present confused situation—I receive telegrams and letters from publishers I have never heard of in regard to arrangements of which I know nothing, acrimonious complaints that the book has been promised them by Rosenthal and taken out of their hands by Girodias—the present situation is entirely my fault. I think that Girodias will make a deal with Barney Rosset on the American edition.[24] As he put it to me straight (over a blackbird pastry) in his new restaurant (and he does come on straight): "This is a complicated business full of angles. I know them—you don't. Let me handle it. You will have to trust me."

So I said, "O.K. for better or for worse, in sickness or on the nod." There is only one way to make a decision: fast and definite. Girodias is not only very smart (and how he snows them with that timid and confused manner), he is also very lucky. I think that he will weather this cancerous restaurant which is gradually taking

---

24. Barney Rosset, the owner of Grove Press and cofounder, with editor Don Allen, of *Evergreen Review*. Rosset bought the American rights to *Naked Lunch* for $3,000.

over the building in which Olympia is housed.[25] Nabokov would have 200,000 dollars to gamble on a restaurant if he had followed my example.[26] If I have made a mistake, I lose.[27]

I rely on your tact to explain the situation to Irving. Well, these are the simple facts of the case. I will write you in more detail later this week. Love to Peter,

Love,
Bill

P.S. You understand my feelings have not changed as regards my debt to Irving, but he did write me and refuse to be my agent.

---

25. Girodias had bought a building on the rue Saint-Séverine, in the Latin Quarter not far from rue Git-Le-Coeur, and turned it into a series of nightclubs, bars, and restaurants under the name the Grande Séverine. The enterprise lost money prodigiously, and he was bankrupt five years later.

26. Olympia Press had published Vladimir Nabokov's Lolita in September 1955. A year later, Graham Greene's praise for it in the Times Literary Supplement provoked enormous public interest, after which Girodias and Nabokov conducted a long and bitter dispute regarding the rights and royalties of the book. It was with his profits out of Lolita, sold to Putnam's in 1958, that Girodias gambled on his restaurant—and lost.

27. In fact, Burroughs' acquiescence in Girodias's plan resulted in the delay or loss of many thousands of dollars, when U.S. and foreign royalties sent to Girodias via Agence Odette Hummel in Switzerland were not forwarded to Burroughs. The Naked Lunch copyright was finally returned to Burroughs' control by an agreement reached in 1967.

Sept. 5, 1959
9 Rue Git-Le-Coeur
Paris 6, France

Dear Allen,

I am terribly rushed right now and no time to breathe. I enclose an open letter to the French Government written by Lawrence Durrell on behalf of Olympia. It is very important and urgent to get some signatures. He wants yours and Jack's especially. Anybody else among *non-French* writers would be worthwhile. But it is question of time since the case comes up in about ten days, and it is very important he have the signatures by then. Please understand that Girodias is in a unique position to publish original and valuable work that more orthodox and committed publishers would not touch. ~~His cause is definitely our cause.~~ Who else would have published *Naked Lunch FIRST???*

So please do your best on this deal . . . If only your signature and Jack's. Those are the signatures in which he is most interested. I mean, don't bother running around town unless you know to whom you are talking and won't be wasting time.

I do not have time to explain the situation here, which is complex. But I am asking this of you not only because of Girodias, but because I am personally involved. It is in the cards that the French Government will proceed against me sooner or later, and rather sooner than later. Love to All.

Love,
Bill

I think the signatures should be in a separate short note and sent to:
M. Girodias
Olympia Press
7 Rue Saint-Séverine
Paris 5, France

Sept. 11, 1959
9 Rue Git-Le-Coeur
Paris 6, France

Dear Allen,

I am suddenly so busy I have to ration my time. One absolute dead-line after the other.

The case has taken a sinister turn. "It is only a mistake that you are not inside now," my Counsellor told me.[28] Telegram from Interpol, Tanger, relative to the Stevens case. God knows I had no connection with those sorry, stupid *bastards*. But it does look bad to a judicial eye. Lund turns out to be a professional rat, and has produced a doctored letter allegedly written by me to him. I have no words to waste on Lund. Wouldn't you? Yes, in his position I would do the same. Anything to salvage the old skin, what? No, I blame myself for knowing Lund in the first place. A mistake that I intend to rectify from here on out as regards Lund and equivalent. Enough of these juvenile delinquents. Write him off.

I am writing a short deposition with regard to *Naked Lunch*. This is essential for my own safety at this point: *Naked Lunch* is written to reveal the junk virus, the manner in which it operates, and the manner in which it can be brought under control. This is no act. I mean it all the way. Get off that junk wagon, boys, it's going down a three mile grade for the junk heap. I am off junk in sickness or in health so long as we both shall live. I will send along a copy of the article (tentatively for *The Express* here.)

Please give your attention to the signatures. You understand this is my own deal as much as it is Girodias's. I do not want to waste my time with all this legal crap and maybe end up with no passport or some other crippling restriction.

The two chapters of *Naked Lunch* that have been described as pornographic are intended as a tract against Capital Punishment in the manner of Swift's *Modest Proposal*. If you want to drink blood and eat hangings, go to it boys. But leave us make it a *Naked* Lunch.

---

28. Maître Bumsell, an English-speaking lawyer, to whom Burroughs was introduced by Girodias.

I hear the boys in the back room say, "Burroughs pulla the switch." Well, maybe. Wouldn't you? I am not playing to lose. In fact, I'm not playing at all. I mean it.

If you can help get the Beatniks off the junk route, then maybe other routes won't be so difficult as they are now. A word to the wise guy. *Quien sabe?* There is no limit. But you can't go in two directions at once.

Second issue of *Big Table* is great.[29] *Kaddish* very good. I think you can go on from there. I mean you have broken the blockade. Love to Jack, Peter, Lucien, Irving.

Love,
Bill

P.S. Dahlberg blew into town needing a dentist and other servicing which I provided.[30] Never saw him again or received so much as a line. No manners. Wrote him off. I am flat on my ass now with this legal bit. Allen, could you please glance through the manuscripts of mine in N.Y. Is there any material, *not* Yage letters, on mythical South American places featuring Carl? Any Scandinavian (Trak) material other than the Carl interrogation? If so, please send along to *American Express—not* here. I need this material for the book I am writing now.[31] I am afraid it may be lost.

[. . .]

Love,
Bill

---

29. The summer issue of Paul Carroll's magazine featured Burroughs' "In Quest of Yage."

30. Edward Dahlberg, the writer. His prose piece, together with Kerouac's "Old Angel Midnight" and Burroughs' *Naked Lunch* episodes, had made up most of the suppressed Winter 1958 issue of *Chicago Review*, and were then featured in the first issue of *Big Table*.

31. The book was *The Soft Machine*, the first version of which was published two years later.

Sept. 25, 1959
[Paris]

Dear Allen,

I have just seen the letter you sent to Girodias and your list. Very thorough, very competent. Thank you. You have done me a solid service. Via Rosalind of *Time,* I am being interviewed by *Life* next week. All this is important for my work, and I agree with you all the way that my work is for me the one important factor. Of course, a certain amount of letter-writing and party-going is part of the job you might say. Every time I go to one of these European gatherings, I gather material for *Naked Lunch.* I mean they are strictly for the book, these characters. My presence protects me from pointless invitations. I am no extra man, no fourth at bridge. No one would invite me anywhere to entertain the ladies. (There are people at these parties whose only function is to entertain the ladies.) So usually I find, if I am asked at all, someone has something definite to say to me and it is always instructive to hear.

The talk in Paris is Reconversion to peace-time economy and cultural renaissance. This is not romantic Bohemian talk. This is politicians and big business talking. The consensus of opinion is, after the Khruschev visit, that atomic war is now out of the question.[32] Reconversion and Renaissance on wheels. I hear that a similar climate obtains in London. What about New York?

The plain fact is that old-style monopoly is not practical, even from a purely economic view-point. The OLD SCHOOL Ties are fading fast.

My case seems to have taken a more or less benign turn.

I decided, on Brion's advice—and he has never steered me wrong—to admit writing the letter to Lund. The judge said: "Look. I don't want to make a big deal out of this. I don't think it is a big deal. But don't treat me like a fool." I mean *exactly* in those words,

---

32. Earlier in September 1959, Khrushchev had addressed the United Nations, visited Camp David and Disneyland, and talked up the peaceful coexistence of capitalism and communism.

you dig. The lawyer did a good job in getting the case in front of this character who seems all right. So I levelled with him. After all, I was telling the truth. I am not engaged in any trafficking and I am not about to be. I don't ever want to see or talk to any of these tiresome underworld jerks again. They work their work, I work mine. Lund is what he is. *Basta*. So I am free on my own reconnaissance [*sic*] and will most likely receive a fine and suspended sentence. Most of my money went into this case. I figure will cost around five hundred d's minimum. Well, it's a good, sharp lesson, and I have learned it well. No more Lunds. No more juvenile delinquency.

I don't think I will see Jack Stern again. Don't misunderstand. I mean he probably does not want to see me, for reasons will appear in next book and in present book as well. The end of *Naked Lunch* is addressed to Jack, as he must know. I don't think we were ever friends, but he acted like a friend. I really learned about Europeans from him. In fact I learned more from Jack than from anyone else I ever knew, except Brion. So by their fruits you shall know them, not by intentions good or bad.

I am working on a sequel to *Naked Lunch*. Maybe *Naked Free Lunch*. Don't know yet. For reasons of mobility I am anxious to make money, at least operating expenses. For example, would like to visit India this Winter. Essential I should have money to get to London when necessary. So I will write pieces of the present work in the form of short stories that can be sold to magazines in the U.S. for immediate cash. If you have suggestions or know of any magazine that might ask for material, I can deliver.

I enclose the article I wrote to cover myself and *Naked Lunch* you might say. There is nothing dishonest about it. I don't intend to do any dishonest writing now or at any time. I do think junk is a bad deal, a nowhere route that never leads to anything but junk. If treated as a public health problem, could be slowly eliminated with no penalizing of existent addicts who, owing to disabilities physical, psychic, or both, are not able to make it without junk— they should have it legally. Most junkies, if given an apomorphine cure and any sort of life away from junk, I think would be glad to pull out. I don't recognise the word theoretical, especially not with regard to junk. When I say I am off junk I mean *off*—not a codeine pill, nothing. OFF JUNK. Suicide. Prefer a bullet. Question does not arise.

Girodias is sending the article to *The Express* here, *Encounter* in England—which has recently got a real shot in the cover—and to *Evergreen*.[33] So best wait to see what disposition before taking any action in N.Y. Of course, I want you to see it in any case, so you will know where I am. So thanks again, Allen, for your efforts in my behalf. This review of Girodias's may turn into a big deal. Love to all,

Love,
Bill.

P.S. I have read your article. Very good and to the point. I think the climate is definitely changing. America will change with the times or find herself left in a long lurch without even power. It is obvious that the balance of power has shifted, and America is no longer the strongest factor. So either America stops, reorients from a course of suicidal and psychotic behavior, or—"Twilight's Last Gleamings." I think the shift may be nearer than you realize.
[. . .]

Love,
Bill

---

33. "Deposition: Testimony Concerning a Sickness"—which became the introduction in all editions of *Naked Lunch* after the Olympia original—did not appear in *L'Express,* but was first published in *La Nouvelle Revue Française* on January 1, 1960, translated by Eric Kahane; the next month, it appeared in *Evergreen Review*.

Oct. 7, 1959
Paris

Dear Allen,

The article is supposed to be what it is and not a cover really.[34]
I am not worried about any fuzz, black or otherwise. "The heat is
off me from here on out," I have written, end *Naked Lunch*.

Remembering has many levels. We remember our operations
under anaesthesia according to *L. Ron Hubbard—DIANETICS—*
went on to *Scientology*, which you would do well to look into. A
run in time, you know. Remember I gave you a tip said the Waiter.

The article is intentionally humorless and moralistic, like I say.
A loveable hepatitis carrier is no ad for hepatitis. The Autumn's
moon shines on everybody except Mohammed. He is off the air
(Koran: "Islam will last forever. *Until man reaches the moon.*" I have
talked to Arabs. The religious leaders in Cairo say: "It is finished.").
I said the junkies were to be pensioned off with junk if they need
or want it—what more do they want from me yet, cold and junkless
charity? If I know my junkies, they are not likely to look a gift
horse in the ass. The Evil Law of which you speak *is* junk. Or more
accurately, and somewhat old fashion way of saying the same thing,
junk is one of the most potent instruments of EVIL LAW.

LIFE was around the other day, several days in fact, took
pictures and concocting a story. Brilliant photography. Two
very amusing and knowledgeable characters. Names: Snell and

---

34. Ginsberg had reacted critically to Burroughs' "Deposition," feeling that it
went beyond the needs of legal protection and was at odds with the spirit of the
book. As the letter indicates, Ginsberg accused Burroughs of adopting an unne-
cessarily moralistic and humorless tone; he also criticized the apparent alibi offered
for the book by Burroughs, who disclaimed authorial accountability in his introductory 'Deposition' [p. *ix*]: "I have no precise memory of writing the notes which
have now been published under the title *Naked Lunch*." See also "Afterthoughts
on a Deposition," p. *xxi*, which Burroughs wrote in 1991 for inclusion in the
Grove edition.

Loomis.[35] Don't know when story out, but they put in fourteen hours already not for nothing. [. . .]

Pick up on the action, pops, and don't forget to give Hubbard a run for his money. He thinks you should and so does

Your Reporter

William Seward Burroughs
"Hello—Yes—Hello"[36]

P.S. Yage letters by all means, but I really *do not* want *Queer* published at this time. It is not representative of what I do now, and no interest except like an artist's poor art school sketches—and, as such, I protest. I can produce any amount *Naked Free Lunch*. Barney Rosset here. Negotiating with Girodias in Frankfurt. Contracts expected momentarily.

Love on the house

---

35. David Snell and Loomis Dean, a reporter-photographer team who greeted him on October 1 with a line adapted from the double-act detectives in *Naked Lunch:* "Have an Old Gold, Mr. Burroughs." The article, by Paul O'Neill, appeared in the November 1959 issue of *Life*.
36. Phrase taken from a Scientology "processing" routine.

Oct. 27, 1959
9 Rue Git-Le-Coeur
Paris 6, France

Dear Allen,

I enclose brief *biographical* note (and recent snapshot), and that is not a malapropism. I think you should read it carefully yourself, since I sometimes feel that you have me mixed up with someone else doesn't live here any more.

[. . .]

The method of directed recall is the method of Scientology. You will recall I wrote urging you to contact local chapter and find an auditor. They do the job without hypnosis or drugs, simply run the tape back and forth until the trauma is wiped off. It works. I have used the method, partially responsible for recent change in management, and policy . . . As for my visions, we don't talk about that. They go into the work. General advice on visions: "Cool it or use it."

It would be great if you could send me some mescaline in a letter. Not against the law here, and no danger of the letter being opened. I am rapidly covering myself with a Man of Letters.

So Mrs. Freud can "drift off at will" can she? Whose will??? The suppressors are not stupid. *"Très grand illusion."* They use pompous and dull ventriloquist dummies is all. I repeat, they are not stupid and not accidental. I have personal relations with some of these ladies and gentlemen, and they don't stay where they are by being dull.

[Dr.] Schlumberger, needless to say, fell overboard like the cook and left several centuries behind.[37]

Allen, I really appreciate all the trouble you have taken on this *Mademoiselle* deal.[38] God knows I do need the gelt. Always broke

---

37. Reference is to an old joke in which a distraught, stammering sailor is told, "If you can't say it, sing it," so he sings: "Should auld acquaintance be forgot and never brought to mind / The fucking cook's gone overboard and left twenty miles behind."

38. For the January 1960 issue, Burroughs contributed to a symposium with other writers on their desires for the 1960s, under the title, "Quo Vadis?"

and what a hassle to squeeze it out of Uncle Girodias. Oh, I sign something every time you understand, and I do have some idea as to what "or else" means. Well, I will pay you back part from *Mademoiselle* money . . . It would be great if you could score for some of this new material. I have heard rumors here and putting out my vine. Love to all,

Love,
Bill

Dear Peter,

Thank whatever Gods may be, you don't have visions. "Mistah Kurtz he dead."[39]

Bill

P.S. L. Ron Hubbard—*Dianetics,* Hermitage House, N.Y. 1950.

Movement now called "*Scientology*"; used more for manipulation than therapy. Known to Russians since long time. Everybody—I mean on top level—now picking up. Southern California camouflage seemingly necessary. Last call to dinner.

I hope you don't have to write an explanation of my biographical note now. Just tell her I am a Beckett-type character says these funny things which is becoming the things to say. You know how to put it down baby. I can't play it straight and stupid any longer. I just can't write one of those autobiographical notes the way writers do, you know about where they live and their pets and . . . I can't I can't I won't. Never no more. Sorry to be putting you [to] all this trouble as interpreter and middle man. Give Huncke my best regards.[40]

Oh uh I don't know what is going on between Rosset and Girodias; he told me it was "premature" to sign a contract. So anything you could find out would be most welcome information in room 32, 9 Rue Git Le Coeur.

Love.

---

39. From Conrad's *Heart of Darkness.*
40. Huncke was by now out of jail again.

Biographical Note on William Seward Burroughs

I have no past life at all being a notorious plant or "intrusion" if you prefer the archeological word for an "intruded" artefact. I walk in passport was allegedly born St. Louis, Missouri, more or less haute bourgeois circumstances—that is he could have got in the St. Louis Country Club because at that time nobody had anything special against him but times changed and lots of people had lots of things against him and he got his name in the papers and there were rumors of uh legal trouble. Remember? I prefer not to. Harvard 1936 AB. Nobody ever saw him there but he had the papers on them. Functioned once. as an Exterminator in Chicago and learned some basic principles of "force majeur." He achieved a state of inanimate matter in Tanger with chemical assistants. Resuscitated by dubious arts he travelled extensively in all directions open to him.

In any case he wrote a book and that finished him. They killed the author many times in different agents concentrated on the road I pass, achieving thereby grey-hounds, menstrual cramps and advanced yoga to a distance of two feet legitimate terrain . . . And never the hope of ground that is yours

william seward burroughs

Oct. 29, 1959
9 Rue Git-Le-Coeur
Paris 6, France

Dear Allen,

Enclose two briefer forms of biographical exegesis, one concentrated by Brion, the other by "myself." I sent along the amended carbon and snapshot yesterday.

I have had it in mind to re-edit WORD. I do not have copy, and missing passages are landmarks for present work. If you will send me the MS. you have, I will re-edit and return.

I have new method of writing and do not want to publish anything that has not been inspected and processed. I can not explain this method to you until you have necessary training. So once again and most urgently (believe me there is not much time), I tell you: "Find a Scientology Auditor and have yourself run."

No vision is ever seen for nothing. Learn to bargain. And remember: "winner take nothing."

First question always: "*Whose vision??*" If you think any vision you see is "yours," go back to First Base and start over. Some people are very very acquisitive of ratings. Others know better. "Keep your bosom unfranchised and allegiance clear," and remember how long Banquo lasted.[41] Who wants to last?? In this game the point is to lose what you have, and not wind up with someone else's rusty load of continuity.

Pay no attention to above. I know you won't anyway, and it isn't written for "you" exactly.

william seward burroughs

[. . .]

---

41. Banquo's words to Macbeth, act 2, scene 1. In the context of the play, Banquo is saying that he (unlike Macbeth) will not be guilty in deeds as he is in "the cursed thoughts that nature / Gives way to in repose." In the "atrophied preface" section of *Naked Lunch:* "You can write or yell or croon about it . . . paint about it . . . act about it . . . shit it out in mobiles . . . *So long as you don't go and do it . . .*" (p. 223, Burroughs' ellipses and italics).

Notes

(Key to abbreviations: al = autograph letter; als = autograph letter, signed; tl = typed letter; tls = typed letter, signed; tms = typed manuscript.)

1 9 4 5 :

July 24, 1945. To Allen Ginsberg. St. Louis. (Place: from envelope.)
lp als. Ginsberg Collection, Columbia University.

1 9 4 6 :

September 1, 1946. To Allen Ginsberg. St. Louis. (Place: confirmed by envelope. Address on stationery.)
2p als. Ginsberg Collection, Columbia University.

October 10, 1946. To Allen Ginsberg. Pharr, Texas. (Place: from letter October 5, 1946. Address on stationery.)
1p als. Ginsberg Collection, Columbia University.
Columbia assumes St. Louis as place of posting.

1 9 4 7 :

February 19, 1947. To Allen Ginsberg. [New Waverly, Texas.]
2p als. Ginsberg Collection, Columbia University.

March 11, 1947. To Allen Ginsberg. New Waverly, Texas. (Place: from envelope.)
2p als. Ginsberg Collection, Columbia University.
(Date: from envelope; poor legibility, possibly March 1.)

August 8, 1947. To Allen Ginsberg. New Waverly, Texas. (Date and place: from envelope.)
2p als. Ginsberg Collection, Columbia University.
Letter dated July 10 by Burroughs, but context confirms envelope postmark, "AUG 8 1947."

1 9 4 8 :

February 20, 1948. To Allen Ginsberg. New Waverly, Texas.
2p als. Ginsberg Collection, Columbia University.

June 5, 1948. To Allen Ginsberg and Jack Kerouac. New Orleans.
2p als. Kerouac Collection, Columbia University.

October 14, 1948. To Allen Ginsberg. Algiers, La. (Place: from envelope.)
2p als. Ginsberg Collection, Columbia University.

November 9, 1948. To Allen Ginsberg. [Algiers, La.]
4p als. Ginsberg Collection, Columbia University.

November 30, 1948. To Allen Ginsberg. [Algiers, La.]
3p als. Ginsberg Collection, Columbia University.

November 30, 1948. To Jack Kerouac. [Algiers, La.]
2p al. Kerouac Collection, Columbia University.

December 2, 1948. To Allen Ginsberg. Algiers, La. (Place: from envelope.)
3p als. Ginsberg Collection, Columbia University.

1949:

January 10, 1949. To Allen Ginsberg. [Algiers, La.]
4p als. Ginsberg Collection, Columbia University.

January 16, 1949. To Allen Ginsberg. Algiers, La. (Place: from envelope.)
2p als. Ginsberg Collection, Columbia University.

January 30, 1949. To Allen Ginsberg. Algiers, La. (Place: from envelope.)
6p als. Ginsberg Collection, Columbia University.

February 7, 1949. To Allen Ginsberg. Algiers, La. (Place: from envelope.)
3p als. Ginsberg Collection, Columbia University.

March 15, 1949. To Jack Kerouac. Algiers, La. (Place: from following
   letter.)
2p als. Kerouac Collection, Columbia University.

March 18, 1949. To Allen Ginsberg. Algiers, La. (Place: from envelope.)
5p als. Ginsberg Collection, Columbia University.

April 16, 1949. To Allen Ginsberg. [Algiers, La.]
3p als. Ginsberg Collection, Columbia University.

May 27, 1949. To Jack Kerouac. [Pharr, Texas.]
2p als. Kerouac Collection, Columbia University.

June 24, 1949. To Jack Kerouac. Pharr, Texas.
3p als. Kerouac Collection, Columbia University.

September 26, 1949. To Jack Kerouac. Pharr, Texas.
2p als. Kerouac Collection, Columbia University. (Address on stationery.)

October 13, 1949. To Allen Ginsberg. Mexico City. (Place: from envelope.)
3p als. Ginsberg Collection, Columbia University.

November 2, 1949. To Jack Kerouac. [Mexico City.]
1p als. Kerouac Collection, Columbia University.
2 lines cut.

December 24, 1949. To Allen Ginsberg. [Mexico City.]
3p als. Ginsberg Collection, Columbia University.

1 9 5 0

January 1, 1950. To Jack Kerouac. [Mexico City.]
3p als. Kerouac Collection, Columbia University.

January 22, 1950. To Jack Kerouac. [Mexico City.]
3p als. Kerouac Collection, Columbia University.
3 lines cut.

March 10, 1950. To Jack Kerouac. Mexico City.
2p als. Kerouac Collection, Columbia University.

May 1, 1950. To Allen Ginsberg. Mexico City. (Place: from envelope.)
8p als. Ginsberg Collection, Columbia University.
Half line cut.

September 18, 1950. To Jack Kerouac. Mexico City.
1p tls. Kerouac Collection, Columbia University.

1 9 5 1 :

January 1, 1951. To Allen Ginsberg. Mexico City.
2p tls. Ginsberg Collection, Columbia University.
"1950" written in error by Burroughs on original.

January 11, 1951. To Allen Ginsberg. Mexico City.
3p tl. Ginsberg Collection, Columbia University.
6 lines cut.

January 28, 1951. To Jack Kerouac. Mexico City.
1p tls. Kerouac Collection, Columbia University.
Columbia dates this letter 1950 as per written in error by Burroughs on
    original.

March 5, 1951. To Lucien Carr. [Mexico City.]
1p tl. Ginsberg Collection, Columbia University.
7 lines cut.

April 24, 1951. To Jack Kerouac. [Mexico City.]
1p tls. Kerouac Collection, Columbia University.
4 words cut.

May 5, 1951. To Allen Ginsberg. Mexico City.
3p tls. Ginsberg Collection, Columbia University.

May 1951. To Allen Ginsberg. Mexico City.
2p tl. Ginsberg Collection, Columbia University.
Postscript signed by Joan Burroughs.
(Date: This letter, and the following, are dated merely 1951 in Columbia;
    their chronology and sequence have been arrived at from textual
    analysis.)

May 1951. To Jack Kerouac. Mexico City.
2p tls. Kerouac Collection, Columbia University.

June 20, 1951. To Jack Kerouac. Mexico City.
1p als. Ginsberg Collection, Columbia University.

November 5, 1951. To Allen Ginsberg. Mexico City.
1p tls. Ginsberg Collection, Columbia University.

December 20, 1951. To Allen Ginsberg. Mexico City.
2p als. Ginsberg Collection, Columbia University.
2 lines cut.

1 9 5 2 :

January 19, 1952. To Allen Ginsberg. [Mexico City.]
2p als. Ginsberg Collection, Columbia University.

March 5, 1952. To Allen Ginsberg. Mexico City. (Date and place: from
    envelope.)
2p als. Ginsberg Collection, Columbia University.
1 line cut.

March 20, 1952. To Allen Ginsberg. Mexico City.
2p als. Ginsberg Collection, Columbia University.
4 lines cut.

March 26, 1952. To Jack Kerouac. Mexico City.
2p als. Kerouac Collection, Columbia University.
1 line cut.

April 3, 1952. To Jack Kerouac. Mexico City.
2p als. Kerouac Collection, Columbia University.
6 lines cut.

April 5, 1952. To Allen Ginsberg. Mexico City.
1p tls. Ginsberg Collection, Columbia University.
4 lines cut.

April 1952. To Jack Kerouac. [Mexico City.]
2p tl. Kerouac Collection, Columbia University.
(Date: from context.)

April 14, 1952. To Allen Ginsberg. Mexico City.
1p tls. Ginsberg Collection, Columbia University.
6 lines cut.

April 22, 1952. To Allen Ginsberg. [Mexico City.]
2p tls. Ginsberg Collection, Columbia University.
(Date: Derives from a typed extract, included with the final version, dated
    by Ginsberg "Received April 25, 52.")
Columbia also holds a shorter draft version (2p tl), parts of which have
    been incorporated for transcription.

April 26, 1952. To Allen Ginsberg. Mexico City.
1p tls. Ginsberg Collection, Columbia University.

May 15, 1952. To Allen Ginsberg. Mexico City.
1p tls. Ginsberg Collection, Columbia University.
15 lines cut.

May 23, 1952. To Allen Ginsberg. [Mexico City.]
3p als. Ginsberg Collection, Columbia University.
(Date: from envelope.)
2 lines cut.

June 4, 1952. To Allen Ginsberg. Mexico City.
2p tls. Ginsberg Collection, Columbia University.

June 23, 1952. To Allen Ginsberg. Mexico City.
2p tls. Ginsberg Collection, Columbia University.

Early July 1952. To Allen Ginsberg. [Mexico City.]
2p als (+ 2p als by Joseph Lucas). Ginsberg Collection, Columbia
    University.
(Date: Context suggests shortly before July 13.)

July 13, 1952. To Allen Ginsberg. Mexico City.
2p tls. Ginsberg Collection, Columbia University.
Letter partially in hand.

September 18, 1952. To Allen Ginsberg. Mexico City.
4p als. Ginsberg Collection, Columbia University.
(Date: from envelope.)

October 6 & 14, 1952. To Allen Ginsberg. Mexico City.
2p tls. Ginsberg Collection, Columbia University.
7 lines cut (from postscript).

November 5, 1952. To Allen Ginsberg. Mexico City.
2p als. Ginsberg Collection, Columbia University.

December 15, 1952. To Allen Ginsberg. Palm Beach, Florida.
1p tls. Ginsberg Collection, Columbia University.
(Date: from envelope. Address on stationery.)

December 23, 1952. To Allen Ginsberg. Palm Beach, Florida.
1p tls. Ginsberg Collection, Columbia University.

December 24, 1952. To Allen Ginsberg. Palm Beach, Florida.
2p al. Ginsberg Collection, Columbia University.
(Date: from envelope. Address on stationery.)

1 9 5 3 :

January 10, 1953. To Allen Ginsberg. Panama.
2p als. Ginsberg Collection, Columbia University.

March 1 & 3, 1953. To Allen Ginsberg. Pasto and Bogotá.
2p als. Ginsberg Collection, Columbia University.
Envelope is franked Pasto, and appears to be dated March 12 (Address on
    stationery.)
1 line cut.

March 5, 1953. To Allen Ginsberg. Bogotá.
2p als. Ginsberg Collection, Columbia University.

April 12, 1953. To Allen Ginsberg. Bogotá.
5p als. Ginsberg Collection, Columbia University.

April 22, 1953. To Allen Ginsberg. Quito.
3p als. Ginsberg Collection, Columbia University.

May 5, 1953. To Allen Ginsberg. Lima. (Place: from envelope.)
1p als. Ginsberg Collection, Columbia University.

May 12, 1953. To Allen Ginsberg. Lima.
3p als. Ginsberg Collection, Columbia University.
(Address on stationery.)

May 23 & 24, 1953. To Allen Ginsberg. Lima. (Place: from envelope.)
1p als. Ginsberg Collection, Columbia University.

May 30, 1953. To Allen Ginsberg. Lima. (Place: from envelope.)
1p tl. Ginsberg Collection, Columbia University.
Half line cut.

June 5, 1953. To Allen Ginsberg. [Lima.]
1p tl. Ginsberg Collection, Columbia University.

June 6, 1953. To Allen Ginsberg. Lima. (Place: from envelope.)
1p tl. Ginsberg Collection, Columbia University.

June 18, 1953. To Allen Ginsberg. Pucallpa.
2p als. Ginsberg Collection, Columbia University.

Early July 1953. To Allen Ginsberg. Lima. (Place: from following letter.)
3p tl. Ginsberg Collection, Columbia University.
Columbia dates letter as "ca. 8 July 1953."

July 8, 1953. To Allen Ginsberg. Lima.
2p tls. Ginsberg Collection, Columbia University.

July 10, 1953. To Allen Ginsberg. Lima. (Date and place: from envelope.)
3p tl. Ginsberg Collection, Columbia University.

August 3, 1953. To Allen Ginsberg. Mexico City. (Date and place: from
    envelope.)
1p tls. Ginsberg Collection, Columbia University.
Columbia dates this letter July 30, 1953. The choice of dates is based on
    two envelopes contained in the same file with a ten-page manuscript
    of *Queer*. The later date seems more likely, given that Ginsberg was
    only asked on July 21 to send a copy of *Junkie*; the earlier-dated en-
    velope, bearing higher postage, is more likely to have been used to
    mail the manuscript to Ginsberg.

August 17, 1953. To Allen Ginsberg and Jack Kerouac. Palm Beach,
    Florida.
1p tl. Ginsberg Collection, Columbia University.
(Address on stationery.)

December 14, 1953. To Jack Kerouac. Crossing the Atlantic.
1p als. Kerouac Collection, Columbia University.
Columbia misdates this letter "14 December '1954'?" Context makes year
    evident. (Address on stationery.)

December 24, 1953. To Allen Ginsberg. Rome.
2p als. Givaudan Collection.
In the late 1970s, Claude Givaudan owned a large collection of Burroughs'
    letters, which he first published in a limited, bilingual edition in 1978.
    Subsequently published as *Letters to Allen Ginsberg 1953–1957* (Full
    Court Press: New York, 1982).

1 9 5 4 :

January 2, 1954. To Allen Ginsberg. Rome.
2p als (+ 1p als by Alan Ansen). Givaudan Collection.

January 26, 1954. To Allen Ginsberg. Tangier.
2p al. Givaudan Collection.

February 9, 1954. To Allen Ginsberg. Tangier.
4p als. Givaudan Collection.
10 lines cut.

March 1, 1954. To Allen Ginsberg. Tangier.
4p als. Givaudan Collection.

March 12, 1954. To Neal Cassady. Tangier.
1p als. Givaudan Collection.

April 7, 1954. To Allen Ginsberg. Tangier.
2p tl. Givaudan Collection.

April 22, 1954. To Jack Kerouac. Tangier.
3p tls. Kerouac Collection, Columbia University.
Note: Letter contains a great deal of marginalia, crossings out, etc.

May 2, 1954. To Neal Cassady. [Tangier.]
1p tls. Givaudan Collection.

May 4, 1954. To Jack Kerouac. Tangier.
2p tls. Kerouac Collection, Columbia University.

May 11, 1954. To Allen Ginsberg. [Tangier.]
1p tls. Givaudan Collection.

May 24, 1954. To Jack Kerouac. Tangier.
1p tls. Kerouac Collection, Columbia University.
Columbia dates this letter 1955 on the basis of (Kerouac's?) annotation on
    letter.

June 16, 1954. To Allen Ginsberg. Tangier.
1p & 2p tl. Arizona State University.
15 lines cut.
First typescript has "June 16" written at bottom of first page, though not
    in Burroughs' own hand (probably added by Ginsberg on receipt of
    letter). Second typescript, also undated, is headed "Tangiers" but not
    addressed. The full content of this retype includes reworking of ma-
    terial from April 7, 1954, letter, establishing year. My transcript uses
    the last paragraph of the second text for its final paragraph.

June 24, 1954. To Allen Ginsberg. [Tangier.]
2p tls. Givaudan Collection.
Typescript is incomplete. First and last pages only.

July 3 & 4, 1954. To Allen Ginsberg. [Tangier.]
2p tls. Givaudan Collection.

July 15, 16, & 22, 1954. To Allen Ginsberg. [Tangier.]
3p tl. Givaudan Collection.
Typescript is missing pp. 3, 4, and 5, and ends incomplete on p. 6.
12 lines cut.

August 18, 1954. To Jack Kerouac. [Tangier.]
4p tl/4p tls. Givaudan/Kerouac Collection, Columbia University.
There are two versions of this letter, one being a carbon made for Ginsberg.
    They both have minor alterations in hand, and I have used both for
    the transcript. The most significant difference is that the signed version
    ends with a longer, typed final paragraph, while the unsigned version
    ends with a shorter, hand paragraph; the former is the one used here.
Columbia incorrectly dates the signed version "ca. June 1954," but the
    copy, where the date has been added by Ginsberg, was enclosed with
    a letter to Ginsberg that is dated August 18 by Burroughs.

August 26, 1954. To Allen Ginsberg. [Tangier.]
2p tl. Givaudan Collection.
1 line cut. Typescript is incomplete.

September 3, 1954. To Jack Kerouac. [Tangier.]
2p tls. Kerouac Collection, Columbia University.

Early October 1954. To Allen Ginsberg. [New York.]
4p als. Givaudan Collection.
Manuscript is missing pp. 1 and 2. 2 lines cut.

October 13, 1954. To Allen Ginsberg. Palm Beach, Florida.
1p tls. Givaudan Collection.
(Address on stationery.)

November 12 & 13, 1954. To Allen Ginsberg. Palm Beach, Florida.
2p als. Givaudan Collection.

December 7, 1954. To Jack Kerouac. Tangier.
2p als. Kerouac Collection, Columbia University.

December 13, 1954. To Allen Ginsberg. Tangier.
5p als. Givaudan Collection.

December 30, 1954. To Allen Ginsberg. [Tangier.]
1p tls. Givaudan Collection.

1955:

January 6, 1955. To Allen Ginsberg. Tangier.
3p tl. Burroughs Collection, Columbia University.
Date and place added, presumably by Ginsberg on receipt. Several hand
   annotations, and notes in hand on reverse of last page.

January 9, 1955. To Allen Ginsberg. Tangier.
1p tls. Burroughs Collection, Columbia University.
16 lines cut (relating to editing of *The Yage Letters*). Note that final three
   words of letter added in hand.

January 12, 1955. To Allen Ginsberg. Tangier.
2p tls. Givaudan Collection.

January 21, 1955. To Allen Ginsberg. Tangier.
2p tls. Givaudan Collection.
Date and place added, presumably by Ginsberg on receipt.
Note: The last two paragraphs of the postscript were incorrectly included
   in the letter dated March 15, 1955, in *Letters to Allen Ginsberg*, p. 91.

February 7, 1955. To Allen Ginsberg. Tangier.
7p als. Givaudan Collection.
Burroughs actually wrote the date as "Feb 7, 1954." But the content makes
   the year evident. Misdated 1954 in *Letters to Allen Ginsberg*. My transcript derives two thirds from Burroughs' original manuscript, pag-
   inated 1 to 4, 6 to 7, with half-page insertion. For the rest, I have
   relied upon a five-page typescript, by "William Lee," of unknown
   date, though possibly made by Burroughs not long after composition
   (Arizona State University), and upon Richard Aaron's transcription as
   used, in edited form, for *Letters to Allen Ginsberg*.
3 lines cut.

February 12, 1955. To Jack Kerouac. Tangier.
3p als. Kerouac Collection, Columbia University.

February 19, 1955. To Allen Ginsberg. Tangier.
4p als. Givaudan Collection.
Manuscript is missing pp. 3 and 4. 3 lines cut.

April 20, 1955. To Allen Ginsberg. Tangier.
4p als. Givaudan Collection.
Manuscript is missing pp. 3 and 4. 4 lines cut.

June 9, 1955. To Jack Kerouac. [Tangier.]
2p als. Kerouac Collection, Columbia University.
Year added, presumably by Kerouac.

July 5, 1955. To Allen Ginsberg. Tangier.
3p als. Givaudan Collection.
Year and place added, presumably by Ginsberg.

August 10, 1955. To Allen Ginsberg. Tangier.
4p als. Givaudan Collection.
8 lines cut.

September 21, 1955. To Allen Ginsberg. Tangier.
3p als. Givaudan Collection.

October 6 & 7, 1955. To Allen Ginsberg. [Tangier.]
2p tls. Givaudan Collection.
(Year: from content.)
Typescript is missing first page.

October 10 & 11, 1955. To Allen Ginsberg. [Tangier.]
2p tls. Arizona State University.
(Year: from content.)
Letter would appear to have been started on October 8, the day Burroughs
    entered Benchimol Hospital. First two pages of four-page typescript
    are missing.

October 21, 1955. To Allen Ginsberg. Tangier.
2p tls. Givaudan Collection.
1 line cut.

October 23, 1955. To Allen Ginsberg and Jack Kerouac. Tangier.
4p tls. Givaudan Collection.

November 1, 1955. To Allen Ginsberg and Jack Kerouac. [Tangier.]
1p tls. Givaudan Collection.

November 2, 1955. To Allen Ginsberg and Jack Kerouac. [Tangier.]
2p tls. Givaudan Collection and Arizona State University.
Burroughs actually wrote the date as "Dec 2, 1955," but "Nov" was
    added, presumably by Ginsberg on receipt. The content does not help
    clarify the date.
Note that the first page was used in *Letters to Allen Ginsberg*, ending
    incomplete at "a tasteless table," and that the second page, a carbon,

was found in a different manuscript collection as a miscellaneous fragment.

1 9 5 6 :

February 17, 1956. To Allen Ginsberg. Tangier.
1p tls. Givaudan Collection.

February 26 & 27, 1956. To Allen Ginsberg. Tangier.
3p tls. Givaudan Collection.
7 lines cut.

March 14, 1956. To Allen Ginsberg. [Tangier.]
1p tls. Givaudan Collection.

April 16, 1956. To Allen Ginsberg. Tangier.
1p tls. Givaudan Collection.
2 lines cut.

May 8, 1956. To Allen Ginsberg. London.
1p tls. Givaudan Collection.

May 15, 1956. To Allen Ginsberg. London.
2p tls. Givaudan Collection.

June 18, 1956. To Allen Ginsberg. Venice.
2p tl. Givaudan Collection.

July 26, 1956. To Bill Gilmore. Venice.
1p tls. Letter from a private collection courtesy of Gary Nargi.
Identity of Gilmore as addressee not certain. 1 line cut.

September 16, 1956. To Allen Ginsberg. Tangier.
2p tls. Givaudan Collection.

October 13, 1956. To Allen Ginsberg. [Tangier.]
5p tls. Givaudan Collection.
Date, repeated at top of next three typescript pages, not in Burroughs'
  hand—presumably Ginsberg's.

October 29, 1956. To Allen Ginsberg. Tangier.
5p tls. Givaudan Collection.

December 20, 1956. To Allen Ginsberg. Tangier.
3p tls. Givaudan Collection.

1957:

January 23, 1957. To Allen Ginsberg. [Tangier.]
1p tls. Givaudan Collection.

January 28, 1957. To Allen Ginsberg. [Tangier.]
1p tls. Givaudan Collection.
Note: Burroughs wrote year as 1956, corrected as 1957, presumably by
    Ginsberg on receipt.

January 31/February 1, 1957. To Allen Ginsberg. [Tangier.]
1p tls. Givaudan Collection.
Note: First date introduced as "received," crossed out, presumably by
    Ginsberg.

February 14, 1957. To Allen Ginsberg. [Tangier.]
2p tls. Givaudan Collection.

March 25, 1957. To Bill Gilmore. Tangier.
1p als. Letter courtesy of James P. Musser.
Identity of Gilmore as addressee not certain.

June 15, 1957. To Allen Ginsberg. [Tangier.]
1p tls. Givaudan Collection.

July 18, 1957. To Alan Ansen. London.
1p tls. Givaudan Collection.

July 30, 1957. To Alan Ansen. Copenhagen.
2p tl. Givaudan Collection.

August 20, 1957. To Allen Ginsberg. Copenhagen.
2p tl. Givaudan Collection.
6 lines cut.

August 28, 1957. To Allen Ginsberg. Copenhagen.
2p tls. Givaudan Collection.

September 20, 1957. To Allen Ginsberg. Tangier.
2p tls. Ginsberg Collection, Columbia University.
11 lines cut.

October 8, 1957. To Allen Ginsberg. Tangier.
2p tls. Ginsberg Collection, Columbia University.
(Date: from envelope.)

October 19, 1957. To Allen Ginsberg. Tangier.
2p tl. Ginsberg Collection, Columbia University.

October 28, 1957. To Allen Ginsberg. [Tangier.]
1p tls. Ginsberg Collection, Columbia University.
2 lines cut.

November 10, 1957. To Allen Ginsberg. [Tangier.]
1p tls. Ginsberg Collection, Columbia University.
15 lines cut.

November 26, 1957. To Allen Ginsberg. Tangier.
2p tls. Ginsberg Collection, Columbia University.

December 4, 1957. To Jack Kerouac. Tangier.
1p tls. Kerouac Collection, Columbia University.

December 8, 1957. To Allen Ginsberg. Tangier. (Year and place: from
   envelope.)
1p tls. Ginsberg Collection, Columbia University.
1 line cut.

1 9 5 8 :

January 9, 1958. To Allen Ginsberg. [Tangier.]
1p tl. Ginsberg Collection, Columbia University.
Note: Date not in Burroughs' hand, presumably Ginsberg's, added on
   receipt.

February 16, 1958. To Allen Ginsberg. [Paris.]
1p tls. Ginsberg Collection, Columbia University.
5 lines cut.

April 18, 1958. To Lawrence Ferlinghetti. Paris.
1p tls. Ginsberg Collection, Columbia University.

July 20, 1958. To Paul Bowles. Paris.
1p tls. Harry Ransom Humanities Research Center, University of Texas,
   Austin.

July 1958. To Allen Ginsberg. [Paris.]
1p tls. Ginsberg Collection, Columbia University.

July 24, 1958. To Allen Ginsberg. Paris. (Year and place: from envelope.)
3p tls. Ginsberg Collection, Columbia University.

August 25, 1958. To Allen Ginsberg. Tangier.
2p als. Ginsberg Collection, Columbia University.

September 28, 1958. To Allen Ginsberg. Paris.
1p tls. Ginsberg Collection, Columbia University.
Half page by Gregory Corso.
Columbia's dating of this letter is supported by a near-identical letter from
    Burroughs and Corso to Peter Orlovsky dated September 24, 1958.

October 10, 1958. To Allen Ginsberg. Paris.
2p tls. Ginsberg Collection, Columbia University.

October 19, 1958. To Paul Bowles. London.
2p tls. HRHRC, University of Texas, Austin.

1 9 5 9 :

January 2, 1959. To Allen Ginsberg. Paris.
3p tls. Ginsberg Collection, Columbia University.
Note: Includes one and a half pages of calligraphy.

January 17, 1959. To Brion Gysin. Paris.
1p tls. Letter courtesy of Robert H. Jackson.

January 17, 1959. To Paul Bowles. Paris.
1p tls. HRHRC, University of Texas, Austin.

February 20, 1959. To Paul Bowles. Paris.
1p tls. HRHRC, University of Texas, Austin.
2 lines cut.

April 2, 1959. To Allen Ginsberg. Tangier.
5p als. Ginsberg Collection, Columbia University.

April 21, 1959. To Allen Ginsberg. Paris.
3p als. Ginsberg Collection, Columbia University.

May 18, 1959. To Allen Ginsberg. Paris.
2p als. Ginsberg Collection, Columbia University.
Note: Drawing enclosed.

June 8, 1959. To Allen Ginsberg. Paris.
2p tls. Kerouac Collection, Columbia University.

Late July 1959. To Allen Ginsberg. [Paris.]
3p tls. Ginsberg Collection, Columbia University.
(Date: from content.)

August 24, 1959. To Allen Ginsberg. Paris.
2p tls. Ginsberg Collection, Columbia University.
(Year: from envelope.)

September 5, 1959. To Allen Ginsberg. Paris.
1p tls. Ginsberg Collection, Columbia University.

September 11, 1959. To Allen Ginsberg. Paris.
3p tls. Ginsberg Collection, Columbia University.
3 lines cut.

September 25, 1959. To Allen Ginsberg. Paris.
4p tls. Ginsberg Collection, Columbia University.
3 lines cut.

October 7, 1959. To Allen Ginsberg. Paris.
2p tls. Ginsberg Collection, Columbia University.
4 lines cut.

October 27, 1959. To Allen Ginsberg. Paris.
3p tls (+ 1p trns "Biographical Note"). Ginsberg Collection,
   Columbia University.
7 lines cut from letter.

October 29, 1959. To Allen Ginsberg. Paris.
1p tl. Ginsberg Collection, Columbia University.
3 lines cut.

Index

Burroughs, William Seward (*cont.*)
225, 234, 256, 307, 309, 312, 318,
325, 351n, 408, 424–25, 427–28,
429

as drug dealer, 25, 33–34, 71, 77, 87,
225, 368n, 427

dysentery contracted by, 168

envy as viewed by, 85–86

Establishment as viewed by, 158

ethical standards of, 42, 67, 79, 254,
331

evil as viewed by, 67, 68, 213–14

expatriation of, xxiv–xxv, xxxi, 198,
254

in extortion plot, 355–56

"factualism" of, 24, 44–45, 68, 71,
136, 226, 334, 415

as family man, xix, 21, 79

as farmer, xix, xxi, 8, 13, 19–20, 21,
22, 23, 25, 28–29, 33, 40, 44, 49,
51, 52, 54, 56, 58, 66–67, 75, 78,
178

finances of, xxx, 143, 152, 153, 209,
217, 228, 229, 238, 252, 262, 264,
267, 268, 271, 277, 278, 292, 307,
309, 311, 322, 323, 342, 364, 386,
399–400, 415, 416, 427, 431–32

finger joint cut off by, 120n, 216, 263

in Florida, 142–46, 188, 238, 251, 252

foreign residence status of, 421

friendships of, xx, 213, 256, 269

guns owned by, 27, 39, 45, 65, 79,
82, 84, 94n, 113, 154, 156, 159, 160,
236, 258, 259, 263, 307

hack work of, 255–56, 258, 259, 270

at Harvard, xviii, 433

haute-bourgeois status of, xxi, 433

hemorrhoids of, 149, 166, 168, 196,
232, 234–35

Henry Street residence of, 45, 78n,
226

hepatitis of, 379, 393

heterosexual experiences of, 45, 88–
89, 171, 326–27, 369–70, 378, 379

as "holy man," 331–34

as *homme de lettres*, xvi, 431

homosexuality of, xxi, 45, 68–69,
84–86, 88–89, 90, 97, 106, 115–16,

119–20, 256, 317, 318, 326, 369–70,
376, 378, 379, 408

humanity as viewed by, xx, 68, 139,
140, 213, 226–27

imprisonment of, 95, 98, 103

as "Invisible Man," xxvii, 405, 419

isolation of, xix, xxiv, 227–28, 245,
246, 257, 273, 274, 337

jaundice contracted by, 97, 109

Kerouac's collaboration with, 107n,
275n, 334n

Kerouac's portrayal of, 105n, 107, 108

knife carried by, 296–97, 344

as landlord, xix, 28, 42, 43, 44, 75

as landowner, xix, 8n, 22, 25, 58, 65,
69, 86, 93

lawsuits of, 41

lay analysis by, 11n

liberalism criticized by, 51, 53, 61, 67

life insurance of, 130

in Lima, 161–86

literary agents as viewed by, 220–21

literature as viewed by, 175

in London, xxxiv, 307, 309, 311, 314,
316, 317–19, 323, 361, 380, 400–
401

loneliness of, 201, 211n

love as viewed by, 111–12, 128–30,
206, 213, 221–22, 226, 229, 230, 235

malaria contracted by, 151–52, 164,
182

as "man of action," 139, 287

marriages of, xviii, xxiii, 8, 14n, 21n,
26, 39, 45, 79, 123

Mayan civilization and language studied by, 69, 78n

medical theories of, xxxv, xxxix, 321–
322, 367, 370, 372, 378, 412

Merchant Marine papers of, 243

Mexican citizenship sought by, 64,
65n, 69, 86, 90

in Mexico City, xix, xx–xxi, 53–141

at Mexico City College, 63, 69, 78,
114

monthly allowance of, xxx, 209, 307,
309, 311, 415

neighbors as viewed by, xix, 41, 63

neuralgia of, 164, 277, 378

Elvins, Kells (*cont.*)
22, 40, 44, 52*n*, 64, 80, 95, 113,
218, 222, 233, 263, 360
in Tangier, 196, 216, 218
Elvins, Marianne Woolfe, 107–8
Elvins, Mimi Heinrich, 218*n*, 360*n*
Elvins, Politte, 52*n*
Empty Mirror (Ginsberg), 112*n*, 280*n*–
281*n*
Encounter, 428
"Epistle to Dr. Arbuthnot" (Pope), 149*n*
Ernst, Max, xxxix
Esmeraldas, Peru, 169, 173
"Essentials of Spontaneous Prose" (Ker-
ouac), 265*n*
Eukodol, 199, 201, 204*n*, 211, 215, 257,
271
Evans, Mary, 393*n*
Evergreen Review, 406, 421*n*, 428
Express, L', 424, 428

Fascism, 67
Fawcett, Percy Harrison, 239, 369
Federal Bureau of Investigation (FBI),
391
Federal Narcotic Farm (Lexington, Ky.),
19
Feldman, Gene, 377
Ferlinghetti, Lawrence, xxxvii, 280*n*–
81*n*, 314*n*, 388, 396
"Finger, The" (Burroughs), 120*n*
Fink, Mike, 263
Finnegans Wake (Joyce), 109
Fiore, Carlos, 368, 370
Fitzgerald, F. Scott, 114*n*
Flanagan, Edward Joseph, 164
Fluke (Stern), 416*n*
Food and Drug Administration (FDA),
52*n*
Ford Foundation, 274, 290
Foster, Stephen, 410*n*
Franco, Francisco, 160, 312
Frechtman, Bernard, 289*n*, 358, 370,
376, 399
Freud, Sigmund, 51, 266*n*
functional therapy, 416–17

Gallagher, Charles Frederick, 273–74,
290, 292, 400
gambling, 303
García Lorca, Federico, 298, 389*n*
Gartenberg, Max, 377*n*
Garver, William Maynard:
Burroughs' relationship with, 8*n*, 12,
13, 19*n*, 20, 21, 38*n*, 58, 63, 65, 70,
104, 134, 136, 137, 139, 141, 281,
294
in Mexico, 58, 63, 70, 104, 134, 136,
137, 139, 141, 345
overcoats stolen by, 8*n*, 58
in Panama, 143–44, 149
Genet, Jean, 124, 289, 292, 358*n*
George Fine Market Research, 145*n*
Ghazal (Allen), 395*n*
GI Bill, 63, 69, 94*n*
Gifford, Barry, xxviin, xxixn, 85*n*, 208*n*,
211*n*
Gifford, Eric, 211, 218, 265, 326, 400
Gilmore, William Scott, 23–24, 70, 368
Ginsberg, Allen:
as archivist, xviii
arrests of, 49, 51
as Burroughs' agent, 83, 95, 107, 111,
112, 117, 119, 134, 164*n*, 240*n*, 285,
294, 299, 315
as Burroughs' correspondent, xvii–
xviii, xxii, xxiv, xxvi, xxix–xxx,
xxxviii, xl, 3*n*, 200, 201, 203, 204,
205, 206–7, 208–11, 216
Burroughs' relationship with, xvii–
xviii, xx, xxiv–xxxii, xxxiv, xxxvi,
xl, 11*n*, 42, 45, 66–70, 71, 85*n*, 201,
205, 206, 211*n*, 213, 232, 235, 238,
255, 269, 286, 287, 292, ·329
Cassady's relationship with, xxvi–
xxvii, 11, 14*n*, 129, 166*n*, 208*n*,
211, 222*n*, 230, 232*n*, 233*n*
Corso and, 181, 335*n*
in Denver, 14–15
European trip of (1957–58), 358*n*,
359*n*, 360*n*, 364*n*, 368*n*, 370*n*, 379,
385, 386*n*, 391
fame of, xxxiv, 327
first sexual encounter of, 283

Hinckle, Helen, xx, 33, 35–36, 37, 38, 40, 42
Hiroshima, bombing of, xvii
Hitler, Adolf, 67
Hoffman, Albert, 104, 105
Hohnsbeen, John, 310
Holmes, John Clellon, 22n, 37n, 145, 221n, 358n
Homosexual in America, The (Cory), 105–6
homosexuality, homosexuals:
  as "fags" vs. "queers," 119–20
  as "fairies," 298
  heterosexuality vs., 85–86, 88–89
  in Italy, 190, 193–94, 239–40
  in *Naked Lunch*, 363, 365
  in Peru, 162, 164, 166, 175–76, 185
  psychoanalysis for, 11n, 24n, 68–69, 115–16
  self-contempt and, xxxii
  social influences on, 97
  in Tangier, 195, 196–97, 198, 199, 204–5, 302–3, 312, 329, 337
  in U.S., 97, 105–6
Hoover, J. Edgar, 146
Horace Mann School, 317n
Horney, Karen, 266n
Hotel Cecil, 355–56
Hotel Muniria, 323
"Hot Rod, The" (Burroughs), 231n
Howard, Brian, 204
"Howl" (Ginsberg), 345n
  Burroughs' views on, 290, 314–15
  fame of, xxxiv, 327
  first public reading of, 293
  publication of, 281n, 314
Howl and Other Poems (Ginsberg), 314n
Huanaco, Peru, 175, 185–86
Hubbard, L. Ron, xxxix, 429, 430, 432
Hulton, Nika, 290n
Huncke, Herbert, 11n, 19, 21, 137
  Burroughs' relationship with, 8n, 12n, 22, 23n, 39, 41, 42, 45, 54, 64, 75
  Ginsberg and, 39, 41, 45
  imprisonment of, 54, 64, 75, 432
  Portuguese counterpart of (Eduardo), 205–6, 217, 257–58

hydrogen bomb, 185n
hyoscine, 280
Hypnoanalysis (Wolberg), 104n

imperialism, 78
Inca civilization, 239, 240
"Indiscretion" (Klee), 290n
Inferno (Dante), 361, 372, 377
insanity:
  as confusion of levels, 71–72, 128
  mystical visions and, 72
Institute of General Semantics, 44n
insurance companies, 79
Interpol, 351, 424
Interpol, xxxvi, 396–97
"Interview with William S. Burroughs, An" (Tytell), xxxviin
Interzone (Burroughs):
  Antonio the Portuguese Mooch in, 205n
  autobiography in, 120n
  correspondence as basis of, 288n
  creativity discussed in, xxxvii
  "Dream of the City by William Lee" routine in, 213n
  "Driving Lesson" in, 231n
  "International Zone" in, 256n
  "Lee's Letters and Journals" in, 222n
  mosaic form in, xxxii
  routines in, 205n
  "Word" section in, 353n, 360, 365, 366, 372, 379, 388, 434
"In the Penal Colony" (Kafka), 140
Invisible Man, The (Wells), xxvii, 190
Isherwood, Christopher, 204
Islam, 244, 342
  Burroughs' views on, 333, 349–50, 429
Istanbul, 364
Istiqlal, 340, 346

Jackson, Natalie, 294n
Jackson, Phyllis, 221
Jaguar and the Golden Stag (Allen), 395n
jazz, 239, 270n, 317n, 362
"Jazz of the Beat Generation" (Kerouac), 276
Jeffreys, Frank "Buck," 89–90

Jesus Christ, 332
jihad, 336, 339–42
Jiu-Jitsu, 222, 297
Johnson, Samuel, 118
Jones, Betty, 239
Jones, Dowell, 387n
Jones, Glenn, 239n
Jones, Leroi, 275n
Joyce, James, 109
Judgment of Paris, The (Vidal), 115
Julius Caesar (Shakespeare), 61n
Jung, Carl G., 266n
Junky (Burroughs):
   autobiography in, xxxv
   Bill Gains in, 8n
   British publication of, 220–21
   Burroughs' arrest described in, 7n,
      48n
   Burroughs' first reference to, 65
   Carr's involvement with, 75, 77–78,
      79, 80, 82, 95, 96, 101, 379
   Cash in, 130n
   Cole in, 48n
   contract for, 117–18, 126, 131, 220–
      221, 223
   dedication of, 105
   in Double Book series, 143, 187
   drug addiction in, xxi, 19n, 65, 70, 83
   drug agencies criticized in, xxi
   Herman in, 12n
   impersonal tone of, xxii
   "Irish" in, 136
   Joan's death and, 118, 135
   Joey in, 78n
   Kerouac's reaction to, 80, 124n
   Lonny the Pimp in, 136
   manuscript of, 118, 135
   Mary in, 11n
   names used in, 136
   narrative of, xxvi, 105
   New Orleans section of, 135, 136
   Old Bart in, 38n, 136
   Pat in, 48n
   publication of, 80, 81, 83, 101, 103,
      107, 111, 112, 115, 117–20, 122,
      126, 131, 143, 152, 154, 157, 187,
      196n, 220–21, 228, 377n

   publisher's introduction to, 117, 119–
      120
   Queer as Mexican section of, 82, 86,
      88, 113
   Queer compared with, xxii, xxvi, 111,
      117, 119, 122, 244
   Reich mentioned in, 82, 83, 88, 92,
      112
   revisions in, 92, 95, 101, 103, 112,
      126, 128, 135
   royalties from, 199, 277
   salability of, xxi
   subtitle of, 143n
   Tige in, 47n
   title of, xviiin, xxi, 105n, 143n
   translations of, 139
   writing of, xxi–xxiv, 65, 70, 80, 81,
      83, 88, 92, 95, 101
Jurado, Bernabé, 65, 91, 95, 103, 110,
   142, 143, 161, 168

Kaddish (Ginsberg), 397n, 425
Kafka, Franz, 140, 411n
Kahane, Eric, 419n, 428n
Kahane, Jack, 327n
Kammerer, David, 7n, 65
karma, 219n
Kelly, John, 236n, 237
Kerouac, Jack:
   boats as interest of, 63
   Buddhism studied by, 213, 219n,
      225n, 392, 394
   Burroughs' collaboration with, 107n,
      275n, 334n
   as Burroughs' correspondent, xvii–
      xviii, 3n, 137, 139, 140
   as Burroughs' houseguest, xxv, 135,
      136, 137
   Burroughs portrayed by, 105n, 107,
      108
   Burroughs' relationship with, xvii–
      xviii, xxxiii–xxxiv, 135, 136, 137,
      139, 206–7, 210, 234, 235
   Burroughs' views on, xxv, 124, 135,
      136, 234, 275, 392–94
   Cassady's relationship with, 33–39,
      49n, 137, 200n, 219n, 392, 394

Nabokov, Vladimir, 422n
Naked Lunch (Burroughs):
"A.J.'s Annual Party" section of, 388, 418, 424–25
anti-dream drug as subject of, 266–267, 268–69
"atrophied preface" section of, 258n, 265n, 318n, 395n, 434n
author included in, 251
autobiography in, xxxiv
"Benway" section of, 330, 362, 363, 365, 366, 369, 372, 377, 388, 412
in *Big Table*, 413, 425n
"black meat" section of, 288n, 293n, 304, 309n
Burroughs' views on, 247, 251, 255, 365, 367, 375, 408, 424–25, 427–28
censorship of, 408n, 409n, 413n, 418, 419n, 425n
in *Chicago Review*, 389, 401, 408, 409n, 425n
chronological arrangement for, 367
comedy in, xxiv, xxx
contract for, 418, 421, 430, 432
"control addicts" in, 365
copyright on, 422n
correspondence as basis of, xxx, xxxiv, 212, 217, 251–52, 259–62, 271–73, 287, 288, 289, 298–99, 304
"Country Clerk" used in, 366, 388
cover art for, 406n, 418
cut-up method and, xvi, 251, 289, 334n
"Diplomat" routine in, 288n
dramatization of, 419
drug addiction in, 365, 367, 369, 370, 372, 376, 378, 388n, 424–25
ending of, 427
expurgated version of, 409, 418
first edition of, 389n
fragmentary quality of, 251
French translation of, 419
Ginsberg's involvement with, xxxv, 270, 356–57, 358n, 409
Grove Press edition of, 421n, 429n
"Hassan's Rumpus Room" section of, 288n, 388, 418, 424–25

"hauser and o'brien" section in, 262n, 267n, 388n, 430n
homosexuality in, 363, 365
"interzone" section of, 211n, 241n, 300, 369, 372, 375, 377, 379
introduction to, 424–25, 427–28, 429
Invisible Man in, xxvii
journals as basis of, 288, 289
juxtaposition in, xxxii–xxxiii, 289
"Leif the Unlucky" routine in, 211n, 218–19
Li'l Abner mentioned in, 157n, 331
manuscript of, 358n, 360, 366, 367, 368, 370, 388n, 408
"market" section of, 300n, 332n, 360, 362, 366, 388
narrative of, xxxiv–xxxv, 367, 375, 377
novel form as inadequate for, 227, 251, 367, 375
Olympia Press edition of, xxxvii–xxxviii, 327n, 356, 358, 377, 406n, 413n, 418, 421–22, 423, 428n
open letter to French government on, 423, 424, 426
"ordinary men and women" section of, 259n, 360n
organization of, 367, 372, 375, 388
pornography in, 388, 418, 424–25
press coverage of, 408n, 409n, 413n, 426, 429–30
proofs of, 418
"Prophet's Hour" in, 332n
psychology in, xxxvii
publication of, xvi, xxxvii–xxxviii, 283, 288, 315, 358, 362, 366, 372, 376, 388, 389
Queer compared with, 367, 372
routines in, xxiv, 299, 300, 322
royalties from, 419, 421, 422n
Scandinavian material in, 367, 369, 375, 377, 379
schizophrenic deconstruction in, xxxv
sequel to, 420, 427, 430
South American material in, 375, 377
Tangier as setting for, 243, 296–98, 300–301

To Leslie,

my girlfriend, my best friend, my wife;

and

To all the women out there

who are mentally hungry—

You have the power!

CONTENTS

ACKNOWLEDGMENTS

My personal gratitude to the following for all of their support and contributions to this project: Tom Huber, Judy Beckett, Ede Slovin, New Directions, Teri O'Shaughnessy, Betty O'Shaughnessy, Linda Kalter, Winter Park Toastmasters Club #3674, and to Kim Kilmer, Debbie Markley, Beth Cunningham, and Roxann Combs at Gulf Publishing Company.

I am not what I ought to be,
not what I want to be,
not what I am going to be,
but thankful that I am not what I used to be.

Author Unknown

PREFACE

What is a Millennium Woman?

A Millennium Woman is a woman who has challenges in her life and is overcoming those challenges with a plan. This woman knows that given the time, understanding and dedication anything is possible to achieve.

Today's world is fast-paced and competitive. Men dominate the industries, businesses and political systems of society. Many adult women need to learn how to gain a competitive edge just to catch up! They need an understanding of how prosperity really comes into our lives. Prosperity that is not just financial but personal and purposeful for our families and eventually their families. How we reap and sow on our path in life is a good indication of how our children will as well.

The Millennium Path has been created to provide a road map that results in creating balances and success in five areas of life: health, personal, financial, family, and education. The Millennium Path is part of the philosophy of the Millennium Woman Foundation.

The Millennium Woman Foundation, a non-profit entity, was created to provide mentors, support and networking for all women who have an interest in self-actualization. This book has become the catalyst for the Millennium Woman Foundation. More can be found at our web-site: *www.millenniumwoman.org*

This book will teach you how to stabilize your life, focus on a direction, and succeed! Personally and financially you will be able to control your own destiny.

This book will enable you to:

- *Create change in your life.*
- *Make your life work.*
- *Free your family from financial burden.*
- *Control your own destiny.*
- *Understand what propels or holds back your life.*

INTRODUCTION

My reasons for writing this book came to me after a
long period of time and observation. My parents
divorced when I was twelve—leaving my mother with six
children to support. While my father met his commitment
toward our financial support, my mother had to become
the main breadwinner and financial planner for our family.
She had had no preparation for this role, however. My
mother began by working two jobs—one as a minimum
wage receptionist and the other as a waitress at night. During the Christmas holidays, she'd even add a third—a
weekend job as a department store clerk. She did the best
she could and we survived. Watching her struggle, however,
made a lasting impression on me and resulted in the creation of Millennium Woman.

Through the course of my business life, I have met many
newly divorced women who have been suddenly forced to
provide for their families with little or no help. For 15
years, as a real estate professional, I sat in women's living
rooms hearing about families who, because of divorce,
death, or poor planning, had no choice but to sell their
homes. These situations always reminded me of my mother's plight.

Without the financial support of a spouse, these women
couldn't maintain their standards of living. Unfortunately,
financial education isn't taught in our schools and many
parents neglect teaching their children financial responsibility. In my real estate business, most of my employees have
been single, divorced, widowed, or are young women just
starting out. I have witnessed first-hand their struggles to
survive. This insight has identified to me the financial tools
that women could and need to utilize to achieve their own
financial independence.

I realized, also, that to create the life she wants, a woman
needs to compete like a man! Men are raised on competition and continue the battle when they enter the workforce.

Our male-dominated society is really just a male-dominated workplace. We live in a male-driven society. Successful female executives have achieved their goals despite childhoods that didn't equip them for tough, competitive work environments. As the late film executive and producer Dawn Steele wrote, "Women then didn't have the experience of winning together. Boys learned these things from team sports. Girls didn't, at least not then." The world's corporations, banks, governments and general social structures are still run by men. If you want to make something happen, you'd better know the game and play by its rules. The purpose of this book is to prepare women to survive and thrive in this world.

Women who want to succeed must learn from inside the lion's den. My building blocks for success work for any woman wanting to raise herself to the next level. This is not a book aimed at turning women into men. It is designed to educate and inspire women in the real world. Women have to compete for the same jobs and in the same environment as men. Women are stronger and deeper than men. It has been well documented that women have a higher threshold for pain. When all is said and done, males are just hunters. Women can be hunters—but they're also capable of so much more. They just need the tools to succeed.

I've always wanted to share with others the lessons I learned on my path to success. This is the book I've always wished my mother had had. *Millenium Woman* will give you the framework you need to create your own financial strength.

Michael O'Shaughnessy

DIAMOND OF SUCCESS

Within this diamond, which of these words dominate your life? Below the midline of the diamond are negative connotations. If any of these words are a part of your life, you'll have a hard time reaching your goals of success. By incorporating into your life the positive words above the midline of the diamond you'll find the strength to attain the rewards you are seeking.

The Millennium Woman's Diamond of Success

Success

Goals

Freedom   Growth

Intellectual-Capital

Accomplishment   Enthusiasm

Experience   Fulfillment   Perseverance

Zen   Balance   Opportunity   Morals   Desire

Knowledge   Technique   Ambition   Health   Action

Time Management   Value Line   Talent   Efficiency   Communication

Environment   Compete   Dreams   Stretch   Provider   Organize

Drive   Uninhibited   Pride   Self-esteem   Love   Plan   Focus   Lioness

Independence   Depth of Strength   Motivation   Education   Attitude   Will

Potential   Humanity   Discipline   Passion   Sacrifice   Captialize   Transform   Character

Impossible   Uncommitted   Risk   Procrastination   Apathy   Worry   Fear   Neglect

Negative   Self-destructive   Timid   Substance Abuse   Barrier

Wasteful Budget   Envy   Lazy   Paper-Tiger   Spendthrift   Debt

Denial   Desperation   Self-righteous   Blocked   Pessimistic

Weak   Prejudiced   Self-pity   Vain   Ignorant

Greedy   Extravagant   Ego-centered

Loss of Humor   Doubt   Jealous

Disloyal   Unreliable   Dishonest

Quits Easily

Failure

Nothing splendid has ever been achieved except by those who dared to believe they were superior to circumstance.

1

YOUR POSITION IN LIFE

Success is a journey, not a destination.
—Ben Sweetland

I understand the process of survival because I've walked the walk. I've been poor and I hated it. I changed my life through sheer determination and will. I have succeeded through failure and have learned that failure is part of the process of success. While growing up, I hated the feeling of never having any money and being the poorest of my friends. My mother had to work two jobs, with the exception of the holidays, when she always held a third job

Not having money affects you psychologically. I felt like I was trapped in a prison. While still a youth, I vowed to make something of myself. People always ask me, "How did you do it?" I tell them it starts with your will.

Your hunger drives your will,
which drives your discipline,
which brings organization
that allows success,
layer after layer.

Money and achievement are a result of discipline. Discipline creates change. Focus on your goals as if you were playing a game. Your first goal, money, will not "buy" you happiness. Only you can provide that with your attitude and outlook on life. Money does, however, buy the time you need to make decisions. If you think of achieving money as a game, one in which you happen to hold all the high cards, that youthful frustration you once suffered can fuel your growth. You, too, can meet any goal.

INVESTMENT AND FREEDOM

Knowing

what to do

with money

and

controlling

the

temptation to

spend it is

not easy for

anyone.

Saving is an investment in the future. Investment for the future does more than sustain a particular way of life—it allows for freedom from wanting the bare necessities. Agesilaus, King of Sparta in the 4th Century, noted that, "Sewing frugality we reap liberty, a golden harvest."

Knowing what to do with money and controlling the temptation to spend it is not easy for anyone. *It is an even more bitter pill for someone who makes a lot and then loses a lot.* The poor have already been there, but the well off are ill prepared to swallow such a loss. I was reminded of that bitterness this past year when I ran into a thirty-something mother I knew from our roaring twenty-something years. She was the daughter of a very wealthy businessman and her lifestyle while growing up was lavish, to say the least. She was accustomed to taking a boat or airplane to the Caribbean at the drop of a hat. I never knew whether I should envy her lifestyle or feel sorry for her. (Why sorry? Because she would never know the joy of having her own financial foundation layered brick by brick.)

Luck had turned on her father and family. They had lost everything. I hadn't seen this woman for about six or seven years, although I'd read about her father's plight and knew it was bad. She had fallen out of the spotlight and, when I saw her, it was a sad sight. She was dressed far below the "middle-American standard" (not for style's sake) and eating at a greasy spoon. With her was her beautiful, wonderful child, running loose.

My friend seemed embarrassed that I had spotted her. Nevertheless, we said hello and exchanged greetings. As she was leaving, she finally broke into honest detail of her current state of being. She was broke, with no friends or family able to help her financially. She had no skills—she had never worked before in her life. She'd rented a room in a house and didn't know how she was going to pay for it. She had never been alone before and was not enjoying the reality of it.

I felt very sad for her. After she left, I thought to myself, "What is the moral here?" What should she do, besides finding a toehold of survival, to help her survive? I came to realize that she had to start again from scratch, find the bottom and work her way up. If she had character, she'd find the way. If she lacked character, she'd need the tools to build it. It was then that I committed myself to writing this book. I wanted her to understand her need to teach and prepare her child for the future. She could no longer afford to be wasteful. She needed to become independent and appreciative of life's gifts.

All people go through cycles, and understanding these values is what holds everything together. That is what Basic Money 101 is all about.

AN OPPORTUNITY TO GROW

One of the most oppressed group of women today are single parents. The majority of these women are stuck in a wretched cycle of need. Mere existence is a colossal task. First, many live paycheck to paycheck. Once a crisis occurs (and it always does), the borrowing starts. As more money is needed, more money is borrowed. Many get so far into debt that only a winning lottery ticket could pull them out. Next, without financial stability, single parents lose emotional stability. Single mothers find themselves spiraling down endless dark tunnels. They have the responsibility for and commitment to raising their children, yet feel their hopes and dreams riding on the winds of luck. They feel helpless.

This is a reality that can be altered. Change comes from within and creating change starts with small, incremental steps. You have the opportunity to grow and imagine your future becoming your reality. Do it! If not for yourself, do it for those most precious to you. Give them the best chance to achieve a life of stability and upward mobility. Refocus your goals and don't give up—you're going to make it.

You can grasp the power of change. It is important to realize that as one door closes another will open. When you understand the forces surrounding your world, you will learn how to control them. You can make positive changes that will overcome all the seemingly insurmountable walls that are now stopping your growth. To do this, though, you must summon the will from deep within you.

THE CHALLENGE

You are just at the beginning of your learning curve. Your first challenge will be to put together a blueprint describing your present life and, most importantly, where you want it to go. Seeing your blueprint in front of you will help you focus on your challenges. You will be able to structure your life in a positive way that will create growth and help you to organize your life and direction. Be aware of exactly which goals you want to set. If you don't, your growth will only come by luck and chance.

How can you effect positive changes? By defining your challenges—the ones you need to face. For most of us, the challenges are:

⦿ Improving financial stability
• Discovering career opportunities
⦿ Letting go of people, places, and things that impact you negatively
• Establishing a long-term solution that will benefit both you and your family while feeling good about yourself and the future of your children.

Change comes from within and creating change starts with small, incremental steps.

To meet these challenges you must have a tremendous appetite for self-help. Say to yourself, "I'm hungry for that opportunity," and mean it! Show you really want to take charge of your life. Begin by taking control of your thought processes and focus on taking these words literally.

Life is about growing, and it's time to break the chains that have been holding you back. Let go of the words "I can't" that act like a stone that is drowning you.

THE POWER OF CHANGE AND CREATING MOMENTUM

Creating positive momentum is a thought process. Society has trained us to constantly be negative. It has overwhelmed us to the point where it is sometimes difficult to see any good. Seeing that good, despite the negativity, is your first step. It must be battled daily for the rest of your life. People of great accomplishment and self-earned wealth possess this bright and cheerful characteristic. My favorite examples are Oprah Winfrey and Whoopi Goldberg. Both have childhood backgrounds that could easily have been used as excuses for never advancing in life. Despite their adversities, however, they both possess a steadfast ability to see the good. They create their own positive reinforcement and assurances. Their faith in themselves has always been unwavering and they've broken any ceilings imposed upon them.

This change of momentum that you create for yourself will, with time, build and take over. It will become a habit. Starting this momentum means becoming positive, enthusiastic, and primed for accomplishment. Your goals must be somewhere on your mind constantly—morning, noon, and night. Those around you will feel the energy and, together, your energies will build a momentum that can't be stopped! People will come into your life because of it. They will be drawn to you. Suddenly, you'll find yourself riding a wonderful swell carrying you into your accomplishments.

The power of change is based on the everyday things you do and don't do. Discipline is essential if you are to take control—you have many needs that are hidden. You must make time daily to cultivate your spiritual and physical

Life is about growing . . . let go of the stone "I can't."

needs. (Positive beliefs and exercise greatly affect your attitudes.) Another good habit is mental preparation. Think things through before jumping in. The habits of positive thinking—such as taking an hour each day to work out or finding that 20 minutes to pray or meditate—will help you build a general swell of energy designed for achievement, accomplishment, and well-being.

Change will come automatically when bad habits are broken and new habits are developed, taking a foothold in your life. It is a gradual process that is life-long. The motivation must come from within. You, and only you, are responsible for raising your level of intensity. No one else can do it for you.

WHAT IS THE MILLENNIUM PATH?

The Millennium Path is your guide to fulfillment. It incorporates five major areas of life: your mental and physical health, along with your familial, educational, and financial well-being. As with all human journeys, the path starts with a commitment—to yourself and to the journey. The path never really ends, but the scenery keeps getting better and better. As you progress, you will see your life improve. The following four levels, the first being Trailblazer, make up the MW path:

TRAILBLAZER

1. Organize long-term goals
2. Organize short-term goals
3. Start a journal
4. Pull your credit file and begin changes
5. Begin credit card reduction plan
6. Eliminate credit card balances to zero
7. Define family goals
8. Create a one-year budget
9. Create a one-month budget
10. Open an account and begin saving
11. Enter into a physical goal and challenge

12. Define negative habits
13. Assess career status
14. Identify positive influences (people and environments), as well as negative influences in your life
15. Make net worth statement
16. Place goals on the mirror
17. Set goals for relationship improvement
18. Identify health goals
19. Read at least three self-improvement books

GUIDE

1. Complete TRAILBLAZER goals
2. Achieve zero credit card debt
3. Define financial strategies for family, college, housing, retirement
4. Live under-budget (positive cash flow)
5. Achieve beacon credit rating of 600 or higher
6. Show educational improvement (class or seminar)
7. Meet one physical challenge
8. Write retirement plan and date of start
9. Show growth on financial net worth
10. Achieve career advancement change or accomplishment
11. Perform public speaking—one engagement, any size
12. Place current goals on mirror
13. Read at least three self-improvement books

LEADER

1. Complete GUIDE goals
2. Maintain zero monthly credit debt
3. Achieve beacon credit rating of 680
4. Professional achievement (award, certification, advancement)
5. Own one property
6. Achieve three public speaking presentations
7. Engage retirement plan
8. Accomplish one new major physical challenge
9. Present a spiritually based speech
10. Enable children to define their own goals
11. Place goals on the mirror

ANGEL

1. Complete LEADER goals
2. Maintain zero credit card debt
3. Achieve zero car debt
4. Obtain beacon credit rating of 725
5. Show educational achievement (degree, license, certification, diploma)
6. Meet minimum net worth of $150,000
7. Give two financial presentations
8. Fund retirement plan
9. Place current goals on the mirror

CHAPTER ONE SUMMARY

Financial investment for the future is the key to the independence and freedom necessary to create the life you desire for yourself and your family.

Analyze your position. Reflect on what changes need to occur and realize that your world is created by you, for better or worse. Small incremental daily changes in your daily routine and discipline start the process of change in your life.

Build your momentum by visualizing your future and what it is you want to accomplish. Change comes from within. All that you need to succeed is inside you already! You must summon the will. You must also, however, have a tremendous appetite for self-help. Let go of the stone "I can't"—because you can! Follow the Millennium Path.

CHAPTER ONE
BLUEPRINT FOR LIFE
WORKSTATION

1. Describe the challenges presently in your life.

a.

b.

d.

e.

2. What changes do you need to make?

3. What vision can you create that shows the world you would like to live in? (Example: Location, Education, Family, Relationships, Personal, Housing)

4. Write a paragraph or more about the life you and your family will live three years from now.

5. What things in your life appear to be holding you back or stopping you from growing? Circle one or more.

Relationships	Family Bad Habits	Lack of Education or Training
Bad Luck	Poor Nutrition	Children's Discipline
Poor Health	Bad Attitude	Financial Needs
No Budget	Not Enough Income	Lack of Discipline
		Lack of Understanding

6. Starting change in your life (creating momentum) begins by separating the good in your life from the bad. By slowly eliminating the bad and building onto the good, your life will change. Name the good things in your life (list as many as you would like).

a.

b.

c.

d.

e.

7. My life will change with a tremendous positive
_____.

8. Name five areas in your life that need greater discipline.

a.

b.

c.

d.

e.

9. Spiritual and physical enrichment help us to feel more positive about our possibilities. Describe how you feel about your faith and understanding of universal laws.

10. a. Name three things you can add to your weekly schedule that can alter your physical well being. (Example: Begin walking, cut out fat from diet, etc.)

b. Define one hour each day, six days a week, that is yours for physical and/or spiritual enhancement. 4 a.m.? 5 a.m.?

11. Name five things you can do daily to help change your life (there are no wrong answers).

a.

b.

c.

d.

e.

12. Who is responsible for change in your life?

13. "One thing that will no longer exist in my life is _____!" (For example: smoking, him, credit card debt, etc.)

THE NEW YOU

All I know is you can get there from here.

You can.

You can walk through the fear.

Travel past what is gone before.

Wake up!

Wake up and get up on the other side.

Dare to become that of your dreams.

Dare!

Dare to believe in your own possibility.

—Mary Anne Hershey

Many times, it is a great failure that gives you the catalyst or momentum to change.

Over time, you will transform yourself. When you look at your vision of "what you want to be," you continually create possibilities. This *positive visualization* and desire will help you become stronger. These changes will happen practically overnight—when you make the decision that your desire outweighs your old life. They will happen

11

simply because you've made the decision to change your life. It is the first step in your quest—it is a revelation inside of you. You've known deep in your heart that, at some point, the change needs to take place. Your attitude will take control. Many times, it is a great failure that gives you the catalyst or momentum to change. That sickening feeling of defeat might come from a broken heart or simply from an event that makes you realize you are alone . . . and that you alone are in charge of your destiny. The important thing is to recognize your own personal catalysts. After all, what made you pick up this book?

Any of these things can be your catalyst, but your attitude is the sole factor controlling your life. Attitude allows the right energy to flow. Energy and time equals achievement. Achievement equals success.

Here are some catalysts from my own past. When I was a young man, I was faced with the challenge of changing my life or becoming forever trapped in it. I'd been a heavy partier during my teen years. I realized, however, that my life was going nowhere. I quit smoking pot and using drugs. Leaving those vices behind saved me—and I knew that this "light switch" change would forever alter my life. *The feeling of change comes from within.*

In my early twenties, I became emotionally devastated when a romance didn't work out. We've all been there. I vowed, however, that instead of feeling sorry for myself, I would change my life. That failed relationship was the catalyst that led to my vow to become successful. I had a clear vision in my mind and I would not accept failure. Constant success and continuous improvement were my goals. No matter how many times I would stumble, I vowed that I would keep that clear vision in front of me.

Use any hardship you are experiencing to your advantage. It has to become fuel. *The new you is focused purely on the future, never in the past.* People who look back will not advance. Whether your past was something glorious and fruitful or something you would rather forget, it is the past. You must be future-oriented to visualize where you are going. To those people who want to live only for today, I say, "Go ahead—but beware!" Remember the tale of the grasshopper who didn't work and plan for the future? The industrious ants had to take him in during the winter because he was starving and cold. There is nothing wrong with smelling the roses and rewarding yourself—but the future will guarantee your efforts. (And your efforts will guarantee your future.) If you can train your mind to visualize your future, you'll someday live like that.

Be aware of what is filtering through your mind. Mental junk food makes slobs of most of us. *Truthful thinking* is a requirement for reaching our goals. It is the willpower that eliminates negatives from entering into a chosen mindset. Truthful thinking is what will move you into action. "I am." "I will." "I will not tolerate less." Your powerful mind controls your actions and your ability to sacrifice, to discipline, to motivate—to win at all costs. Truthful thinking must always be followed by *automatic action.* Automatic action is the force that helped Kerri Strug make her successful vault on a broken leg during the 1996 Olympics.

Automatic action means always being prepared. Truthful thinking and automatic action, when used correctly over time, dramatically increases your probability of success. The average person thinks at a rate of more than 1,000 words per minute, yet about 75% of those thoughts are negative: "things are always wrong," "why me?" "I'm no good." Most people, to counteract this negative thinking, try to trick the brain with a single positive thought. While this may work temporarily, it will not last. If you're a professional speaker or an actor, you know it takes truthful thinking and automatic action working together as a reflex to give you the confidence to succeed. Your thoughts and your actions have to be rehearsed and utilized over and over. During that fateful vault, Kerri Strug may have thought, "I've done this already and I will do it again!" Her thoughts were truthful and her actions automatic.

GETTING INTO THE ZONE

Getting into the zone is a way of thinking. It is that time when you are focused and getting closer to your goals. *Being in the zone means that you are constantly concen-*

trating your efforts toward success, accomplishment, and achievement. Athletes understand this concept because when they get into the zone, all things work for them and they feel mentally invincible. They are not distracted by life's mundane junk. They see only the solution. In your case, instead of reflecting on the negative, such as a broken marriage or a difficult boss, your vision should be focused straight ahead toward your glorious future.

When you are in the zone, this positive force builds. Soon, your momentum grows stronger and you find yourself breaking through any barrier in your path. *You've created a positive high cycle.* Without your being aware of it, all will go right in your life. Be it financial, family, career, or business development, you'll suddenly see progress on all fronts. And not only will this positive-high cycle carry on for an indefinite period of time, it will also repeat itself!

While you are in the zone, you feel good because your focus is strong. Getting into the zone and staying there will pull you along because negative factors are fended off by this self-installed "reflective shield."

SELF-PRESERVATION

Self-preservation is self-love. Loving yourself means accepting yourself as you are and realizing that you're a very unique individual. No one on this Earth is like you— no one. You are uniquely gifted and able to give the world talents only you possess.

If you are like most of us, you were taught at an early age that having an ego means being conceited. *Having an ego, however, simply means appreciating yourself.* Unfortunately, many people are torn down by the negative influences in their lives. Their egos have become so trampled and smothered that they live only for the pleasure of others. When you appreciate yourself, however, you'll start to do more for yourself. It begins with you and, once you have taken care of yourself, your attitude will transcend to the rest of the world.

Loving and appreciating the *new you* means stepping away from anything negative you may have previously

You are uniquely gifted and able to give the world talents only you possess.

been part of. Remember—the past is the past. We can all grow and change . . . if we want to.

Everyone has a sad tale to tell, has suffered from a broken heart, or has experienced hardship. You have a choice. These experiences can either rule you or you can throw them into your locomotive fire to stimulate change. Get over it and move on! If you treat yourself like a champion, the rest of the world will, too.

Self-visualization is important. How you see yourself is how other people are going to see you. I remember a young woman that, to this day, I don't know anyone who'd had more hardship in her life. She couldn't go a day without some major catastrophe happening. The people around her treated her like she had problems—and she treated herself the same way. In fact, she chose to see herself as a person with insurmountable problems; she never did succeed. If you feel, act, and think you're a champion, you will become one. Unfortunately, this concept also works in reverse. The ability to overcome obstacles is what sets each of us apart and each situation will either beat you down or make you stronger. How you respond to life's challenges is what makes the difference.

Pure and simple, you determine how people see you. It all has to do with the self-image you send out. Be strong, be direct, and be powerful. Know your mission and your goal path. Stand up in your life—building confidence comes from practice, experience, and knowing. Remember your first time driving a car? How nervous were you? Are you nervous now? It's like that with your first speech or your first day on the job. Trust yourself. It will all come together. Your eyes need to sparkle. You send a very strong message when other people see that trust in your eyes. What does your soul want? *You* make that decision.

Confidence is a by-product of experience. You get it from putting yourself into uncomfortable roles that make you "stretch." Once you've experienced that *stretch,* you realize you didn't die from it. It wasn't so bad—and you're a better person because of it. Each time you stretch and accomplish your goals, your confidence will increase.

Here's an example from my life. I grew up with a terrible stuttering problem and I hated it. Because of my communi-

However you see yourself is how other people are going to see you.

cation problem, people thought I was either aloof or not interested. After finishing college, I decided I would become a very good public speaker. That's right—I knew that by throwing myself into speaking situations, I would be forced to stretch my experiences and make myself into what I wanted to become. After five years, I became a tolerable speaker—and after 10, I was good! Today, I speak professionally. I felt as if I had given myself a "get out of jail" card. Stretch your experiences! You alone determine your image and your personal perception.

SELF-REWARD

Stand up in your life— building confidence comes from practice, experience, and knowing.

After any long run of hard sacrifice, you need to take care of that most important person—yourself. You are worthy and must reward yourself accordingly. Have you earned a bonus? Go out and buy yourself something! You must pay yourself for all your discipline and sacrifice. Dip your toes into the cool waters of reward. Life is about enjoyment after the toil and trouble. Most people have it backwards—they enjoy and reward themselves before they have achieved anything. They either wind up with nothing or reward themselves too much and later pay for it.

Your reward is a personal gift. It is directed toward you and not toward the group you're pulling along. Be firm and independent in this. You've earned it! But remember, you must also exercise conservatism since the reward has an impact on your finances and budget. You might make your reward something as simple as a day trip to the beach. The reward is special to you because you earned it!

SELF-RESPECT

Self-respect comes from living up to your own personal standards. If your standards and morals are high, you probably have a heavy dose of self-respect. Wealth and success do not automatically give you self-respect. It comes from your actions and your honor. Walk the good walk and your positive path will always prevail.

Self-worth comes from the values you employ in your everyday life. *Self-worth is knowing you're making a difference in the lives around you while continuing to better your own.*

From self-respect and self-worth finally comes self-esteem. You're either proud of yourself, full of confidence and direction—or you're not. If you don't have high self-esteem, you probably lack goals and purpose. Find your mental compass and map out a path toward wherever and whatever you want to achieve. The purpose of writing your goals is to give yourself direction and purpose—raising yourself to a higher level of human experience.

SELF-LOVE

Love is the single most powerful and important ingredient in life. Children and animals are motivated by love. They thrive on love . . . and mentally die without it. Today's dysfunctional youth is a direct result of poor emotional support. Many children today get their "love" from a television—but does it nurture them? Can it help them get through life's ever-changing challenges? Love is a force, just like gravity and magnetism. It attracts positive forces and can be your most powerful ally. Your love for yourself empowers you to build upon your *truthful thinking*. **Accepting others and reaffirming yourself are two ways you can experience love.**

As you challenge yourself each day, tell yourself just how unique you are! You are one of a kind. If negative people cross your path, ignore their attitudes. Loving yourself and others brings happiness. Master this one thought and you won't need anything else in life. I heard a speech once about the power of a smile. To try it out, one day I tried smiling at everyone I met. I smiled during tough business negotiations. I smiled while on the phone. Everyone I met that day received a smile and the warmth of love I felt was amazing. If you possess that love, your radiant happiness will brighten your life and the lives of those around you.

If negative people cross your path, ignore their attitudes.

WHAT ARE YOU CONSUMING?

What you consume, mentally and physically, will affect your everyday attitudes. If you eat the wrong foods, you can become depressed and lazy. Our society has gotten fat from its self-indulgent eating habits. Foreigners are often shocked at how fat Americans have become. Over the last 50 years, our eating habits have changed and so has the level of our depression and anxiety.

What you consume can become the cornerstone to rebuilding your mental and physical health. A stockbroker friend of mine gave the book *The Zone,* written by Barry Sears, to an overweight client. The client read it, but that's all he did. His wife, however, also read the book and planned menus based on its suggestions. Simply by eating what his wife prepared, the man lost 40 pounds! The amazing thing is, he lost the weight without even one minute of exercise!

Developing good eating habits takes discipline, time, and persistence (even if it is as a result of your spouses' persistence). Today, our diet contains many fats and chemicals. If you're depressed or tired, your eating habits could be what is causing the problem. Gergley's Rule is, *"You are what you eat."* (Jerry Gergley is a three-time Ironman.) If your body feels good, your mind feels good.

Your health begins with what you're digesting and ends with physical activity. Both proper eating and exercise combine to keep you young—and must be done daily. Most people completely ignore this advice. Your physical well-being, through both diet and exercise, is imperative for success.

You must also feed your brain. Junk in, junk out. Put down the tabloids, turn off the television, and ignore the negative news! Start reading educational material that will make your life better. When I started my professional career, I was totally ignorant about how money worked. I knew that in order to succeed, I had to literally consume magazines that could teach me about business. *Money* magazine taught me the basics of financial savvy. *Success* magazine convinced me that I could become successful. *Entrepreneur* and *Inc.* magazines helped me understand

> What you consume can become the cornerstone to rebuilding your mental and physical health.

and create new ideas. *The Wall Street Journal* gave me a global outlook on the big picture of money and how it affects the world. I forced myself to read publications that would teach me about things I would need for my chosen path. You might pick a different route and need different reading material. Be selective. Your efforts *will* pay off and once you push yourself through this process, there will be many rewards. ***You are what you read!***

To change the big things in your life you must start with the little things. What I have just suggested will have an enormous impact. If you're in your car, turn off the radio and plug in an educational tape. You're in a growing mode and this intense self-feeding practice will push you up the ladder of success. If you're consuming mental rubbish, which the majority of Americans do, you're wasting your time. A few years ago, my days seemed to be starting on a negative, slow note. It occurred to me that I had gotten into the habit of reading all the junk in the local section of the newspaper. It was filled with depressing news about people's problems. I stopped reading it and found that my mood soon improved.

Negative thoughts, no matter what the source, will take the snap right out of you. The bottom line is that you are what you consume both mentally and physically. All these little acts of discipline will add up and will eventually transform your life.

CHAPTER TWO SUMMARY

The new you has found the past a valuable learning experience that is never to be repeated. Are your thoughts in a positive or negative place? Remember, positive attracts—negative repels. Only one of these thinking modes enhances your life for success.

Truthful thinking is your ability to see the rewards and to react automatically through experience. You are one of a kind—uniquely different from any other human. You are a gift to life, so love yourself and pursue a higher level of existence. Confidence is a by-product of self-love and experience. You need to stretch your experiences to grow.

Junk in, junk out. Put down the tabloids, turn off the television, and ignore the negative news!

Respect and self-respect come from a standard of moral and ethical values that need to be high. Most importantly, what you consume mentally and physically affects your life. Consume only positive and educational material! Healthy food consumption leads to a healthy lifestyle. Exercise is an outlet that allows the mind to massage itself.

CHAPTER TWO
BLUEPRINT FOR LIFE
WORKSTATION

1. My catalyst for change is_____.
   (The turning point that is motivating you to change your life.)

2. Energy and time =_____.

3. Which is better: a) to remember the past, or   b) to look toward the future?

4. Truthful thinking is followed by_____.

5. The_____is a form of momentum.

6. I like myself because:

7. I am unique because:

8. Write down five things that make you different from everyone else in a very unique and positive way.
   (Only you know yourself.)

9. Is liking yourself and having an ego a good thing or a bad thing?

10. On a 3 x 5 card write the following statement, then tape it to your bathroom mirror and say it out loud three times each morning in front of the mirror for the next 90 days:

**I am working from my present power.
I draw my power from my positive attitude.
Each day I will challenge myself to achieve the
things I never thought possible.
I will, I can,
I am, I have faith.**

11. List five things that are holding you back.

    a.

    b.

    c.

    d.

    e.

12. List five things that you will overcome.

    a.

    b.

    c.

    d.

    e.

13. What three things can you think of that could be a reward to you (for example: a trip to the beach, membership to the health club, etc.)?

    a.

    b.

    c.

14. I want to achieve the following in the near future (for example: education, money, a balanced relationship): _____.

15. In one year, I will_____.

16. In five years, I will_____.

17. List 10 things that you love (for example: my child, sunrises, sunsets, cool swims at the spring):

   a.

   b.

   c.

   d.

   e.

   f.

   g.

   h.

   i.

   j.

CREATING A PATH FOR CHANGE

Life's journey should be one of constant improvement. Before you can make anything better, however, you must understand where you are right now. This begins with an honest look at your feelings—how you operate in life. Do you have any weaknesses? Can you turn them into positive life changes? Do you continually allow these failings to destroy your opportunities? Here are some faults many people have—faults that should be on your list to avoid:

- Not saying what you mean
- Abusing alcohol or drugs
- Allowing people to manipulate you
- Not having any plan or goal beyond today
- Being disorganized
- Not planning to better yourself through education
- Keeping bad habits, such as smoking
- Indulging in self-pity
- Not making quality time for yourself or loved ones
- Having little faith in yourself
- Not being punctual
- Not being focused
- Not developing a financial plan or budget
- Being submissive
- Not letting go of guilt

Before you can make anything better . . . you must understand where you are right now.

*You must either make the proper
adjustments in your life
or you will always
be handicapped.*

Here's an example. Someone with promise and talent has a "small" drinking problem. After awhile, that "small" drinking problem slows her ambition, preventing her from even trying. There's nothing worse than someone's passion only coming out when they are drinking. *"I could have."* *"If only."* Your ambition needs to come out now! Don't let old habits get in the way of your future path.

KEEPING A JOURNAL

Creating and maintaining a daily journal is a prerequisite to finding your way. Simply put, it's an opportunity to talk to yourself about your trials and tribulations. Solutions will surface. **Write down those things you should be doing in your life.** Write down, as well, those things you are doing but aren't doing so well. This journal will help you stay focused and on track. It's also fun to go back and read how hard times were and to confirm the amount of growth you've experienced. I began a journal 15 years ago and it has become a friend that helps me understand myself. Your journey will be a challenge and your journal will help stabilize your thoughts. Many times, you will find solutions to your problems by looking at what you are writing.

Each day you will find an achievement or opportunity if you know how to look for it. Your life will move according to whether you follow that achievement or opportunity. All it takes is planning, setting goals, and concentrating on taking positive action. Discovering what held you back before will help you concentrate on which actions you need to take now.

To create the big picture for your life, you must be true to yourself. If you are tenaciously true to your pursuit of success, I guarantee you that the laws of our universe will

Creating and

maintaining

a daily

journal is a

prerequisite

to finding

your way.

deliver your dreams. The one necessary ingredient is time. While there is no way to determine how long or how fast the realization of your inspirations will take, with time and a strong work ethic, they will happen.

Each day gives you an opportunity to challenge yourself, to make yourself better. Some days you'll get knocked off your feet, slammed so badly you'll wonder whether anything good will ever happen. Soon afterward, though, you'll realize it's really just a short-term disappointment. A new day and a new life are upon you. Keeping your journal will help you organize what is happening—both the good and the bad. Soon, you will discover a new, clearer path. By being able to see your problems (and the ways out of them), refocusing yourself toward the big goal will become easy. Your journal is your best tool for both introspection and evaluation.

THE POWER OF GOALS

Written goals are the cornerstone of a progressive and positive life path. You must have a defined direction—and this is how you do it. Goals are your opportunity to create the life that you want before it happens. When I was 24, I had a life-altering experience when I realized that I could actually create the future that I wanted by positive visualization and writing down the things I wanted. Giving yourself advance direction allows you to move forward instead of in circles.

Start by thinking and writing down in your journal what you want in life and what excites you. Where do you want to live? How do you want to live? Ten years from now? Five years from now? One year from now? What are you willing to give up in order to receive these things?

In a study done by Harvard University, a survey of graduating seniors showed that after 30 years five percent of the graduates who had written down their goals outperformed 95% of the graduates who had not written their goals. That is, the net worth and achievements of the five percent was greater than the combined net worth and achievements of the 95%. *This certainly illustrates the importance and success of writing down your goals!*

Your 90-day goals will reflect bits and pieces of all those long-term goals. Here's one example: Begin with the long-term goal. Now write your short-term goals leading to how you will eventually achieve that long-term goal.

Long-Term Goal = A number of short-term goals

Long-Term Goal: Graduating from college

90-Day Short-Term Goals:

1. Visit a college campus or community college.
2. Set a goal to enroll officially.
3. Apply for financial aid.
4. Look for scholarship opportunities.
5. Arrange a lifestyle for the challenge ahead (for example, childcare).
6. Discontinue any bad habits that could hinder the ultimate goal of getting this degree.

These small pieces build up to the huge but achievable goal of getting that college degree.

THE WOMAN IN THE MIRROR

Who are you? What do you see when you come "face to face" with yourself? For centuries, women have gone to a mirror to find their value. Appearances have received as much focus in women's lives as inner growth. It is an old habit—and today's woman is bombarded by many pressures. They hear everything from promises of age-defying makeup and clarifying lotions to being everything they can be. In truth, what needs to be "clarified" is the inner path—the goals and direction to take in life.

If you walk away from this book with only one action, let it be to write down your goals—personal, professional, and financial. Post them on your bathroom mirror. It is a hollow vision to only see value in beauty and appearance.

Why put your goals on a mirror? To many women, a mirror is where they find reassurance. They still have the

While there is no way to determine how long or how fast the realization of your inspirations will take, with time and work they will happen.

false notion that looking pretty = having a man = security. You don't need that. Now you'll gain strength from the goals on your mirror and your security will be your self-confidence. You'll look at where you're going at least twice a day: first thing when you wake up to brush your teeth and last before you go to bed. Your goal list is a reminder of your process of transformation and how much you can accomplish today.

ORGANIZING YOUR GOALS

So now you are saying to yourself, *"How can I find the time for all these things?"* Each day offers you 24 hours. Learning time management will give you the skills you need to fit everything in. It will always be a struggle— ambitious people always have more to do than time allows. By using and studying your journal, however, you can figure out what and how you are doing, and ways it might be done more efficiently.

Only three percent of people write down their goals. The average person does not even take the time to form any! By simply writing down the things you want to achieve, you plant a seed in your subconscious. All successful people have goals and know their power. Why then don't more people capitalize on this power of focus? I don't have a definite answer to that. It's amazing, however, how the act of writing down the things you want in your life can cause your conscious and subconscious efforts and energies to deliver these things to you.

My personal experience with goals began when I was 24. Up until that point, my life had had no direction. I was all over the board, always in trouble, and had never done anything meaningful. In search of my future, I went to visit my father in Charleston, South Carolina. One day while he was away at work, I came across a list of things he was planning to do that year taped on his bathroom mirror. He was going to "pay off a credit card," "organize a family reunion," "save $5K," and "take a ski trip to Colorado." I was amazed that someone could actually write down what they wanted for the future and make it happen!

Your goal list is a reminder of your process of transformation and how much you can accomplish today!

Goals were my answer. Reading this list turned a light on in my head. I immediately ran down to the kitchen and wrote my own list of things that I wanted to do, things that would in some way improve my life. Here's part of what I put on that list:

- Obtain a gas credit card
- Pull and review my credit file
- Pay off a $500 car loan
- Enroll in real estate school
- Open a savings account
- Quit smoking
- Begin a payment schedule for my student loans
- Train for a road race
- Get a teaching job
- Develop my faith

There were more items on the list, but you can see where I was in my life at that time. At age 24, I had a negative net worth of about $20,000. That means that if I had died that day, I would have left behind bills totaling 20 grand.

My list of goals finally gave me the direction I needed. I didn't know it was in me, but I later learned that making goals is an ability everyone possesses. We all want things in life. If we just sit down and think for awhile, then take the time to write things down, almost any goal can be delivered to us. The conscious and subconscious will massage and manipulate our thoughts until an opportunity is presented. A strong work ethic, discipline, and hunger will pull it in.

During the next couple of years I became obsessed with goals. I soon realized that my goals were taking me someplace and were my lifeline to future security, rewards, and experiences. I rewrote those goals every 90 days. Initially, I used specific categories, areas where I thought I needed growth. I was very raw when it came to business acumen and skills. I had no real knowledge and terrible money habits. I was a case that needed work, so I concentrated and focused on the improvements I needed. Over the years,

I continued to form new lists until, eventually, I perfected the art of writing my goals.

Here is an example of some of my former 90-day financial goals:

- Read three books about business
- Read only the business section of the newspaper
- Go to three financial seminars
- Learn real estate contracts and their contents
- Purchase a house
- Take out a subscription to *Money* magazine
- Work off the monthly budget previously formulated
- Pay principal toward any credit card debt

AREAS OF GROWTH

My original goals were based on five areas of need. (Personally, I have since added others.) These are the basic ones I recommend for most people:

1. Financial
2. Educational
3. Business development/career
4. Personal
5. Family Development

I would write 10 to 15 goals under each heading, no matter how trivial. As long as I could grow from it, that goal was something I wrote down.

Over time, I discovered that I wasn't able to achieve every goal I listed. If it continued to be important, however, I would include that goal on my new list until it was achieved. (It took me two years of consistently writing, "Quit smoking!" before I actually did quit. I had smoked for 14 years. Quitting was one of the best things I have ever done for myself and it was all because of the goal I persistently wrote down.) Eventually my goals evolved and started looking like this:

- Open a real estate company
- Buy three properties

All successful people have goals and know their power.

- Open a mortgage company
- Buy a new car for cash
- Run a full marathon
- Join Toastmasters to learn how to communicate better and stop stuttering
- Go to a financial seminar
- Save $100,000

Yes, as you can see by my increasing goals, my life was changing. This dumb little piggy was going to market. I would usually have about 45 things I wanted to do in 90 days. Achieving 65% of them was usually about all I could do. As stated before, if something wasn't achieved but remained important, I would add it to the next list. As time went on (literally, within five or six years), I had become financially independent (net worth of $1 million). I owned two homes free and clear of any debt: a personal residence and an ocean-front home. Here I was in my early thirties and life was good. I could do no wrong because of the goal-driven engine I was running—so I stopped writing goals.

To this day, I am not sure why I stopped writing goals. Things started to change. I began losing money—$700,000 on just one business deal. I felt as if I was all over the board again with no true focus. I'd lost my path and direction in life. Then it finally came to me—I'd quit growing because I had gotten away from setting goals. So, once again, I sat down to renew my quest. After thinking about it, I came to realize that if you're not growing, you're dying. And I wanted to grow again. Goals had been the rudder of my sailboat and I wanted that direction back again. You might have the energy, but you need the rudder that goals provide. Having good energy blowing your sails is only part of it. You'll find yourself going in circles if you don't have the direction of goals.

I have been able to experience a much fuller, richer life thanks to goal setting. During the past few years I trained for and completed an Ironman triathlon, which includes a 1.2-mile swim, a 112-mile bike ride, plus a 26.2-mile run, wrote one book and have another in the works, traveled to Fiji and the Hawaii's north shore to surf the biggest waves of my life, and competed in Southern California's famed

If a goal wasn't achieved but remained important, I would add it to the next list.

Catalina Classic, a 32-mile, open-ocean paddleboard race. I even accomplished the goal of becoming an Irish citizen for dual citizenship. As you can tell, these personal goals have been life experiences. In order to maintain this lifestyle, however, I also set and advanced many financial goals. The day I decided to focus on my written goals, my life received the rewards and experiences I desired.

To this day, you can find my 90-day and one-year goals written on a sheet of paper taped to my bathroom mirror. This reminds me of the experiences I will be rewarding myself with this year.

Anyone who has achieved success knows the importance of goals. If you want success or anything meaningful in life, goals come with the territory.

HOW TO CREATE GOALS

It is not difficult to begin your first list of goals. Start with the most basic things that need changing and follow these rules:

1. You must write them down.
2. Don't shoot too low; always stretch.
3. Make them measurable.
4. Put them where you will see them every day (for example, on your bathroom mirror).
5. Break down your larger goals and goal time frames into smaller, more manageable pieces. They should build on each other.
6. Rollover any important unfulfilled goals onto your new list.

Different goals can have different time frames. There are:

- 5-year goals
- 1-year goals
- 90-day goals
- 30-day goals

Daily goals are also useful. The first step is to write down what you want to achieve. For daily goals, try to

Different goals can have different time frames.

write them on a legal pad the night before. Carry that pad with you, so that you are constantly reminded of what you want to accomplish. Take your time when deciding what you want and what steps are necessary to achieve them. In your overall goal plan, you should have a minimum of five goals for every category listed in the previous section.

Here's an example:

90-DAY GOALS
July 20–October 20
(Always put in a start date and an end date)

Educational

1. Take a computer class
2. Read a book on negotiation
3. Read a family planning goal book
4. Take a night class
5. Take a parenting class

Financial

1. Open a savings account
2. Direct deposit 10% of paycheck to savings
3. Read only the business section of the paper daily
4. Complete a financial net worth statement
5. Break down where money goes each month
   (fill out a budget)
6. Reduce principal on credit card debt

Family

1. Organize a family walk in the park once a week
2. Devote at least three hours per week with each child
3. Write family goals together and review weekly
4. Have cookout with family
5. Read to children at bedtime—or have them read to you

Business Development

1. Have conference with boss about advancement
2. Identify three ways to become more valuable at work
3. Ask for company to provide development class or seminar
4. Attend seminar for development
5. Go to local junior college career placement center and determine what is available now

Relationship

1. Have one live date a week/go out with a friend/attend a social gathering or ask someone out to a social event
2. Read a book on relationships
3. Do something nice for someone every day
4. Kiss and hold spouse every night before going to sleep
5. Try not to fight in front of the kids
6. Say I love you daily to each member of your family, once in the morning and once at night

Personal

1. Eat better; read a book on nutrition
2. Work out for 45 minutes per day at least five days per week
3. Go to a spiritual event with the family
4. Try and give a smile to everyone you meet
5. Converse with other women. Join a support group, etc.

ONE-YEAR GOALS
(Begin at date you are writing goals)

1. Take three computer classes
   a.
   b.
   c.
2. Put 10% of total income into savings
   (Total income x 10% = savings)
3. Take a family vacation
4. Help children get good grades
5. Teach kids about goals and have them write down their own goals
6. Run/walk in a partial or whole marathon
7. Have at least one date or social activity each week
8. Pay off car
9. Clear up credit
10. Exercise or dedicate time to a fitness program/hobby/something of personal interest
11. Achieve zero credit card debt

1. Have $50,000 in the bank or equity in a house
2. Become a successful businesswoman
3. Maintain a permanent relationship
4. Have happy, healthy kids
5. Attain a college education, degree, or a career-driven license
6. Become computer literate
7. Volunteer in the community regularly
8. Own your home
9. Own your car free and clear—no payments
10. Have a great job
11. Develop healthy habits
12. Achieve zero credit card debt

Now, your accomplishments will keep growing. You should put your old goals in a file and religiously write new ones. Keep them visual and observe them daily. You'll see an amazing change over time. I warn you, however: be careful what you write down—you just might get it!

Discipline creates change.

DISCIPLINE: THE KEY

Discipline is the key to your advancement. Most people possess very little. They're given discipline as children growing up—yet, when they become adults, they lose this discipline. This stops them from achieving. Discipline is a key element for creating change.

I read an article in the July 27, 1995, edition of *The Wall Street Journal*. The subject was the transformation of young recruits from impoverished backgrounds going through basic training. Entering the military, they were prejudiced, irresponsible, and drug addicted. After eight weeks, these same young people came out despising drugs and their former lackluster attitudes. Their vigor and can-do spirit enabled them to conquer any obstacle.

You, unfortunately, do not have a drill sergeant to whip you into shape. For you to conquer anything in life, you must have focus. To have focus, you must have discipline. For our purposes, this discipline can be called *an action*. It is an action of your will—an action that allows you to meet your challenges every day. When actions are repeated over and over, they become a habit. These habits lead to forming your new character.

Discipline is something you practice over and over. It can be as simple as putting on your seat belt every time you get into a car. You will grow from these good habits. My completing an Ironman Triathlon required extreme discipline and focus. I trained 4½ hours each weekday for five months, and each Saturday and Sunday I put in an additional eight hours daily. Without that discipline, I would never have achieved my goal.

In today's pampered society, people wonder why their lives (or those of their children) are such a mess. It is because of a lack of discipline, both physical and mental. Discipline shows in your every action. It could mean making your bed every morning. Or consistently writing in your journal. Or setting aside $20 of your $100 paycheck for savings. Discipline means keeping your focus on your goals. Discipline is learning to consistently produce. Discipline is organizing your life so that you can succeed! It's hard—but the rewards are great.

Let's start by looking up the word discipline in the dictionary so you know the word's true definition: Discipline = (go look it up!). Write the word and its definition in your journal. *Warning to the weak: You cannot travel the journey of this book without the acceptance of this concept. It is the driving force behind all the changes you will make in your life. Discipline creates power.*

THE KEYS TO PERSONAL POWER

Your personal power comes from within—it's all up to you. It doesn't matter how bad your life is now. You can improve your situation without depending on anyone else. It all starts with small steps of understanding.

A woman's place in our society is controlled by her knowledge. This isn't, however, only book knowledge—it's also what she has experienced in life.

> You can improve your situation without depending on anyone else.

Knowledge = Experience + Education

Anyone can gain this "knowledge" if she has the discipline to make it her goal. You will gain experience simply by trying new things. If you overcome your fear of facing new challenges, you will have won half the battle. Just walking down different roads gives you tremendous insight about achievement. Education comes from the information you put into your head. If you want to think and compete like a businessman, read *The Wall Street Journal.* Notice, I said *businessman*—because *he* is your competition. Stop wasting your valuable time by listening to and reading junk! Anything that does not help you with business, financial, or personal growth must be dropped from your busy schedule. No junk radio. No sitcom television. No *People* magazine. Can you tell me what one more cover story about Julia Roberts can do for you? Zero—zip—nada. We live in the real world. We need real-world building blocks for self-help.

This new competitive education will come from your determination. Your previous schooling and society's expectations may have done a poor job of preparing you for success. It will take tremendous intensity for you to break free from your old mold. You can do it—especially if you follow the advice in this book.

BECOMING AN ACHIEVER

Some people get more out of life than others—they make every minute count. They do more, think more, laugh more, play harder, and are more financially successful. They are passionate, uninhibited, enthusiastic, and exhilarating to know. While so many of us barely skim the surface of human potential, these people dive deeply into the realm of the seemingly impossible and emerge with a treasure trove of life's experiences. These achievers have developed an attitude of "go get 'em" and a belief that each dawn is a new opportunity to move closer to their goals. How do these super-achievers accomplish so much each day, while others stand still, bleary-eyed with toothbrush in hand, just staring into the bathroom mirror? Where do achievers get the energy, drive, and ambition to "go get 'em?"

There are three basic areas that motivate people: money, love of family, and personal fulfillment. The reason most people do not succeed is that they have not clearly defined their goals for these areas. Setting goals, both short-term and long-term, is the key to your personal power.

You must be willing to perform extra tasks—work that others don't want to do. *Achievers have learned to dream constructively, to establish clear goals.* They stretch themselves beyond their comfort level. Achievers are clear about who they are, what they want out of life, how much they want it, and what plans they need for attaining it. For example, many people have trouble speaking up for themselves. They are afraid they will look foolish. The person who effectively communicates, however, is someone who gets noticed. You must learn to speak both one-on-one and in front of an audience. By doing this, you will learn to think more clearly and you will become articulate. These skills bleed over effortlessly and beneficially into every area of your life.

Each step and each day brings the achiever closer to her dreams. Achievers don't waste time worrying about yesterday's flops or tomorrow's potential problems. They have adopted the Zen principle that within each problem there is a lesson. Nothing seems to daunt them. When an achiever comes to a barrier, she pauses. She then steps back for a moment—but only to size up the situation. The true achiever proceeds on and finds a new solution. *Achievers are tenacious. They don't give up. Like well-trained athletes, they understand the need to practice and persevere. These people believe in themselves! They don't wait for opportunities—they create them. Achievers know there are no guarantees in life and that to risk is to grow.*

Mickey Rooney, when asked how he felt about his life's highly publicized ups and downs, once said, "It's not a sin to fall down. It's a sin to lie there." There is no shame in taking a risk and failing. The dishonor comes from not trying again!

High achievers feast at the banquet of life. They are enthusiastic about work, learning, and play. They know

> The true achiever proceeds on and finds a new solution. Achievers are tenacious. They don't give up.

that balancing their time between all three areas is good for them. No regrets, no guilt. Like those who follow the teachings of Buddha, they appreciate that only the present external "now" moment is real. Realizing that the past cannot be changed nor the future controlled, they devote themselves fully to the rich experience of the present. **High achievers love themselves and trust their own abilities.** They don't waste time seeking the approval of others. They know their own worth and have learned to pat themselves on the back. They are not conceited or selfish—they merely have pride in their own independence and unique qualities.

Sooner or later, each of us needs to decide what we want and how much we want it. Are you willing to enjoy the freedom of success and also assume the personal commitment necessary to achieve that goal? In your journal, ask yourself these four basic questions: 1) Who am I? 2) Where do I want to be? 3) What is in the way? 4) How will I overcome those barriers?

For some, the answers seem clear. Others are not as sure of their personal ambitions. To reach goals successfully, life is a journey—and one worth pursuing. You need to understand yourself and these questions before you can take the first step. Let's begin by taking a long, hard look at your hopes. What are your unique strengths? What weaknesses have stopped you in the past? What can you do to avoid these in the future? What handicaps do you need to overcome? Once you have learned to be honest about your abilities, you will be ready to select a path. Choose one that capitalizes on your talents and strengths.

Set personal goals and target dates for achieving them. Hazy goals produce hazy results.

IF NOT NOW, WHEN?

You alone are responsible for your actions and reactions. Only you are in charge of your life. Shakespeare wrote, "All the world is a stage, and we are but players." You're the author of your own script. You choose your role. Knowing that life is limited to only a certain number of days, you must grasp each moment as an opportunity to live to your fullest. Life is a maze and many rules are arbitrary. We are not meant to have all the answers, but we should know which questions to ask.

Set personal goals and target dates for achieving them. "If you don't know where you are going, any path will lead you there." Hazy goals produce hazy results. After you have decided where you want to be in life, write down your goals with a clear step-by-step plan. Perhaps the future will not happen exactly that way—it rarely does. But establishing a blueprint for achieving results keeps your efforts on track and gives you a reference point from which to work.

Develop your abilities and commit yourself to excellence. *Opportunity is often difficult to recognize because its favorite disguise is hard work.* Wishing alone cannot make things happen. Planning, persistence, and a burning desire to succeed are essential. You need to acquire experience, skills, and knowledge—only then will you have the ability to succeed. No carpenter ever built a house without tools and knowing where and how to use them.

THINK POSITIVELY

Be confident. *Learn to trust your ability to succeed.* There will always be educated risks—don't be afraid to take them. How easily we limit ourselves. Have you ever heard someone say, "Oh, I could never do that." There is a difference between the words "cannot" and "will not." Every time you want to say, "I can't do that," substitute the words, "I will not." Notice the difference between the two in meaning! When you say, "I can't," there is usually a way it *can* be done. It is *you* who is setting a limit on yourself, choosing not to pursue a certain direction.

Amelia Earhart was a great example of not limiting herself. When she was 23, she received her pilot's license. Seven years later she got a call asking if she would be willing to fly across the Atlantic Ocean. She responded with, "How could I refuse such a shining adventure?" Of the previous 15 pilots to attempt this feat, only one survived—a man by the name of Charles Lindbergh. In 1928, Earhart became the first woman to cross the Atlantic—but she was embarrassed. The pilot and co-pilot never let her touch the wheel. In her own words, she was "nothing but a sack of potatoes," yet this experience still inspired her. Four years later, she took off again. The 15-hour flight in her single engine plane was harrowing. There was rain, fog, and ice. She had zero visibility, frozen wings, instrument failure (both her tachometer and altimeter stopped working), a leaky fuel gauge, and a cracked manifold that shot flames into the night. Somehow, Earhart managed to land in a cow pasture in Northern Ireland. She had less than 100 gallons of gas remaining in the tanks. When asked why she did it, Earhart replied, "I flew the Atlantic because I wanted to. . . . To want in one's heart to do a thing for its own sake . . . against the opposition of tradition, neighborhood opinion, and so-called common sense—that is an Atlantic. . . . Everyone has his own Atlantic to fly."

Earhart went on to break records for the rest of her life. She always wanted to go further, farther, and faster. We all have our own Atlantic to cross. All we need is the confidence, the courage, the conviction, and the tools to begin our own shining adventure.

CHAPTER THREE SUMMARY

Your commitment requires you to identify changes that need to be made in your life. Making the proper adjustments through your will to change is the second step.

Developing a journal will help you because the journal will allow you to revisit your problems mentally while suggesting solutions at the same time. When these things take written form, they begin to become a reality. Every day is an opportunity to create change—and to create opportunity.

The *power of goals* is the cornerstone that defines your progressive path. They must be written down by category. They must be made visible daily and must be measured daily. They must have time frames.

You can gain momentum and direction in life by simply looking at your mirror and reminding yourself about your reasons to energize today.

Discipline is the lone word that creates change in your life. When discipline is created in one part of your life, it transfers to the other parts.

High-achievers love themselves and trust their own visions. They do not waste time seeking the approval of others. They are clear about who they are and what they want from life.

You alone are in charge of your life. If it is to become successful, no other person can hold you back. Life is limited to only a certain amount of days and hours and you must grasp each moment as an opportunity to live life to its fullest. Think positively and learn to trust your ability to succeed.

"Everyone has his own Atlantic to fly."

CHAPTER THREE
BLUEPRINT FOR LIFE
WORKSTATION

Develop your abilities and commit yourself to excellence.

1. Write down five weaknesses you would like to eliminate (for example: stuttering, eating habits, smoking, negativity).

   a.

   b.

   c.

   d.

   e.

   Which of these might be limiting your potential?

2. The five most important things in my life are (for example: my faith, my family, my future, building financial security, going back to school, losing five pounds):

   a.

   b.

   c.

   d.

   e.

3. Start a scrapbook (this is *not* your journal). Every time you read an inspiring personal story about someone achieving and overcoming, cut it out and paste it in your scrapbook.

4. Now, write in your journal. Date it and begin: "This is how I feel and here are the different aspects of my life." Write what you think is right and wrong in your life for 10 days. What must you do to improve your situation? View this as a conversation with yourself—try to write down different solutions and options. Write something each day for 30 days.
5. Make a list of five tangible things that you want. (For example, a new car, home, etc.)
6. Write what your life will be like five years from today.
7. Now, it's time to write your one-year goals. Take your time and come back if you need more time. Feel free to write more than five goals for each category—since there should be more—but list a minimum of five.

Financial

a.

b.

c.

d.

e.

Educational

a.

b.

c.

d.

e.

Business Development

a.

b.

c.

d.

e.

Family Development

a.

b.

c.

d.

e.

Personal

a.

b.

c.

d.

e.

8. Now, duplicate the above process but using 90-day goals.

9. Put these on a separate sheet of paper and tape them to your bathroom mirror with a start date and a finish date.

10. The definition of discipline is_____.

11. Who am I? (Be descriptive.)

12. Where do I want to be?

13. What is in the way?

14. How will I overcome those barriers?

15. Go to your mirror.
    a. If you have written goals taped to the mirror, collect $200 and pass go!
    b. If there are no goals written and taped to the mirror, reread this entire chapter.

BREAKING THE CYCLE

B reaking the cycle means changing your patterns and the way you look at things. Ever feel like you are constantly spending money? It's important to realize that you and your family are direct targets of the most creative advertising in the world. Even people with vast incomes and salaries are lured into buying more than they really need or can afford. Advertising seduces you into thinking you just have to own that item. It's like nicotine and cigarettes: you really can't help yourself.

DEPROGRAMMING THE CONSUMER MENTALITY

While returning something at the mall recently, I suddenly felt this tremendous urge to buy a particular item. What could I do to resist this urge to buy? Stay away! If you have no immunity, don't go near places that are going to challenge your willpower. (The same can be said about people. If you associate with friends who are bad influences, you'll eventually become like them. Your best defense is to avoid them.) Breaking the cycle means destroying the way you've always done things in the past.

If you have no immunity, don't go near places that are going to challenge your willpower.

The first step on your path toward success is to become mentally alert. Think about what you really need. Make a shopping list. Develop the willpower to go into a store, any store, and only buy the things on that list. Becoming tight-fisted is a real art. It will control those impulse-buying reactions and help you control your budget. It is usually the small, unnecessary items purchased that make the difference between being over- or under- budget.

Most Americans have only one thought process when it comes to shopping—buy it! Numbed from constant advertising and told to think we "deserve" it, we lose all common sense. We're the richest people in the world and the choices are phenomenal, but many of us are also in debt. Most consumers carry credit-card debt for years—a dead weight on their quality of life. Financial pressure makes for short nerves and stress. You might be happy with a new car—but what about the $500/month car payment? Do you really need all those bells and whistles on it?

The key to financial stability is to change the way you think. Make a game out of seeing what's behind the creative advertising. Try to expose the hustling sales techniques. All they really want is to suck the money straight out of your pocket. I've always enjoyed identifying a salesperson's closing technique, and then saying, "Wow, that was a good one—that should work on someone else."

Practice these words: I'm not a buyer. Phone solicitors are the best-trained salespeople. Most of us don't like to hang up on strangers. It is not impolite, however, to simply cut them off and say, "I'm not interested, but thanks for calling." Separate yourself from the herd—become independent and not a consumer. It's the only way you can move on to the greater financial decisions awaiting you. You cannot afford to think like the masses—you are now on your own independent path toward prosperity. Break this cycle of dependent consumerism!

Let me hit the consumer mentality right between the eyes. Consider the shoe industry and all the NBA hype aimed at our children—with shoes costing over $100 a pair. If we'd let them, our kids would buy a new pair of sneakers every month. Stay alert. Rise above the needless buying. Become more reasonable and stay on budget. I'm

Breaking the cycle means destroying the way you've always done things in the past.

sure you're saying to yourself, "Well, *you* try saying 'no' to my child!" That child, however, gets his information from television and magazines aimed at teaching him to spend, spend, spend. It's your job to educate your child. Just as you teach him to cross the street safely, you must teach him to live within his, and your, means. Love means teaching him to say "no"—and meaning it! Make all your children "team players" by teaching them healthy consumer habits. It will help each child become more responsible and, eventually, a better adult.

If I didn't already say it, let me say it again. *Start with turning off the television.* We are raising a generation of drones that behave like trained seals. Me, me, me. I want, I want, I want. Be smarter than television advertising campaigns trying to affect your decision-making process. Turn off the television and watch the creative, self-entertaining side of your family take over. Get rid of the boob tube and take advantage of the quality time its absence will give you.

TIME CONTROL: FINDING THE TIME

Ever notice how some people have more time than others? While there is no way to create time, some people have a better handle on controlling it. Organization and discipline can help identify waste. (This is especially true for single parents who seem to need a 28-hour day.) *You need to make a list every day.* What do you hope to accomplish today? Now, work from that list! Identify things that are time wasters. Maybe several small things can be combined and/or completed together. Writing down that daily sequence of events will help you gain control.

It is important that your family also make a master schedule. Working together toward mutual goals will give you focus and help draw all of you closer. Once your children see you trying to help them, it will all become smoother. Also, you are teaching them valuable skills they can use in school, as well as later in life!

Time efficiency is an awareness that allows you to do more and achieve more in a controlled fashion. If you're

Turn off the television and watch the creative, entertaining side of your family take over.

going to change your life, you'll have to find ways to juggle and carry more load. It is when your tasks aren't organized efficiently that you feel overwhelmed. Thinking through the process to *find the time* will help you become more efficient. Once you see the possibilities, you will become more confident that you're on the right path. Reading books about time management will help give you greater insight into the art of time efficiency. Here are two possible starts:

How to Get Control of Your Time and Your Life
   by Alan Lakein
First Things First by Stephen R. Covey, A. Roger Merrill, and Rebecca R. Merrill

ORGANIZATIONAL LEVELS

There are several levels of organization. Once you create discipline on the first level, you'll be ready to organize the second level, and so on. As stated previously: *organization = growth.*

You have organizational influence. This means you can change things around you to make them fit your needs. Your personal life is your first level of organization: your family, home, automobile, desk, bedroom, closet, etc. The second level revolves around friends and money: how you produce income; your debt; the boards, clubs, and associations to which you belong. This second level of organizational influence allows you greater opportunities for contacts and ways to create new opportunities. Widening this sphere of influence is important—you will be exposed to more opportunities for success. The third level of organizational growth is future planning: the ability to see and plan well into the future.

You must find ways to organize before the future becomes reality. Right now, you're building a bridge to that future reality. My goal of writing this book didn't just happen. Over a period of 10 years, I jotted down ideas and saved articles I thought might be pertinent. When I was finally ready to put my thoughts into action, I had all the materials I needed. If those organizational efforts hadn't been taken, this book wouldn't exist. It was my ability to see far into the future—my third level of organizational skills—that got me to this point. Develop that third layer and start dealing with your future now.

Your ability to create and plan will become easier as you begin to experience success. If you are now on the "survival" level, you are only concentrating on the innermost layer: yourself and your surroundings. People of great accomplishment have many, many more layers of organizational abilities. What steps can you take to put yourself on to the next level of organizational growth?

SACRIFICE:
TAKE THREE STEPS BACK

Transforming your life and that of your family requires sacrifice. If you want more time and more "stuff," you must be temporarily willing to give up some of the luxuries you now enjoy. You must reorganize your finances for the short term so that you can ultimately achieve the greater picture. Here's an example: I was helping a woman reorganize her finances to get out of debt. The first thing I told her was that she would have to shut off her cable. She was very unhappy about losing her favorite drug (television) but she understood. She knew that sacrifice was necessary if she was going to help herself. She realized that she was gaining something from that sacrifice: quality time and extra money to pay off her credit card debt.

Right now you're probably hanging on dearly to surface appearances and "keeping up with the Joneses." *Get over that mentality and go back to the basics.* Economize, restructure, and grow. What's sinking you is letting others make your standards. Set your own priorities. They don't happen overnight but changes will come—and they will be good changes.

For a number of years I "house sat" by living in someone else's home while they lived abroad. I saved every dollar I might have used toward my personal house payment and used it to purchase other properties (income-producing apartments and/or houses). It might have looked better to

You can change things around you to make them fit your needs.

others had I been living in a "keeping up with the Joneses house," but I got more in the long run. I was keeping my expenses down and investing in income-producing assets with the money I saved.

To get something, you have to give up something. It is a simple universal rule. What are you willing to give up (sacrifice) in order to receive? Eating rice and beans for one year may allow you to eat steak for the rest of your life! The false props of comfort that may have been given to you by a former husband can be your handicap. They've given you false values—ones that you cannot currently afford. Once you get your priorities in order, you will understand that you need to give up some of them now . . . but, remember, you will gain far more luxuries later.

MAINTAINING MOTIVATION

Trying to maintain motivation while making sacrifices isn't easy. You must remember that you will conquer your goals if you simply stay on track. Maintaining this motivation is a skill and there are a number of ways to do it. Your internal motivation will come from pride in your achievements. You are getting better and better all by yourself. You are developing the self-esteem and confidence that will lead you on the right path.

External motivation can come from many sources. Physically, you can surround your personal life with possibilities: pictures on the refrigerator of things you are striving for (these can be daily and nightly reminders of things to come)—the scrapbook of "possibilities" you are compiling. For mothers, a source of motivation can be their children. Each night go and sit quietly by your child's bed for a few moments and watch him or her sleep. That observation should inspire your commitment to protect what is important for you to achieve. Other external sources of motivation could include:

1. **Mentors:** Speak to a mentor about your quest—someone who has traveled the road you wish to take. I have enjoyed many calls from people looking for their path

and I have also had mentors during my own journey. It's a chain: as I become one to you, you will become one to someone else—sharing your travels and the experiences of your journey. (Most people will be flattered to be asked to be your mentor. Don't hesitate to approach someone for advice.)

2. **Write it down:** Look daily into your mirror at your goals and remind yourself, "Wow, I'm on my way! I'm really going someplace if I stay on this track."

3. **Motivational materials:** Keep a constant flow of motivational seminars, books, tapes, and programs on your schedule.

4. **Create a "scrapbook of dreams":** This scrapbook consists of all the things you want in life. Cut them out of magazines and newspapers. Look at the pages you have constructed as often as needed to refuel your motivation.

5. **Be healthy:** If you are polluted with alcohol, tobacco, unhealthy foods, or a bad living environment, you must consider cleaning up. These things will pull you down!

Many people live and dwell on their pasts—glorious or sorrowful. The achievers (and those rewarded with time or material wealth) get there by living for the future. They have goals and use them as steps toward progress. You can do it, too!

CHAPTER FOUR SUMMARY

Define your thinking now. You're not one of the "consumer cows" in our society, looking to spend all the money or income you receive. Be mentally alert to the fact that money, for now, should buy only the necessary. After that, get rid of your debt (including the principal). The rest should be saved for future investment and security.

It is imperative that you teach your children fiscal responsibility every year of their young lives. If you do, they'll probably never be in debt.

Turn off the television—listen to the whining for awhile, and then watch human creativity and self-entertainment develop! Television robs time and is a drug that you don't need.

You must remember that you will conquer your goals if you simply stay on track.

Time efficiency is the organization of your life in motion. Organization equals growth because it creates time and space. We all must constantly try to achieve higher levels of organization. When we do, our lives surge ahead. Three levels of organization bridge the space between the future and now. You must think for the future. When you do, your life will become the future you envisioned.

There is nothing wrong with streamlining your life financially, sacrificing now for a better tomorrow. What will you sacrifice now in order to receive more later?

Motivation comes from your will to change, from your love, and from your goals for your family. It comes from your own dogma to give yourself the life you deserve—and shall receive!

CHAPTER FOUR
BLUEPRINT FOR LIFE
WORKSTATION

The achievers get there by living for the future.

1. Go to a very large, sell-all type consumer department store. It must be large and should sell everything from hardware to housewares to clothes. Sit down for 30 minutes and observe what people are buying. Make your own judgments as to what these people can live without. Do the buyers look like consumer cows?
2. Get out a sheet of paper and list, in sequence, the things you will do tomorrow to improve your life. Small things—things that just need to be done. (For example, monitoring your daughter's homework or going to the grocery store.) Fill up the page. Write your daily goals the night before.
3. Identify two people you consider successful, and whom you feel you can approach. Call them. Tell them you admire their success and respect them as a person for what they've accomplished. Ask them if they can spare 10 minutes on the phone or in person. Make an appointment for this time. Say that you'd like to listen to their opinions about the process of success. Take notes on what they say. (They should be flattered and they may be a mentor down the road for your problem-

solving solution needs. Successful people are usually open to this.)

4. Go to the bathroom mirror and read your goals out loud. If you can't do this (because you haven't written them yet), consider it confirmation that you are stopping yourself from growing.

5. Create a scrapbook consisting of 10 to 20 pages of pictures. Cut out only pictures of things you want in your life.

6. Make a list of five things you will do that will affect your health in a positive way (they can become goals).

7. Enter into the next 5K road race as a walker in a beginner's level of competition. If you don't have the entrance money, trail at the end or on the sidewalk.

YOUR FAMILY

You cannot change without the full cooperation of your family unit. This involvement can be positive for each family member. For you, your family can create an extra power force enabling you to battle the task ahead. For the others, your success will become a valuable lesson in life and a role model for them to learn from.

YOU ARE THEIR ROLE MODEL

In everything you do, the family follows your lead. The actions you take now will influence all your future generations.

If you have a child always asking for money (and they all do), teach him to organize his priorities. Children's money needs can usually be categorized into two areas: (1) basic necessities: food, clothing, and school supplies, and (2) optional: Little League registration, dance classes, money for snacks, a new basketball, and video games. While you are obligated to provide the basic necessities, the other things are *optional*.

Your child needs to *earn* the things on the second list, whether through extra chores, behavior, good grades, or outside jobs. Is this being too hard on your child? No. This is a lesson in life. If you want something, you can achieve it. The reality is that no one gives you anything. Parents who give too much to their children ruin their chances for independent survival. The mind and the heart will find constructive ways to satisfy the desire. Having your child do his or her share of the work will help him or her gain more respect for the things you provide. *Children grow when they do things for themselves—never when someone does something for them.*

CHORES

Make your child responsible for work chores around the house. Chores are not done for extra income. It is your child's duty as payment for the things you already provide. If you do decide to pay for certain duties in cash (as opposed to paying for an after-school activity or sports equipment), 20–30% of that money should be saved in the child's name. This will be seed money for other items they will need for the future. Consider what could happen if you were to grant your child's every wish. Instead of growing up responsibly, he would become like everyone else—uneducated in money matters and thinking he deserves things simply because the world owes it to him. Imagine that you have a 16-year-old. How different would it be for his self-esteem if you were to 1) give him a car, or 2) if you had him make payments every month himself. Think about what each payment would teach him! If children are taught that they will receive things without any effort, they can turn up at age 40 still living at home, continuing to sponge off mom and dad.

Responsibility is a great attribute and a highly prized characteristic in your child's character. Providing an allowance and the chance to earn extra money through additional household chores is one of the best ways to teach financial responsibility. But, beware! Don't tie an allowance to the performance of routine chores. It frequently backfires. Parents often tie themselves in knots making sure the chores get done so that they can give their children money. They don't

If you want something, you can achieve it. The reality is no one gives you anything.

want to pay a child before the chores are completed, but time goes by and the chores are undone. When you require chores independent of payment, it teaches your child that everyone in the family has jobs around the house.

I know a friend who to this day (at 43 years of age) cannot do his own laundry. His mother always did it for him, so he never had to learn. During the course of his marriage, his wife did all his laundry. Last year, when he became divorced, he was helpless. Learning to become independent for your daily needs means survival and self-reliance—a great gift to your children. I found myself realizing at an early age that if I wanted something to wear, I had better be able to wash a cycle of clothing. Self-reliance. Thanks, Mom!

You appreciate things that you *earn*. Children who are given things usually do not respect their value. It's the same with credit. Picture this: you walk into a store and buy something for cash. If you walk into a store, however, and are given an item that you don't have to pay for, it has actually been bought on credit and you *will* pay (and pay and pay), but you won't really own it for three years. You purchased on credit—you were given something you didn't earn. This is the difference between buying something and taking it out on credit.

TEACHING KIDS ABOUT MONEY

American children spend over $7 billion a year on candy, clothing, snacks, cosmetics, CDs, and video games. How do they get the money? Some get it from allowances, babysitting, mowing yards, or part-time jobs. Others are just given the money. Our children learn their values and work ethics from us, their parents. They absorb attitudes toward money and our beliefs about saving and spending every time we make a purchase. Financially responsible children come from financially responsible parents—parents who have taken the time to instill those values. Not only do you have to set an example, you must also sit down with your children and show them the details of money management (even if they have just been given their birthday money).

Children are never too young to begin learning how to save.

Providing an allowance and creating chores from which young children can earn money is one of the easiest ways to teach financial responsibility. All too often, however, parents don't stay within their own rules and guidelines. *It is extremely important that you stick with the discipline of only paying your child when your child has met his or her responsibilities.* What you're really trying to do is instill the values that come from handling money: discipline, responsibility, and dealing with the frustration of having to make choices.

Your children must realize that structuring money and making budgets is not an option or a choice. It is a requirement. They have to become responsible for their own spending decisions. If they choose to blow their entire month's allowance on an expensive pair of basketball shoes, that's their choice—but they will have to live with the consequences. Children are never too young to begin learning how to save. Give your small children piggybanks and encourage them to deposit whatever change they find.

Older children usually receive real allowances. Encourage them to save part of it! Instead of handing your child $20, for example, give him the money in $1 bills so part can be set aside for savings. If your child wants a big-ticket item such as a trip or car, take the time to sit down with him and work out a goal-plan. See how much he must save. If he wants something that costs $1,000, divide that amount by some number of payments. Show how much money needs to be saved or earned and for how long. For example, if an item costs $365, he'll need to save $1 per day for one year, or $2 a day for six months. You can also work out a weekly payment schedule. Ask your child how or what he can do to earn that money to meet that financial goal. Also, where will he put his savings?

Your children need to learn how to evaluate products and costs and you are responsible for teaching them.

THE ART OF SHOPPING

Shopping is an art—and one that has to be taught. Figuring out the best value is a skill children must develop. Don't allow impulse purchases! If your child wants a CD, take him to three different stores before letting him buy it.

Show him that different stores have different markups and similar products. The money spent at the counter should come from his pocket, not from your purse. Take him shopping with you when you are ready to buy something important. Discuss how you plan to make that final decision and show him how, when, and why you decided to buy it. Your child needs to learn how to evaluate products and costs and you are responsible for teaching him. For more information on teaching your children about money, I recommend the following publications:

Kids, Money and Values: Creative Ways to Teach your Kids about Money, by Patricia Schiff-Estes and Irving Barocas, Betterway Books, 1994.

Money Doesn't Grow on Trees: A Parents' Guide to Raising Financially Responsible Children, Neal S. Godfrey and Caroline Edwards, Simon & Schuster, 1993.

Piggy Banks to Money Markets, Kidvidz, distributed by Price, Stearn, Sloane, Inc. For this video, contact Price, Stearn, Sloan, Inc. at 1-800-421-0892.

The Real Deal: Playing the Buying Game. This is a 12-page publication designed to show elementary school-age children "how to read between the lines to buy smart." The booklet, published by the Federal Trade Commission and the National Association of Attorney Generals, costs 50 cents. For a copy, write to Consumer Information Center, Department 382C, Pueblo, Colorado 81009.

AFTER AGE 10, IT'S OVER: MAY LUCK BE WITH YOU

Start young! If you want to impress *your* principles and values on your children, get an early start. Psychologists have found that even the youngest infant has an enormous capacity for learning. Why does society start your child's public education at age five? You can teach valuable lessons much earlier—your child's mind is being molded even at age three. It is your responsibility to create disciplined habits for life.

But discipline is not enough. It takes love, too. Compare your child's learning control to learning algebra. While it's great to have a calculator, you need to understand the math first. You have to pay attention to your child now, while she's young. You can't put off making time for your child. You won't be able to reach her when she's older—she'll be more influenced by peer pressure. Communication is the ultimate tool and it must start at an early age. In the morning, at night—a few moments acknowledging the love you have for each other will nourish both of you. It is the only way.

Take Tiger Woods—a wealthy golf pro while still in his teens. Why does he behave so humbly and respectfully toward others? He has said that whenever he had a question for either of his parents, they would put down the paper or turn off the television. They would stop whatever they were doing and answer his question. Sometimes the dialogue would go on for hours even though he was only a small child! The wisdom, understanding, and love poured into that child had tremendous results. You get the most out when you put the most in.

How do you begin, however, to bond with each other? For starters, when serving dinner try to have everyone eat together. Openly discussing conquests, problems, and desires will help bring your family together and will help your children develop better speaking skills. Turn off the television. Children who watch television during the dinner hour waste precious development time. If you want them to learn your values, you have to get their attention. Turn off the tube and show your children you care about *them!* Your values will soon be recognized, realized, and honored now and years from now.

MAKING THE MOST OF THEIR FREE TIME

Keep your child active and learning. Temptations to be lazy are overwhelming. If she has nothing to do at 14, she will find others with idle time. Sooner or later, she'll find opportunities to explore sexuality (maybe before you'd like her to), alcohol, or drugs—and by then you will have lost your influence.

Participating in extracurricular activities, such as sports, will give your child a chance to experience some of life's most important aspects: teamwork, success, failure, goal setting, discipline, organization, and overcoming odds. The greater your child's involvement, the higher the value of transfer in his or her life. No involvement = MTV = brain mush. Perhaps you could contact your local Girl Scout or Boy Scout office. Find out about local YMCA, judo, soccer or Little League programs. They're out there and will help to instill confidence in your child.

If you think there will be a time-pressure problem because of your work schedule, try to find other single parents to join you. They could help with researching programs or car pooling. Or, perhaps, begin a program closer to your home. (Find a way—it can be done!) A parent's goal is to help her child become self-supporting, happy, and competitive. A child needs all three to survive in today's world. Don't overpressure your kid's life, however. Today's parents often go overboard, programming every minute of their child's time. Overworked and overstressed by age 12, the children become burned out.

HAPPINESS: A STATE OF MIND

Unlike Charlie Brown, happiness is not a warm puppy— but that *is* part of it. Happiness is having love. It is an ingredient that has to be nourished daily. Your children can never get too much because love can outperform and conquer everything else. Unfortunately, most of us just don't get enough of it or exude the amount we should. *Love rules over attitude and good attitude can survive anything!* Love rules over anything negative, including a bad attitude. A good attitude can survive hardship and let us feel perpetual happiness. Many cynical children do not understand this.

I, personally, used to have a nonemotional attitude that I showed to the world. I projected an image based upon my macho psyche. While I loved deeply on the inside, I didn't

Happiness is having love. It is an ingredient that has to be nourished daily.

let it show on the outside. What a loser! Ever hear this excuse? "My parent's weren't emotional, so I'm not and my kids aren't going to be either." That's a tragedy. The following excerpt from an Ann Landers' column (reprinted with permission) is a story we can all learn from.

Dear Ann Landers:

This is for "Feeling Guilty in Woodbridge, VA. She said her adult children wouldn't forgive her for the lack of affection they experienced growing up. When I read that letter, I said to myself, "That's me."

My father worked six days a week, and my mother was always cleaning, cooking and doing laundry. They both came from undemonstrative families with parents who never showed any affection and never told them they were loved. So, of course, this explains why they didn't know how to give affection or express it in words.

My life changed at age 9 when I stayed overnight at a girlfriend's house. Her mother kissed us both good night and tucked us in. That did it. I was so moved by that loving gesture I couldn't sleep. I thought, "This is the way it is supposed to be." When I left, I was angry at my own parents for a while, but I couldn't hold it against Mom and Dad for the way they were.

This is what I did to reverse the process: I began kissing my mother so often that I got her to laugh about it. I married at 17 and had two children before I was 20. I kissed them until their little cheeks were red. When I talked to my mother on the telephone, I would say, "I love you, Mom." After a while, she finally said, "I love you, too." I'd never heard her say that before.

After a few weeks, when I'd go to see Mom, she would say, "Where's my kiss?" When it was time for me to leave, she'd say, "I love you, you know that, don't you?" I'm so glad I was able to change things because my precious mother passed away not long ago. I cherish the many letters from her saying, "I love you."

So to that person in Woodbridge who feels guilty, I say, I hope your children read this. It's never too late to change, and I promise you, it works.

-Sun City, Calif.

A good attitude can survive hardship and let us feel perpetual happiness. Many cynical children do not understand this.

STRESS AND YOUR CHILDREN

Don't transfer any stress you may be feeling to your children. When you're angry and frustrated, it's easy to take it out on them. After all, they are closest to you: and you know you can win them back after you calm down. This strain, however, will stunt their growth and hurt your relationship. If you've raised your children right, they know discipline and what that tone of voice means. They know when you are serious—and you need not say it more than once. It's important to find other ways to relieve your stress.

JUNK IN, JUNK OUT

Whatever you're putting into your head is what will eventually come out. Read enough Stephen King novels and, sure enough, you'll start to think scared. Stop reading pop novels, and turn off that radio and television! Listen to motivational or educational tapes instead and watch the way you act and react. You'll become like the morning bird, chirping away and happy, if you fuel yourself with positive energy.

My personal growth took off when I read a book that told me to unplug my television and put it in the closet. What would your children do without television? Maybe their homework? Perhaps start a butterfly, stamp, or coin collection? Learn a sport or craft? But, you say, "That's how I keep them quiet." Maybe the problem is you. Perhaps you need to become more authoritative and instill more discipline.

In my opinion, today's juvenile crime has a lot to do with the child-raising practices popular during the last 20 years and what's been going into kids' heads via the entertainment media. Junk! Now, think of the alternatives if your child used her time wisely. She might discover her talents and gain self-esteem and self-confidence. Tapping into her abilities and having to think independently would be quite a change from her normal diversions—especially if they are Grade B slasher movies and rap records!

The hazards of drugs and alcohol are well known. These vices rob you and your children of productive lives and of any likelihood of success. You must be vigilant against substance abuse. If you live in an area infested with this pestilence, move! Find an apartment in the best school district possible. You may have to fight to get to a more habitable environment, but it will be worth the effort. I would rather raise my children in a one-bedroom safe environment than a four-bedroom bad environment, no matter how elegant the home. If your will is strong, you will find a way and things will work out. Open communication between you and your children is imperative. They know what is going on.

BREAKING THE GENERATION CYCLE

Whether you like it or not, you are probably following in the footsteps of your parents. Through the generations, no one may have been given the knowledge they needed to pass down to you: fiscal responsibility, budgeting, how to make money creatively, how to invest, or where to save. You must ensure that this doesn't happen to your children. Break the cycle—learn so that you can teach them! My favorite understanding of this concept was provided by Heady Green, the "Witch of Wall Street." At the time of her death in the 1930s, she was the wealthiest woman in America. Her estate included more than $100 million in cash, 8,000 parcels of real estate, and several railroads. How did she gain this wealth? She attributed her ability to make money to something she had learned at the tender age of eight. Her grandfather, with whom she lived, had lost his eyesight. Every morning it was her duty to read him *The Wall Street Journal*. She recalled that, by the time she was 14, she could outpick any hot shot Wall Street stockbroker. She'd learned it all purely from her years of reading *The Wall Street Journal!*

Most likely, your children will eventually keep house like you do, pay bills like you do, and maintain the same lifestyle. This is why it is imperative to analyze all aspects of your household to make sure that all is in order and improving on every front. How you lived as a child doesn't have to be passed on to them! If something was lacking in

> Whether you like it or not, you are probably following in the footsteps of your parents.

important moral or ethical standards in your own child-hoos, change it. Educate yourself to find better standards. Your children are depending on you!

CHAPTER FIVE SUMMARY

Analyze

all aspects

of your

household

to make sure

all is in

order and

improving on

every front.

How you

lived as a

child doesn't

have to be

passed on to

them!

Your family must be made aware of which way the rope needs to be pulled—and that all hands are needed. Remember that your actions influence your family and *their* future families. Everyone must pull their efforts in the same direction. This is defined by your family's goals and by your children's individual goals.

Your child grows by learning to be independent. Learning to clean, cook, and wash are good things. They are lessons in self-reliance. Chores and family responsibilities should not be tied to wages or allowances. These are required tasks.

Appreciation comes from earning, not gifts. Responsible children come from responsible parents. It starts with you.

Budgets and money matters are not an option. They are a need and a requirement to guide the family toward stability and prosperity.

Communication is the only real two-way street between you and your child. Keep it open even when things go wrong. The challenges of life will make this difficult but they still need you. They need you more than either one of you realizes. Love and *showing* that love is the most important action you can display. Love conquers all and is above all.

When things are tough, keep your frustrations away from your children. Try to display courage, patience, resolve, and a positive attitude that your faith will prevail.

Throw your television away and curb your children's computer time. Get them to interact with their creativity in the backyard. Raise your children as if you had only one shot to make and mold the next generation.

Your will, your inner strength, will guide your way!

CHAPTER FIVE
BLUEPRINT FOR LIFE
WORKSTATION

1. Post a family meeting notice on the refrigerator and verbally announce that there will be a family meeting. Sunday evenings are often a good time, but make it a time when all can be there. Have a "topic" agenda. Discuss with them the things they would like to achieve as a family this year, this week, and this month—along with problems and solutions. Let everyone have a chance to speak. Family goals may include a trip to the beach, a trip to Grandma's for Thanksgiving, or the creation of a family hour, curfews, etc.

2. Help your teenage children make a list of things that require money. Figure out some things they can pay for themselves. Discuss their income opportunities. Be creative. Teaching your kids to become self-sufficient is the greatest gift you can give them.

3. Make a rotating list of duties around the house that can be shared by all. Can you teach them how to wash clothes correctly? Explain to everyone that you are a family and you move as a family. You all help each other.

4. Explain the difference between:
   a. Buying something, then paying for it.
   b. Paying for something, then buying it.

5. Create a cost list of what your child spends or needs for one day. For one week. For one month. For one year. (Do this with them. It is a financial education opportunity.)

6. Help your child create a large goal and work out a solution as to how he or she may financially obtain it. (Example: new bicycle = $200.00. Six months =180 days = $1.11 needed to be saved per day. How can he or she create income to achieve that?)

7. Hand the child a paper or magazine that will include savings information or coupons and ask him to cut out the ones you and your family can use.

8. Make a schedule of when dinner will be for whole-family participation. All noisemakers must be off (televisions, radios, etc.) Create a weekly food menu for meals. Work with your children so they can understand your budget needs. See if you can work together and find ways to control these costs.
9. Pick a time that meets everyone's schedule of availability. This will be "family time." Do something together at least once every week (a baseball game, picnic, walk in the park, dollar movies).
10. Get the business section of the newspaper. Ask your child to find something specific in that section. Make a game out of it—with a reward. Do this daily.

ADVANCEMENT IN LIFE THROUGH CAREER OPPORTUNITIES

According to the census bureau, the typical American working woman is paid 71 cents for each $1 earned by a man. Over a lifetime, that can add up to a gap of $420,000! This is money that could have bought a home, educated a child, or allowed a woman to prepare for retirement. African-American and Hispanic women face an even greater pay gap. They only earn 64.2% and 53.4% respectively to what men earn. We need to get into the next millennium and change some of these figures. It starts with you!

YOUR HANDS OR YOUR HEAD

If you make a living using your hands, you will always be limited by how fast and how many times you can move your hands in a given day. Your income will be limited to the speed at which you can work. If you own a company in which others use their hands, you have more room for growth but are still limited by time and the movements of your employees. Even a professional, such as a lawyer, is limited if she practices independently. She can only bill for a limited number of hours each day. Your best future lies in creating a career that earns income while you're sleeping,

Your best future lies in creating a career that earns income while you're sleeping.

using your head instead of your hands. **If you use your mind to make a living, you become limitless.**

Finding, deciding upon, and pursuing your optimal career—one that offers "income while you sleep" or income from your thoughts—takes a long time to develop. Constantly massage your thoughts until the right opportunity comes along. Your thoughts about the pursuit, changes, and improvements are the beginning. Then, tear down your thoughts (daily) and rebuild those arguments. This is what your "daydreaming" should be! Think about long-range plans, but also consider where you might make a relatively safe first stop.

It is hard to make that first leap. Before deciding on your direction, talk to people whose opinions you respect. Interact with people who seem smarter than you and who work in those industries that seriously interest you. This is called improving your *"intellectual capital."* Once you have your information about this industry, you will be ready for that better leap. You can change careers with confidence. *Intellectual capital is a resource of knowledge that builds over time.*

BREAKING THE GLASS CEILING

Recent studies have shown that a significant number of women start their own businesses because they hit a "glass ceiling" (an invisible barrier to advancement) in their former jobs. They feel unchallenged, unappreciated, or underpaid. Women coming from the corporate world seem particularly frustrated. Many say their employers don't take them seriously or value them. Nearly 60% of women who own their own businesses (after leaving the male-dominated corporate culture), say nothing would induce them to return—including more money or flexibility. This research explains the explosive growth of the United States' 8 million women-owned businesses. **One-third of all U.S. firms are now owned by women! They are being created at twice the rate of all others.**

According to Sheila Wellington, president of *Catalyst* (one of the groups involved in this study), frustration with the work environment has pushed a significant number of women into entrepreneurship. *"They leave to get more flexibility. . . . They feel their advancement opportunities are not valid."* As might be expected, nearly half of all women business-owners started their companies because they had a winning business idea or they wanted to turn their skills into a business. Sixteen percent of all women business-owners cited a glass ceiling as significant motivation for becoming entrepreneurs. Eleven percent identified a lack of challenge in past careers as a deciding factor.

Let's break it down: work for yourself or work for someone else. Working for yourself means *you* control your time—if you work more, you get more. Being an independent contractor is a form of self-employment. It allows you true freedom. Simply put, your ability to earn is only limited by your actions and intensity. Some of the greatest rags to riches stories have come about because of this limitless opportunity. Your value grows as you learn how to mass-produce and exceed your quotas.

Here are some examples. Glen Turner was a sharecropper's son. Yet, starting out selling pots and pans on the dirt roads of South Carolina, he advanced his career and became a multimillionaire many, many times over. Other people who have also developed large sales organizations are Mary Kay Ash of Mary Kay Cosmetics, Rich DeVoss of Amway, and Joe Girard—who is listed as the greatest salesperson of all times by the *Guinness Book of World Records.* They all embody the reward of limitless self-employment, where prejudices and glass ceilings are reduced to an almost nonexistent level.

Please don't think that all your opportunities are limited to sales. They're not. In order to succeed, however, you have to be able to "sell" yourself to others. Those who master the art of "selling" themselves control their own destinies. The playing field becomes level with the better "salespeople" winning the turf war. In corporate or company-controlled environments, favoritism and prejudices might exist. Some glass ceilings cannot be broken. Don't put yourself in a corner by working for a company notorious for its prejudices. Find a path that rewards hard work. If you work for any state, federal, city, or county municipality, you will only have a roof over your head and an existence. You will never find true wealth or independence working for the government. Remember: Competing is a mental thing. *This book is about transforming your mentality from that of a paper tiger into a lioness.*

ADVANCING IN A WHITE MALE-DOMINATED SOCIETY

The good news is that changing attitudes are opening doors for those who have been unfairly held back in the past. The bad news is that despite these changes you may still have to deal with workplace discrimination during your lifetime.

As recently as the 1970s it was unusual for a woman to be employed outside of a secretarial, teaching, or nursing occupation. Today, it is possible to bypass any limitations placed on you. You must, however, outperform your competition. Look toward your goals and seek career opportunities that have no ceilings and are worth your effort. Many times, these opportunities will be in sales where it's the numbers, not what you look like, that count. Don't find yourself trapped. Take pride in turning in a heavier load. Hard work pays off. Create value for your employer and you will eventually be recognized—or financially able to start your own company.

A few years ago I watched a young, talented woman drop out of law school to take an excellent job with a large super-regional bank. Sounds great, doesn't it? The job she took, however, had a ceiling. Becoming an attorney would have given her freedom. She knew the super-regional bank was well known for its Southern, good-old-boy hierarchy— but she took the job anyway. Although her new career gave her more immediate income, the long-term results were not as positive. Look at the whole picture when considering your future!

What are the ingredients for winning the battle and becoming successful? Education, persistence, and an entrepreneurial spirit. You must find your way into a good sales career, provide a service better than the next guy, or refocus your corporate career. If you don't, you'll be forced to

Those who master the art of "selling" themselves control their own destinies.

accept a more limited job. Whatever you do, if you want more, you need to know where you are going. If you are on the right path, success will come to you far more easily. Find your niche and become the best!

KEYS TO ADVANCEMENT: ADDING VALUE

Add to your worth. If you want more from an employer, give them a valuable commodity they can't afford to lose—you. I've always told my employees that it was important to make themselves so valuable that I couldn't afford to lose them. My greatest example is a young woman I hired on a part-time basis. Soon, part-time became full-time. Before long, this former waitress became my office secretary and then my office manager. One day I looked at her and said, "You're worth so much more than the $25,000 per year I'm paying you."

She needed more money, but her job classification only paid $25,000. We talked and both decided she should change career goals—she was a valuable employee and needed to be paid her true worth. So she decided to go back to school and obtain her real estate license.

One day, after her first month in sales, I came in and found her crying about her lack of sales. Instead of consoling her, I asked her about her sales methods. What was she was doing every day? She responded with all the right answers (calling prospects, following up on leads, etc.) I told her that all would work out if her pursuit was true. Within a week of that meeting, she broke through with four sales! By the end of that year, she had made about $40,000. Last year she made $85,000. I have since written her commission checks totaling more than $35,000 in income (and that was for one month). Today, she represents herself well in her field and has an established career.

Create value! Risk with preparation creates the new opportunity. Creating value comes from being two steps ahead of what's expected of you. You have to do your homework. I was once able to attract and receive a very lucrative consultation agreement because I knew what was

Create value for your employer and you will eventually be recognized— or be financially able to start your own company.

needed. When I went to the CEO of that company, I knew he would want certain information—and I had it. He trusted me to do the work because I had made the extra effort of finding out more than everyone else. My value was enhanced. Every employer wants to think of future success. Show him what you can do!

If you feel you're not being paid what you are worth, remember that it is always best to put out feelers for a new job while you're currently employed. Your value is higher while you're employed. (The new boss may think you're a real catch!) Employers are sometimes hesitant to hire someone without a job since they're never sure if it's going to work out. They will also try to get away with paying you bottom dollar if they think you are desperate.

PUBLIC SPEAKING SKILLS

If you don't have them, get them. It's that simple. The ability to speak in public is the single most important attribute you can possess in any business dealing. You cannot grow if you don't present yourself and your concepts well. Most people would rather swim with sharks than speak on a public platform. *In any company setting, it is the employees with superior speaking skills who are offered positions of leadership.* This also happens in social and community organizations.

Depending on how good you are, you can literally drive yourself all the way to the presidency of our country. Look at Bill Clinton and Ronald Reagan. Their superior communication skills allowed them to talk themselves all the way to the presidential platform. Okay, so you don't want to be the president. But you do want to be successful and you do want to advance. Take yourself down the really challenging path and work toward becoming comfortable speaking in public.

My lack of public speaking skills during my early adult life caused my first career failure. I was a teacher who was not asked back for a second year. Every time my peers evaluated me, my poor speaking skills caused me to bomb miserably. I could handle speaking in front of the kids—but I couldn't handle speaking to the adults. Years later, after improving my oratory skills and challenging myself to become a better speaker, my career opportunities soared. I've since given college graduation addresses. It's ironic. I now make my living in public speaking where, once, I was an utter failure.

My growing public speaking skills have become my most useful tool. When I was young, I wanted to own a company but I questioned how I could do that if I couldn't communicate with my employees. I forced myself to grow. I'll admit it. Beginning was hard, challenging, and scary—but the ultimate reward was so great! I learned how to stand up and speak in front of a group through Toastmaster's International. Every sales, professional, and entrepreneurial position requires you to communicate both one-on-one and in multiple-person settings. Raising your skill level allows you the opportunity for more sales and contacts. The more people you meet in your business, the greater your potential for income. These skills will open many doors if you just find the courage to go down this path.

If you need to improve your public speaking skills, I suggest you join an organization like Toastmasters International. Toastmasters is a fantastic communications self-improvement program you can do at your own speed. It's a "grow as you go" environment. There are literally thousands of clubs worldwide and all are easy to access. *Toastmasters* is the single most important developmental tool I've used to build my confidence, knowledge, and presentation skills. There might be many such clubs in your town, so find the one with which you are most comfortable. By sheer osmosis, going there will advance your life. For further information on Toastmasters International, contact:

Toastmasters International, Inc.
23182 Arroyo Vista Rancho
Santa Margarita, California 92688
Phone: (949) 858-8255
Fax: (949) 858-1207

Now is the time to concentrate on improving any personal weaknesses or skills. Your life should be a process of constant change. Focus on molding and improving yourself!

If you feel you're not being paid what you are worth, put out feelers for a new job while you're currently employed.

CAREER AND JOB OPPORTUNITIES

The following is a list of career opportunities. (Remember: to succeed you must live on less than what you make. This is just a guide.)

Women planning careers should have a general idea about their expected average annual earnings before committing themselves. The following chart shows basic salaries for workers in a number of occupations based on 1998 averages—not entry-level rates but yearly earnings for all people currently employed in each field. I've also listed the minimum levels of education required to be successful. In many cases (such as flight attendants, physical therapists, and paralegal employees), additional education is common and an asset when job hunting.

HIGH SCHOOL TRAINING

Bank Teller	$15,200	Police Officer	$32,900
Cashier	$11,700	Receptionist	$16,400
Construction worker	$19,700	Taxi driver	$16,200
Flight attendant	$26,300	Telephone operator	$20,100
Garbage collector	$18,800	Truck driver	$23,100
Mail carrier	$32,900	Waiter/waitress	$12,000 + tips

SOME COLLEGE OR VOCATIONAL SCHOOL TRAINING

Appliance salesperson	$23,300	Licensed practical nurse	$22,600
Auto mechanic	$21,900	Paralegal worker	$27,900
Computer repairer	$30,500	Preschool teacher	$18,400
Dental hygienist	$28,600	Secretary	$20,100
Funeral director	$36,500	Surveyor	$28,700
Hairstylist	$36,500	Welder	$23,600

BACHELOR'S DEGREE

Army officer (captain)	$43,800	Financial planner	$55,100
Bank officer	$43,000	High school teacher	$32,500
Civil engineer	$55,800	Pharmacist	$47,500
Computer systems analyst	$42,700	Physical therapist	$27,200
Electrical engineer	$59,100	Property manager	$26,600
Elementary school teacher	$31,000	Registered nurse	$35,700

MASTER'S DEGREE

Geologist	$50,800	School counselor	$33,000
Hospital administrator	$36,000	School principal	$57,300
Librarian	$29,500	Social worker	$26,600
Management consultant	$61,900	Urban planner	$42,800

DOCTOR'S OR PROFESSIONAL DEGREE

Chiropractor	$77,000	Lawyer	$60,500
Clergy member	$26,000	Physician	$143,000
College professor	$45,000	Psychologist	$53,000
Dentist	$93,000	Veterinarian	$46,900

ENTREPRENEUR—ZERO TO $100,000+ PER YEAR

EDUCATION IS THE KEY

The more knowledge you have, the better your career opportunities. How sad it is, once you understand the value of education, to see an 18-year-old stop her pursuit of a higher education to enter the job force! It's not just that a college education would provide her with knowledge. College also teaches how essential it is to understand and meet deadlines—a valuable life skill. One of your goals should be the taking of a class at a community college. Take one that will challenge you. It might require you to write a book report or learn some new skill. Let it help prepare you for real life—so you can deliver what will be asked of you from your employers.

As an example, I remember once being at a bank board meeting where everyone was asked to give a presentation about his project. I thought to myself, "Wow! This is just like school." In reality, everyone there was being graded even though we were not handed report cards. And just like school, if you didn't produce at that higher standard, you failed. Every professional giving a presentation is ultimately graded on her job performance. You will show your quality and advance to better paying jobs more quickly if you continually educate yourself.

Single mothers who are forced to leave school early must fight their way back to completing their educations. Single mothers not only have the responsibility of their children—they also have a responsibility to better their lives. Your task will be hard! Focusing on that long-term goal of personal educational growth will allow your economic engine to grow.

Any education that propels you toward a structured career and enhances your real-world problem-solving solutions is useful. I watched one woman for about 15 years, who wished the whole time for change in her life. She wished and hoped—but that's all she did. She lacked the courage to make any changes. You only advance when you find the confidence and the courage to act.

Another woman I know decided, at age 29, that she wanted to become an attorney. She was married and could have succumbed to the security of being taken care of for the rest of her life. She could have remained a homemaker, relying totally on her husband *(something you never, ever want to do)*. Instead, she made the decision to attend law school at night. She graduated last spring—and is looking forward to a fascinating career. She made it happen. She took the time and invested in herself. The bottom line is that she can now be self-sufficient. You must always have the ability to be independent.

LIFETIME CAREER OPPORTUNITIES

The easiest way to focus on what will make a difference in the way you live is to complete a Personal Values Inventory. You can find one through a career counselor or in career guidance books. *Life Center,* a new library service, offers an excellent, free values assessment quiz by Dr. Darryl Laramore. Ask your librarian about it. When you answer the questions, don't try to just breeze through it. You should develop a long list of occupations you'd like to explore, then match your values, educational requirements and budget against each possibility. Take the time to find a good match between your career and your goals.

You will show your quality and advance to better paying jobs more quickly if you continually educate yourself.

How do you find the details about each occupation? There are many ways, but a reliable one that just keeps getting better and better is the Department of Labor's *Occupational Outlook Handbook* (ISBN 0-16-049348-X). The new edition shows each occupation's best points before each of hundreds of occupational briefs. For example, *"Occupational Therapy offers a good job opportunity and high pay."* Also, websites are available for each occupation allowing you to scout out even more information. The handbook, 528 pages long, is a prime source for people in the decision-making mode and is available at most libraries. You can also buy your own copy from the Superintendent of Documents, Post Office Box 371954, Pittsburgh, PA 15250 for $44 (call 202-512-1800). Alternatively, you can read the handbook online for free at http://stats.bls.gov/emphome.htm.

CONTINUING EDUCATION

Continuing education refers to any kind of short-term education. It is designed to give you a quick shot of content in a specific subject. (Remember, your goal is to learn not only facts, but to find out what you don't already know) You may think you have sufficient knowledge, only to learn how much bigger the world really is. Most cities have some form of adult learning facility. A vast variety of courses, from debt counseling to spiritual healing, are available. These seminar-style education forums are like a one-stop shopping center. If you are confused, they can give you the boost of information you need and point you in the right direction. Take the time to discover what's available. The class sizes are generally small and you just might find a friend with whom you can share your common goals and challenges.

WORKING FOR THEM OR WORKING FOR YOURSELF

What are your career options? For whom do you want to work? Do you want to work for a structured system of

You must always have the ability to be independent.

hierarchy (a real corporate job)? Or do you want to create your own destiny? In the corporate world, performance, dedication, and loyalty should advance you—but there are no guarantees. A corporate takeover might boot you out the door. On the other hand, there may be benefits, stock options, and relative security (remember, no one can just fire you anymore—there are too many federal laws). Many people choose this route and it might suit you—*as long as you're taking some of your salary and splitting it into two areas after living expenses: (1) pure savings and (2) a rainy-day fund.* Remember, you must strive to live on only a percentage of what you make. The majority of the work force operates in these controlled structures. It's controlled because you have a boss.

Your other options are becoming an independent contractor (usually in sales) or an entrepreneur (owning your own company). *Be forewarned—most people cannot handle the freedom and liberal nature an entrepreneurial or independent sales contractor opportunity provides. They find it gives them too much freedom and allows them to do anything but work. Self-control and self-discipline are essential!* If you are considering this option, you can make a smoother transition into entrepreneurship and test the waters by developing it part-time in the evenings and on weekends. If you find yourself going nowhere because you have the "I'm off work" mentality, keep the day job. Let the Henry Fords of the world have the cake and icing that sometimes come along with owning your own company.

CHAPTER SIX SUMMARY

Look at your career. What are your long-range goals? Plan to advance through educational advancement. Sit down with your employer and work through the challenges you need to face. Do you even like what you are doing? If not, begin the steps to change.

Intellectual capital builds over time, which means that each month and year you will broaden your knowledge in your field or industry. Create value through your superior knowledge. One day, it will pay off.

Good speaking skills will advance anyone. Be prepared for leadership and advanced roles if you show you can speak in public. Develop your skills and use them to manipulate more opportunity.

When working for someone else, concentrate on becoming more valuable and reliable. While working for yourself, find ways to become more disciplined. Organize your output and production on a daily basis.

Knowledge is power that will continue to advance your journey.

CHAPTER SIX
BLUEPRINT FOR LIFE
WORKSTATION

1. Figure out the answer to this math problem: If a person makes $25,000 per year and puts 10% of that away each year, how much will she have saved if that savings is allowed to earn 8% annually for 20 years? (Find help until you receive the answer.)
2. What is intellectual capital?
3. Obtain a schedule of classes and career preparation opportunities from the nearest community college or local university. Enroll in 1 class from that school.
4. Schedule an appointment with your boss (or someone with authority) in your company. Explain to her/him very nicely and professionally that you'd like to become a more valuable worker. Tell them you'd like to know what advice she/he can give you on becoming more valuable because you're interested in growing with the company.
5. Go visit three *Toastmaster International* groups and join one.
6. Stay in *Toastmasters International* until you've completed at least the first basic manual.
7. Go to a local college, university, or public library and prepare a report on a career that interests you. Determine what incomes can be expected from them.
8. If you like a certain profession and feel as if you'd like to pursue a career in that profession, pick someone in

the community who practices that profession. Ask her/him if you could possibly job shadow them for a day or speak with them about their particular career. (This should be easier than it sounds.)

9. Roughly add up how much you spend each month. Make as many categories as you'd like and compare that with your combined income for that month. Is there any money left?

10. Go to a local college or junior college and walk around the campus. Get a feel for the growth these institutions represent. Stop in the Administration Building and pick up a Course Catalogue.

11. Identify three seminars or short-term classes offered through the local newspaper (just identify them, you don't have to attend).

    a.

    b.

    c.

12. Identify the percentage of what you can start saving. (1%, 2%, 5%, 10%?)

13. Inquire with your employer or bank about the possibility of having direct deposits taken from your paycheck and put into your savings account automatically.

14. Order the *Occupational Outlook Handbook*. Review it and, if not needed for yourself, pass it on to a friend in need. You can also view on-line what the handbook has to offer.

7 RELATIONSHIPS

After awhile you learn the subtle difference
Between holding a hand and chaining a soul,
And you learn that love doesn't mean leaning
And company doesn't mean security,
And you begin to learn that kisses aren't contracts
And presents aren't promises,
And you begin to accept your defeats
With your head up and your eyes open,
With the grace of a woman, not the grief of a child,
And learn to build all your roads
On today, because tomorrow's ground
Is too uncertain for plans, and futures have
A way of falling down in mid-flight.
After awhile you learn that even sunshine
Burns if you get too much.
So you plant your own garden and decorate
Your own soul, instead of waiting
For someone to bring you flowers.
And learn that you really can endure . . .
That you really are strong
And you really do have worth.
And you learn and learn . . .
With every goodbye you learn.

Anonymous

Get rid of anyone who puts a drag on your life. You have work to do and a lot of it.

81

I'm going to keep the advice very simple. *Either the person you're with is good for you or he's not. Either the person in your life adds value to your life or he doesn't. Either the person you're with supports you spiritually, mentally and physically, or he drains the reservoir of energy out of your body.* It's that simple. Get rid of anyone who puts a drag on your life. You have work to do and a lot of it. You cannot swim this sea with a lead weight around your ankle. If your significant other truly loves you and wants to be with you, he will respect you for your new strength and goals. If this so-called spouse or boyfriend does not support your growth individually and your growth together, get rid of him!

Many young people sacrifice their development years by choosing the wrong person. If you are in a bad relationship, get out! When you become someone successful, you can pick and choose healthier relationships. Once you reach that point, supportive guys will come out of the woodwork! *Don't ever lower your standards when choosing the man you want.* Honesty, loyalty, support, friendship—why settle for anything less? Direct your time toward your children, if you have any, and your personal growth. Don't accept a life of stagnation or abuse.

BAD ONES: GO BACK TO START

How many mothers have you known who have been forced to begin the business- and income-learning curve at age 30 or 40? Never exposed to any business training, they're now expected to compete. All these years they've been saddled with children to raise or they've helped build their husbands' businesses. Now they're on their own and are lost. Their problem's began with two false assumptions: 1) Mr. Right was really Mr. Wrong, and 2) they didn't develop and focus on their personal growth when they were young. They thought they would always be taken care of by their husbands.

I can't stand it when I hear a woman say, *"I'm looking for a rich man to take care of me."* Wrong, wrong, wrong! It's like all those lottery winners. They all eventually end up broke and in bankruptcy.

Choosing Mr. Wrong happens. Many women marry young, before age 25. (Being young, they don't see patterns of infidelity or the real personality of the man they thought was wonderful.) Suddenly, they wake up and see that the fun, pot-smoking jokester they married isn't fun anymore. Accept your mistake! Don't be afraid of the changes it will bring. Focus instead on your growth and on your children—what you can do to enhance your education, financial career, and personal life.

This "new life" of knowledge can begin at any age. James Nesbitt, author of *Futuristic Living Patterns,* says that, as humans, we will one day be able to live much longer lives, perhaps as long as 100 to 150 years. If this happens, we will be required to retool ourselves at 50 and 60 and again at 90 and 110, just to keep up with the fast-moving world. You can and must regenerate a new path, image, and expectation for your life.

If you suddenly find yourself out on your own with more responsibilities than answers, look to education for a new beginning. Local community colleges, vocational tech programs, and private institutions are sources for your advancement. If money is an immediate problem, there are loans, grants, and scholarships. Find a decision maker at that college or institution and discover what funding is available. Perhaps you can find employment at that institution as well. Most schools offer free or greatly reduced classes for employees. Talking to your present employer is another possibility. Go to your supervisor and remind him that the better mentally equipped you are, the more value you can bring to his company.

PROTECTING YOURSELF FROM BAD RELATIONSHIPS

Consider where you met "Mr. Right." That will go a long way toward determining the class and standard of that individual. I know a wonderful young professional woman who wanted nothing more in life than to meet Mr. Right. The truth is, I met her when she was 18. She is now 35 and she has never stopped looking . . . in bars. Deadbeats and losers occupy these grounds! Hold your standards high. A man deeply wants to find a woman he can respect. If he doesn't, you'll eventually see the ugly side. Hold the line on your standards of truthfulness and values. If he doesn't understand your true worth, he is a dead-end loser and you need to move on.

While at the beach recently, I observed a young couple. All seemed to be going smoothly until he put the moves on her in a very physical way. I was close by and didn't look up, although from the corner of my eye something drew my attention. I saw her struggle, move away, and then take control of the situation. She grabbed all her things and walked hastily back to his truck. I guess he had become too fresh too quickly. She sat by the truck for about 40 minutes while he lay in the sand a couple of hundred yards away, defeated.

His male chauvinistic attitude stopped him from going over to her and making up. What a terrible attitude to have! I could see his thoughts and read his mind. His attitude was *"I am the man and should get what I want."* This is dominance. In the end, he picked up his things and went to the truck. He seemed to try and console her. After two or three rounds of sometimes-bullish attempts to effectively coerce her, he still didn't succeed. She wasn't budging on the moves.

In my opinion, this lady is a catch if I ever saw one! If he is smart, he will realize the power of her convictions. This could be a valuable asset in his life. A good man will crawl back for forgiveness. The moral of this story is that she set the tone and held on to her values. This is what you must do. He lost out because of his stupidity and lack of understanding. She will receive her desires because she refuses to settle for any less of life's standards than those she sets.

My own relationship works because I deeply respect my wife. I realize that she is smarter than I am in most decision-making areas dealing with the guidance of our relationship. We go with that flow because it is in both of our best interests. (Sometimes she'll use her secret code of communication to make sure I'm doing the right thing.) In return, she respects my areas of expertise and listens to my opinions as much as I listen to hers.

GOALS FOR RELATIONSHIPS

Each relationship must have goals. If you are in a relationship, think to yourself: where is this relationship heading? Is there a long-term picture? Are you best friends? Can you both see the path? Goals will tell you the answers to these questions. Is the relationship compatible with your career? Is the relationship compatible with his career? Are your pleasures and his pleasures compatible? The importance is in finding a balance. Are you happy on a trip with him once a month? A date once a week? Find the balance and plug in the dates and times. You both must grow. When one does and the other doesn't, problems arise—for you will stray from your path toward success. Start planning. Keep your life moving toward the future. By helping him achieve, you will be rewarded with a more loyal partner. Don't forsake your own growth, however. Take the time to plan, just as you do with career goals, and you will have a relationship with more zest and a stronger sense of companionship.

WHERE TO LOOK FOR THAT COMPANION: DO YOU REALLY WANT TO SNAG A MAN?

A lot of books and articles have been written on this subject. As a man, I know how men think—and it might not be what you imagine. Obviously, relationships cannot be forced but finding opportunities is not as hard as you think. If you want a bum, hang out in a bar. If you want a professional, hang out where professionals go: meetings, seminars, associations, and professional affiliations. Your active participation in life is a requirement in this process.

Older men tend to be more educated, experienced, and financially secure. They are also more set in their ways, can be bothersome, and sometimes old-fashioned. But if you are dead set on finding a rich man, go where rich men hang out: yacht clubs, tennis clubs, auctions, etc. Younger men, depending on their age, also present problems. Sometimes,

A man deeply wants to find a woman he can respect. Hold the line on your standards of truthfulness and values.

they need training and experience. In the end, however, it is shared values that will make your relationship long-lasting.

When beginning a relationship, don't hide the fact that you have children if you have any. *The man who wins your heart must also have a true heart for your child.* Since your child could be the future brother or sister of children with this man, he must accept the joint lifelong responsibility of your child's upbringing. On *your* end, educating children about and developing their attitudes toward a new potential member of your household must be discussed on a regular basis. Happiness, at the end of the day, comes from having a companion who is your best friend, for better or for worse. Don't settle for a blue-plate special.

Unfortunately, my mom and I did not have this discussion when I was a teen. I chased off any new suitors who came to court my mom. If only she had sat down and said, *"Hey—this is who I am and these are my needs,"* life would have been much more pleasant for both of us.

WHAT DO MEN WANT?

The trick with men is that, without knowing it, they need their wife (or girlfriend) to be their best friend. A best friend to a guy is someone they can just hang with, do things with, go fishing with, etc. (Be aware: hanging out does not always include lots of conversation.) Be careful not to always be doing everything for him. This will make him respect you less. You must be equals.

Women, on the other hand, consider their best friend someone with whom they can talk for hours and hours. I once watched my wife talk nonstop with her best friend from college for six hours straight (she hadn't seen her in a few years). Meanwhile, I sat and watched television with the best friend's boyfriend. We just hung out together and didn't talk much to each other. Women *need* someone to talk to. It's great for a man to hear the heartfelt communication you're giving him. Just remember, however, *it may be a turnoff for the guy.* Most guys just want to hang out or go do stuff.

How do you get a man? Quit searching! You are meeting people every day. People are watching you all the time. When you least expect it is when it will happen. Right now, the most important thing is to focus your energies on what you are doing for yourself and your family's welfare. If you are not sure about your value system, read a book about values. Pursue those strengths and your harmony will put something together for you—I promise. I know, I was single and lonely during my twenties. I focused on getting rich—and when I least expected it, I met the woman who held my dreams. It happens. Don't look for it and don't settle for less!

YOUR FRIENDS

Choose your friends wisely. True friends are a precious gift—we are all like branches of a tree, growing and crossing paths, and sometimes never seeing each other again. True friendships can be maintained with notes, cards, and calls. There are other "friends" we should let go, like other mistakes we've made in our past. Look at where you are spending your time. This is what influences you and impacts your growth. A simple rule to live by is the old adage of "guilt by association." Essentially, you are who you hang around with. Find and keep the "good" friends, even if they are fewer in number.

I once knew a young man who fought and defended his number-one theory: "keep the old gang alive." The years passed and inevitably he went from being 22 to 35. His friends were good people, growing in their lives. They found jobs, married, and succeeded financially. He, however, was left behind. Eventually, his circle of friends became so small that the only ones left were the nonachievers. His main focus had been upon his friends, not his advancements, and he never grew.

Although I have tried to keep my personal testimony in this book to a minimum, here's my story as an example. I grew up closely bonded with the gang from the old neighborhood. There were a lot of us and we stayed pretty close even after we had all grown up. We began our adult lives

You are who you hang around with. Find and keep the "good" friends, even if they are fewer in number.

frequenting the same local pub and practicing the same bad habits we had as youths. I felt very close to my friends, but realized that I couldn't grow unless I left the antichange environment we were in. My leisure time was spent drinking and fighting, hanging out from afternoon until long past midnight. I had to change my ways!

I now look back, 15 years later, and know that some of my so-called friends resent me now. I have grown into a much more promising life. I look at them, however, and see that most still haven't changed or improved their lives despite all the years that have passed. At 40, some still live with their parents! Their circle of experience was and is very limited. I wanted more out of life and didn't like the way I was drifting. I'm no better than my old friends. . . but my life choices are grand in comparison. That is ultimately what success gives you—the ability to make choices.

When I parted company with my old friends, I wanted to become successful. I purposely worked and lived in a wealthier part of my town. I wanted to learn what successful people thought and how they made their decisions. I wanted a better life. I found that self-made people have huge reservoirs of knowledge. These were the people I was attracted to! I found that people who were given or had inherited their wealth were, usually, superficial or financially ignorant. They were limited in their knowledge and would probably lose their wealth within a couple of generations. I also found first-generation overachievers that I could emulate and learn from, if not be motivated from.

Keep your goals! Seek friends who share your same attitude toward positive growth. Don't hold on to the past. Your opportunities in life will come from your connections—and your friends will provide those opportunities based on your attitude, aptitude and honesty. If your friends or family have a problem with your self-improvement, they aren't very good for you right now. Some may be jealous—something you will often find when you are growing. You are reminding them of what they are not doing with their own lives.

Don't hold on to the past.

CHAPTER SEVEN SUMMARY

Share your path and goals with your partner. This is a team effort, if there is a team. Don't lower your standards during your search for a relationship, however. Get out a sheet of paper and list the pros and cons of your current relationship. Ask yourself all the hard questions in advance. Is there a problem? Is that significant other in your life a hindrance or an asset? React from there.

Choosing the wrong person happens. Someone close to me has said that she wasted 15 years of her life trying to make a good man out of a bad one. A loss of time and valuable energy—what a waste!

You can identify a bad relationship very simply: is it healthy? Are you best friends? Is honesty the ruling word? If you lower your standards or have a blind eye, you'll pay for it with wasted time.

Each relationship must have goals. If you're searching for Mr. Right, get active. Your active participation in life is required.

Associations with friends should not keep you from growing: you are who you hang out with.

CHAPTER SEVEN BLUEPRINT FOR LIFE WORKSTATION

1. If you're involved in a relationship, take your journal and create two columns: good and bad. Make a list in each column for that person. Take your time and think through that person's habits, actions, morals, and characteristics. (Make sure that you are being honest!)
2. If the bad is heavier than the good, my advice is that you probably need to stop the relationship. Do you agree?

3. Write down in your journal what makes a good relationship and what makes a good partner. Share this exercise with your partner, if you can.
4. Identify five good places where you might meet a moral and responsible person.
5. List 10 things that you think would make a fun date (make it simple and no less than 10). Example: bowling, picnic, feeding the pigeons in the park, etc.
6. Identify five places in your area where quality men go to enjoy themselves. Could you fit in with this group comfortably?
7. Name five things you want out of a good relationship.
8. Name three people on whom you can depend (don't be disappointed if you can't).
9. Consider moving to a better part of town (start by looking at rentals; remember, you'll have fewer square feet but more quality of location). Where could you go?

SUCCESS

Why are there so many different definitions of success? Because success is very personal. To define success is to define your path toward achievement. Success is constantly changing, just as you are constantly changing. For me personally, my definition of success changed as my level of achievement changed. At one point, I wanted to graduate. Then, I wanted to get a real estate license. Next, I wanted to buy a house. And then, another building. Later, I thought success was having a million dollar's worth of real estate. Now, it's about physical challenges and creating a women's learning foundation. For you, success could initially mean running a 5K walk, and then it could be running a marathon. Success continues to change—and your definition must also constantly change. This is the only way you can continue to grow.

LAWS OF SUCCESS

Your success in life depends both on your ability and training and on your determination to grasp opportunities that are presented to you. You yourself, either now or in the past, have created all the opportunities in your path.

If you use all available means, as well as your natural abilities, to overcome every obstacle in your path, you will succeed. You have unlimited power, given from a higher

> You have unlimited power: the power of thought and the power of will. You must utilize these divine gifts.

being—the power of thought and the power of will. You must utilize these divine gifts.

THE POWER OF THOUGHT

You will succeed or fail depending on how you think. Your thoughts and your attitude become habits. If you are usually in a negative state, one positive thought will not make much difference. When you are entrenched in positive thoughts, however, you will find your goal despite the darkness you might occasionally feel.

Have a problem? Don't dwell on it! Let it rest a short while—and it may work itself out. This is why your journal will work for you. It will allow you to review the problem until solutions materialize.

WILL POWER

You must use your will power, as well as your positive thinking, if you want to succeed. Every outward manifestation is the result of will. The dynamo of all your powers is volition—or will power. Without it, you can't walk, talk, work, think, or feel. In order not to use this energy you would have to be completely inactive both physically and mentally. Even when you move your hand, you're using will power. It is impossible to live without using this force.

There is *mechanical will*, as well as *conscious will*. Mechanical will is your automatic use of your will power, similar to "truthful thinking." Conscious will is a vital force accompanying determination and effect—a dynamo that should be visibly directed.

As you train yourself to use conscious (instead of mechanical) will, be careful that your power is being used constructively. Do not use it for harmful purposes or for useless acquisitions.

The combination of your conscious and mechanical will is your dynamic will. This is something that must be created by determination. To create dynamic will, you must try new things, accomplish tasks you've never thought of before. Attempt simple tasks at first—for example, a 5K walk or a short hike. As your confidence strengthens, you

You will
succeed
or fail,
depending
on how
you think.

can aim for more difficult accomplishments. Be certain you've chosen a worthy goal and refuse to submit to failure. Devote your entire dynamic will to mastering one thing at a time. Do not leave something half done!

Your mind is the creator of everything. Guide it to create only good. When you grab a thought with dynamic will, it finally assumes a tangible outward form. When you always employ your will for constructive purposes, you become the controller of your destiny.

FAILURE

Even failure can act as a stimulant to your will power, along with your material and spiritual growth. *The season of failure is the best time for sowing the seeds of success.* Though circumstances might bruise you, keep your head up. Always try once more, no matter how many times you fail. Fight when you think you cannot fight any longer, or when you think you have already done your best. Don't give up until your efforts are crowned with achievement!

New efforts after failure bring true growth. These efforts, however, must be well planned and charged with an increasing amount of focus and dynamic will power.

The successful person may have experienced more serious difficulties than the one who has failed, but she has also trained herself to reject the thought of failure. You must transfer your attention away from failure and toward success. You must go from worry to calm, from mental wondering to concentration, from restlessness to peace. When you obtain this state of self-realization, the purpose of your life will unfold.

I would like to acknowledge "The Law of Success" by Paramahansa Yogananda as well as many other writers and philosophers who have contributed to my understanding of how we go about creating success in our lives. These formulas are there for everyone.

WHAT IS THE PROCESS?

Success is a process. It's a continuing cycle of failure, work, and goal setting. It's layer upon layer of challenge, defeat, and resurrection. Let's understand the basic foundation:

When you always employ your will for constructive purposes, you become the controller of your destiny.

DISCIPLINE	ORGANIZATION	WORK ETHIC	GOALS

You build your life, career, and aspirations upon these four blocks.

1. Discipline—a cornerstone to the base of success

Discipline is a key building block. It alone creates change in your life. Discipline allows you to become organized. That organization allows you to grow. When you grow, you achieve—success! It is a very simple formula:

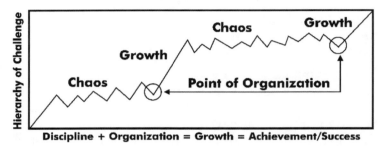

Discipline + Organization = Growth = Achievement/Success

Most people in our society are not disciplined. They're plagued by continual problems and lack motivation—things discipline can cure. Your ability to discipline yourself is what sets you apart. It drives you to your goals. It allows for organization—the next step in your growth process.

2. Organization—the second building block in the base of success

Chaos is something that happens when our lives become overloaded. It doesn't matter if you're a sales clerk raising three kids or a company president sitting on several boards. The bottom line is that *you will always experience some degree of chaos from time to time*. It comes again and again, over and over. Your ability to organize leads you out of this chaos. It will push you to a higher level of achievement. How can you organize and get rid of the chaos? Systemize what you're doing, whatever it is. Find a better way to do your work. Become more efficient.

Early in my real estate sales career, for example, I started carrying a notebook. Each page in that notebook represented a prospect. Pretty soon, although I seemed organized, I

Your

ability to

discipline

yourself is

what sets you

apart.

was overwhelmed. My prospects outnumbered the pages of my inefficient notebook. So I switched to putting prospects on a 3 x 5 index card and started carrying a card file with me. That was great until I started to have more than 500 clients/prospects. (The box was getting heavy!) So I next moved on to the computer—a new system of organization for me. And then that system needed to be modified . . . so I upgraded and improved again. *In order to grow, you must organize and reorganize if you want to reach a higher level.*

Organization starts at home. It can begin with your closet, your car, your bill-paying systems, your budget, your income/expenses, or your net worth. Don't forget to look at the way your family is operating. It is possible that you could all work more closely together. The more you organize, the more you will grow. You will find your achievement.

People in our community who serve on multiple community boards and supervise hundreds of employees, still find the time to be wonderful husbands or wives. They find the time to have fulfilling personal lives and to be great parents. They have an edge on the rest of society, and that edge is their ability to organize. They have super-organizational skills.

If you want change, discipline is the key. If you want growth, organize!

3. Work Ethic—the third building block of success

E + M = WE. Your **Energy** driven by your **Motivation** equals **Work Ethic.** This must be the main component of your drive toward success! For years, I've not only had an office desk but also a desk at home. Before I go to bed every night, I plan and organize how I will spend my next day. Even on weekends at my beach house, I have a desk so I can produce work. The message is: *you must put in the time.* But what are you putting the time into? If it is work you hate, you will never find motivation. Your work must be a labor of love. If it's not, you should question the career path you're on. If it's just a stepping-stone occupation (using it to get to another, better job), that's one thing. But if you're doing something you don't like—I'll guarantee you that you'll have an unhappy life. Change what you're doing through planning and goals. When you find your

The more you organize, the more you will grow.

path there will be a sense of freedom. There won't be enough hours in the day, but it will be fun and exciting to produce your life's work.

4. Goals—the cornerstone for the base of success

Your goals are your path to achievement. Goals mark a path for you to follow. Almost every chapter in this book mentions goals. Every successful person knows about them and uses them. If you don't know where to begin, re-read the goal section as many times as you need to begin this process of having goals in your life.

ACHIEVING SUCCESS

Most importantly, success is about failure. How? All successful people experience failure. It's really part of the cycle. The difference is your determination to pick yourself up and continue on your path. You'll get your reward if you keep picking yourself up—I promise!

During the 1998 NBA playoffs, a favorite television commercial showed Michael Jordan walking into the gym greeting people. In the commercial, you could hear him talking to himself inside his head. He talked about all the failures he had had in his life. He talked about being cut from his high school basketball team. He thought about his failure at professional baseball and his failure to make the winning game point 38 times in his NBA career. Then, at the end of the commercial, he looked into the camera and said, *"That's why I'm successful."* What a powerful message!

ATTITUDE AND ACHIEVING AND POSITIVE SELF-EXPECTANCY

Positive self-expectancy is simply optimism or enthusiasm for whatever it is you're doing.

Winners always expect to win. There was never a winner who didn't think he was going to win. Their positive thought or visualization ends in a physical reality. Life is a self-fulfill-

There was never a winner who didn't think he was going to win.

ing prophecy. You get what you expect in the long run. If you focus on the negative or on fear, you will not advance.

Tara Lipinski, winner of the gold medal for ice skating at the Nagano Olympics, told her father, "I'm going to do it." She said this just before her medal-clinching program, "I have confidence and I believe in myself." This is a great example of positive self-expectancy! She expected to win and she did. You have to go toward your goals with the same attitude.

The effect of the self-fulfilling prophecy is one of the greatest phenomena of human nature. Don't stand on the street corner and ask everyone's opinion about your business. This is letting others become the source of your confidence. And they are not you. Let your energy and the desire within you be your inspiration. Always expect the best. Focus on a positive outcome and work toward that positive self-expectancy. It is more important for you to believe in yourself than for others to believe in you.

THE MAJOR FORCES: DESIRE AND FEAR

The first major force is desire. Winners are driven by desire. We become what we think about the most—we make that vision a reality. I have experienced this many times in my life. Most recently I wanted to become an Iron-man athlete. I would manipulate my thoughts daily in order to unlock training solutions and accomplish it. The same thought process should occur when you set any goal for yourself.

Desire is a craving for something—and it leads to motivation. Your motivation is an inner drive or impulse that causes you to act. It comes from inside of you and cannot be "pumped in" from friends, relatives, or motivational speakers. You have to have that need from within if you are going to succeed. What is your motivation? Children? A better life? Becoming debt-free? Stability? A desire to show the world you must be counted?

There is an opposite to desire: fear. It is the most powerful negative motivator of all. It is the great inhibitor. It

We become what we think about the most—we make that vision a reality.

restricts, tightens, and panics. And worst of all, it defeats goals.

Desire is a positive energy and it acts like a magnet. It pulls, attracts, reaches, and directs. It allows you to achieve your goals. **Fear comes from the past.** Desire is what you want the future to become. If you want to succeed, focus only on the desire and how it can happen. Winners dwell on the rewards of success, not the penalties of failures.

If I told you all you had to do to get a $50 bill was to walk toward the end of a plank (which was only two feet off the ground), you'd go and retrieve it. Your only focus would be that reward and the desire to be $50 richer. Now, place that same $50 bill on a plank that is 20 feet high. You're probably hesitant. Why? Because of the fear, the negative, the what if? If your focus were true (and balance excellent), there'd be no problem. Focus on the positive! Tell yourself "I can."

A friend once explained this positive thinking theory to me with a story. She was a good skier and was on her way to the nationals. At the championship tournament, a slight northeast wind picked up on the course just before her turn. An advisor said to her, "Watch out for the wind" (a negative). While on her run, she was doing fine going through the first five buoys. Then, for just an instant, on the sixth buoy she remembered the wind. And she fell. Many years later, she was watching a skiing competition and overheard a respected skiing coach caution against those same conditions to another skier. This coach, however, said, "You'll be fine on the first four or five buoys, but coming out of turn five I want you to dig hard and give it everything that you have." This was great positive advice that avoided the negative! Sure enough—that skier was successful.

Winners in life know that all their actions will be controlled by their thoughts. You can't lose weight if you are thinking how heavy you are. You can't stop smoking if you are thinking about smoking. You can't get rich if you are worrying about your bills. The things we fear the most will come to pass because of ourselves—if that is the way we think. **A burning desire is the only thing that can dispel fear.** Success in life is not reserved for the talented. It doesn't depend on a high IQ, a gifted birth, or on ability and having the best equipment. ***Success is almost totally dependent on desire, drive, and persistence***—using that extra energy to try and try again. Desire or fear, which is your choice?

CHAPTER EIGHT SUMMARY

Success is defined by you. It is obtained by very simple, yet life-changing, words: discipline, organization, work ethic, goals.

The Law of Success: Opportunities are created by your thoughts and actions. You must grasp them when they present themselves.

You demonstrate success or failure by your habitual trend of thought. Every outward manifestation is the result of will.

Experiencing failure is part of the path to success.

Self-expectancy is knowing that things will work out—your committed attitude.

When driven by desire, we become what we think about the most.

Fear defeats goals. It repels. You must have faith. All will work out. (It will if you are true in your pursuits.)

Winners in life know all their actions are controlled by their thoughts.

CHAPTER EIGHT
BLUEPRINT FOR LIFE
WORKSTATION

1. Name four building blocks for success.

2. Discipline + organization = _____.

3. Redraw the graph of organization showing growth.

4. It's important to know that everything is a cycle. Identify where you are in this cycle for each of the following categories: personal, financial, educational, relationship. Put these in your journal.

5. The two major forces in success are:
   a. Desire (explain):

   b. Self-expectancy (explain):

6. List five things in your life that need better organization.

   a.

   b.

   c.

   d.

   e.

7. Read your goals out loud.

8. Close your eyes and visualize each goal.

9. Success is all about _____.

10. "_____ will hold me back from obtaining personal and financial success."

11. List 10 things that will guarantee your success.

   a.

   b.

   c.

   d.

   e.

   f.

   g.

   h.

   i.

   j.

12. Write in your journal a short essay (one page). Write as if you are telling someone else what they must do to become successful.

MONEY 101

What is the key to wealth? It's probably the opposite of what you think. If you study the lifestyles of the truly rich (those who have earned it and will in all likelihood keep it), you'll find a common *frugal* lifestyle. Sensible cars, practical watches, sensible homes—the profile of the typical millionaire is quite different from what most people imagine. The main thing wealth gives them is the ability to make decisions about their time. This is wealth's most important attribute: **Wealth gives you the ability to make choices.**

THE KEY TO WEALTH

Exclusive hideaways, Leer jets, and lavish spending are quick ways to lose a fortune. The short time of enjoyment they provide is not worth losing what could be a lifetime of comfortable security. The truly wealthy make a game of their money. They make it grow instead of showing off what it can buy. The idea that millionaires are all celebrity jet setters is not reality. A real-world millionaire is an entrepreneur businesswoman who owns her own company and who focuses her attention on that company. She has no aspiration to be portrayed on *Lifestyles of the Rich and Famous*. Although you need money to flow into your life as the by-product of your work ethic, it is the small but

Americans have forgotten the discipline of saving. They have become financially upside-down.

mountainous habit of saving that will make you a millionaire and keep you there.

People magazine expressed this concept vividly. Shown on the cover of the February 24, 1997, issue were multimillionaire celebrities who became broke, going from a net worth of millions to zero. This included Burt Reynolds (who filed bankruptcy after reaching a debt level of $4.5 million), Kim Basinger (who had to sell the Georgia town she had purchased for millions years ago), M.C. Hammer (from $33 million to zero), Shannon Dougherty (with multiple bounced checks), Dorothy Hammill (who lost her ownership of The Ice Capades), and Loni Anderson (who was hit with a $565,000 tax bill). **Wealth can easily be lost if it is not appreciated and protected.** Appreciation for and protection of your money is the basis for building wealth.

YOU, TOO, CAN MAKE IT!

Early in the 19th century, English clergyman Caleb Cotton noted that *the secret of making money is saving it*. He went on to say that one's income does not matter. "It is the relation of his expenditures to his receipts that determines his poverty or wealth."

A prime example of spendthrift discipline is Gladys Holm, a secretary who earned $15,000 per year. Holm made a fortune in the stock market with guidance from her boss, and left $18 million to a children's hospital upon her death in 1996. She had no children of her own and no known surviving relatives when she died at the age of 86. Holm bequeathed all of her money to Children's Memorial Hospital for research—the biggest gift in the hospital's 115-year history, surpassing a $10 million donation from McDonald's founder Ray Kroc.

Holm had lived her life alone in a modest two-bedroom apartment in Evanston, Illinois. Few people had suspected she was rich. Jan Jennings, President and CEO of Children's Memorial Hospital, told the media, "We were all stunned and surprised by the magnitude of her generosity. It's breathtaking."

Knowing what to do with money and controlling the temptation to spend it is not easy for anyone.

Holm had previously given the hospital $200,000 over a 25-year period. She was known around the place as the "Teddy Bear Lady," for handing out stuffed toys. Holm retired from the Evanston-based Hospital Supply Co. in 1969 after working as secretary to its founder, Foster C. McGaw, for 41 years. By the time Holm retired, the company had become the largest distributor of health care products in the world. (It has since been acquired by Baxter International.)

Looking back, co-workers estimated Holm earned a career-high of $15,000 per year prior to retiring. She said she had amassed her fortune by living frugally and investing wisely. Her one apparent luxury was a classic red Cadillac Eldorado with fins. (A friend said Holm drove the large car because she had arthritis—it allowed her to get in and out comfortably.)

Somehow, in the last two generations, Americans have forgotten the discipline of saving. They have become financially upside-down. I compare it to driving a new car off the lot, financed to the max. You'll soon owe more for it than it's worth.

Our self-indulgent society has taken the rather Epicurean view that today is what matters and tomorrow will just have to take care of itself. Irresponsible, frightful, nearsighted? Commentators on frugality and spending smart would respond with a resounding "Yes!" English educator Edward Parsons Day wrote a century ago, "To acquire wealth is difficult, but to spend it wisely is most difficult of all."

ACQUIRING WEALTH WITHOUT EFFORT

People who are given money (through lotteries and inheritances) will usually have a hard time holding on to it. I remember reading a study about lottery winners of the past 20 years. Amazingly, all were broke—all of them! Most instant lottery winners are paid over 20-year pay schedules and most of these winners never developed any financial skills during those 20 years. Because they'd wasted that time and didn't retool and refine themselves toward making money, they'd lost it all. You have to work at making money. I have a theory that it takes the third generation of an industrious and successful family to lose the base the first generation creates. This isn't always true, but it is for many. The first generation employs the discipline, work ethic and creativity needed to make a fortune. The second tries to hold on to the reigns. And the spoiled third generation squanders it because they never knew the character it took to build it.

GUNS AND BUTTER

People who are given money through lotteries and inheritances will usually have a hard time holding on to it.

When buying something for yourself, it's related to either "guns" or "butter." I'm sure the MBAs of the world would have a field day with this theory and my version of it, but it's my theory and it is directed to you and your prosperity—and not to the MBAs of the world.

"Guns" are solid things that will appreciate or go up in value, and will earn you silent equity or income. "Butter" includes things that depreciate or go down in value, evaporate, or have little or no value after their life of use.

Some examples:

BUTTER	GUNS
Automobiles	Real estate
Televisions	Antique furniture
Stereos	Stamps
Most household furniture	Coin collections
Pleasure items	Some collectable cars
Boats	Stocks (blue chip)
Clothes	Savings account
Computers	Rental property
Electronic equipment	Bonds

The idea here is to wake you up when you are making a purchase or spending money. If you *have* to spend, try and make it on items in the gun category. Two examples:

1. *Outfitting a living room with collectible antiques versus showroom model furniture.* The latest trend showroom furniture will be out of fashion within the next three to five years, have zero value, and will eventually be put out on the curb to be picked up by Goodwill. The collectible antiques will have increased in value and will continue to increase over time. **Buy things of value that will retain value—or don't buy!** Reupholstering a classic piece of furniture is often cheaper than purchasing a new one.
2. *Purchasing a new car or a collectible.* One person bought a late model car for between $5,000 and $10,000. In five to seven years, however, it will have to be hauled to a junkyard. A friend of mine, on the other hand, purchased a '64 Dodge Dart convertible for $1,200, then spent an additional $3,000 on a rebuilt engine and paint job—for a total investment of $4,200. It is fabulous! It's an all-time keeper and its value will keep increasing. This year, she decided to sell it after driving it for seven years. She sold it for $6,500! (Compare this to the average medium price of today's cars at $21,000+)

That's the concept of purchasing a "gun" or purchasing "butter." Again: One will retain its value. Purchasing the "gun" is a form of savings. It's simple economics.

LEVERAGE

Leverage allows you to use other people's money to maximize your investment.

This is a simple term that allows you to use other people's money to maximize your investment. Remember: Always cover yourself on this one because leverage means payments. You must be able to cover your payments, even on a rainy day (your overall goal is to become debt free), but leverage allows for greater growth in the long run. A simple understanding: Let's say you want a house that costs $100,000. One way to buy it is to pay $100,000 and own it free and clear. A better way to purchase it is to use leverage. You put in $5,000 of your own money and let the bank invest $95,000 (it holds the mortgage). You have used $95,000 of the bank's money to buy a $100,000 house. Your own investment is only $5,000. If you sell the house for $125,000 in five years, you will have made $25,000 on a $5,000 investment!

GOOD DEBT VERSUS BAD DEBT

Debt is never really good, but you can consider leverage to be *good debt* if it is on a "guns" asset. Bad debt is debt on anything that is "butter," an asset that will go down in value. When you pay by credit card and don't pay off the balance in full, you're losing twice. For example, say you have a high-interest credit card debt of $3,500 and pay the minimum monthly payment. Reaching a zero balance (without paying any additional principal when you make your monthly payments) will take many, many years. This is *very* bad debt.

Here's a real world example of what can happen to a $3,000 credit card debt. Let's say you bought a large-screen television. You have a $3,000 principal balance at 19.8% interest listed as owing on your credit bill. But you pay only the required minimum payment of 2% of the balance or $15 (whichever is greater). You now make no new purchases using that credit card. It will take 39 years to pay off that debt! And you will end up paying over $10,000 in interest charges (more than three times your original debt!). THIRTY-NINE YEARS! It's no wonder people continue to struggle.

Another example of losing value is the purchase of an automobile on credit. The value of the car depreciates to zero in a few short years and you pay a high interest rate.

BUDGETS

If you don't have one, try, try, and try until you make one and *stick with it*. This can be very scary because it will force you to see where your money is going. The goal here, though, is to slow your flow of money (spending), no matter how large or small. After you tighten the controls, principal debt (your credit cards) can be paid off. Then, seed money for investments and security can be started.

To begin your budget, list all your expenditures in a month. If you have a yearly cost, divide that number by 12 to find the monthly cost. Don't leave anything out. Come back to this at least every other day so you can account for what you are buying or spending each month. During the next year all this should be put into a three-ring notebook. You will review this over and over, each time finding where you can save a dollar here and a dollar there. Now, look at your monthly income after your taxes have been paid. Are you losing or gaining? Don't be alarmed if you're in the negative—most people are. The important thing is to begin today to get hold of the situation and start saving.

We have to find out where the "fat" is (more income than debt) in order to find seed money for investments. Nobody really likes the "B" word . . . budget. It sounds like too much trouble, too much sacrifice—which is partly true and partly false. It's not too much trouble if you keep it simple. Keep your first budget in a journal or use a legal pad. Start with the same categories you used to determine your spending. Ask a bookkeeper or an accountant for possible lists, or use the one listed below. If you tell them you may use their services for future business, I'm sure they'll provide this to you. Any office supply store can also be of help if you want one that is pre-printed.

Jot down your expenses for a few months, making a conscious effort to both eliminate overspending and reduce waste. Use your checkbook to refresh your memory about bills—and don't forget about the ATM machines and all those withdrawals!

Where is most of your money going? To pay monthly bills for credit card minimums? How many expense "extras" are on your list? Chances are, you'll immediately see some areas that seem out of line. For most people the real shocker is cash. It's amazing how much money you can go through in a week! Everyone's had the experience of withdrawing $50 on Monday and $50 on Wednesday, and finding that by Thursday you don't have any more money—and you don't have anything to show for it.

When you pay by credit card and don't pay off the balance in full, you're losing twice.

Taking control of your money means controlling what you spend—from car washes to quick runs to the store, to magazines at the checkout counter when you're buying groceries. Think about how to rearrange what you spend, however, and find ways to save. The more you live with the budgeting process, the more you'll decide what to spend and what to adjust. Pretty soon it will become second nature and you'll begin to control your expenses instead of your expenses controlling you.

You need to keep your priorities straight in your mind in order to succeed. Advertisers are well aware of the lure of impulse buying. Don't walk through the mall; send someone else to get what you need. The next time you're at the grocery store, notice how the store positions all the tempting candies at the checkout aisle. It's so easy to grab a handful as you check out, even though you aren't even looking for candy. The same is true for the "sale" signs in stores. It's easy to be tempted by a 50% off sign, but the bargain you get may be something you didn't even want or need.

Be sure to make photocopies of the following. You do NOT want to write in this book. You will be changing these numbers on a periodic basis.

Family Budget	Monthly	Yearly
Income		
Wages or Salary		
Alimony/child support		
Social Security		
Pension		
Other earnings		
(Commissions, interest, tips, dividends, etc.)		
Total Income		

Taking

control of

your money

means

controlling

what you

spend—from

car washes to

quick runs to

the store.

Expenses	Monthly	Yearly
Giving		
Church		
Poor		
Other		
Other		
Transportation		
Gas and Oil		
Automobile Insurance		
Repair and Maintenance		
Licenses/Registration		
Parking and Tolls		
Medical		
Doctor		
Dentist		
Prescriptions		
Glasses		
Health Insurance		
Other		
Children		
School Tuition		
Allowances		
Tutoring		
Music/Dance Lessons		
Sports		
Babysitting		
Other		

Insurance	Monthly	Yearly
Life Insurance		
Disability		
Other		
Food		
Groceries		
Eating Out		
School Lunches		
Other		
Clothing/Grooming		
Purchases		
Cleaning		
Hair Care		
Toiletries/Cosmetics		
Other		
Housing		
Rent or Mortgage		
Property Taxes		
Property Insurance		
Electricity		
Heating/Gas		
Water		
Garbage Service		
Cable TV		
Telephone		
Cleaning		

Housing (continued)	Monthly	Yearly
Repairs/Maintenance		
Supplies		
Improvements		
Furnishings		
Other		
Debt Repayment		
Credit Card Acct. #		
Credit Card Acct. #		
Credit Card Acct. #		
Credit Card Acct. #		
Credit Card Acct. #		
Recreation		
Adult Allowances		
Vacations		
Magazines/Newspapers		
Books/Tapes/Records		
Hobbies/Pets		
Entertainment		
Gifts		
Christmas		
Birthdays/Anniversaries		
Weddings/Showers		
Graduations		
Office Gifts		

Personal/Business	Monthly	Yearly
Education		
Clubs, Union, Dues		
Accounting/Legal		
Financial Services		
Other		
Total expenses		
Total Income Less Expenses		
Savings or Principal Repayment (This should equal the figure above)		

KNOWING THE SCORE

To begin this financial journey, I'm going to ask that you keep a ledger. One section can be about credit and what you're concentrating on cleaning up. Another can be about the budget. A third section can list expenses and payment records. Most important, however, is that you complete a financial net worth statement each year. It may look bad or upside down (a negative net worth), but that's okay. We're going on a fast track and when you start using the suggestions in this book, your negative net worth will reverse itself and you'll soon start to grow financially.

It's very exciting to track your growth each year, but you need to know the exact score. To do that, you must complete a financial net worth statement every year (including this first year)—which you can pick up at any local bank in the loan department. By completing a net worth statement, you will start to see what's missing from your ultimate financial portfolio. These things include stocks, insurance, and real estate, etc. In the future, you will want to obtain those missing items.

Soon, in a year or two, your discipline and concentration will be rewarded—you will show tangible assets on your net worth statement. Remember: When figuring out your net worth, it's important not to exaggerate the value of the assets you have. In the future, your financial statement will be a key factor for approval when filling out applications for credit and credit lines. Investors do this on a regular basis.

CHAPTER NINE SUMMARY

Money 101 is the process of recognizing where your money is coming from each month and determining how it is being dispersed in your life.

Setting controls through this budget process allows you to identify waste or excess. The monies that are left over can be used as "seed money" for future investments.

The purpose of having money is to give you the ability to make decisions about your time and what you want to do with it. Wealth can be lost if it is not protected and appreciated. Safeguard all the money you are able to—this is the only way it will grow. Becoming financially independent is, and should be, a game. Treat it like a game and it will become fun to win.

Savings should be a disciplined part of your life. One day, it will pay off—big time! Be conscientious when making every purchase. Buy for value and longevity. The money you spend will either melt away (butter) or grow because it was directed toward an appreciating asset (gun).

When leverage is used on a "real" appreciating asset (for example, a house), the equity ($) grows. When leverage is put on a "butter" investment (for example, a car), the value of this so-called asset decreases more quickly than the debt used to purchase the item (leverage).

CHAPTER NINE
BLUEPRINT FOR LIFE
WORKSTATION

1. The Key to Wealth is _ _ _ _? (four letters, one word)
2. If you won the lottery, you would (circle as many as you like):
   a. Invest wisely
   b. Continue to earn money and make a living
   c. Continue to educate and refine yourself in business

d. Not get lazy for 20 years

e. All of the above

3. When purchasing a "gun" item, the value of that item will go:

a. Up

b. Down

4. Write a detailed one-month budget.

5. Write a detailed one-year budget.

6. If you were 40 years old and had a $3,000 credit card balance at 19.8% and paid the minimum monthly requirement, your age when the balance becomes zero will be:

a. 44

b. 79

c. 50

7. Define, from creating your budget, 10 things which could be reduced or eliminated to create extra cash flow for yourself.

8. Keep a hard, detailed budget for six consecutive months.

9. What is the average cost per meal to feed your family on any given day of the month?

10

UNDERSTANDING DEBT

BECOMING DEBT FREE

Credit can be your best friend or it can take your legs right out from under you. If you use credit for every purchase, you will become dependent on those credit cards and—all of a sudden—you will find yourself a prisoner to credit debt. *Carrying too much credit debt is one of the worst financial decisions a person can make.* The consumer mentality has led Americans to carry between seven and 10 credit cards and have a collective family debt average of nearly $3,500. We spend about 20 percent of our disposable income paying off debts with, obviously, little outcome.

According to the Federal Reserve Board, American consumers now carry over $3.8 trillion in debt, including mortgages. How do we get out of this? Well, it's easier to dig the hole deeper than it is to get out. I remember an occasion when I was asked to assist someone up to her ears in credit card debt. After I started to show her what would have to be done, she was scared. She didn't want to face the reality of what needed to be done, which included cutting off the cable TV and eliminating her teenage daughter's phone.

If you are not ready to make sacrifices in your life, this book can't help you. You must focus directly on your prob-

The consumer mentality has led Americans to carry between seven and 10 credit cards and have a collective family debt average of nearly $3,500.

lems, how you got there, and how you can solve those problems—and prevent them in the future.

HOW DO YOU KNOW WHEN YOU'RE IN TOO DEEP?

- Do you incur credit card interest charges because you're not paying off your balances in full each month?
- Do you pay your bills late?
- Do you take out new loans to pay off old loans?
- Do you ask for extended payments, from 30 to 60 to 90 days?
- Have you reached the maximum credit limit on any of your credit cards?
- Have you ever bounced a check?
- Do you just look at the minimum monthly payment and pay that amount, and not any more, on your credit card bill?
- Does life without credit seem impossible to you?
- Are you currently drawing from your savings accounts to pay your regular bills?
- Do you use cash advances on one credit card to make payments on another credit card?
- Do you now borrow money for purchases you used to pay with cash?
- Is the portion of your income allocated to debts rising every month, preventing you from contributing to a savings account?

The first goal is to get completely out of credit card debt.

If you've answered yes to any of these questions, you need to focus on getting out of debt. Debt will stop you from having the free life you so desire. If you see your debt for what it is (something *you* can control), you become competitive. Make a game out of your plan—*The Debt-Free Game*—and see debt for the temporary state it can be. This begins your walk toward financial freedom.

THE SLOW DESCENT INTO DEBT

According to the American Bankruptcy Institute, the number of consumers and businesses filing for U.S. Bankruptcy protection has risen dramatically, hitting a record 335,073 in the late 1990s. How do people get into debt and work themselves eventually into bankruptcy? You have to understand about debt. Debt comes in three stages, each step becoming worse than the previous one.

- **The first stage of debt is when income is being used to pay off principal.**
- **The second stage of debt is when income is used to pay interest while the principal remains the same or increases.**
- **The third stage of debt is when income is insufficient to pay even the interest.**

My recommendation is to buy your car free and clear, even if it means buying an older car.

Our United States Government has been in the third stage of debt until very recently. It has been borrowing money to pay interest on what it already owes—just like if you were to borrow money on your Visa card to pay your MasterCard bill.

The nation's level of personal bankruptcy filings is at its highest level in decades, but more will be coming. It is estimated by the Regional Financial Associates based in Webster, Pennsylvania, that more than 1.5 million individuals will file for bankruptcy in the year 2000.

BASIC PHILOSOPHY FOR GETTING OUT OF DEBT

Credit cards should be your first concentration in your efforts to become debt free. The interest and nature of the beast will keep you buried. You must list all your credit card information, payment plans, due dates, etc., in your financial ledger. Any time you have any bit of excess money, you must apply that payment to the principal on those designated credit cards and identify it in your ledger. The first goal is to get completely out of credit card debt. If you can't meet this goal, you can't accomplish anything else.

The second phase of getting out of debt concerns your automobile. The money you were paying toward your credit cards should now be applied toward the principal on your automobile. Ultimately, when you find your credit card and car debts gone, you will have money to apply toward savings, investments, and other opportunities. To accomplish this tremendous task and to keep your daily focus, I recommend putting up some kind of graph or chart on your refrigerator or bathroom mirror where you will see it every day. Take great pride in checking off any small payments, no matter how incremental, whenever they are made.

You cannot solve your financial problems until these two forms of consumer debt are eliminated. Reaching this goal will allow all other opportunities to grow. Once those objectives are accomplished, you may want to apply additional money toward your 30-year mortgage. You should find out what it would take to convert your 15-year mortgage to a 15-year payment plan. This can be achieved not by refinancing, but by making a separate payment each month. You can write out a second check for "principal only" and put it in the same envelope as your mortgage payment. If you stay on course, this "double payment" will save you hundreds of thousands of dollars by reducing the mortgage payoff time. (The additional monies needed should be between $70 and $100 per month).

Your focus should be to establish your budget and determine how you can live within it. Any excess should go toward paying off the principal on your credit card debt.

CAR DEBT

If you're financing a car for more than three years, you can't afford that car. My recommendation is to buy your car free and clear, even if it means buying an older car. Also, make sure it is a good, sound investment and a reliable brand. It might have to last you a long time! Take a look at the *Consumer Auto Reports* (found in your library or at the local newsstand) and think about which car you would purchase now if you were in the market. This magazine is used to determine the recent history and auto

Learn to use credit cards only for purchases you can pay off within the next 30 days.

mechanic's comments about all makes and models. The information is consumer-friendly and reliable.

USING CREDIT CARDS

Each month, compare your credit card receipts with your billing statement. It's a great reminder of exactly what you're spending—and what you have to focus on. Learn to use credit cards only for purchases you can pay off within the next 30 days. Vow never to pay another penny of credit card interest! Use credit cards for convenience, not for installment loans.

Married couples should agree on the amount each spouse can charge without consulting the other (both partners will have to limit their spending). Each partner should be committed to debt-free service (no balances carried over into the next month). This is one of the biggest problems in marriages. Deciding in advance what you plan to buy and how you plan to buy it will help avoid those "impulse" purchases that can get you in trouble. Keep your plan firmly in mind.

The majority of Americans are in debt, along with our great government. The 5% who are not have an enviable peace of mind. If you want to begin your financial freedom, start by focusing on your debt, getting out of it, and staying out. Before you can begin to grow financially, this first step of having a zero credit card balance must be met.

Married couples should agree on the amount each spouse can charge without consulting the other.

CREDIT CARD DEBT

Any time you "find" extra money (perhaps from tax returns, overages, birthday money, or extra income money), *apply these extra monies to your debt.* Get rid of any credit card balances you may be carrying from month to month. Pay them off until the balance carried over hits zero! Another hint: every time you make monthly payments on your credit cards, round up the amount you pay to the next highest $25 or $50. Eventually, you will get that credit card paid off! Then go on to the next card and the next. The object here is to pay off additional principal every month—not just the interest. Otherwise, you will stay in debt forever *and the mental anguish will ruin your spirit.*

In your journal, keep track of your debt—and also keep a list of your credit card balances. As you pay down a credit card each month, draw a line through the balance and write the new, lower balance beside it. Keep marking through these balances. This focus and this attention to what you're doing will move you closer and closer to your goal. I personally remember having about seven credit cards all the way up in the $5,000 and $6,000 balance limits. Each month I felt I'd scored a victory every time I was able to pay off a little bit of that principal. What a feeling of gratification! About 14 years ago I got those balances down to zero—and I've kept them there ever since.

THE HOME EQUITY TEMPORARY SOLUTION

The next thing to do is to quit using credit cards! **If you can't control yourself and don't intend to use credit cards for investment purposes (the availability of funds for a quick investment), get rid of them!** If you do need to charge something, make the commitment to pay off the amount you've charged *in full each month.* One way to consolidate your debts is a home equity loan (assuming you own your own house). Check and see if you qualify for a home equity loan large enough to get rid of all your credit card debt. This would cost you a lot less interest on your debt and would allow you to comfortably make new, hopefully lower, payments (as well as to allow you to deduct the interest on your income taxes). Do not allow this new loan on your house, however, to make you feel richer! Yes, you've brought your other credit cards back to zero. *This does not mean you have more money.* In fact, you have now put your home in jeopardy should you miss a loan payment. If you do consolidate your loans this way, be sure to tear up all your credit cards. When making payments on your new equity loan, again pay some money toward the principal each month.

I would rather you have zero credit card debt and no savings, than to have credit card debt and savings.

CUT THEM UP!

Get rid of any extra credit cards! When you cut up a credit card, however, just don't throw it away. You must write a letter to the bank card company (Visa, MasterCard, etc.) and formally request that your account be closed. Also request that they inform the credit bureaus they report to that you have closed that account.

WORKING YOUR WAY OUT

If you are currently in debt and have some savings, think about using some of your savings to pay off those credit cards. *You have to look at debt that is constantly charging interest as making your life go backwards financially.* When you have equity or money that is making interest, it means you are going forward financially. My advice is that I would rather you have zero credit card debt and no savings than credit card debt with savings. If you're way over your head in debt and don't have the money to even make the minimum payments, it's time to contact your creditors. Write a letter explaining your financial problems and commit to a payment schedule in that letter. Even $5 a month might be enough. Your creditors might give you added help by applying more of your monthly payments toward your principal. If you contact them and make a show of good faith, they will certainly be more willing to work with you than if they had never heard from you. In many cases, if you ask, they will even lower the interest rate being charged to you. Send what you can until you get back to zero. Make bankruptcy the absolute last option.

Bankruptcy is not a cop-out way of not facing your fiscal responsibility. It may just be a quicker way for you to get back to zero.

BANKRUPTCY

Bankruptcy. It's not as bad as you might think. It's our federal government's way of saying you've made a mistake and need to start again. In theory, it is supposed to take the pressure off and allow you a fresh start. In most cases it works—people learn (the hard way) how to control their finances. You may have a heavy burden of debt from a previous marriage, escalating because of high interest rate credit cards. And the mountain may just be too high to climb. Bankruptcy is not a cop-out way of avoiding your fiscal responsibility. It may just be a quicker way for you to get back to zero.

Bankruptcy laws are changing every year (even as this is being printed), mainly because of abuses to the system. If you are considering declaring bankruptcy, it is imperative to seek material on the subject from your state and, of course, from federal agencies. Local libraries have a wealth of information on the subject and the business section of most bookstores will carry pertinent information. Also, you should seek opinions from at least two professionals before deciding to proceed. Bankruptcy will affect your ability to get credit for many years.

The most important issue if you decide to clear the books with bankruptcy, is that from that time on **you must never again be late, delinquent, or miss a payment to a creditor.** Building back your credit is imperative to regaining financial strength. If you decide to declare bankruptcy, you must put together a plan for keeping yourself out of debt. You cannot make the same mistake twice! A list of credit counselors who can help you structure a plan is available. Look in the business pages of your local telephone book for the closest office of the Consumer Credit Counseling Service (a nonprofit United Way organization) or the Christian Credit Counseling office. Either can help you structure your financial rebuilding at an affordable price. See page 128 for more information.

Building back your credit is imperative to regaining financial strength.

CHAPTER TEN SUMMARY

Consumer debt, and especially credit card debt, will prevent any financial growth no matter how strong your will is. Your first mission is to put any excess cash flow ($5, $50, $500) toward this high-interest-rate debt. Debt will stop you from having the free life you so desire.

Home equity loans can allow you to consolidate your credit card balances. Don't let this new, lower monthly payment fool you into thinking you no longer have that debt. Stop using your credit cards—it will just create more debt.

Protect your credit rating from this day forward. Be ahead of your bills. Your positive credit rating is power.

CHAPTER 10
BLUEPRINT FOR LIFE
WORKSTATION

1. If you own your own home, calculate how much additional principal has to be paid each month if you were to pay off your loan in 15 years instead of 30 years (you may need to contact your local banker for this "secret" mortgage formula).
2. Answer the questions on the first page of Chapter 10.
3. Analyze your automobile debt. Make a schedule to determine if any principal is being paid off each month. (Again, contact your banker for help. You will need to show them the terms of your loan.)
4. Eliminate/tear up/cut up all your credit cards with exception of one gas credit card.
5. Do you have a credit card list in your journal? Are you using the "additional principal paid" column?
6. Purchase or get from the library a book on getting out of debt. Read it!
7. Can you consolidate all your credit card debt? What is the average rate you pay on all your credit cards? Look into getting an equity line loan. What is its rate? What would be the difference between your payments on the equity line loan and your current payments on your credit cards?
8. Bankruptcy—seek two professional opinions. Decide whether this would help your financial situation.
9. Make a time-line showing when you will be able to pay off all your credit cards.

THE POWER OF CREDIT

If you boast that you pay cash and have never bought anything on credit, you're way behind.

Acquiring credit and maintaining a good record should be one of your most important goals. **Credit is power. To live nowadays, you don't need cash but you do need credit.** If you boast that you pay cash and have never bought anything on credit, you're way behind. I recommend owning certain assets using leverage as power (such as a house), because it multiplies how much credit you can get—and credit is the key to it all. In our economy, where a car loan is standard equipment, where a credit card can be more acceptable than cash, and where a mortgage figures into most families' dreams, your economic well being can rise and fall on your ability to get credit. This "rating" determines both your ability to qualify and the interest rate you will be charged.

Years ago, during the '60s and '70s, obtaining credit was very easy. There were assumable mortgages and just about anybody could get anything. It was easy to manipulate the system and grab as much cash and leverage as you wanted. Things changed in the '80s with mortgages becoming nonassumable and harder to qualify for. Because those once-abundant nonqualifying opportunities were too easy for the average investor to manipulate, the system changed. Today, if you have blue-chip credit and if you are sophisticated about what you're doing, you can still obtain whatever loans you need for investment. This is because when credit tightened in the early '80s, financial institutions became creative and extremely competitive. They began offering adjustable rate mortgages, reverse amortizing mortgages, and credit cards with initial teaser interest rates (and higher rates later on). Lenders from California to New York were, and still are, willing to give you lots of money if you have the credit. Today, companies beg, borrow, and steal lists of good credit prospects.

Let me share with you a personal story about credit. About 12 years ago, I read a book discussing the importance of credit. After reading this book, I became very intense about building credit with one theory in mind. If I were offered a real estate deal in which I could purchase a property for $100,000, but with a real market value of $200,000, would I be able to raise that cash in one day? Most people couldn't, and I myself couldn't at the time. I'd probably have to share the deal with someone else and reap a much smaller profit. If you're able to access large sums of money, you can participate in much better deals for yourself. The goal is to build your credit and your availability of cash. I started with credit cards that had available balances of just a few thousand dollars. In 10 years, I had an availability of over $1 million.

RULES OF THE
CREDIT CARD GAME

Rule 1: *Never, ever make a late payment.* Don't be one of those people who pay on the first if it is due on the first! If the mail isn't delivered on time, you could easily get a negative mark on your credit. You don't want to ever come close to that or have to explain any negative entry on your credit report. *You just want good triple-A-rated credit.* You want the person who's reviewing your report and making the decision as to whether or not you'll be granted a credit opportunity to say, "Wow, this person is an automatic to get a triple-A rating." Some advisors say you should hold on to your money and your payments until the due date (hoping to earn every bit of interest out of your money), but why chance this? I'd rather build credit because credit is king. For years, I would pay well in advance so that I could get an edge on my debt and my responsibilities.

Rule 2: *Pay off your balances at the end of each billing period.* The only reasons you shouldn't pay your balance in full are either 1) dire situations or 2) extremely creative business opportunities. You don't want that high interest rate eating away at your equity! Keep your balance at zero and you'll always be in control. If you get out of control, be forewarned that bad credit will take you out of any financial game. It will all be over before the race even begins. **It's imperative that you control your debt instead of your debt controlling you.**

Rule 3: *Multiplying your credit starts with one card.* You can draw cash from that credit card and then immediately go pay off the principal you created with that same cash. For example, if your credit line is up to $500, draw out $500, then turn right around and pay it off. Note: this will cost you a small transaction fee. In a couple of months write a letter to your creditor and ask him to review your credit. It will show him that 1) you paid the loan off early, 2) your balance is zero, and 3) you've maximized your credit limit several times. They will now extend your credit limit from the original $500 to maybe $1,000 or $2,000— and, eventually, up to $5,000. Some credit cards will offer a credit line of $25,000 to $50,000. Here's a sample letter you might send to your lender:

> *Dear Sir:*
>
> *I am requesting a higher limit on my credit line. As you can see, I am an honorable patron with good credit standing. Please check your records. My credit availability was $500 and I would like to request a credit availability of $2,000.*
>
>
>
> *Sincerely,*
> *Millennium Woman*
>

Find that limit, work yourself through it, and keep raising your credit. Again, you never know when you're going to need to raise $100,000 because you've been offered a $200,000 upside opportunity (a deal).

As the financial provider for your family, you need to carry the credit stick in business affairs.

OTHER WAYS TO START

A quick and easy way to obtain a credit card is to add your name to someone else's card (such as your father's or another relative's). It works very well with a family member. Tell that person that you're "riding" with your name on their card and promise that you won't use the new card. (They don't even have to give you the card.) You just want to "ride" their credit to establish yours. In time, other credit card companies will send you applications—and you're off and running on your own! It's just that easy. If you have a bad credit rating, however, and you are trying to reestablish good credit, check with a credit counseling service before attaching your name to someone else's card.

Theoretically, you could raise your credit limits across the board by making a deposit, borrowing against it, and continuing the practice with as many banks as you wish. Deposit in one account, then borrow against it. Put that borrowed money into your checking account—and pay the loan off early. There might be some nominal interest costs involved but, again, your goal is to build credit, not make money (at least not yet). Multiple credit lines, both secured and unsecured, give you the purchasing power to strike when rare opportunities present themselves. You're building a power base with your credit.

THE BEST CREDIT CARD DEALS IN THE U.S.

Credit Cards	Rates	Annual Fees	Telephone #
Cards with the lowest rates according to Money Magazine, May, 1999			
Wachovia Bank (Delaware)	7.75%	$88	1-800-842-3262
Huntington National Bank (Ohio)	7.75%	$39	1-800-480-2262
USAA Savings Bank	8.75%	$45	1-800-922-9092
(The rest of the cards listed have no annual fees.)			

Multiple credit lines, both secured and unsecured, give you the purchasing power to strike when rare opportunities present themselves. You're building a power base with your credit.

Credit Cards	Rates	Annual Fees	Telephone #
Capital Bank One (VA)	9.90%		1-800-822-3397
Wachovia Bank (Delaware)	9.90%		1-800-842-3262
Bank One/First USA	9.99%		1-800-451-2491

BAD CREDIT

Pay your bills on time and don't go over your credit limit. You can be hit with penalty fees and rates as high as 25%!

If you are hopelessly behind on paying your bills and creditors are badgering for payment, seek professional help. The Consumer Credit Counseling Service offers educational programs and debt repayment programs and most are free. To find the closest, call 1-800-388-2227. Also, Bankcard Holders of America offers the Debt Zapper Kit to help consumers figure out a personalized credit card payoff plan. To order, send a check for $15 to BHA Debt Zapper, 524 Branch Drive, Salem, Virginia 24153.

Attack any credit card debt from your past—get free! You cannot become a Millennium Woman until you are truly free from the land of debt. If you have bad credit now, make an appointment with a credit agency and find out what you need to do to clear up your rating. Be persistent about this. You should set the goal twice yearly to review your credit report. Pay the necessary $7 to $12 fee to find out how clean (and accurate) it is and what a lender will see when he looks at it.

If you find a problem, two very important resources are available to you. Each individual has the right to place an in-depth statement, usually up to 40 words, into her credit report explaining any bad credit or reasons for discrepancies. You might not be able to change or stop a bad mark on your credit record, but you can state a reason. As an example, it might be your husband who ran up the credit card bill before the divorce. You can state that you've since reestablished credit (which can be shown from a certain date of separation) after which there is no bad report with your name on it.

Here's another example: you have been making late payments after your separation. If you have moved, you can honestly tell them that the credit card company mailed your statements to the wrong address and you were not receiving them in time to make the payment date. *You should tell the credit agency* **in writing** that you value your credit and honor your responsibilities and that, as of this date forward, you will never again be delinquent about any financial responsibility. Use all the space given to you so that you can sound professional and mature. This explanation will help sell the fact that you are starting anew.

The next thing you can do is determine that from now on you will live without ever being delinquent. The professionals who review your credit report will see when (and if) you have turned over a new leaf—and if you have any backsliding tendencies. Bad credit reports will stop you dead in your tracks. A good credit report is most vitally needed when you are trying to use leverage or obtain credit. You need it when you are desperate. You want the people who will be reading your credit report to always think you're a safe risk. You will be termed an "automatic" if your history reflects numerous loans, all of which have been repaid on a timely basis. It takes years to build such a strong credit base, so start as soon as possible. When most people are young, they don't pay much attention to bounced checks, overdrafts, and late utility payments. These will all catch up with them, however, when they decide to start moving their lives forward financially. At some point in time, everyone must start to live right. And today is your day. On-time payments grease the tracks toward accomplishing your financial goals.

CREDIT REPORTS

It's useful to understand how lenders qualify you based on credit reports and information. Your knowledge of credit reports can have a direct impact on your bottom line. Finding false information on a credit report isn't unusual. (That's why I recommend that you review your report twice yearly.) In fact, the data is a far cry from perfect. A recent study conducted by the National Association of Independent Credit Reporting Agencies (NAICRA) showed that 85% of the files reviewed contained outdated information and 44% were missing information regarding balances and payments. The chance for errors soars if your name is John Smith or Mary Jones. And there is no such thing as a universal credit rating. Lenders make up their minds about us in their own inscrutable ways and no two of them use identical criteria. Most of them do, however, get information about credit applicants from the files of the nation's 1,200 consumer credit bureaus.

HOW WE ARE JUDGED

You should set the goal twice yearly to review your credit report.

A mistake in your credit record can make you ineligible for an auto loan, a credit card, or a mortgage. These days, most lenders decide whether to grant you credit through a process called *credit scoring*. To score, statisticians study the personal traits and payment histories of previous customers of a given lending institution. Each trait that seems pertinent (excluding gender, age, race, religion and nationality, all of which are illegal grounds for refusing credit) is then assigned one or more points depending on its apparent importance in identifying desirable borrowers. No single profile of the faithful borrower emerges from credit scoring. Indeed, scoring systems can differ remarkably from city to city and even amongst lenders in the same vicinity. The traits that help to determine your acceptability are likely to include the following:

Your age. People in their forties and early fifties, the peak spending years, tend to lose points here.

Your occupation. Blue-collar workers tend to score lower than white-collar workers.

How much money you earn.

How much money you have in the bank.

How much money you owe and to how many lenders.

How promptly you pay your installment debts.

Your scoring total, when combined with other agencies, is called your "beacon credit rating." It is a point total and a synopsis of your credit history. A score of 600–700 is excellent. A score of 800 is outstanding.

REPORTS

For more information about credit reports, you can contact the following:

Merchants Association Credit Bureau
P.O. Box 3307
Tampa, FL 33601
1-800-226-6214

Experian Credit Data
P.O. Box 2350
Chatsworth, CA 91313—2350
1-800-682-7654

Credit Data Services
Consumer Association
800 North Magnolia Avenue
Orlando, FL 32803
1-800-749-7576 or 407-246-7615

Each report will cost $8. It is well worth the money to see your financial standing and the accuracy of that information. If you have been denied credit within the past six months, you may request these reports for free.

> A mistake in your credit record can make you ineligible for an auto loan, a credit card, or a mortgage.

DIVORCE VERSUS CREDIT: HOW DIVORCE AFFECTS YOUR CONSUMER CREDIT

When you are given credit while married, you usually don't think about the possibility of divorce. But divorce and your credit rating can cause headaches for the unwary. Joint accounts mean joint liabilities. Some divorce decrees don't pay attention to the remaining joint credit obligations (and it's only fair that the credit grantor collect what is due from the credit agreement both you and your former spouse entered into). But where does that leave you if your spouse won't pay? When you obtained your credit, you signed a contract agreeing to pay your bills. A divorce decree doesn't change that contract. There are ways to re-establish your own credit lines in your own name after the divorce. Listed below are ways you can prevent credit obligations from making divorce more difficult.

1. **Talk it out.** Communicate with your soon-to-be ex-spouse. Even in good times, many couples find it difficult to discuss money issues. You have to try and find a way to put the bitterness aside and make as clean a financial cut as possible. Unfortunately, a lot of spouses use their debt obligations as an ax to grind.

2. **During divorce negotiations keep your joint bills current,** even if it means paying your spouse's share for awhile. If you don't, your creditors could become more reluctant to release one party from the joint liability. Remember, joint bills are joint responsibilities. You obtained the credit based on the income of both parties. It's only fair that the grantor of the credit collect what is due.

3. **Communicate with your creditors.** Decide which debt belongs to whom, then ask each creditor to transfer the debt to the name of the person who will be responsible. (Creditors don't have to do this and they may defer a decision until you prove you can handle the payments alone.) This is an excellent way to protect yourself from any new liability. It is also a good way to reestablish credit for yourself.

4. **Make it legal.** If your ex-spouse assumes the major joint debt, this should be recognized as part of the support agreement. If you can't convince your creditors to remove you from the liability and your ex later files for bankruptcy, you may be able to sue for that money should his creditors pursue you. Support agreements aren't dischargeable in bankruptcy (he still has to pay the debt).

5. **If your spouse runs up large amounts of debt,** you should cancel as many of the accounts as possible. Inform all your creditors in writing that you are not

Some divorce decrees don't pay attention to the remaining joint credit obligations.

responsible for these debts and his actions. (This may not prevent them from trying to collect, but it does show that you attempted to act responsibly.)

6. **Upon your divorce settlement,** close your joint accounts and establish or reestablish credit in your own name.

7. **Limit your liability** by ensuring that your soon-to-be ex-spouse cannot charge on your accounts. Ask the credit grantor to remove your spouse's name as an authorized user of your credit cards.

8. **Keep both eyes open.** Even if your marriage is proven and secure, it can pay to take note and stay alert to your credit situation. If divorce looms, watch out for those bank cards, the mortgage, and the home equity loan. For a separated couple, each of these can be a recurring pain that is resistant to all but the most courageous financial antidotes.

Article from The Sanford Herald

CHAPTER ELEVEN SUMMARY

Your true financial power lies in your credit. The higher your "beacon credit rating," the stronger your position to demand better interest rates when making loans.

Never, ever be late on making your payments on anything.

Credit reports very frequently have inaccurate information. You should pull your report now, and do this at least once every year.

CHAPTER ELEVEN BLUEPRINT FOR LIFE WORKSTATION

1. Call or write for two credit reports about yourself. Review and understand what they mean and say.

2. Make necessary changes and explanations. Be sure, with your explanation, that you write in how you are attempting to have future great credit.

> Keep both eyes open. Even if your marriage is proven and secure, it can pay to take note and stay alert to your credit situation.

3. If you have proven by this time that you are responsible about handling your credit, contact your lenders and ask that your credit limit be raised.
4. Make all credit card payments within three days of your having received the bill. Include additional monies to pay off any principal that may be owed—or pay it down to zero.
5. See if you can lower the interest rate you are paying on any of your current cards by calling and negotiating.

SECURING YOUR FUTURE

Financial planning is extremely important. One way to approach financial planning is to find a good financial planner you can trust and discuss your goals with. (I would, however, prefer that you educate yourself through publications such as *Money* magazine.) Your goals can include things like how you will want to live 25 or 30 years from now. How will you put the kids through college? How will you buy them braces? Will you have to work when you'd really rather slow down? Up until now, you've learned how to get rid of your debt and why you need credit. Now, it's time to start setting money aside for your long-range plans of attack.

You might have to learn to live on only $12,000 per year instead of $30,000—at least for awhile.

FINANCIAL PLANNING

Hopefully, you've reached the level of discipline where you are living on less than what you make. You have extra money at the end of the month. What should you do with that extra money? Consider direct-depositing part of your income into some form of savings. This keeps you from the temptation of using your money for anything other than savings. You might say to yourself, for purposes of planning, "I want x amount of dollars by the time I'm __ years old." Now, you might not be satisfied once you reach that level, but putting down that specific amount of money as your goal gives you a starting point.

The questions you need to ask yourself are:

- How much financial security can allow me to support the people in my life?
- How can my work sustain me personally, as well as professionally? I want to work in a field that keeps me happy and lets me live well.
- How can all this come together in a way that doesn't deny the present? I don't want to feel that I am constantly struggling. I want to be able to enjoy life.

We live in an age where frugality and simpler living are often discussed—but, historically, this movement doesn't have a lot of staying power. *To make financial planning work, you must make careful choices about how you spend your money.* You might have to learn to live on only $12,000 per year instead of $30,000, at least for awhile. Or you may need to change where you are spending your money. The actual dollar amount that you spend every month may not change, but the areas that you spend it in might. For example, instead of buying cigarettes, you might be paying for a course at the community college. Having goals and an idea where you are headed gives you the motivation to think more about your spending and savings. This is what financial planning is all about. You are the steward of your ship, so start learning now—either on a self-taught basis or through the help of a financial planner.

FIVE THINGS THAT KEEP YOU POOR

What happens to all those millions of dollars made by the average American over the course of his lifetime? The reality is that most people literally live paycheck to paycheck. They know it's important to save, but they "need" things today. They allow impulse buying and the intense demands on their money to take over. While it's nice to buy

Most people literally live paycheck to paycheck. They know it's important to save, but they "need" things today.

a new bike or the latest exercise gadget, they know there are other, better places to put those spare dollars. They are pulled in a million directions at the same time: mortgage payments, car payments, school expenses, food, utilities, bills, bills, bills. There's no planning going on, so money seems to just disappear. That's why most people are devastated by the unexpected emergency or by the loss of their job. It doesn't have to be that way! A few simple principles and a little discipline can change everything.

Five Things That Keep You Poor

Lack of understanding about how money works

No financial goals

No financial plan

Overpaying for basic items

Procrastination or inactivity about changing your present situation

If you see yourself in this list, you're not alone. Most of America is also there. When you learn to overcome these mistakes, you'll be on your way to a more secure future. Why do many people fail? They don't believe in themselves! **The most important thing anyone can do to solve her personal financial challenge is to believe that a solution is possible.** Many people don't make the effort—they're trapped in the maze of not enough time and too much work. But that's just not true.

Do one or more of the following excuses apply to you?

1. *You don't think you have enough money to manage.* Either you have more money than month (you already have learned how to save) or more month than money (not enough money to pay all the bills at the end of the month). Everyone can find ways to free up some money. **There is no reason not to begin to manage your money, no matter how little you are earning!**
2. *You don't think you have the time . . .* after all, books on money management can be three inches thick. It

takes too much time to read when you are busy running through life balancing the demands of work, family, and recreation. Wrong! The only way to create time is to find the time to learn about wealth.

3. *You don't think you have the knowledge and don't know where to get it.* Many people think the rich know something they themselves can never learn. They think the techniques and methods that trained advisors dole out for hefty fees are simply not available to someone making $20,000 a year. Would you believe there are a lot of cheeseball seminars charging more than $5,000 for information that is just a joke? **The truth is that the same money management principles and techniques that the wealthy use are available to everyone.** *Frugality* is one of the big ones. The reason people who have personal money managers do well is simply because those money managers know and apply the basic rules of how money works. *They know the keys to gaining maximum value for the minimum price.*

FOUR KEYS TO BUILDING WEALTH

None of us wants to face the basic rules of managing money.

Rule 1: *You can't have everything.* You have to make conscious decisions and choices about your purchases.

Rule 2: *Distinguish between "wants" and "needs."* Do you need a new car? Or do you just want a new car? Do you need a bigger house, or is it a luxury you'd like to have? It's easy to convince yourself that "wants" are really necessities, but an important part of the budgeting process is learning to separate the two. If you're working toward the security you need, you may have to postpone some of your wants for a while—at least at the beginning. Ever know someone who seemed to have limitless money, yet, when tough times hit, were financially ruined almost overnight? These are people who focus exclusively on their "wants," spending all their money (and all their credit) on luxury and enjoyment—but ignoring their need for savings and a healthy balance sheet. They leverage their future for a present of fun and end up paying a dreadful price.

Rule 3: *Procrastination is the biggest dream-killer of all.* The most important part of your financial plan is getting started. Nothing happens until you take action. Don't worry if you can't do everything at once! It's amazing what you can do after you begin moving. Every single thing you do toward building for your future will pay off. Don't become discouraged. Keep moving forward and ultimately you'll make it. And it's okay to start small. Just remember, any start is a good start!

Rule 4: *The First Step to Future Financial Security: Pay Yourself First.* Everyone intends to build financial security. In reality, many people are doing little or nothing to reach their financial goals. According to statistics, Americans save less than citizens of virtually any other major country. Strangely enough, the first step toward financial security isn't more money. The first step is putting yourself at the head of the line. This means putting your family's future ahead of the landlord, the electric company, and all the other demands on your money. Paying yourself first is good common sense. Before anyone else gets a claim to your money, pay yourself by putting a set amount aside in a savings or investment account. A standard rule of thumb is to save 10% of your income. Every time you get a raise, adjust your savings amount up to 10% of your new income. If you can save more, that's even better, but 10% will get you going in the right direction.

> The most important part of your financial plan is getting started.

THE POWER OF TIME

Someone once said that life gives you only two things: opportunity and time. Time is, indeed, one of life's most precious gifts. Except for unforeseen tragedies, most people will have many years on this planet. That amount of time can literally work financial miracles—time may be the most underrated commodity in a financial game plan! It can overcome a million shortcomings: a modest income, a modest rate of return, and even poor habits. If you have time, even a disastrous financial situation can be made right. **Time, combined with two other important elements—rate of return and consistency—is a powerful key to achieving financial security.**

Take a simple example. Suppose your parents deposited $1,000 on the day you were born. Assuming a modest 6% rate of return, that $1,000 would become $44,000 by the time you reached age 65—without your ever having added another penny! (Einstein once said that compounding interest is an amazing principle!)

The biggest financial mistake most people make is assuming they don't have any money to save. Time can also be the answer to that problem. The truth is, almost everyone can find some way to save. It doesn't take much. What if you could save just $5 a week, beginning at age 25 until your retirement? Within a year, you'd have more than $260—and that amount would just keep growing! It's never too late to start, but you have to be consistent. What if you could afford to save more? That brings us to another key factor influencing the growth of your money: the dollar amount. *The more you manage to save weekly, the more effectively time can work its magic.*

Savings and time and consistency will make your financial engine grow!

CHAPTER TWELVE SUMMARY

You will be amazed at how secure your future will become if you discipline yourself. Save at least 10% of your income each paycheck. The compounding of this money over time will give you a secure retirement.

Frugality and simpler living means the possibility of that financially secure future.

There is a solution to all your financial challenges. Believe it, and work on those solutions and goal-setting until it all becomes a reality.

Save 10% of your income. Every time you get a raise, adjust your savings amount up to 10% of your new income.

The secret to financial security is putting your family's future ahead of paying anything else (with the exception of high-interest consumer debt).

Time, combined with the consistency of your putting money aside, is the key to achieving financial security.

CHAPTER TWELVE
BLUEPRINT FOR LIFE
WORKSTATION

1. Pretend you are 75 years old. Create a budget for your needs.
2. With that estimate of financial need at age 75, determine how much money needs to be in the bank (earning 8% annual interest) to meet that standard of living.
3. Circle the investments or cash-flow solutions to meet that figure:

Stocks	Mutual Funds	Social Security
Rental Property	Savings	Mortgages Held
Employment	Pension	

4. What is the first step toward financial security?
5. What are two powerful steps to financial security?
6. If you save 10% of $30,000/year income for 30 years, at an 8% annual return, how much money will you have?
7. Go to an educational book store and purchase a financial workbook. This will give you the answers to the above financial questions—and others you should be thinking of.

13
CREATING A FINANCIAL BASE

There's something I like to call *The Tycoon Mentality*—you want more in a big way! There's only one other financial method of thinking. It's what I call the *consumer mentality*, which describes the vast majority of people in the U.S. This is not a group you want to join! Three percent of the people in this country control all the money. The other 97% are consumers buying and watching televisions and spending money on "butter" items. *If you want to succeed, you must begin today to think like a tycoon. A tycoon is someone with ambition and drive. She places herself in a position of importance.*

Tycoons invariably bring forth to the world a product or service that people want—a "something" for which people will willingly part with their money.

THE FINANCIAL MENTALITY

People with tycoon mentalities have more fun than the average "wage slave" at her routine job. And they find creative ways to make money from the consumer mentality adopted by the rest. When you (as a tycoon) see an opportunity, it's like a bulb suddenly being lit in your head. Don't worry about the consumer—he's happy to buy what you're selling. It's his way of life. **You must believe in your** *tycoon mentality* *if you want to rise above the financial oppression surrounding most of society.*

Some individuals can never be tycoons because they thwart themselves right from the start. They make excuses like, "I'm not smart enough," "I don't have enough money to start," or "I have no business sense." These are all copouts! With the right attitude, anyone can become a tycoon.

You may not think you are smart . . . don't worry about it! Most entrepreneurs/tycoons have only average I.Q.s. The "straight-A" students go on to become attorneys and accountants. *They end up taking care of the entrepreneurs of the world.* (The other "A" students are employed in teaching jobs or in the corporate arena.)

It is possible to begin with little or no money and still become financially successful. Most of today's millionaires were poor at their beginnings. As for having no business sense, well, this book is a start and will probably teach you more about basic finance than all the academic years you spent in school. Whatever financial acumen you lacked before today, you'll have tomorrow—so relax.

HOW TYCOONS SUCCEED

A tycoon on the way up is always able to motivate herself, her family, her possible staff, and any possible partners who work with her. Once you start buying property or running a company, you'll find the importance of being enthusiastic and loyal to your staff. It's important because, as your fortunes grow, a loyal staff becomes essential. Some people respond best to praise and titles, others to money. You must be creative and generous with "bonuses" if you want to keep the best staff. You'll find that, although you're starting out small, you're going to end up with a lot—and you'll need help.

On the home front, the same rules apply. Give recognition and daily compliments to the people around you. You'll be amazed at what people will lay on your doorstep simply because they like you. Your happy, enthusiastic attitude will draw them to you. For example, at a meeting, a colleague might come up to you and say, "I really like you

Tycoons invariably bring forth to the world a product or service that people want—a "something" for which people will willingly part with their money.

and I know that you're looking for a good deal. Let me share some information with you." When you give your positive attitude in a genuine manner, it will be received and returned. Your life will be richer if those you live and work with know that you like them.

The tycoon mentality is nothing more than the way you look at things. You have to make a complete break with your old attitudes about money. After all, you're no longer looking at spending every last dollar on material things. Once you've caught up and paid off some principal debt, most of your money should go toward pure solid investment.

The tycoon mentality will accomplish your goals for you. Here's an example: If someone were to give you $200 today, what would you do with it? Would you take the girls out for some cocktails? Would you go out and buy a new watch? How about a night on the town? Now try $20,000. What would you spend it on? A terrific car? A trip around the world? Now suppose someone gave you $2,000,000. What would you do with it? Think about it. Would you go give it to the Trust Department at the bank? Answering these questions is where having that tycoon mentality comes in. A tycoon is going to think of what products can be produced with that money, what services can be provided, and what needs can be filled. Thoughts like those will help make you a millionaire!

One thing you have to understand about tycoons—they act a lot differently than "regular" people. *They don't have unnecessary conversations.* They don't waste time sitting around shooting the breeze for hours on end. If you notice, some "regular" people talk about other people while others talk about current events. Tycoons talk about creativity, making things happen, financial enterprises, and "what ifs." They don't gossip or make idle conversation.

Also, the tycoon doesn't brag about herself. She doesn't need to toot her own horn—her success shouts for her. If you look around, most people just move along in life. The tycoon, easy to spot, is busy asking for things. "How much do you want for that square? "How much do you want for that house?" "How much do you want for that business?" If you were to make a very low offer on a specific property

Persistence

and

enthusiasm

are a tycoon's

most

important

tool.

to eight different property owners, you'd be amazed—one person out of the eight would make a deal with you! That's where you make your money.

PERSISTENCE AND ENTHUSIASM

Persistence and enthusiasm are a tycoon's most important tools. You can only learn how to do something right by first doing it wrong. You must look at all your mistakes with a sense of humor. See them as "educational experiences" that will someday do you some good. I've mentioned before that I lost $700,000 in an investment deal. I call that my "Harvard Education." Never again will I part with money via that same mistake! Every failure is a valuable learning experience—problems are just exciting challenges. Pay no attention to negative people! You're going to find that as you start to grow and acquire wealth, people will try and knock you down. Even your own family members and friends might start holding you back. You must stay focused! Remember—*your greatest successes will come because you never quit.*

YOU CAN NEVER HAVE TOO MUCH INFORMATION

A tycoon is always alert for changes in the economy. She always keeps up with the latest financial news and understands what the financial markets are doing. You're not going to be able to do this at first. If you concentrate all your reading habits purely on business improvement and understanding, however, you'll soon start to get a feel for the water. You'll understand the changes in the financial arena and, once you've built up a base, you will know how to take advantage of those changes.

During recent years, the stock market has been on a bull run. If you knew what you were doing, you could have taken advantage of this run. A tycoon always maintains a historical perspective on things, however. She knows that after a boom comes a bust, and that everything runs in

> Every failure is a valuable learning experience. Pay no attention to negative people!

cycles. You ride high when the cycle is going, but you also watch your backside for the time when the cycle will stop.

Here's an example from real estate. The last couple of really bad cycles I remember were in '73 and '74—real estate was a bust. In '79, however, the real estate cycle moved up. People doubled and tripled their money on any real estate investment. Then from '80 to '83 the market dropped and you couldn't give property away. Next, from '84 to '89 or the first half of '90, the market was on a tear and price appreciation was in double digit gains again. After '91 and the Persian Gulf War, the real estate market stopped. A lot of values were lost. In '94, '95, '96 and '97, the real estate markets and the financial markets went on a bull run once again. In '98 and '99, they were really roaring.

So what's next? Understand that there are opportunities in all markets, and all cycles. From 1986 to 1994, the commercial real estate market in this country was flat on its back. If you had the financial wherewithal, understanding, and experience to take advantage of the situation, you could have easily become a multimillionaire many times over. Even in a down market people were willing to sell at 50% of today's value. The point is that you have to understand your investments. You have to be ready to take advantage. You have to put yourself in the position to both understand and be ready to pounce!

THE TYCOON LEAVES THE SLAVE MENTALITY

Becoming a true tycoon starts with your mindset. While you may acquire wealth using the methods listed in this book, if you want to become a true tycoon you must be in charge of your fate. Only an entrepreneur or an independent contractor has that type of control over her time and production. In these positions you are compensated in direct proportion to your output—the more you work, the more you will earn. Most people have a 9-to-5 job. They may feel secure while they're on the job, but they're never really safe because they are not in control of their own destinies. How could anyone know that the easy-going job

If you concentrate all your reading habits purely on business improvement and understanding, you'll soon get a feel for the water.

they currently have won't soon be taken over by a machine or a computer? Or a corporate takeover? Suppose the company hires the boss' daughter and she wants that job?

Even if you have what you think is a secure 9-to-5 job, you still have time to do something on the side. If you want to become any type of tycoon, you've got to get your mental mindframe working for you. This is the only way you can ever achieve financial security. When you feel financially secure, you won't worry about being laid off (because you're the one who probably owns the company). Now, you might say that social security and your pension fund are always there. Don't think about pensions and social security as being fail-safe! As far as social security is concerned, you should really consider it "social insecurity." I personally doubt that it will be available by the time you and I retire. After inflation, your dollar is really worth about half of what you thought it was. Who knows how much you will really be able to purchase if you collect only your social insecurity at retirement?

WHEN IS A DEAL A DEAL?

You're going to be purchasing a lot of things during your lifetime. You might as well start by trying to get the best deal for yourself because you, literally, save money when you do. Here are some basic concepts about making a "deal," using real estate as an example. You never really know when you have a "good deal" unless you can determine its value against the real market (what other people would pay with no pressures on either party to buy or sell). Here is my evaluation on buying real estate or real property. This measurement can be used for most things you buy.

Understand that there are opportunities in all markets and in all cycles.

_____Stole it
_____Great Buy
_____Good Buy

_____Fair Market Value ◄——— above or below this point shows whether you have lost or gained

_____Top Dollar
_____Overpaid
_____Ripped Off

You can pay top dollar for a property and still make out well financially if the market forces are pushing prices upward. That is because time is on your side and this is an investment. Obviously, when buying, you will want to pay no more than fair market value. The valuation process listed on the previous page comes from knowing the market. You must educate yourself about the items you're buying—be it a car, house, or even ceiling fans. You make money by knowing about comparables (comparables are similar to sales that have already happened). Let's say you are buying a '65 Mustang and the seller wants $4,000—and you know of four other cars in similar condition that sold for $5,000. In this case you know you will be getting a good buy. You'll still want to use some negotiating techniques to work your price, but you know you will be getting a good deal since you could (based on comparables) resell the car immediately and make a profit.

When you are

negotiating a

sale, always

take your time.

When negotiating a sale, always take your time. If it is meant to be it will happen—but it should only be on your terms. If you buy something blind you're bound to lose. I overpaid $20,000 on the first house I bought. I hadn't done the research and lost all the way around. Don't learn the hard way! Your money has been earned by hard work, so you've got to protect it. No one else will. Don't buy unless you know you're getting at least a fair deal.

HOW TO LOSE YOUR MONEY

It's easier to lose money than it is to make it. I was once fat and happy, then I got stupid, and made investments out of sync with my basic investing principles. A quick $700,000 loss brought me back to my senses. After that, I once again became a lean, mean, and focused machine. In another venture, a so-called "hot stock pick," I lost $48,000 in a week. I obviously had not learned as much as I had thought! Learn by what you're reading now. Stick to this advice. Listed below are some situations which you should never, ever, become involved with. Steer clear of these and, hopefully, you won't ever have to experience the unpleasant loss of your hard-earned money.

HOW TO WIN

Michael O.'s Rules of the Game

1. Never be the only investor with money in the deal if there are other partners.
2. If you give money to someone for something, consider it gone. For example, if you give money to someone for them to make an investment and they're in control of it, it's gone.
3. Don't invest in something outside of your area of knowledge and expertise.
4. Prefer the investment to be asset-based or secured by an asset.
5. Don't loan money to family, friends, and people. That should cover everyone.
6. Multiply by three any estimate you make for a financial guesstimate as to the costs of your investment. This applies to starting a new enterprise.
7. Keep your money matters to yourself! (Exposure brings out the sharks.)
8. If you have a project or an idea, money is easier to get from other people. Leave yours alone.
9. Don't invest in the business unless you are in the middle of it.
10. Stay in control, if it's a business, or your money is gone.
11. If you have any doubt, just say no, no, no! This protects your money.

HEDGING

When you start to accumulate savings, it's a good idea to have a mix of assets. This allows growth and gives protection against market cycles, be they boom or bust. An example of this hedging would be dividing your assets and putting 20% into savings, 25% into stocks, 50% into real estate, and 5% into retirement pension plans. You can change the percentages any way you want—this type of mix is called "hedging." Finding a good mix helps when the bull (a good market) is running. As an example, for the past eight years, the stock market has been on a tear. If you hadn't participated in stocks during this period, you'd have lost out on one of the greatest runs of all time. Markets change without your realizing it, however, and you never know how long the change will last until it's over. That is why it's best to have diversification—an assortment of investments in different financial markets.

SNAKE OIL SALESMEN

What else can I call all those *get rich quick* people who flaunt their lifestyles and tell you that "you can, too?" (Since you're reading this book, you've probably wondered whether I fit into this category. I don't. You can't get rich quick, and, if you did, you would have little appreciation for it.) Most financial gurus do have some degree of success, but not the type of quick success they're trying to portray. As far as the "no money down" guys go, you can learn something from them. They have, at some point, really bought a piece of property with little or no money down. It is unusual, however, to be able to constantly do this— otherwise, why would they be letting you in on their secret? If their secrets were as good as they say, they wouldn't be sharing them with you. They're making more money selling their tapes, books, and snake oil than with any of their investments.

There is no true get-rich-quick opportunity unless you win the lottery. It takes years to understand the creativity and inner-workings of the financial concepts these guys are hawking. *It takes great determination and persistence— something they always forget to tell you.*

I know you're hungry for good information. That is why you are reading this book. The most reputable and reliable information is usually found in bookstores. Financial seminars can also be very helpful—but only word-of-mouth regarding these sources can attest to their credibility. All knowledge is good but it must be filtered. The "cheeseballs" don't tell you about the real guts it takes for finan-

When you start to accumulate savings, it's a good idea to have a mix of assets.

cial improvement. They fail to tell you that it takes time—lots of time and many, many years of experience.

When you put time and experience together, it's the start of making things happen for you. Then you have to add a lot of persistence, low offers, patience, and more persistence—all the while educating yourself financially. Then, and only then, you'll be on your own. What these snake oil salesmen say can be done, *is* possible . . . but not with the ease they suggest. It's as if someone is telling you, "Oh, it's easy to have a baby." Let an experienced mother tell you how *easy* it is—from the morning sickness to the last of the contractions. Yes, it can be done, but it's never easy.

YOUR ECONOMIC ENGINE

You are the economic engine. You are the ultimate power pulling the wagon. If you're depending on someone else for financial support, take their money and put it away *unspent.* You have to realize that at the end of the day you can depend only on yourself. *Your economic engine is your career or how you produce income.* This engine needs to be adjusted annually because you want to increase your income. And changes will happen to this engine if you want to improve your financial motor power. Ask your boss what you can do to earn more income. Ask your employer how you can improve to meet that goal. Can you be rewarded more (get a raise) and how can you produce more? Let them know what you're thinking and that you want to improve!

Here's an example: an educator with a teaching degree continued her education by obtaining a master's degree. This allowed her to both earn more income and have a higher value. If she were to go on and pursue a doctorate, she could find greater, higher paying, opportunities. She could, for example, write a book—making her "an authority" as well as giving her additional income. Paid speaking engagements at seminars and training sessions, boards and affiliations—all this came from a single teacher trying to increase her value.

The most reputable and reliable information is usually found in bookstores.

Your economic engine is fueled by your income production or growth toward that goal. Every year, your value, be it in the form of education or an increased bottom line, must grow. While you're learning to live on a percentage of your income, the money you are setting aside should be considered "seed" money to create other forms of income (rentals, stock dividends, interest, etc.). If year after year you stay level and have no growth, you're falling behind. Inflation takes care of that. Growth is where it's at.

It takes persistence, hard work, and time to gain that precious tycoon mentality. Start your journey now!

CHAPTER THIRTEEN SUMMARY

The financial mentality is an attitude that is fueled by your desire and hunger. You have to believe you will be one of the 3% who control the money.

It doesn't take a great intellect or good grades to become financially successful. It takes will, experience, and the tycoon mentality. A tycoon is positive and will motivate herself and those around her. She looks for opportunities and is always asking people if they would like to sell their "gun" assets. A tycoon understands that there are opportunities in all economic cycles.

Becoming financially prosperous is the result of purchasing assets at *better* than "fair market value."

It is easier to lose money than to make money.

Be leery of snake oil salesmen touting the latest get-rich-quick scheme. There is no way to get rich quick. It's similar to a movie star's becoming successful "overnight." The public thinks it happened in an instant with a certain hit. In reality, that actor has had 10 years of mind-boggling rejection, trials, and challenges.

You are the ultimate economic engine that pushes your life-train. Continue to work at it. You'll do fine—just not overnight.

CHAPTER THIRTEEN
BLUEPRINT FOR LIFE
WORKSTATION

1. Describe the tycoon mentality.
2. What would you do with a gift of $200,000?
   Be specific.
3. Describe the two adjectives that are the tycoon's tools.
4. When is a deal a "deal"?
5. List five ways you can lose your money in an
   investment.

   a.

   b.

   c.

   d.

   e.

6. How do the "get-rich-quick, multigillionaire
   infomercial people" make all their wealth?

   a. Selling junk to you?

   b. Doing what they are selling?

7. Can you make a fortune easily?
8. Name three ways you can improve your economic
   engine.

   a.

   b.

   c.

HOW TO BUY REAL ESTATE

Building and holding on to real estate, you can create (through time) tens of thousands of dollars of additional income each year.

Homeownership—why? Because it is a secret savings account. It is an asset that builds equity (money) over time. I have learned in my long real estate career that even a bad real estate investment in time reverses itself.

In my career, I've witnessed a poor widow or couple who (although not financially savvy nor income productive) had—after all those years—a small fortune in the house they were living in. Through time, your house pays itself off and usually appreciates in value. (This only works when you don't pull out equity.)

When I was a young broker in real estate, I was able to create a yearly commission income of $75,000–$100,000. But as a private individual versed in the game of real estate, I could easily make between $100,000 and $300,000 part-time per year in additional income. Building and holding on to real estate, you can create (through time) tens of thousands of dollars of additional income each year.

Real estate only discriminates if you are not knowledgeable. For those who have the work ethic and desire, it can create a tremendous cash flow.

Real estate is the secret of the "have-nots" who want to be the "haves." It's an excellent vehicle to financial prosperity, allowing for leverage and, over longer periods of time, stability. For tycoons, real estate can become an amazing game of leapfrog. It allows you to own hundreds of thousands of dollars worth of equity while having put very little down. One of your written goals should be to educate yourself about this financial vehicle. Understanding real estate and how to leverage it will speed your growth toward success.

TEN WAYS TO BUY REAL ESTATE

Here are 10 basic ways to purchase real estate. Some are more creative, but all will work. You should consider buying a home. With today's interest rates, renting is more expensive than owning! Remember: leverage allows you to use other people's money!

1. *Seller-Held Financing*

Have the Seller hold as much of the mortgage as possible. Make sure your payments don't exceed your comfort level! Sellers will privately hold your mortgage if they own their properties free and clear. Both of you win because they get a higher rate of return than what they'd get by putting their equity into a savings account. And you don't have paperwork, up-front fees, and rigid qualification standards that banks and mortgage companies demand. Private mortgage holders sometimes charge a slightly higher interest rate than what you'd pay if you went to a bank but, if you can afford the payments, it is still a wonderful option.

Suggestion: If you have been a tenant for a long time, ask your landlord if he will sell the property to you and hold the mortgage. Tell the landlord that if he does this, he won't be responsible for the property's upkeep anymore. If you've established an excellent credit and payment history (meaning that you've paid every month on time) he might consider it—and with 100% financing. Anything is possible; you just have to ask. This deal is difficult to find but is a real diamond when you do. Remember: Don't pay more than the market value of the property. To find out the market value, get an appraisal. Be prepared, however, to pay top dollar for the property. This type of financing is worth paying a little extra if you think you would have trouble making the initial down payment.

Real estate is the secret of the "have-nots" who want to be the "haves."

2. *Contract for Deed*

This option is usually good if you have a bad credit history. In this case, the Seller usually owns a problem house that has been on the market for awhile. You've had trouble buying—and he's had trouble selling—a match made in heaven. A Contract for Deed shows the selling price, lists an interest rate, and leaves a balance that will be payable in the future. The advantage to the Seller is that the property is out of his hands, including any repairs and landlord responsibilities. The Seller can still write off the interest he can collect for his taxes, just as you are allowed to write off the interest you are paying him. You may also file for a Homestead Exemption, if your state has one.

To keep yourself safe, you must have in your contract words that state it is a recordable contract. This type of sale can also be done with little or no money down. There are no closing costs until you actually close on the property (when you make the "balloon" payment). Meanwhile, you are assured that if you make the payments, the principal will be paid down. The deed (title) to the property transfers only when you pay the "balloon" or pay the entire principal amount—they are the same. Be sure to use an attorney to draft the contract. You and the Seller can split the costs of that attorney's expertise.

Also, be sure you purchase title insurance (you only want a good, clear, marketable title with any property). Don't pay or contract for more than the property is worth; make the deal subject to an appraisal. This transaction is sometimes known as a *land contract*. **Remember: only buy property you think will significantly increase in value.** When the "balloon" comes due, you have the option of either refinancing or selling the contract for a profit.

3. *The Good Old-Fashioned Lease-Purchase*

A lease-purchase gives you the right to purchase the property you are leasing (renting) at a predetermined figure. When writing this agreement, the contract states a specific time in the future by which the contract must be completed. This is not to be confused with an "option to purchase." An "option to purchase" gives you the right to purchase by a certain time *without penalty* if you decide to exercise this option.

Approach your landlord and ask if he is willing to sell you the property you are living in. Lock in a competitive price and try to negotiate. For example: Will the landlord pay mortgage points? Will the landlord hold the first or second mortgage? If you're looking for a down payment, ask the seller to credit you a certain amount of your rent each month which will go toward your down payment and closing costs. After a time, this "credit" will build toward your total down payment and closing costs, so that you will not need any cash when you close the contract and purchase the property. Remember—you can educate yourself as to the minimum amount of money you will need by getting a "good faith" estimate from a mortgage broker (this is a free service).

Having the seller hold the mortgage is the least expensive way for you to purchase. Explain to the landlord that he'll never have to fix another repair and that he'll still receive his monthly cash flow. If you've made all your rental payments on time in the past and have shown that you are a good credit risk, they may hold the first or second mortgage.

Always make sure you are getting the best price by finding comparables or getting an appraisal. And always get title insurance to make sure the title is "good" and "warranted." This is probably the easiest way to purchase a property. Some points you should include in this contract are: (1) the contract price; (2) the closing date (it can be years from now if you wish); (3) if some or all of your lease payments (rent) can go toward reducing your eventual down payment; and (4) if some of the costs of this transaction can be paid by the Seller.

Emphasize to the Seller the regular money he will be receiving from you and how good a tenant you have been. Remember: In five years that property could be worth quite a bit more, but you will only have to pay the Seller the price you contract for now. See an attorney for your final paperwork but negotiate the deal yourself.

4. Co-Equity

What a deal! With this form of purchasing, you do not need any down payment. You find a deal and verify it's a "deal." Find an investor who makes the initial down payment (usually a relative or close friend). You will be responsible for making the payments and maintaining the property. After a specified period of time, say five to 10 years (possibly 15), you sell the property and split the profits. You water it and it grows. This allows someone to help you and, at the same time, invest in a money-making venture.

Have an attorney draw up your arrangement. Make a good purchase, discuss your arrangement, and **make sure it's in writing.** Let the legal beagle look over your paperwork to protect your interests. This is an excellent way to purchase property if you have bad credit and no money. It's a great way for a family member to participate in an investment while you carry the debt service. You do, however, need to be able to make the monthly payments. Further note—put in a clause with your co-equity partner saying that you can "buy them out" at a predetermined rate of return. Make this rate one they will be happy with.

5. *Their Money—Your Credit*

In this case you have a relative or friend who wants to help you, but doesn't want to make the down payment a "gift." This plan only works if you have a good credit history. Talk to your relative or friend and make a payment plan stating that you will pay him back with interest. Offer him a Promissory Note for his financial seed money. You will be the one who will have to "qualify" for the loan (unlike the co-equity) and you are the one who will make the payments both to the mortgage company and to the relative or friend. Who benefits? You own the property 100% and they get an investment with a return! Make sure the property is a "good buy." Don't just buy for the sake of buying! Work through a mortgage broker to understand what is needed when you receive gifts from any relatives. This is an excellent way to buy with no money—but with your own credit. You must have established income (history) to qualify for this type of loan.

6. *Government Financing Plans*

Federal Housing Administration and Veterans Administration acquisition loans allow you to buy a property with sometimes as little as 1% down! These federal programs are designed to assist people who have minimal cash yet are capable of qualifying (they can make the payments). There are many different government programs for FHA and VA. You can learn about them through a mortgage broker or by telephoning an agency such as the Federal Housing Administration. (Put learning about these programs on your financial goal list of "things to do.")

7. *State, County, and Municipality Programs*

Our good-natured society provides assistance in many, many ways. There are down-payment assistance programs for community-built project homes. Find out about them and get on the list! Dig and dig until you find something. You'll be amazed at the number of opportunities available with little or no money or with county, federal, or city assistance. Special buy-down programs for interest rates make owning a home a reality for many people. (Many of these programs lower the interest rate you will have to pay.) Almost all of these programs require you to have credit and qualifying ability, however. Start by asking a couple of mortgage brokers where to go and then call the appropriate government agencies. (Once again, it pays to have good credit!)

8. *Assuming a Balance*

Some people literally do not want their property anymore. They may also owe more on the mortgage than what their property is worth. (Be sure to get an appraisal to protect yourself from overpaying.) Being able to qualify for a loan really pays off here. It's possible that the Seller is so motivated, he'll pay the assumption costs for the mortgage! He wants his name off the mortgage and the note. You would be shocked at how many opportunities exist out there in this category!

The Seller might also be willing to hold a second mortgage or a note, making this a 100% financed transaction— with no money down from you! If there is a gap between the mortgage balance and the purchase price, the Seller might be willing to hold a second mortgage. Just make sure that you're not paying too much. Credit is king once again, because no one will consider selling to you with this type of purchase unless you have an excellent credit history.

9. *Foreclosures*

Buying a foreclosed property is a lot trickier than it seems. It is very easy to pay too much. Why else would someone just let it go when selling it could have saved their credit? I liken foreclosures to panning for gold. You have to sift through the pebbles and the dirt to find the flecks of value, eventually finding a nugget here or there. It takes quite a bit of work and a lot of persistence. FHA and VA foreclosures also take a lot of persistence and luck. In most cases, you'll be submitting sealed bids. If you are interested, contact large banks and have their REO (real estate owned) department send you a list of their foreclosures. (The bank might look into doing the financing if your credit is good!)

Unfortunately, most foreclosures are in undesirable areas and, personally, it's not my cup of tea. I like location-driven properties in good school districts. Some people, however, have made money on foreclosures. *Remember: You must pay lower than fair market value if you hope to make anything on this type of purchase.* Many times you do not know the true condition of the property and it is easy to get burned! Once again, you must have a good credit history to qualify for the mortgage you will need.

10. *The Conventional Method*

This is how most people purchase a property. Your down payment (usually 5% or more) and your qualifying for a mortgage (this is why you've worked toward a good credit history) will get you the deal. First, you must negotiate with the Seller for the best price. Try to get the Seller to pay all or some of your financing costs (this will lower the amount of cash you need at closing). A good broker can help you, both with negotiating the sale and with obtaining financing.

WHERE TO LOOK

Before you even begin to look for a property, talk to a good mortgage broker. Have her look at your credit history and pre-qualify you. Get her to do a good faith written estimate of how much it will cost for the loan. Use your

---

Unfortunately, most foreclosures are in undesirable areas. You must pay lower than "fair market value" if you hope to make anything on this type of purchase.

top qualifying numbers (sale price) and only look for properties costing less than this number. If you do this the other way, by looking for properties priced at more than what you qualify for thinking that someone will come down on their sales price, you're only fooling yourself. *If you have the total cash saved and can qualify for an amount that equals your top purchasing price, you'll be able to pick and choose from the whole market up to your price range.* Using conventional financing, every property is available to you. The other financing options previously mentioned have limits on both inventory and selection.

TEN BASIC POINTERS ON ALL YOUR DEALS

1. You should pay for a building inspection that includes the roof, pool, plumbing, electrical appliances, mechanical, and possibly structural elements. In your contract, you could use the following generic clause:

   The Buyer shall have the right to inspect all aspects of the Property, including, but not limited to, the right to investigate the zoning affecting the Property, the physical condition of the improvements located on the Property, the environmental condition of the Property (including, but not limited to, investigating whether asbestos is located within the improvements on the Real Property), and to conduct all inspections, examinations, tests and such other investigations as the Buyer deems necessary and/or desirable, including, but not limited to, having the Property inspected by a certified building inspection and a termite inspector, for a period of ten (10) days after the Effective Date of the Contract (the "Inspection Period"). If for any reason whatsoever, in the Buyer's sole, absolute, and arbitrary discretion, the Buyer is not completely satisfied with all aspects of the Property, the Buyer shall have the right to terminate the Contract by written notice to the Seller within two (2) business days after the expiration of the Inspection Period. If the Buyer so terminates the Contract, then the Deposit shall be immediately returned to the Buyer,

Before you even begin to look for a property, talk to a good mortgage broker. Have her look at your credit history and pre-qualify you.

and thereafter each of the parties shall be released from further liability to the other.

2. Have an out clause. This gives you an unconditional out should the inspections find something wrong or should something else happen in your life and you just want out of the deal. (Perhaps you've gotten a better job in another city!) Your deposit should be 100% refundable. The previous clause can serve as an out clause, or you may opt to add the following language: *This contract is subject to the Buyer's attorney's review and acceptance.*

3. Qualify yourself through a mortgage broker before you waste your time or anyone else's—a *must first step*. This is a free service—it is also critical. Your credit report should be pulled in advance for a thorough review.

4. Have someone really knowledgeable, not your dad or your brother (unless they are more than qualified), review the contract and the deal. An attorney or good real estate broker working for you can review what you have found and how you are writing it up. It's important to have someone look at your legal wording. These words are binding! If you can't get your attorney, insert a clause that states, "This contract is subject to my attorney's review and approval." (This can get you out of the deal or change what might not be a good deal for you!)

5. Be sure you have at least a fair deal and that you're not paying too much! I overpaid by over $20,000 on my first home. Ouch! You can easily get an appraisal or make your contract subject to an appraisal. Make sure you use a good, conservative appraiser who will verify that your value is at least fair if not better.

6. You must get Title Insurance. This is the only way you will have a clear, marketable title at the end of the day of your closing.

7. Before you close, get a new survey to make sure there are no encroachments or clouds on your Title. (This usually doesn't cost much money and an ounce of pre-

vention can save you pounds of headache later.) Know your property's boundaries—you need to know what you're buying. Updating a Seller's survey is satisfactory if you know that it is newly certified. Don't take anyone else's word for it. The proof is in the Certified Title.

8. Get the Seller to provide a Seller's Disclosure. This way, you're informed in writing about problems with the property. Any real estate company should be able to provide you with a Seller's Disclosure. It is mandatory that Sellers disclose any latent defects that could affect the material value of a home. You need to know exactly what you're buying—up and above what the inspectors say.

9. Add up how much it will cost you to correct any imperfections in the property. Now, multiply this number by three—because that's really what it will cost. Another solution is to negotiate with the Seller which imperfections he is responsible for fixing. Put this in when writing your contract. For example, if you have a house that needs all new flooring, insert a clause that specifies the Seller is to replace the carpet with a carpet allowance up to x amount of dollars. The Buyer is to choose the color and the company. The company can be paid from the Seller's proceeds or the Seller's contribution can be put into an escrow account to pay the carpet company. There are many ways to work this. Get creative and see what you can do to save yourself some money!

10. **Buy right.** Realtor's fees aren't cheap and there is always the possibility of losing money (especially if you are forced to sell sooner than you anticipated). Make sure you are making a good deal for you. Realtors can provide comparable information. Today, you should be able to access comparable information yourself on the internet. Look for your county's tax assessment office's webpage.

Make sure you are making a good deal for you.

CHAPTER FOURTEEN SUMMARY

Buy Real Estate!

I highly recommend learning more about real estate so that you can make the best choices for yourself. Most people are afraid to make this type of investment. Go to seminars and read books. Real estate can easily be your most profitable investment—and home ownership builds a very strong power base. It has, literally, given me the foundation and security I enjoy today.

CHAPTER FOURTEEN BLUEPRINT FOR LIFE WORKSTATION

1. Purchase a book from the bookstore about "buying your first home" or go to the local library and pick out a book on this subject.
2. Read a second book on the same theme, by a different author.
3. Get the local daily newspaper and read the real estate classified ads every day for one month.
4. During the second month, call a mortgage broker and ask them to pre-qualify you for getting a mortgage. From that communication, discuss with that mortgage broker what it would take to purchase a home within your comfort range. Get a good faith estimate based on today's quoted rates.
5. Every day for a minimum of 90 days call all the "For Sale by Owner" ads in the newspaper and ask various questions about the properties, provided they appear in your price range or the location you want. Ask them these questions:

   a. How much are you asking?

   b. Will you hold a mortgage?

   c. Will you contract a long-term lease purchase?

d. Can you help me purchase your home with some financial assistance (such as paying some costs for obtaining a mortgage, or holding a note or a second mortgages)?

e. Will you do a Contract for Deed?

f. Which school district are you in?

g. How much do you pay in taxes?

h. What is the general condition of your home?

i. How old is the roof?

j. Are there any Seller disclosures, etc.?

Please note: Don't worry about not knowing what you're talking about and making a fool of yourself. These people have advertised their homes and have opened up their doors for everybody and anybody to call them with both stupid and valid questions about their homes. Obviously, there are many other qualifying questions that need to be asked (they can be found in the start-up books I've recommended you to read). Your purpose is to start talking and understanding the lingo. Don't worry about not knowing anything. Engaging in real estate conversation will quickly bring you up the knowledge curve.

6. Starting the second month, dedicate three to five hours each weekend to looking at assorted properties: duplexes, quadraplexes, and residential houses. Know the market in your area.

7. After your third month, contact several real estate brokers or agents in your area. Tell them you'd like to be kept in mind for problem properties. These require creative financing solutions in order to sell. You're looking for a good buy!

8. Do not purchase, contract, or make an offer for a home until you are nine months into this relentless program. Continue your calling and be patient. You'll get a good buy once you're extremely knowledgeable.

9. Purchase only after the deal has been reviewed by someone who is competent to give you representation and protect your interests (an attorney or

knowledgeable real estate broker). Confirm it is at least a "good deal" with an appraisal.

10. Read the newspaper, including all real estate articles every Saturday and Sunday. They are usually in the real estate section.

11. After three months, define *in your own words* the 10 different ways to purchase a home I have listed in this book. List these ways in your journals.

12. Inquire with local municipal, state, federal and county agencies about their financial assistance programs for first-time home buyers. The blue pages in the phone book is a good place to start. Make a call and ask whoever you get on the line where else you can call for information.

15

UNDERSTANDING INSURANCE

Don't wait for the knight in shining armor to save you. Buy insurance! There's just one catch: for insurance to protect and defend you, you have to buy it when you don't need it—if you wait until you need it, you can't get it.

This is the logic of insurance. If you're already disabled, you can't buy disability insurance. If the burglar has come and gone, you can't buy homeowner's insurance to pay for your losses. If you're seriously ill, forget about buying life insurance to protect your family. But if your life is going great, this chapter is critical. A single gap in your insurance could destroy a lifetime of sacrifice and saving—so don't give in to your inclinations and skip this chapter! *Read each word because every modern woman needs this knight in shining armor.*

WHAT TYPE OF INSURANCE DO YOU NEED?

Insurance is simply your way of passing on the financial risks to someone else should disaster strike. The amount of insurance you need depends on your age, your property, and your dependents. Here is a list of the most important kinds of insurance and how each protects you:

TYPE OF INSURANCE	YOUR PROTECTION
Health Insurance	Protects you from out-of-pocket costs for health care and large cash outflows during major illnesses.
Homeowner's Insurance	Protects you from cash outflows for replacement of your home and its contents.
Renter's Insurance	Protects you from cash outflows for replacement of personal possessions if they are stolen or damaged.
Automobile Insurance	Protects you from large cash outflows for damages resulting from an accident or from theft.
Disability Insurance	Replaces part or most of your income should you become unable to work.
Life Insurance	Protects those dependent on you by replacing part or most of your income after you die.

Insurance is your way of passing on the financial risks to someone else should disaster strike.

A woman needs insurance for the same reasons a man does—to protect her wealth, her health, and her heirs. You have many options. Before you choose the policy that's right for you, take a few minutes for the following little *Insurance 101 mini-course.*

HEALTH INSURANCE

Choose your health insurance company as if you were making the choice for a lifetime. If you or anyone in your family becomes ill, you will be relieved that you spent the time shopping for a quality company rather than the one with the lowest premium.

Conventional Health Insurance

Most health insurance policies offer three basic types of coverage: medical/surgical insurance, hospitalization insurance, and major medical insurance. The basic medical/surgical insurance covers visits to or from a doctor for an illness, prescription medicines, and specialized tests. Most have a front-end deductible (you have to pay everything up until a certain amount of money has been paid).

The second part of most health plans is hospitalization benefits. This part of the plan pays for all or part of in-hospital procedures, testing, and surgery. Most require you to pick up 10 to 20% of the cost up to a maximum of, perhaps, $3,000. After you have paid that $3,000, the insurance picks up 100% of the rest for that calendar year—until you reach your policy limit.

When the regular hospitalization runs out, the major medical portion of the insurance begins to pay. That's why it's smart to check the top limit your plan will pay. A limit of $100,000 may sound like a lot, but can easily be exceeded if you or someone in your family has a lingering illness.

HMOs

The other option is to join a health maintenance organization. More than 40 million Americans are currently covered by HMOs. Here's how they work. When you join, you pay a yearly premium (typically around $2,500 for a family of four—much less than the usual $4,000 cost for the standard medical/surgical policy for the same family). You usually receive coverage for all medical visits. You do not have any deductibles or claim forms, and you do not have to wait for reimbursements for out-of-pocket costs (many conventional insurance plans make you pay first and then reimburse you!).

There is a trade-off for these advantages, however. You must see your HMO doctor first every time (there is usually a "gatekeeper" primary care doctor who decides whether you get to see a specialist . . . and when) and you must use a hospital designated by the HMO. When evaluating an HMO, the facilities should be convenient, the list of doctors extensive, and the procedures allowable (the ones they are willing to pay for) should be generous.

When evaluating an HMO, the facilities should be convenient, the list of doctors extensive, and the procedures allowable (the ones they are willing to pay for) should be generous.

HOMEOWNER'S INSURANCE

There is tremendous variation between types of coverage when shopping for homeowner's insurance. First, make sure the policy you sign says that you have purchased "replacement value" coverage on your home and its contents rather than "actual cash-value." Replacement value will cover the actual cost of replacing your home or contents. "Actual cash-value" subtracts depreciation from the amount you're given to replace your home and belongings. In other words, you would not be given all the money needed to replace that damaged item. You would only be given what the insurance company thinks the damaged item was worth. The amount you need to insure (the cost of replacing your house and its contents) should be refigured every year when the policy is renewed. This is especially true if you've increased the value of your home or contents with additions or improvements.

AUTOMOBILE INSURANCE

Most states require car owners to have some form of auto insurance. Your best advice is to read your current policy carefully and ask questions about coverages you don't understand. There are six basic types of coverage:

- *Bodily injury liability*—pays claims and legal defense as a result of injuries to pedestrians, people riding in other cars, and people in your car. It also covers you and your family when you are driving someone else's car with permission and usually covers anyone driving your car with permission.
- *Medical payments insurance*—pays medical and funeral expenses resulting from injuries to you, your resident family members, and guests in your car regardless of who is at fault.
- *Uninsured motorist coverage*—pays for your injuries if you're hit by another motorist who doesn't have insurance.

- *Property damage liability*—pays claims if your car damages the property of others.
- *Collision insurance*—pays for the damage to your car if it rolls over or collides with another vehicle or object.
- *Comprehensive insurance*—covers losses from theft or other damage from various forces such as fire, vandalism, or weather conditions.

The premium you pay depends on where you live, your age, your sex, your driving record, and the deductible amount (how much you are willing to pay before the insurance pays anything).

DISABILITY INSURANCE

Most people recognize that they need health insurance, auto insurance, life insurance, and homeowner's insurance. But many forget about income replacement or *disability insurance*. **Disability insurance is the one insurance that protects your way of living.** If you became sick or hurt, how long would it take to go through your savings without any income? More homes are foreclosed upon (the people can no longer make the mortgage payments) because of a disability than for any other reason. If you think it can't happen to you, consider this: a 35-year-old stands a better than 50% chance of being disabled for 90 days or longer! If you are single or if your family depends on your being able to earn money, income replacement is essential to keep your financial security intact.

You can buy disability insurance for varying lengths of time. The average policy is for five years and usually pays up to 60% of your income. Disability insurance usually doesn't start immediately after the time you stop working. (Many times, it takes three months before you get the first payment.) You may believe Social Security will cover your income for you. In reality, Social Security denies more than 65% of all claims for disability benefits. You *need* private disability insurance.

In reality, Social Security denies more than 65% of all claims for disability benefits. You need private disability insurance.

LIFE INSURANCE

If you have dependents, you should purchase life insurance. The amount depends on how much would be needed if you were to die prematurely. The number of children you have and their ages will dictate how much life insurance you need. If you don't have dependents, it's still wise to have some life insurance. Your family will have to pay for funeral and burial expenses, as well as any debts and taxes you may owe at the time of your death.

There are so many life insurance options! The right one for you has everything to do with your individual situation and your other financial strategies. Whichever option you choose, your premium will be based on these three components:

1. **Mortality cost:** Defined by an actuarial table that projects the number of people fitting your profile (age and health risk) who will die each year.
2. **Administration cost:** Charged for managing and servicing the plan.
3. **Investment cost:** If you buy a plan that offers a savings component.

Your insurance broker can help you determine your individual needs.

If you have dependents, you should purchase life insurance.

HOW TO CUT INSURANCE COSTS

Here are invaluable tips from financial experts guaranteed to trim the cost of your insurance premiums:

. . . On Your Health Insurance

1. If you're young and in good health, consider taking a $1,000 deductible policy (rather than paying a higher premium for a lower deductible). Full coverage can cost you an extra $50 each month (that's $600 a year). If you only go to the doctor twice a year, you don't need the full coverage. If you do end up paying the full $1,000 deductible, why not pay for it when you need it rather than in advance?

2. If your health insurer requires a second opinion on surgery, be sure to follow the guidelines. Unless you need emergency surgery, many insurers will penalize you up to $1,000 for not getting a second opinion!

. . . *On Your Homeowner's Policy*

1. By installing an alarm system in your home, you get a discount on your homeowner's insurance. Some insurers reduce premiums from between 2 and 10% if you install a burglar alarm and take another 2% off for heat smoke detectors.
2. Nonsmokers often get a reduced rate, too, because they lower the risk of fire damage.
3. You can lower your premium if you accept a higher deductible. As a rough guideline, you can reduce your premium 5 to 10% by choosing a $500 deductible. A policy with a $1,000 deductible will be approximately 15% less than a policy with a $250 deductible. Experts advise being protected for the "worst-case" scenario and to self-insure the small stuff.
4. Ask for discounts for being a loyal customer. Some insurers offer 10% discounts to customers who've been with them for longer than five years.
5. Ask for a discount if you insure your car and home with the same company.
6. Don't include the value of land when you get your home appraised for a homeowner's policy. Your land isn't likely to be stolen or destroyed by fire.
7. Some insurance companies give discounts to senior citizens.

Nonsmokers get a price break that can add up to $100 annually—so stop smoking!

. . . *On Your Automobile Policy*

1. Compare rates. You can save as much as 10% just by shopping around.
2. By raising your deductible to $500 or $1,000 you can save up to 30% on your premiums.
3. If your car is worth $2,000 or less, experts say to drop the collision and comprehensive coverage. That will cut your bill by as much as $250 in some states.

4. Ask about discounts for antitheft devices, antilock brakes, and airbags.
5. Make sure all the drivers in your household have taken driver's education or a defensive driving course. You will save between 5 and 15% on your automobile policy.
6. To lower your premium, have your teenager drive your oldest and cheapest car and be sure to tell your insurance company which car your child is driving.
7. Ask about discounts for special groups. For example, drivers over 50 and women drivers over 30 get special price breaks.

. . . On Disability Insurance

1. Shop for the lowest-priced disability policy that is renewable, that cannot be cancelled, and that is indexed to inflation.
2. Nonsmokers get a price break that can add up to $100 annually—so stop smoking!
3. If you have enough savings to get you through 90 days to 180 days of no income before you need disability payments, your premium will be much lower.
4. Lower your premiums by reducing the time you must be paid benefits. Will you really need disability payments after you reach retirement age?
5. About one-third of the disability policies sold by major companies are sold to women. The insurance companies report that women have a higher disability rate than men, making the premium for women up to 30% higher. Look for companies that have "unisex" rates.

Look for companies that have "unisex" rates.

. . . On Life Insurance

1. Consider "term life insurance" instead of a "whole life" if you need coverage to protect dependents at the lowest possible cost. A 35-year-old nonsmoker would pay a $125 premium the first year for $100,000 of coverage with a term policy. That same $100,000 coverage of "whole life insurance" would cost $1,000 to $1,500 for the first year's premium. Term insurance rates go up every year on an annual renewable policy.

You can buy five- and 10-year renewables to lock in lower rates for longer time periods.

2. Check with your insurance company as to which mortality table they use to assess your charges to cover the risk of death. Most use the Commissioners 1980 Standard Ordinary table. Some use the 1958 table. You'll pay higher mortality fees if your insurer uses the 1958 table.

CHAPTER FIFTEEN SUMMARY

Insurance helps you cope with sudden losses and other challenges that life sometimes throws at you.

Review each category of your life in which insurance is concerned. Are you adequately covered?

CHAPTER FIFTEEN BLUEPRINT FOR LIFE WORKSTATIONS

1. Sit down and read all of your insurance policies. (Make sure you include those that you receive from your employment and as credit card bonuses.)
2. Make a checklist of the policies you most need and can afford.
3. Place all your policies in an organized, easy to access file. Make copies of these and give them to a friend or family member to hold in a separate location (in case of fire).
4. Determine if you can or should increase the deductible on your policies. (This will lower your payments.)
5. For each policy, contact two competing insurance providers and obtain two bids prior to that policy's renewal date. Make sure you are getting the most for the least.

FURTHER FINANCIAL CONSIDERATIONS

Financial security for retirement takes a long, calculated plan.

Assumptions are a dangerous . . . assumption. Retire at 65? Maybe—but you should definitely assume you'll live past 75. Given recent advances in nutritional and medical care, Americans might soon have a life expectancy exceeding 100. Many people also assume they will have sufficient income if they save for retirement only during the final five to seven years of their careers. It doesn't just happen like that. Financial security for retirement takes a long, calculated plan. Preserving principal is not so much the issue—it's earning income and creating interest on the principal you have. And don't assume your workplace's pension plan will match inflation. Miracles aren't likely to happen. You must create your own miracle by funding and being conscientious about long-term financial goals.

Miscellaneous 2%
Investment and Savings 35%
Part Time Employment 25%
Retirement Savings Plan 20%
Social Security 18%

WHERE'S THE MONEY FOR RETIREMENT?

Social Security currently provides less than 25% of the income most retirees need. Many of these "retirees" have to depend on part-time jobs to fill in the gaps. In the future, Social Security payments will probably become an even smaller percentage of your retirement income. The Social Security Administration estimates that combining the income from both Social Security and pensions provides less than half of what the average retiree needs today. So how do you make it happen? How will you survive? A 49-year-old who contributes $500 a month to a retirement fund will never catch up with a 30-year-old who contributes $100 a month! *The power of an early start is absolutely essential to a healthy retirement plan. Strange as it may seem, you will have more money at age 65, saving from age 21 to 28, than from 29 to 65.*

The nation's top financial planners listed these strategies as musts for a comfortable retirement:

- Start investing for retirement at an early age
- Make regular and consistent contributions

You've probably said time and time again, *"I don't have enough time and I don't have enough money."* Not true! The younger you start, the better you'll live. A golden retirement is mostly just putting time to work for your future. Unfortunately, most of us choose to put it elsewhere. A large percentage of people living in poverty today are elderly women. *Two out of every five older women (41%) are poor.* While 33% of men 65 and older collected pension benefits last year, only 12% of women did.

The average woman steps out of the work force to care for children or elderly relatives for 11 years over her lifetime, compared to 16 months for men. That gives women less time to build a retirement fund—even though they will need it longer. Women live an average of seven years longer than men. *The only person who is going to take care of the older you is the younger you, right now.* No matter what your age, you have a lot of years ahead. Current actuarial tables used by the insurance industry say that today's 40-year-old non-

Social Security currently provides less than 25% of the income most retirees need.

smoking woman can expect to live until age 86. She has over half her life left—and more than 20 years beyond retirement. *It's time you started making those 20 years golden.*

CHILDREN AND FUTURE PLANNING

You must have a will, no matter how little you think you own. If you die without a will, your assets will be distributed according to the laws of your home state. Since you have not indicated your wishes, the state will decide where the money will go. More importantly, the state will also decide who will take care of your children. If your husband is still living, some states dictate that half your assets will go to your children and half to him. This means that minor children (those under age 18) could become wards of the state. In this case, even though the children are living with their father, he would be required to account to the court for every penny spent on the children's behalf. While you might like this idea, if you and your ex did not get along, it is not the best of circumstances. Once your child came of age, he would be entitled to all the remaining money. with no strings attached. Remember: your child will only be 18 years old when this happens! Dying without a will is not in the best interests of either your children or your husband.

SOCIAL SECURITY NOW

Social Security, despite its gaps, has an "up" side. An article by Jane Bryant Quinn, a columnist with *The Washington Post* Writers' Group, stated that, *"While Social Security will probably not last until the next generation, it is a safety net for today's women."* This is because the program favors dependents and lower earners, most of whom are women and children. Some proposed reforms, however, might take this advantage away. These reforms include investing Social Security funds individually, rather than paying Social Security taxes. What is often forgotten by reformers is that your Social Security taxes buy other benefits. For example, when a worker dies, his spouse and

You must

have a will,

no matter

how little you

think you

own.

young children are eligible for monthly benefits. In this case, Social Security provides a form of life insurance.

Retirees who have had low or spotty earnings during their working years (usually women) don't personally get much out of Social Security. They can, however, collect greater benefits through their spouse's account (or former spouse's if they have been married for 10 or more years). The divorced person can collect personal benefits based on the earnings of her former husband's higher-earning account if their marriage lasted at least 10 years. This means a divorced woman *who hasn't remarried* isn't necessarily financially abandoned in old age. These payments to the former wife don't take one penny away from the worker's account or his current spouse. It is divorce insurance and it includes inflation insurance! Your check rises annually with the inflation rate. If you had to buy this insurance privately, it would be costly. Social Security, as currently formulated, is an important safety net.

THE "NEW" SOCIAL SECURITY

Many of the reform proposals currently being talked about would slash these forms of social insurance. They would use part or all of your Social Security tax for some form of mandatory 401K. Money would be diverted from your paycheck into a personal account. You would be given the choice to decide where to invest it and your standard of living in retirement would depend on the size of this nest egg.

How would life differ for women under these privatization proposals (if they came into being)? If you are an entrepreneur, you would probably be in favor of the privatization of Social Security. If you live from hand-to-mouth, however, the changing face of Social Security could hurt you. Each proposed plan has different results. Here are some guesses from the General Accounting Office.

1. Benefit Payments

Women, on an average, earn less than men. A woman's personal investment account would be lower than the average man's. Social Security currently helps low earners by raising their benefits a bit. That wouldn't happen if every-

Social Security, as currently formulated, is an important safety net.

one's money was in private accounts. The gap between men's and women's retirement income would grow.

2. Investment Returns

Women tend to be more conservative investors than men. If the individual investment account was in stocks, and stocks did poorly for a long period of time, a woman's natural conservativism would pay off. (She would probably have put her investment account into bonds or annuities.) But if stocks did well, the woman's cautious investing would leave her further behind.

3. Longevity

Women with the same earnings and investments as men could wind up with lower monthly incomes. This is because they tend to live longer. Each woman would have to draw less from her account to be sure the money she has will last her entire lifetime. Under the current Social Security program, people who have equal incomes get equal monthly benefits for life.

4. Divorce

None of the plans provide monthly payments to an ex-spouse. My personal crystal ball sees more impoverished divorcees. Some reformers would split the investment account at divorce. This is bad because 1) it helps the ex only at the worker's expense, and 2) there is no guarantee the ex will get the same income that Social Security currently pays.

5. Spouse Protection

When a worker dies today, a spouse is entitled to 100% of that worker's monthly Social Security benefit for life. With private savings, the retired worker can take money as needed in a lump sum and/or as a lifetime annuity. Spouses get no income guarantees. A private investment account might give a spouse more than Social Security pays—or it might give less. That depends on life's tragedies (death, divorce), how the money is invested, and how the stock market behaves. We all need private savings. Dependents, however, also need a Social Security guarantee.

As you can tell, I am in favor of both protecting yourself and having a governmental safety net. For those who follow the path and their goals, there will be no problem. For the rest, let there be some form of Social Security.

CHAPTER SIXTEEN SUMMARY

Retiring comfortably is the result of a long, calculated plan. The "seeds" should be planted as soon as possible—and will fully bloom in 25–35 years. You must start early.

Your future can only be as secure are your plans to make it secure. Take the time to plan—and stick to that plan.

Women have less time to gain assets than men because of their nurturing responsibilities.

There is no promise of Social Security. If it is there when you retire, it will only represent 10–20% of the income you will need.

Millennium Women live comfortably now because of the efforts and the plans they began in their lives years earlier.

CHAPTER SIXTEEN
BLUEPRINT FOR LIFE
WORKSTATION

1. Find out what it would take to pay off all mortgages you currently hold in half the time listed on their current amortization tables. (This is a repeat question from a prior workstation.)
2. Make a will with the help of a professional.
3. Make sure your spouse (if you have one) has a will.
4. Identify a "true" retirement plan. Look at the length of time between now and when you are age 65. Construct a plan for a comfortable retirement.
5. Identify in your budget how much you can devote to this plan.
6. Call up the Social Security Administration and request that they mail you a benefits package on your name and Social Security number.
7. Calculate how much equity you need to have invested to achieve $35,000 per year annual income when you retire.

17

WHAT EVERY BRIDE, EX-WIFE, AND WIDOW SHOULD KNOW

Keep records

of everything!

The key to a healthy economic partnership today is knowledge and participation. Marriage counselors say that disagreements concerning money is one of the most common reasons for marital problems. The bottom line? The more you know, the better off you'll be with your spouse. Here are some interesting statistics:

- One-half of all recent first marriages will end in divorce.
- Half the widows who are poor weren't poor until the death of their husbands.
- The average income for women at age 65 is $6,300 per year.
- Fifty percent of all women older than 65 in the United States are widows and remain widows for 15 years after their husbands die.
- One-third of all widows in 1985 were under age 50 when their husbands died.
- Women outlive men by an average of seven years.
- The remarriage rate for divorced women ages 45 through 64 is about one-tenth that for divorced women under 25.

Remember, what you don't know about finances will hurt you!

FOR THE NEW BRIDE

The best time to talk about money is before you get married. Sit down, just as you should do periodically during your marriage, and discuss all financial issues. Here's a checklist of some money matters that you need to discuss with your intended spouse:

- Talk about both your incomes.
- What are each person's assets and debts?
- Who is going to control the overall plan?
- How will income be handled after you're married?
- Will there be a joint checking account?
- Will both of you have separate accounts?
- Will both of you contribute equally toward retirement and what proportion should be saved for that retirement?
- How will debt be handled during the marriage? Will each be responsible for paying debts incurred before marriage or will they be lumped into a common pool?
- Will one party pay all the debts in full?
- Will pre-marital debts be paid from the joint account after marriage?
- How will credit be handled after the marriage?
- Will you have joint credit—and will credit be reported in both names?
- Will you change your name on your credit card but keep your credit separate?
- Will you keep your previous name and separate credit cards?
- How will you save for major purchases, such as a house or a car?
- Will you make purchases whenever one or both of you have enough cash?
- Will you create a separate money market account to be signed by both parties?
- How will you structure investments?
- How much risk is each of you willing to take or should you take?

Never sign a contract that you haven't read or that you don't understand.

- Will the one who contributes the most make all the decisions?
- Will the one with past experience make all the decisions?
- Will decisions be made jointly with both parties equally responsible for understanding the risks and investment strategies?
- How is your estate set up?
- Do you have enough insurance?
- Does each of you have a will?
- How will the assets be divided in case of divorce? Does this include future income and assets?
- How will money management be handled in the household?
- Will one person always be responsible for bill paying?
- Will you rotate the responsibility from month to month?
- Will bills be divided as previously agreed and paid out of separate checking accounts?
- Who will have the monthly responsibility for paying the bills, writing the checks, and balancing the checkbook(s)?

These are very important questions. I witnessed a couple, neither of whom had very good financial acumen or organizational skills, struggle for many, many years. In a marriage, someone must take the lead. If it is your husband, you must still be knowledgeable. I recommend that you to take the time to learn about financial matters through books or classes—or hire a bookkeeper to do the things you can't handle. When I was young, I was notorious for never being able to balance a checkbook. Later, I recognized the importance of organization and knowing exactly where each penny was. I hired a bookkeeper—and she's been doing all my books ever since. I knew what was needed and I did something about it.

KEEP RECORDS

Keep records of everything! Make copies of all your tax returns and organize yourself. On a sheet of paper, write down both of your social security numbers, your bank accounts, insurance policy numbers, brokerage account

There's nothing wrong with having your own money and your own assets separated even when you are married.

numbers, and money market accounts. Keep these records in a special file—and make sure it is accessible to you. Or keep a separate copy for yourself in case an emergency should arise. You don't want to be helpless should something happen to you or your spouse!

Never sign a contract that you haven't read or that you don't understand. You must be able to understand everything. When you have separate property, think carefully before putting that property into a joint account. There's nothing wrong with having your own money and your own assets separated even when you are married.

THERE IS BOTH A ME AND A WE

Develop your individual credit rating. Don't be afraid to open your own bank account or get loans and credit cards solely in your name. It is important that you maintain your own separate credit.

One of the biggest problems wives make is not openly discussing with their husbands what the money situation is. They believe it is not "romantic" to talk about money. Even if you have decided that your husband is in charge of your joint monies, finances must be a mutual undertaking. Both partners must understand what is happening. There should be special times when you sit down and talk about goals, update your records, and discuss everything. You should do this not because of the possibility of divorce or becoming widowed, but if you don't do this, you'll still become dependent and vulnerable.

This book is about becoming independent. If you haven't sat down with your husband to discuss 1) how much he owes, 2) what your family assets are, 3) what your insurance status is, 4) how much he spends, and 5) how he has structured his will, you must make this discussion a family priority. The checklists must be marked off. You can't afford to know only what your salaries are and think that this is sufficient information. You've got to understand how it flows through your family so that you can budget. What would happen if he wasn't there?

IRS AND SPOUSE TAX LIABILITY

Under the current law, each spouse is responsible for the full amount of income tax due when you file a joint federal tax return. This is a legal concept called *Joint and Several Liability*. **The IRS is legally allowed to pursue one spouse for the payment of back taxes if the other is unavailable.** There is, however, limited relief for spouses who can prove they didn't know a tax return contained an error or under-statement of taxes. In any case, do not sign your joint tax return unless you fully understand it.

Divorced women have been and are responsible for their ex-spouse's tax consequences. A safeguard against such future tax surprises is to file your own, separate tax return after you marry. This prevents the IRS from holding you responsible for your spouse's or ex-spouse's tax liability.

COLLEGE FOR YOUR CHILDREN

In most states, the parent's legal responsibility for his child stops at age 18.

Studies have shown that a person with four or more years of college will earn approximately $250,000 more over a lifetime than a person with only a high school diploma. If you want to give your child that kind of increased earning power, start planning *right now* to give him or her a college education. There are many scholarships and low-interest-rate loans, as well as grants. College is more accessible than you think. Remember: in most states, the parent's legal responsibility for his child stops at age 18. This means that unless it is specifically written in the divorce decree, your child has to pay for his own college education.

Some states have a pre-paid college tuition program. See whether your state has a program like this for educational planning. The cost of a college education is significant and has outpaced inflation. Today's one-year-old can expect to pay more than $100,000 at a public university and more than $200,000 at a private college if this rate of education-al inflation continues! Before you go into shock, though, there are ways to make covering the costs easier. Time is your greatest ally—invest now. *If you follow the path laid out in this book, you and your family will be able to have all your dreams.*

FOR THE EX-WIFE

Credit

Many times the former wife does not understand the financial state of the marriage. Husbands have been known to hide huge amounts of debt prior to the divorce. *This is debt with your name and obligation to it.* You must take these immediate steps to protect your credit and your financial interests.

1. Request a copy of your credit report.
2. Look at the number of credit cards and check for outstanding balances in joint accounts.
3. Immediately close all of your joint accounts and start establishing separate credit from that day forward.

Typically, a creditor cannot close an account because of divorce unless they have evidence that you are unwilling or unable to pay the debt. You do not, however, want your ex to be able to continue charging purchases on that credit card. Cancel that card! If you want a new card, the bank might ask you to submit a new application, however. This is especially true if the original application was based on your husband's income. When figuring your credit worthiness, a creditor can include alimony and child support as part of your income. *You do not, however, have to disclose these monies unless you need them to obtain credit.* In any case, inform the credit bureaus in writing of your new marital status and request that your credit information now be reported only in your name.

Child Support

If your former husband neglects to pay the designated child support (as agreed to in your divorce decree), your state might be able to help. There are agencies that can find him through Social Security payments and other official records. You can seek this information by contacting your local librarian.

Divorced women have been and are responsible for their ex-spouse's tax consequences. A safeguard against such future tax surprises is to file your own, separate tax return after you marry.

Tax Considerations

If you receive alimony, you must pay income taxes on it. If you pay alimony to your former husband, you may deduct it and he will pay taxes on it. You do not pay income taxes on money given as child support. Property settlements are not taxable. If you sell joint real estate or your house, however, there may be a taxable gain depending on how long you have owned it, lived in it, and how much you've sold it for. The IRS has a free publication you may request called "Tax Information for Divorced, Separated Individuals," Publication No. 504. Call 1-800-TAX-FORM to order this brochure. It can help.

If you are a widow, check to make sure you've taken all the allowable deductions on your income taxes. This is especially true if your husband has had a lengthy illness. See if he left a "living will." Examine insurance papers to see if your husband took out coverage to cover debts in case of his death. American Express and other credit card companies carry this type of insurance. They also sometimes give accidental death insurance policies as "freebies" for accepting a new credit card. Call them to see if you have missed any monies that might be owed to you. Check to see if his health insurance policies included death benefits. Go over the insurance papers and look at your pension plans carefully to make sure no benefits have been overlooked. Talk with the officials at the Social Security office to see if you or your children qualify for payments. Children under 18 and students under 22 probably qualify. If you're over 60 or are disabled you probably do, too.

If you and your husband had a joint safe deposit box, you may wish to empty it before his death. This will save you the inconvenience of not being able to remove documents conveniently after his death. The bank closes all joint assets for a given time after a death. Destroy your husband's credit cards and make sure, in writing, that his name is taken off all those accounts.

Typically, no estate taxes are owed to the federal government on any amount a husband leaves to a wife. States vary in their tax requirements, however, so be sure to review the laws in your state. If your estate is substantial,

When divorced, inform the credit bureaus in writing of your new marital status and request that your credit information in the future be reported in your name only.

however, you might want to pass it on to your heirs. Taxes are higher when a single person dies (and you are now single). With an estate over $1,000,000, see an attorney about estate planning. Above all, *avoid making any major changes in your life for one year after your husband's death.* Your emotional condition is likely to prevent the kind of rational thinking required for major financial decisions.

Children and Taxes

The main connection between children and taxes is the tax credit. *You are entitled to a tax credit if you're working, looking for a job full-time, or attending school full-time. This is not a deduction but a tax credit subtracted directly from the amount of taxes your owe.* If you pay someone to care for your child (and your child is under the age of 13), you may be able to take a tax credit of up to 30% of the amount you paid. The credit works on a sliding scale ranging from 30% of your qualified expenses if your income is below $10,000 to 20% of your expenses if your income exceeds $28,000. The maximum amounts you can deduct are $2,400 per year for one child and $4,800 for two or more children. IRS Publication 503 gives detailed information on claiming this tax credit.

You can also qualify for "head of household" status to lower your income taxes. This is true even if your divorce decree says your former spouse is the parent who can claim the child as a deduction on his income taxes. If the children are living with you, you have child care obligations—especially with young children. When you pay someone to take care of your children outside of your home, you are not required to pay Social Security taxes on your day-care payments. The day-care center does this paperwork.

The rules are different if you hire someone to come into your home to take care of your children. In this case, you are responsible for Social Security taxes on the caretaker's salary if that salary is more than $50 per quarter. This amount is subject to change as well as the method of payment. Check with your Social Security office to verify the current amount. You may either withhold half the Social Security tax from your employee's pay (and you pay the other half) or you can pay the entire tax yourself. You must file Form SS4 with the IRS. You will then be assigned an Employer Identification Number and must file Form 942 four times a year. These will be mailed to you by the IRS. There may also be some state forms required.

CHAPTER SEVENTEEN SUMMARY

Marriages end in divorce many times because of financial distress and the mismanagement of money.

Keeping an eye on all financial responsibilities is a safeguard for your marriage's financial prosperity.

Organization is the key to growth, and none is more important than in financial matters. Make files and records of your entire cash flow (both incoming and outgoing) and be on top of the game.

Make a goal of discussing all the checklists in this chapter. It is imperative that you get your credit straight and under your name as quickly as possible.

Never, ever sign anything, whether happily married or divorced, unless you have read every line.

CHAPTER SEVENTEEN BLUEPRINT FOR LIFE WORKSTATION

1. In your journal, copy the checklist on the first page of this chapter. Answer all the questions and write them in your journal.
2. Now, go over the same list with your spouse (schedule a financial meeting of the minds).
3. Go to an office supply store and purchase the necessary organizational helpers. You want to organize all the financial categories in your life and put them in order.
4. Open up some lines of credit solely in your name. Use a different variation (such as using your initials, T. M. O'Shaughnessy vs. Thomas Michael O'Shaughnessy) of your name.

If you follow the path laid out in this book, you and your family will be able to have all your dreams.

5. Request a copy of your credit report, if you haven't done this previously.
6. Contact the IRS and order Form 504 (1-800-TAX FORM). Read it.
7. Make sure you are using all the tax credits to which you are entitled. Call an accountant and make an appointment.

EPILOGUE

I hope that this book has helped you on your rightful path to prosperity.

Never lose control of being able to secure your own life. Life will always present challenges to you. It's how you react and deal with those challenges that makes you a Millennium Woman.

Always remember, you are a beautiful human being who deserves all that you receive and what you receive is controlled by your perception and vision.

I wish you much luck and most of all, that you will be able to share your success with others. It's going to happen for you!

Michael O'Shaughnessy

May the beauty of God shine through you,
May the light of God surround you,
May the love of God enfold you,
May the power of God protect you,
May the presence of God watch over you,
Where ever you are, God is . . .

Charles Clayton Jr.

PERSONAL GROWTH TERMINOLOGY

Accomplishment	Achievement, to get something done
Achievement	Equals success
Action	Your physical momentum
Acumen	Business intellect
Ambition	The desire to go forward to obtain a higher level
Attitude	Mental strength (that which conquers all)
Balance	Finding stability among the different areas in your life
Barrier	Nothing more than a temporary obstacle that you will go over, under, around, or above
Capitalize	Taking advantage of
Character	Something that you obtain after a lot of trial and error
Comfort	Achieved goals
Communication	The key to advancement in society, corporate or private sector
Compete	To challenge yourself
Competitive	To challenge others
Concentration	Equals focus

Consumer	Something you don't want to be
Depth of Strength	Your reservoir
Desire	Something that must burn inside of you
Determination	Internal strength
Discipline	Your mental focus that allows goals to be obtained
Dreams	Mental visions
Drive	An internal hunger that must be quenched
Economize	Something we must all constantly do
Education	A process of enhancement
Efficiency	Something we must implement daily to allow a better life
Enthusiasm	The positive energy one must possess to obtain success
Environment	That of which you are a part and of which you are a product
Exercise	Use it or lose it; needed for mental strength
Exhilaration	The feeling that you get from succeeding
Experience	Revelation of a new meaning and greater understanding
Failure	The keys to success—a lot of failures equal a lot of successes
Faith	Trust in a higher power; includes the belief that good things will happen in time
Fear	The uncertainty of not knowing
Focus	That mental vision that allows you to see only your goal
Force	Something that you have within you
Freedom	Independence
Fulfillment	Satisfaction. Goal accomplishment. A higher state of being.
Goals	The marked path to a pre-determined achievement
Guts	Something you have a lot of

Habit	Something that you are used to doing (good or bad)
Hard Work	Pays off!
Health	Your most important concern
"Impossible"	The attitude of someone who doesn't strive for success
Improvement	Something we do daily
Integrity	Being true to yourself
Intellectual Capital	Your understanding of how all these words relate to your life and how you control your destiny
Introspection	Something you do with yourself and/or a higher power
Involvement	You and life
Knowledge	Power. Wisdom and understanding. The key to obtaining what you want.
Lean, Mean, Focused Machine	You—what you are about to become
Learning	An educational opportunity
Lesson	An opportunity to be educated about a specific thing
Lioness	You
Love	The highest form of power
Luck	The product of hard work and determination
Management	A form of organization
Mental Strength	Focus, vision, and belief
Mom	Love provider, mentor, caretaker—the hats you wear will never end. It is the greatest responsibility you will ever assume. Moms are the flowers that seed the next generation of life.
Money	That which humans use to purchase time and material things
Morals	Something we all need to live a little bit more by
Motivate	Something you use to give you mental energy

Motivation	Something that comes from within
One Hundred Million Dollars	A lot of money
Opportunity	Hard work plus luck (hard work brings luck)
Organization	A form of management. A key in the building block toward success. It creates growth.
Paper Tiger	Someone without any strength behind him
Passionate	Heartfelt feeling
Patience	Time cures everything
Perseverance	Time equals accomplishment
Persistence	Tenacity—not giving up
Plan	A marked path
Potential	Something everyone has, even if it has not yet been developed
Power	Your ability to choose
Practice	What you do to obtain a habit
Pride	Sense of accomplishment
Progress	Something you do daily
Reaction	The ability to bounce back
Respect	Universal law—something you earn through dedication
Responsibility	What we all have to ourselves and to our families
Restructure	To grow
Results	Come in direct proportion to your applied energy
Risk	To learn
Self-Esteem	Mental strength and confidence
Smart	The description by which you should always expect others to characterize you
Strength	Something you have within you
Stretch	The ability to throw oneself into an uncertain situation and come out stronger (because of the growth you achieve)

Talent	Something each individual has that is unique
Technique	Business acumen that allows you to gain and advance
Time	Something we all need more of
Transformation	Something you're going to go through
Uninhibited	Self-expression, fearless
Uniqueness	You
Universal Forces	Natural laws of life
Value	[1] Material: Your monetary evaluation of an item. [2] The importance you put upon your internal or spiritual understanding
Wealth	A mental state of being
White Anglo-Saxon Male	Someone you compete against, but occasionally need for personal purposes.
Willpower	A reservoir of strength
Work	How you choose to make a living
Worry	A negative attitude
Zen Principle	Being true to your thoughts

DEFINITIONS OF FINANCIAL TERMS

Appraisal	An estimate of value, not to be confused with true value. This is just one person's opinion
Appreciation	Something that is growing in value
Asset Based	Based on a certain asset, or tangible entity
Balloon Payment	When all the debt comes due at one time
Budget	An understanding of what you're spending
Bear Market	A contraction of the stock market. People are losing money—possibly jumping out of windows
Bull Market	When things are running extremely well. People are making money.
Butter	A depreciating asset
Ceiling	Something that you can't go through, must find a way around, or must break
CEO	Chief Executive Officer
Clouds on a Title	These are imperfections that make a title unmarketable
Co-Equity	Shared interest in a property
Contract	An agreement between a Buyer and a Seller. This should be in writing.

Contract for Deed	An unconventional method to purchase a home—very similar to a modified lease-purchase
Debt Service	A reoccurring service on a debt or payment structure, usually monthly
Economic Engine	Your financial motor power
Educational Experience	1. Value added to your life's knowledge base 2. Any failure that you may have
Equity	The amount of money that may be in an asset you own, usually refers to a real estate property
FHA	Federal Housing Administration
Financial Vehicle	Something that will carry you through a financial process
Foreclosure	Not necessarily a great buy, but somebody's misfortune that could be your opportunity
Guns	An appreciating asset
Hedge	An assortment of investments, diversified so that if you lose in one you could possibly not lose in others
Investor	Someone who knows how to manipulate a dollar
Knowledge Shop	A short-term educational opportunity offered in a local or community type of environment
Lease Purchase	A form of right-to-purchase a property under a specific time frame
Leverage	A form of multiplying what you have invested in a project to increase your growth potential
Lottery	Something we all wish we would win
Market	What a buyer will pay and a seller will sell for given no adverse conditions
Marketable Title	A deed or a title to a property that is clear and unencumbered. Title insurance is purchased for this entity.

Masters of Business Administration (MBA)	These are people who went an extra step in the college process. They are a dime a dozen, unless you are one.
Negative Net Worth	That means you're worth less than zero. You would have to pay to get out of life.
Net Worth	Your monetary value at any point in time. Includes all your assets: real property, stocks, bonds valuables, collectibles, cash, etc.
One-Hundred-Percent Financing	Financing that covers 100% of the asset. Example: A house for sale at $100,000, has a mortgage of $100,000
Parsimonious	Someone who is real tight-fisted with money
Principal Reduction	The principal portion (debt without interest) of a loan that is being reduced
Promissory Note	A promise to pay
Qualifying	The ability to be greenlighted into a loan opportunity because you have met certain lender's standards for the processing of the loan
Seller Financing	Where the owner will hold a mortgage. (He creates money for you to leverage that opportunity.)
Seller's Disclosure	These are disclosures that a seller must make of any items that could affect the value of the property you are purchasing from that seller
Subject To	A condition in the contract tying up the property, putting the property under a contract or agreement, which protects you
Survey	A boundary surrounding a piece of real estate that is designated by a surveyor and is the legal description
Title Insurance	Insurance that protects the value of your deed or ownership of a piece of property
VA	Veterans Administration

INDEX

ABOUT THE AUTHOR

A firm believer in goal setting, **Michael O'Shaughnessy** has created a book of inspiration and advice specifically aimed at women. He became aware of the specific needs of women by watching his own mother, friends and clients struggle to find their financial way. Using his own hard-luck beginnings, failures and ultimate success as a guide, O'Shaughnessy helps women attain the happiness, success and security they so richly deserve through his book *Millennium Woman*.

A ninth-grade dropout, O'Shaughnessy went back and finished school and started his own real-estate business at 26. By the time he was 31, he was a self-made millionaire. He credits his success to tenacity and to the ability to set and reach goals. A severe stutterer as a child, he forced himself to join Toastmasters International when he was 28. Conquering his fear of public speaking, he became a Distinguished Toastmaster, won several international speech competitions, and today is a professional public speaker. O'Shaughnessy is also an Ironman Triathlete, an avid surfer, and has twice completed the famed Catalina Classic, a 32-mile open ocean paddleboard race. He also led the Quiksilver/Silver Edition Key West to Cuba 92-mile open-ocean paddleboard expedition in June of this year.

Michael is married and currently lives by the sea in Ponce Inlet, Florida, in a house called "Ebbtide"—a house that he once only dreamed about owning until he dared to make it a goal.